Land of the Midnight Sun

Land of the Midnight Sun

A History of the Yukon

Ken S. Coates & William R. Morrison

Hurtig Publishers
Edmonton

Hurtig Publishers Ltd.
10560-105 Street
Edmonton, Alberta
Canada T5H 2W7

Canadian Cataloguing in Publication Data

Coates, Kenneth, 1956–
    Land of the midnight sun

Bibliography: p.
Includes index.
ISBN 0-88830-331-9

1. Yukon Territory—History.   I. Morrison,
William R. (William Robert), 1942–   . II. Title.

FC4011.C62   1988   971.9′1   C88-094300-9
F1093.C62 1988

*Editor/*Sarah Reid
*Design/*David Shaw
*Composition/*Attic Typesetting
*Manufacture/*Friesen Printers

Edited, designed, typeset, printed, and bound in Canada

Contents

Preface

We come to this book from very different directions. One of us was raised in the Yukon; the other in Ontario. One was drawn to the study of Yukon history by the absence of historical analysis about a region he viewed as his homeland; to the other, the Yukon provided an opportunity to study the evolution of Canadian attitudes and policies towards the north. This book represents a union of these approaches — an attempt to see the north from both the inside and the outside.

We have tried to incorporate the entire Yukon into our investigation. In the past, the activities of newcomers to the Yukon — explorers, traders, miners, and government officials — have attracted most of the attention from researchers and writers. The Indians have, unfortunately and unnecessarily, been relegated to the background. The irony in this is obvious, for the Yukon Indians have persisted in occupying their corner of the world, while non-natives, as a group, have demonstrated surprisingly little commitment to the Territory, moving in and out as the seasons and business cycles dictated. The history of the Yukon should be one of both groups, and of relationships between them. We have tried to bring these often-separate strands of Yukon history together, in the hope that natives and whites will recognize how their histories — and their futures — are very much intertwined.

This book also reflects our belief that the history of the Yukon Territory is far more than the experience of the Klondike gold rush and the building of the Alaska Highway. In the past, these dramatic events have drawn most of the attention given to the Yukon, to the detriment of our understanding of the complexities of its history. While giving them their rightful due, we have also covered the full range of the Yukon experience. It is in this larger picture that the major themes of Yukon history become particularly evident: native persistence, the transiency of the white population, formal and informal processes of racial segregation, the boom-and-bust cycles of the economy, the debilitating effects of colonial status, and the Yukon's inability to control its own destiny.

This study is dominated by our understanding of the Yukon Territory as one of Canada's colonies. The political, cultural, and economic realities of being a colony within Canada have had a major impact on the Territory's evolution over the past century. Rooted deep in the past, the struggle to shed the bonds of colonialism and to gain a full measure of local autonomy dominates contemporary politics and government in the Yukon Territory.

Our work on this book has been greatly aided by the encouragement and assistance of others. Mel Hurtig greeted our initial proposal with enthusiasm, and has maintained his interest in the project throughout. We have been fortunate to have had several excellent research assistants. Lucy Bashford was of invaluable assistance at all stages of the research. Her professionalism and enthusiasm are greatly appreciated. Sarah Reid, our editor, has done a masterful job of giving this book much of its coherence. While we thank these people, and Judith Powell and Peter Cross for their assistance with the last phases of the project, they carry no responsibility for any errors or problems it may still have.

Our research activities have been assisted by the financial support of the University of Victoria and Brandon University. Our wives, Cathy Coates and Linda Morrison, have been remarkably understanding of our long research trips, weekends in front of word processors, and many days of consultations. As always, we are grateful for their unflagging support for our research and writing activities. To our children, Bradley, Mark, and Laura Coates and Claire and Ruth Morrison, we offer apologies for time spent away from the family; we hope that they will, in time, accept this book as suitable compensation for our absences. We would like to also thank Con and Dot Lattin of Whitehorse, whose home has always been available to us on our northern research trips, and whose love for the north is a constant source of inspiration.

We would like, finally, to dedicate this book to the native people of the Yukon Territory. Major strides have been made in the past two decades in responding to the Indians' struggle for justice within the Yukon Territory. Far too much, however, remains to be accomplished. It is our hope that this book, which we trust places the Indians' story firmly within the mainstream of Yukon history, will play a small part in helping all Yukoners understand the nature of native life in the Yukon. The contemporary Yukon is, in large measure, a creation of a past that has not been kind to the Yukon Indians. An awareness of this history is an essential component of an equitable and just future.

NATIVE PEOPLES

DANIEL 87

CHAPTER ONE

The Natives' Yukon

Yukon—what a vivid image the word evokes in the minds of people all over the world: miners and gold, snow and hardship, Mounties and Dangerous Dan McGrew. But these things, while rooted in fact, reflect only a single dramatic episode occurring over a few years of the long and generally little known history of the region. An irony of a land rich in historical irony is that the Yukon, one of the youngest parts of North America as far as European civilization is concerned, was almost certainly the first part of the continent to bear the footprint of humankind. It is a young land, yet at the same time almost unimaginably old.

Non-Canadians sometimes have vague and confused notions about the Yukon. Many Americans, for instance, believe that the Territory is part of Alaska, and, lumping the Klondike gold rush with the later one in Nome, think of the two as one large northern gold frontier. But Canadians should not be smug about this; as modern-day Yukoners will attest, they too are often pretty vague about the Territory, thinking of it and the Northwest Territories as a kind of undefined "north." Indeed, the ignorance and neglect of their homeland on the part of outsiders is one of the main complaints that Yukoners have about their treatment by the rest of the country.

The neglect may seem strange, for Canada is a northern country. The north — the True North, strong and free — is the symbol of our identity and our future. Our national myth is that it is the north that has given a special quality to our character. Leading nineteenth-century Canadian thinkers claimed that the future belonged to northern peoples, arguing that the country's character rested in the hardiness, fortitude, and inventiveness demanded by the winter climate.[1]

Such ideas may have been fodder for academics and the occasional politician, but they do not reflect the realities of Canadian life. Even during periods of national navel-gazing, when Canadians have agonized about the alleged lack of a national identity, little public attention has been devoted to

1

the northern nature of this identity. Has the north in fact shaped the Canadian character? Is it truly a part of Canada, in the sense that it is part of a Canadian homeland? Or is it a place to exploit, a national treasure-house, where people can seek their fortunes in order to return with their wealth to southern places? The north means different things to different people. To some it is a place to be pillaged. To its native inhabitants it is and for millenia has been simply a homeland — a fact that should be obvious, but that seemed to surprise the nation when it received wide publicity during the Mackenzie Valley pipeline hearings in the mid 1970s.[2]

To Yukoners, southern Canada is "the outside" and its residents are "outsiders." But perhaps "outsiders" equally well describes how Yukoners see themselves in their relations with the rest of their country.

This book is a history of a northern region that has been created by geography and by legislative fiat. The borders of the Yukon Territory are partly natural (its southern three-quarters consisting of the upper Yukon River Valley and its drainage basin) and partly artificial (its western border at the 141st meridian reflecting nothing more than European power politics of a century and a half ago).

There are several explanations of the origin of the Territory's name. John Bell, the first European to stand on the banks of the upper Yukon River, said that the Indians called it *Youcon*, or white water river. It has subsequently been suggested that the term derives from the Kutchin word *Yu-kun-ah*, meaning great river. The Hudson's Bay Company wrote the name of its river and its fort as had John Bell, but when they withdrew in 1869, the Americans opted for the more concise spelling that remains in common usage. Most of the other geographic features of the Yukon, however, bear not their original names, but those given to them by European explorers.[3]

The Yukon Territory covers 186,100 square miles (482,000 square kilometres), of which about one per cent is inland water and more than half is wooded. Its elevation varies from sea level on the northern coast to 19,500 feet (5,951 metres) at the top of Mount Logan, the highest point in Canada. Much of the Territory is mountainous, the chains running from the northwest to the southeast. The highest peaks, including Mount Logan, are in the spectacular Kluane region of the Yukon's extreme southwest corner, and it is these mountains that effectively cut the Territory off from the Pacific. Whitehorse, although only a hundred miles from tidewater, has a climate very different from that of the Alaskan coastal settlements of Skagway and Haines. A geographical oddity worth a question in Trivial Pursuit is that the entire Territory lies further west than Vancouver. Beaver Creek, a highway community near the Alaskan border, has the distinction of being Canada's most westerly community.

Top left: *Much of the Yukon remains as it has for centuries, untouched by human development. This caribou is a member of the Porcupine herd, which numbers around one hundred thousand head.* YUKON GOVERNMENT PHOTO

Lower left: *The Yukon is carved up by a series of imposing mountain ranges, such as the Ogilvie Mountains, located north of Dawson City.* YUKON GOVERNMENT PHOTO

Below: *The harvesting of large animals, particularly moose and caribou, provided the basis for native habitation in the upper Yukon River basin.* YUKON GOVERNMENT PHOTO

Despite the proximity of the ocean, the climate is continental. The brilliant, intense summer months are warm, with temperatures occasionally recorded in the mid-thirties Celsius, but the winters can be paralysingly cold; the lowest temperature ever recorded in Canada was in February 1947 at Snag, northwest of Kluane Lake, when the mercury plummetted to –63C. In the southern parts of the territory, the winters are often broken by chinooks, gusts of warm Pacific air which push across the mountains, raising the temperature (and the spirits of the residents) dramatically in a matter of hours. Yukoners find some solace in the fact that their periods of extreme cold, unlike those in the eastern Arctic, are generally not accompanied by bone-jarring winds.

The semi-arid climate keeps rainfall to a minimum, and helped create the "world's smallest desert" just outside Carcross. Permafrost is present everywhere north of the Porcupine River, and occurs here and there throughout the Territory.

The Yukon possesses a striking geographic diversity. Along the southern border, a series of major lakes, tucked neatly among the mountain valleys, dominates the landscape. For many centuries, the native people have inhabited the shores of Kluane, Aishihik, Dezedeash, Kushwa, Bennett, Tagish, Marsh, Laberge, and Teslin lakes. In the extreme north, the Arctic coastal plain slopes gently down from the mountains to the Beaufort Sea. Just off the coast is Herschel Island, the northernmost part of the Yukon. At some almost unimaginable time in the past, when this part of North America was closer to the equator, great deciduous forests covered the land that now lies under these waters. Over countless centuries these were turned into the oil which has for some years past been the target of numerous exploration companies.

Different natural forces gave the Yukon its other treasures. Rich lodes of silver, lead, copper, and other ores lay locked in the mineral-rich hills of the Yukon River Valley. At some far distant geological period, gold was deposited in the rocks not far from present-day Dawson City. Later, water eroded these rocks, ripped the gold from them, and glacial creeks carried sand, gravel, and finely ground gold away from the original location — the mother-lode — and deposited them in creek beds. But that part of the Yukon — the Klondike district — was never glaciated, so the gold stayed in the creeks where it fell; otherwise, it would have been torn from the bedrock and deposited many miles to the south, and there would have been no Klondike gold rush. Over thousands of years the creeks shifted in their beds and more sand and muck buried the gold. It lay until Europeans and North Americans, who valued gold almost more than life itself, came to search for it.

In its primeval state, the Yukon was well-stocked with wildlife — moose and caribou, mountain sheep and goats, bears, and animals that later supported the commercial fur trade, such as marten, beaver, and fox. A variety of fish, including Pacific salmon migrating from the Bering Strait, greyling, lake trout (char), whitefish, and northern pike could be found in the Yukon's many rivers and lakes.

Much of the Yukon is well (although not densely) treed, with spruce, poplar, and lodgepole pine the most common species. In areas where the ground thaws deeply in the summer, the spruce can grow as tall as 120 feet. In the parts of the Territory that escaped glaciation there are plants which occur nowhere else in the Canadian north. It comes as a surprise to the non-botanist, who might think that the Yukon's official wildflower, the ubiquitous fireweed, is the only flower in evidence, that the Territory contains at least a dozen species of wild orchids.

The most notable feature of the Territory is the great river that gives the region its name. The southern three-quarters of the Yukon, part of British Columbia, and much of Alaska — an area of 325,000 square miles — is drained by this broad and mighty but fairly placid river, as it flows from its source, less than 20 miles from salt water at the Lynn Canal, 2,000 miles to its mouth near St. Michael on the Bering Strait. The fact that it is easily navigable from its mouth almost to its source has been a great advantage to the region; like the other great northern river, the Mackenzie, the Yukon has provided a ready (though long and slow) avenue of transportation into the interior. Unlike the St. Lawrence, the Yukon has no great rapids in its lower reaches to hamper commerce and travel, although river navigation was never trouble-free; Miles Canyon and the nearby Whitehorse Rapids blocked most river steamers from travelling the entire route. There were several smaller impediments — Five Finger and the Rink rapids — and the constantly shifting sandbars in the river would present major difficulties for all but the most shallow-draft vessels.

The Yukon together with Alaska is the oldest continuously inhabited part of North America. It is almost universally accepted that mankind, in some dim past, came to this continent across a land bridge from Asia. Therefore, people first entered the hemisphere through western Alaska and migrated via the Yukon into the rest of North America. This may have taken place before the beginning of the last ice age, about twenty thousand years ago. Thus, human habitation of what is now Canada began not just in the Yukon, but in one of the most northerly parts of the Territory — the Old Crow basin. Through an irony of geography and climate, during the last ice age, while much of the rest of what is now North America was weighed down by a heavy layer of glacial ice, the Old Crow basin was free of ice in the summers, probably because the snowfall was too scanty to breed glaciers.

There is a great deal of uncertainty about when the first Alaskans and Yukoners arrived. Most North American archaeologists accept that these people first reached the regions south of the ice sheet in significant numbers

Top left: *For generations, the coastal mountain range blocked and limited communication between the Lynn Canal area and the upper Yukon River basin. Passes once controlled by the coastal Tlingit Indians have now been developed as rail or road routes. The South Klondike Highway joins Skagway, Alaska, and Carcross, Yukon.* YUKON GOVERNMENT PHOTO

Top right: *The Porcupine caribou herd, here seen north of Old Crow, migrates between Alaska and the northern Yukon. The people of Old Crow derive much of their food supply from this herd, as have their ancestors for generations before them.* YUKON GOVERNMENT PHOTO

Lower right: *The southwest corner of the Yukon Territory is a land of contrasts — broad valleys and massive mountain ranges, including the highest peaks in Canada. This river is the Tatchenshini River, a rich salmon spawning stream.* YUKON GOVERNMENT PHOTO about 11,000 B.C., although some would put the date very much earlier than that. But there is considerable controversy as to when people first reached this continent and how long they stayed in the northwest before spreading south.[4]

Some of the most interesting and controversial Canadian archaeological finds have been made in the valley of the Old Crow River. The excitement started with the discovery in 1966 of a caribou bone that had been worked by hand into a flesher — a tool to scrape hides — as well as other bones that had evidently been altered by humans. Radio-carbon dating gave a date for the flesher of 25,000 B.C. This was a find with sensational implications; to uncover in the northwestern-most part of Canada evidence of humankind's activities in North America thousands of years older than any other accepted find — such a discovery would revolutionize the understanding of the pre-history of North America. Even as the debate started, scientists, particularly teams led by Richard Harrington and William H. Irving, returned to the field, hoping to find further confirmation of the existence of early humans in the Yukon.

But there were two difficulties with this discovery, neither of which has yet been resolved. First, though it was obvious that the flesher was man-made, there was no way to tell whether the work had been done on a bone from a freshly killed animal, or on one perhaps thousands of years old, picked up somewhere already fossilized. As for the other bones that had seemingly been worked by human hands, it was suggested that they had been cracked by large carnivores, by freezing and thawing, or perhaps they too were tools made from fossilized bones. None of these artifacts had been found in the locations where they had originally been dropped; they had all been carried in some way, probably by water, from their point of origin to where they were found, so geological dating was of no use. (The shifting sands of the Old Crow flats are geologically unstable, meaning that the location of a particular item at a specific depth cannot be readily tied to a specific era.) Many experiments were done with caribou bones — throwing them to lions, freezing them, and breaking them in various ways. While those who believed that the flesher was indeed 27,000 years old were convinced that the results of these experiments proved their theory, others were skeptical. Their doubts were justified in 1985, when more sophisticated radiocarbon tests indicated that the flesher and some of the other bones dated from about 1000 A.D., though others were indeed at least 25,000 years old. What was needed was further proof, perhaps indisputable evidence of a campsite, fire, or human dwelling.

In 1975, a number of limestone caves were discovered in the Old Crow region. In them were deposits of dust, bones, pollen, and debris which, when deciphered by palaeontologists, gave a record of the natural history of the region for the past 20,000 years. At the beginning of that time period, the rock flow of the caves had begun to fill with *loess*, or fine, wind-blown dust. This accumulated at the rate of less than a millimetre per year for about 10,000 years. Analysis revealed that at first the land was tundra, inhabited by horses, mammoths, caribou, muskoxen, bison, mountain sheep, elk, wolves, and bears. About 14,000 years ago, the climate warmed appreciably, permitting shrubs and small trees to grow. Then, the pollen in the layers of dust in the caves showed, about 10,000 years ago the area became forested with spruce trees, the loess stopped blowing as vegetation covered the northern Yukon, and the large animals disappeared from the region.

Unfortunately, nothing in the caves suggested a human presence. The oldest incontrovertible traces of man are some flint artifacts dating to about 10,000 B.C. There are a few *suggestions* of human activity in the form of flint flakes dating to 14,000 B.C., as well as massive numbers of bones which seem simply too numerous to have been brought to the caves by any animal other than man. But there are no traces of fire from the 16,000 B.C. level of the caves, nor any tools — the things that are necessary to convince the doubters. The search continues, and the Old Crow region remains a hot-bed of archaeological research.

A glimpse into Yukon pre-history over several millenia is provided by Catherine McClellan's sensitive and evocative vignettes of native life at different periods. The earliest one, titled "late winter on a branch of the Porcupine River, 11,000 years ago," shows a people engaged in a hunter-gatherer way of life. The chief difference between their lives and those of later generations is the lack of tree cover and thus firewood in that era. Nonetheless, they were successful in hunting caribou and bison (and the occasional mammoth, though these were disappearing from the country), from which they obtained food and clothing:

> Bison meat is rare at this season of the year. In summer, everybody in camp can help to drive a herd over a cliff or up a narrow canyon by setting fires in the grass and then running and shouting behind to scare the animals. The dogs help in the drive too. Bison that break their bones as they fall over the cliff, or bunch up at the head of a canyon, can be quite easily killed by the hunters. In winter it is not so easy. The hunters had to follow the herd on foot for many miles before they had a chance to make this kill, but it was a specially good one. Butchering the cow, the hunters found an unborn calf in her—just the kind of food to give to the two wise but nearly toothless older men on whose knowledge the welfare of the group depends.[5]

The more recent prehistory of the Yukon, however, is better known. Sites have been investigated in the northern part of the Territory which indicate that the prehistory of the last few millenia is that of Inuit rather than Indian peoples as the artifacts dating from that period are common to the Inuit of

Alaska and elsewhere on the Arctic coast. In the part of the central Yukon which was unglaciated in the last ice age scientists have found fossils of great antiquity. A caribou antler punch found near Dawson has been dated to 21,900 B.C.; the same questions arise about it, however, as about the flesher found near Old Crow. The southern part of the Yukon, on the other hand, was almost completely covered by glaciers during the last ice age, thus the earliest traces of human occupation, found at a site along the Alaska highway near the Aishihik River, date to about 5,200 B.C.

In more recent times, there have been a number of distinct, but related, native peoples in the Yukon. Inland Tlingit, related to the Tlingit Indians of the Pacific northwest coast, lived in the area of the southern lakes. To the far north, the Inuit occupied the Arctic slope and Herschel Island. The Athapaskan peoples, divided culturally into the Kutchin, Han, Tutchone, and Kaska, covered much of the Territory. The Athapaskan peoples are racially, and in some cases linguistically, akin to native people living to the west of them in Alaska and to the east and southeast of them in the Mackenzie Valley. It is not possible to link these people with those who were in the Yukon during the glacial period, but it does seem that their direct ancestors were living in the Yukon by at least 8,000 B.C.[6]

Some of the history of the pre-contact Athapaskans — or Dene — particularly the migration of different subgroups, can be deduced from a study of linguistics. The linguistic history of the Dene suggests that as late as about 700 B.C. they were a single, closely-related group of people with a homeland in east-central Alaska and the adjacent part of the Yukon. After this date the Dene began to disperse, a movement into the present groupings that was not completed until about 1400 A.D. The native people of the Yukon are thus part of a large, widely dispersed Indian grouping. Because they traditionally did not observe rigid geographical boundaries, and their languages shade into one another through various dialects, attempts to divide them into distinct tribes or bands are arbitrary; most of the names given to them are the creations of Europeans.

The natives were hunters and gatherers, their lives governed by the natural environment and the changing seasons. The Kutchin people led lives centred around the hunting of large game animals, particularly caribou. Winter hunting was done on foot, and snowshoes were an important item of manufacture. The mainstay of the hunt, the Porcupine River caribou herd, was hunted intensely during the fall migration. The technique of the hunt was to construct two long rows of wooden sticks in the path of the animals, thus funnelling them into an enclosure, or surround, made of branches. Snares made of hide were set, and when the animals followed the path of sticks, or were frightened into it, they ran into the snares and were killed with bow and arrows. Sometimes the caribou were driven into a lake and then speared. Both techniques were highly effective, and if the migration

9

occurred when and where it was expected to, produced an abundance of food and useful animal products.

Although other animals, including moose, bear, hare, and ptarmigan, were hunted, the caribou was to the Kutchin what the seal was to the Inuit — food, clothing, and a host of other necessities. They thus had to live, at least in certain seasons, where the caribou lived. Particularly, they had to wait for them at river crossings and other likely places during the fall migration, when the animals were at their fattest and their hides were in the best condition. They also ate fish, which they speared or trapped in weirs. The Han Indians, who inhabited the west central Yukon, were particularly adept at this, developing the Klondike fishing grounds into the mainstay of their seasonal round. Indians further supplemented their diet with berries, roots, rose hips, and other wild plants.

Top left: *"A Co-Yukon Deer Corral," drawn by Frederick Whymper in 1865 clearly shows the traditional native technique of driving caribou into a "surround." The two rows of branches funnel the animals to the enclosure where they are easily killed.*

Centre left: *Kutchin Indians dancing, from Alexander Hunter Murray's journal of 1847–48.*

Lower left: *Kutchin winter tent of caribou hide, half-banked with snow and protected by a windbreak of trees, drawn by Alexander Hunter Murray.*

Murray's portrait of a Kutchin, with facial tattooing, wearing typical ornaments and beads, probably of European manufacture.

In each area of the Yukon, the Indian people adapted their eating habits, seasonal movements, and lifestyle to make the best use of the available food resources. The Indian groups, therefore, differed quite markedly. In the Alsek River drainage, in the Yukon's southwest corner, the Indians maintained regular contact with the coastal Indians and built their life around the abundant salmon stocks. The Kaska, on the other hand, relied on non-migratory fish and the hunting of large game animals. In all cases, poor fish stocks, a decline in the number of large animals, exceptionally cold winters or wet summers, or unpredictable changes in animal migratory habits could bring suffering and even starvation. In such instances there was usually recourse to smaller game — squirrels and rabbits — or berries, roots, and other plants to sustain life until the returns from the hunt improved.

The Yukon Indians pursued a way of life which has been described as "restricted wandering." Such people identify a particular territory as being their own, and take measures to restrict the access of others to the resources of that territory. As the seasons passed, the Indians moved about freely, according to no set pattern, in pursuit of food. The largest social unit was the local group or band — either a single extended family or a small number of related or friendly families. At certain times of the year, perhaps when a seasonal fish run or a caribou migration ensured that food supplies were plentiful, a larger number of families might live and hunt in one location. An intense social round of activities followed, including games, ceremonies, and even the launching of raids and attacks on neighbouring Indian or Inuit groups. Such sites were found along all the major rivers and lakes, and, logically, many later became the sites of fur trading posts and Indian villages.

The Indians' social structure was egalitarian — there were few differences in status, and although there were men who were recognized as leaders, their leadership was informal and largely advisory in nature — they had no means of enforcing their wishes.

The native peoples were intensely spiritual, although not in a way that Christian missionaries would readily acknowledge. They had few public religious forms except for shamans, who had a particular relationship with the supernatural that enabled them to cure illness, place spells on enemies, or bring good luck in the hunt. The Indians' world view, however, was filled with spirits — they suffused all animate and inanimate objects — and much of their behaviour was rooted in a strong awareness of the presence of spiritual forces.

The Inuit living on the Yukon's Arctic slope followed a very different lifestyle. The Arctic had been inhabited in a series of waves separated by many generations as the people adapted to changing environmental conditions and the development of new technology. Partly because these people lived in treeless regions, making their campsites and artifacts easier to find than those of people who lived in the forest, their prehistory is easier to trace. The Inuit of the western Arctic, unlike their relatives of inland Alaska, lived largely off the resources of the sea, which provided a rich foundation for their adaptation to a harsh and unforgiving environment. Theirs was a unique society — Europeans would marvel at its simplicity and yet wonder at its complexity, for the Inuit were able to live well in a land that white men found most inhospitable.[7]

Long before the first European actually set foot in the Yukon River Valley or along the Arctic slope, the native peoples had learned of the existence of white men. The various native groups — coastal Tlingit, Tagish, Tutchone, Kaska, Han, Kutchin, and Inuit — had for centuries been regular traders among themselves, bartering surplus goods from their own region for supplies not otherwise available. When Europeans — Russian in the 1740s and the British in the 1770s — arrived along the Pacific northwest coast, news of their appearance travelled quickly inland.

The Indians' desires for the new trade goods, especially the metal products like knives, axes, and pots, ensured an enthusiastic response to the advance of Europeans along the coast and down the Mackenzie River. The Kutchin Indians of central Alaska shifted significantly to the east, to better exploit the trading opportunities. Long-established inter-tribal trading networks were abandoned, altered, or expanded to carry manufactured goods into the Yukon and furs out to the Europeans.

The white men were making their presence felt, even though they had not yet advanced beyond the periphery. The trading Indians unwittingly carried European diseases into the interior, killing an untold number of Indians who had yet to see a European face-to-face. T. H. Canham, an Anglican missionary who worked in the Yukon in the late nineteenth century, was told by the Indians that the "great diminution during the past century in the number of native inhabitants" was due to "the ravages of smallpox communicated from the southern indians soon after the date of the earliest explorations."[8] The Yukon Indians, who numbered from seven to eight thousand before the Europeans arrived, declined rapidly in subsequent years; the loss of many elders and young adults to the devastating diseases was an incalculable loss to a society that relied on oral traditions.

By the 1830s, the upper Yukon River Valley was one of the few blank spots on the European maps of North America, sharing that status with parts of the eastern Arctic and the Arctic archipelago. Such gaps could not be tolerated, particularly when the unknown lands might hold commercial opportunities. It was therefore, only a matter of time before European traders and explorers breached the mountain barriers and entered the Yukon basin. The Indians of the interior, dependent on other natives for manufactured goods, eagerly awaited the fur traders' advance. The written history of the Yukon was about to begin.

FUR TRADE and
EXPLORATION of
THE YUKON

0   100   200
                          Miles

SIMPSON and DEASE 1837

JOHN FRANKLIN 1826

Firth River

N

Rampart House
Porcupine River
BELL 1845
Fort Youcon
(1847-69)

Lapierre's
House

McDOUGALL 1872

Peel's River Post (1840)
(Fort MacPherson)

BELL 1842

YUKON
CAMPBELL 1851
RIVER

Peel River

Klondike R.

Stewart River

Fort Selkirk
(1848-51)

CAMPBELL 1843

YUKON R.

Pelly River

White River

Kluane
Lake

Aishihik
Lake

INDIAN TRADE ROUTES

Teslin R.

Marsh
Lake

Teslin
Lake

Tagish
L.

Atlin
L.

CAMPBELL 1840

Frances Lake Post

A. MacKENZIE
MACKENZIE

GREAT
BEAR
LAKE

Keele River

1789
RIVER

Fort
Simpson

Nahanni River

Liard River

McLEOD

Dease R.
MCLEOD 1834

Dease
Lake

1831

Stikine River

DANIEL 1987

14

CHAPTER TWO

The Fur Trade

The European advance into the Yukon was surprisingly slow, given the voracious appetite of the fur trade companies for new areas to develop. Indians from the Mackenzie River Valley, the Lynn Canal region, and the lower Yukon had passed along stories of the area's riches, and urged traders on the periphery to expand their operations further inland, hoping that the establishment of trading posts would break their reliance on other Indian tribes for their European supplies. The economic realities of the North American fur trade, however, slowed the European commercial powers as they moved toward the far northwest.

The Russians, struggling to maintain their tenuous base on the lower Yukon, could not afford to mount a major expedition inland, and the British advance across North America was stalled by battles between competitive traders. The wintering partners of the North West Company, creators and protectors of a proud tradition that stressed strength, daring, and success at any cost, led the trade across the continent. Alexander Mackenzie, searching for a navigable passage to the Pacific Ocean, followed the river which now bears his name, but it turned north, not west, and he called it the "River of Disappointment," for the vast, underpopulated lands draining into the river seemed to hold little prospect for profit. Faced with competition to the south, however, the North West Company decided early in the nineteenth century to test the value of Mackenzie's discoveries. Posts were established at Fort Liard and Fort Good Hope, providing good returns to the company.[1]

The expansion did not solve the North West Company's many financial woes. Company traders treated the Indians badly, forcing them to trade at their posts, mis-using alcohol, and disrupting native settlements. On occasion the Indians struck back, burning company posts; more often, they simply avoided them. Yet the returns came in, swelling the North West Company's domination of European markets. Volume did not mean profit, however, for the company's trade lines, stretching from Montreal to the Mackenzie, were seriously over-extended, while the Hudson's Bay Company, firmly based in its posts, had expanded less aggressively, surrendering much of the trade to the Montreal traders. Since neither company seemed to be winning the cut-throat and increasingly violent competition, economic logic and the strong urging of the British Colonial office dictated an end to the rivalry and a consolidation of the fur trade enterprise. Lengthy negotiations followed, complicated by the intense personal animosities remaining from the years of competition, resulting in the 1821 merger of the North West Company and the Hudson's Bay Company.[2]

The task of co-ordinating the unwieldy fur trade of the northwest now fell to George Simpson, governor of the Northern District of the Hudson's Bay Company. Armed with an authoritarian outlook — Peter C. Newman calls him "a bastard by birth, and by persuasion" — an acerbic pen, and a relentless determination to improve the firm's profits, Simpson moved quickly to rationalize the fur trade.[3] Years of competition had swept much of Rupert's Land barren of furs, forcing the company to look elsewhere for the pelts needed to supply European markets. The recently opened Mackenzie Valley offered just such a prospect, and Governor Simpson was determined not to miss the opportunity. Simpson ordered the re-establishment of abandoned North West Company posts and the opening of new establishments along the Mackenzie and its major tributary, the Liard.

In 1825, Russian and British diplomats negotiated a boundary line separating their North American territories. Both sides accepted the 141st meridian, plus the "panhandle" — a vaguely-defined strip of land extending southward along the coast to 54° 40′ North latitude — seemingly settling a long-standing dispute over economic jurisdiction in the region. This line, set by uncaring diplomats half a world away, would become the permanent boundary between the Yukon Territory and Alaska. At the time it was drawn, no one knew about the land that it bisected. In later years, when Canadian and American governments gave substance to the political division, the Indians of the Yukon River Valley would be forced to choose a national allegiance. For now, the 1825 boundary was simply a European convention, of no importance in the north.[4]

The Russian American Fur Company maintained a series of posts along the coast and on the islands of the panhandle. To augment the declining returns from the depleted coastal fur stocks, the Russians encouraged their Tlingit trading partners to maintain and extend their trading contacts with Indians in the interior. The coastal natives did so with enthusiasm and skill, for the middleman trade brought considerable profit and allowed them to extend their domination over inland tribes. By the early 1820s, the Russian-Tlingit trade reached well inland, drawing thousands of pelts annually from British territory in what is now the Yukon. The Hudson's Bay Company's discovery of this trade angered Governor Simpson, who demanded immediate retaliation.

Top: *A great deal of the work in the Indians' camps was done by women. In addition to domestic duties, they helped transport supplies, hunted for small game, and dried fish and meat. This photograph was taken near Rampart House,* c. *1919.* YUKON TERRITORIAL ARCHIVES

Centre: *Lapierre House, opened in 1846, was the first Hudson's Bay Company post west of the Richardson Mountains. It was abandoned when the firm retreated from the Yukon River trade in 1893.* YUKON TERRITORIAL ARCHIVES

Below: *Originally a headquarters for the Hudson's Bay Company's trade in the upper Yukon River basin, Fort Youcon was taken over by American traders in 1869 and renamed Fort Yukon. The trading depot was, as the Hudson's Bay traders knew only too well, located well outside of British territory.* YUKON TERRITORIAL ARCHIVES

17

Top: *Frederick Whymper drew this scene at Fort Yukon in 1865, four years before the Americans arrived to order the Hudson's Bay Company out of United States territory.*

Below: *Alexander Hunter Murray's portrait of Kutchin hunters shows European influences — rifle, powder-horn, knife — as well as indigenous native artifacts.*

Under the 1825 treaty, British subjects had the right to travel on rivers originating on British soil which passed through Russian territory to the sea. In 1833, Simpson sent Peter Skeene Ogden aboard the *Dryad* to exploit one such river. He was to sail up the Stikine River, and establish a trade post, Fort Drew, on British territory. The fort would, Simpson believed, prevent the coastal Indians from "raiding" British territory and protect the returns from the Mackenzie River district. The Russians, however, ignored the terms of the treaty and refused to let Ogden pass upstream, touching off a diplomatic furor that soured British-Russian relations for much of the decade.[5]

Simpson then sought another means of penetrating the Russian trading zone. Fortunately for the Hudson's Bay Company, explorations undertaken earlier by Murdoch McPherson and John McLeod had pioneered a practical route. McPherson had travelled along the mid Liard River basin in 1824, reaching as far as the Beaver River. The company moved slowly to exploit the discovery, establishing Fort Halkett on the Nelson River in 1829.

John McLeod's voyages proved even more crucial. In 1831, McLeod had been commissioned to "to get some information on the sources of the West Branch of the Liard River." He and his party left Fort Simpson and the Mackenzie River on June 28, 1831. Their journey covered more than five hundred miles, through lands previously unknown to Europeans, along one of the most treacherous rivers in North America. McLeod's exploration ended at Lake Simpson, located slightly west of the Frances River, in what is now the southern Yukon. The trip diary and accompanying maps were forwarded to Governor Simpson, who confidently declared that the territory was "perhaps the richest Beaver country in America." McLeod was more cautious than his superior, emphasizing the difficulties of travelling the Liard and the great distances involved in reaching the district.[6]

The combination of McLeod's discoveries and continuing Russian encroachments on company trade spurred Governor Simpson on. He ordered further exploration of the Liard basin, hoping to find a route to the northwest coast. John McLeod returned to the field in 1834, unknowingly travelling on the heels of Ogden's failed attempt to break through the Russian blockade on the Stikine. His efforts were once more successful, for he ascended the Dease River, crossed Dease Lake and portaged into the Stikine River watershed. McLeod learned that the end point of his journey, along the Tuya River, was the principal meeting place between the coastal and interior Indians. Upon his return, he once more dispatched a full report of his journey to Governor Simpson.

Simpson reacted with enthusiasm to the discovery that the company could strike back overland at the Russian traders. The journey would be hard, and transportation costs would eat up much of the profit from any post established in the area, but the company believed that a small post would gather considerable trade from the "poor timid Indians of the Interior."

The task of establishing the post fell in 1836 to John Hutchinson, then stationed at Ford Halkett. Four days out of his home post, Hutchinson learned from his native companions that the Nahanni Indians intended to attack the brigade. He beat a hasty retreat, only to suffer a blistering attack from the pen of Governor Simpson: "The Governor and Committee consider it a stain upon the character of the concern that the Russians should so long be allowed to drain the country of its riches," Simpson wrote, "while we remained paralyzed by terror in Mackenzie's [District] through the childish reports of a nervous creature who was never calculated for the enterprising life of an Indian trader."[7]

Simpson passed the vital duty of westward expansion to Robert Campbell, a dour, God-fearing Scot. Campbell was one of that legion of ambitious fur traders who did so much to make the world aware of the interior of British North America. Born in Perthshire in 1808, his interest in the fur trade was sparked by tales told by his cousin, a Chief Factor with the Hudson's Bay Company. Hired by the company at the age of twenty-two, Campbell was employed at the experimental farm at Red River. He found supervising cabbages and sheep uninteresting and petitioned the company to send him north as a fur trader. When a position was finally offered, Campbell leapt at the chance for adventure, fueled by dreams of glory and fame as a North American explorer. In 1837, he reached Dease Lake, where he built a small post and settled in for the winter. The antagonism of local Indians, a harsh winter, and a lack of supplies brought on near starvation and forced Campbell to retreat in the spring. Ever stubborn, he demanded permission to return to Dease Lake the following year.[8]

However, following the *Dryad* affair, Hudson's Bay Company and Russian American Fur Company officials, aided by their countries' diplomats, had sought a negotiated settlement. An agreement was reached in February 1839, permitting the Hudson's Bay Company to lease the Alaskan panhandle for an annual payment of 2,000 land otter pelts and other benefits. Company ships and coastal posts could now collect the furs from the northwest coast, rendering further expansion inland along the Liard totally unnecessary. Robert Campbell and his crew were effectively rendered superfluous and faced absorption into the regular trading corps.

As exploration in one direction ended, a new avenue developed. In 1837, two company explorers, Thomas Simpson and Peter Warren Dease, seconded to scientific surveys in the Arctic, had been sent to chart the coastline west of the Mackenzie River district. Officially undertaken for "the acquisition of scientific knowledge and information, and unconnected with a view towards advantage from Trade,"[9] the Simpson and Dease expedition was actually carefully calculated to enhance the Hudson's Bay Company's image before an increasingly critical British public. In covering the distance left unexplored after the Franklin expedition a decade earlier, Thomas Simpson casually observed that "The Colville [River] separates the Franklin and Pelly Mountains, the last seen by us; and probably flows in a long course through a rich fur country, and unknown tribes in the west side of the Rocky Mountains."[10]

The discovery was a revelation to the always alert Governor Simpson. He quickly ordered a two-pronged expedition toward the Colville River. John Bell, then stationed at Fort Good Hope, was sent in 1839 to explore the Peel River, discovered earlier by John Franklin. He returned the following year and established Peel's River Post (Fort McPherson) to tap the lower Mackenzie fur trade and as a base for explorations to the westward. His initial attempts to cross the mountains were thwarted by the eastern Kutchins' unwillingness to share the secrets of access to the west. Even after he had successfully crossed the Richardson Mountains in 1842, descending perhaps as far as the Porcupine River, his Indian guide abandoned him, forcing Bell to retreat to the security of his post. The Peel River Kutchin dominated the trade with western Indians, not allowing them to visit the H.B.C. post for the purposes of trade. Reluctant to surrender their profitable position, the Kutchin interfered with Bell's progress whenever possible. However, Indians from the west — without furs — did visit the post, encouraging Bell to continue his efforts to reach across the mountains, holding out the promise of bountiful fur returns if the explorations proved successful.[11]

The workman-like but cautious John Bell was reluctant to proceed alone into unknown districts, where all but local guides had consistently proved unreliable, but he could not ignore Governor Simpson's repeated demands to continue the search. He set out again in 1845, this time taking Indians from the mid-Mackenzie River basin. In August of that year, he was able to report to Governor Simpson, "I have great pleasure in informing you that I have at length after much trouble and difficulties succeeded in reaching the 'Youcon,' or White Water River, so named by the natives from the pale colour of its water." Like McLeod before him, Bell cautioned that transportation difficulties would impede the trade, but he also reported that the Yukon appeared to be a rich fur trade district. If further incentive was required, and Simpson's excited reaction to Bell's discovery suggested that it was not, Bell also learned from the Indians that Russian trade goods had reached well up into the interior.[12]

John Bell was not left alone to carry on the search to the Colville. Robert Campbell, recently freed from the Dease Lake trade, was delegated to follow John McLeod's early exploration along the West Branch of the Liard, hoping to find the "Toucho" or Great Water River reported by the natives. Campbell set out in the early summer of 1840, accompanied by several of the men who had travelled with John McLeod almost a decade before. Upon reaching the Frances River, Campbell continued past McLeod's farthest point — the junction of the Simpson River — and on July 19 reached Frances Lake. Leaving most of his men to build a small cabin, Campbell proceeded with the exploration. After crossing the Finlayson Lakes, he reached the banks of a large river which he named the Pelly.[13] Unlike McLeod and Bell before him, Campbell wrote enthusiastically about the prospects for trade in the new district. "Few places," he wrote, "present a more favourable appearance for establishing a post than Frances Lake." Although Campbell would later regret his sanguine analysis, the Hudson's Bay Company now had two routes into the as-yet-unknown valley of the "Colville."[14]

One further effort was made to identify a quick access to the river valley to the west of the Mackenzie River. Chief Trader Lewes dispatched Andrew McBeath in 1843 from Fort Norman to explore the headwaters of the Gravel (later the Keele) River and to locate a pass through the mountains. Mc-Beath, like Bell, encountered trouble with his Indian guides, who abandoned him several days' journey into the hills. He attempted to press on alone, but reluctantly admitted defeat after several days of fruitless effort. This exploratory thrust, undertaken without Governor Simpson's approval, marked the limits of Hudson's Bay Company interest in westward exploration. The company had two routes into the new district; the time had come to exploit the opening.[15]

Robert Campbell set out first to expand the company's trade. From the beginning the trade was hampered by difficulties with navigation along the Liard River, the animosity of local Indians, and a shocking lack of country provisions in the area. A shortage of men in the Mackenzie River district stalled the construction of a post at Frances Lake until 1842. Campbell had standing orders to continue his explorations, but several times the near-starvation of his men forced him to cancel his plans. Robert Campbell did descend the Pelly to its junction with the Lewes (Yukon) River in 1843. Governor Simpson had arranged with the Russian American Fur Company to receive Campbell if he was able to continue his exploration further into Alaska. When Campbell learned from his native guides that Indians on the lower river planned to attack his expedition, he called off the more extensive exploration and returned to Frances Lake. Governor Simpson was disappointed with Campbell's reluctance to proceed — native rumours of violent Indians downstream were commonplace when guides did not wish their employers to continue — but he authorized him to establish a trade at the junctions of the Lewes and Pelly. The achievement of that goal would wait another five years.[16]

The push west from Peel River was more successful. In 1846, one year after Bell's final exploration to the Youcon, the company opened Lapierre House on the Bell River. The factor, Alexander Hunter Murray was accompanied by his new bride, the first white woman to enter the Yukon.

The following summer, Mrs. Murray, due to deliver her first baby, remained behind at Lapierre House when Murray led an expedition to the junction of the Yukon and Porcupine rivers and, two miles upstream, erected Fort Youcon, the largest and most important post in the new district. That the new post was probably inside Russian territory and hence in direct violation of an 1839 undertaking to the Russian American Fur Company, occurred to company officials, but did not deter them.[17]

Much of the Yukon River Valley still remained unknown to Europeans, but the Hudson's Bay Company had little interest in further discoveries. Robert Campbell, reluctant to settle down to the business of trading furs, requested permission to explore toward the Pacific Ocean, but Governor Simpson, after initially authorizing the journey, recognized the dangers inherent in such an exploration: "If we obtained our supplies from thence, we should be opening a communication to the most valuable part of the Northern Department by which strangers might find their way thither, and with our supplies we should be obliged to introduce the extravagant tariff of the N.W. Coast."[18]

The prospect of exploring the lower Yukon River similarly held little attraction. Shortly after arriving at Fort Youcon, Alexander Hunter Murray learned from the Indians that the Russians were but a short distance downstream. Recognizing the possible diplomatic and legal ramifications of further encroachment into Russian territory, Governor Simpson postponed fur explorations in that direction. With Fort Youcon established and Robert Campbell's men advancing along the Pelly, the company could now develop the local fur trade.[19]

Murray soon received further confirmation of Russian designs on the trade of the middle Yukon basin. Beginning in 1847 and continuing annually thereafter, the Indians kept him appraised of his competitors' movements along the river. In 1849, Indians travelling downstream laden with British trading supplies reported to Vasilii Deryabin, manager of the Nulato post, who was travelling upstream at the time, that rival traders had established a post upstream. Deryabin dispatched a note to Alexander Murray, and returned downstream to report the British advance to his superiors. Murray could not read the Russian script and passed the message on to Fort Simpson. From there it went to Governor Simpson. After more than a year, during which time the Hudson's Bay Company men braced for the imminent arrival of the Russians and a forced retreat from their post, Governor Simpson wrote to Murray that translators in London had deciphered the ill-written message. The note, which may have been an identifying jacket covering a longer letter which Murray never received, simply identified the writer and contained no threats or warnings. The Hudson's Bay Company men could rest easy. If the Russians were coming, they were not likely to be belligerent.[20]

With the threat of immediate expulsion settled, the Fort Youcon trade soon proved to be a most profitable addition to the corporate empire. The same could not be said for Robert Campbell's effort to the south. The Frances Lake–Pelly River trade proved a major disappointment from the very beginning. In the first year, the lack of food near Frances Lake forced Campbell to break up his establishment, sending three men to winter at Fort Simpson and a fourth to Fort Halkett. The men returned the following spring, permitting Campbell to make his foray down the Pelly. Governor Simpson was most anxious that a post be established at the junction of the Pelly and Lewes, and sent a major expeditionary force in 1845 to assist Campbell. Like so many of the company's plans in the southern Yukon, this one failed. Campbell had trouble getting his supplies up the Liard River, and the Fort Frances area did not generate enough country produce — fish and wild animals — to support even a few men. Once more, Robert Campbell sent a number of his men to Mackenzie River posts, placing unanticipated demands on posts already struggling to meet their own food needs. Unsure of the prospects of expanding the trade, Campbell called off the expedition to the Pelly and Lewes, declaring that the Indians from that area would bring their furs to Frances Lake.[21]

Governor Simpson, however, ordered Campbell to continue his expansion, and arranged for the men and supplies necessary. Campbell stalled once more and proceeded to Fort Simpson to secure further aid for his expedition. Murdoch McPherson, in charge of the Mackenzie District, was perturbed by Campbell's unauthorized appearance and wrote to Governor Simpson that the man "has a strong reluctance to go down the Pelly, which he has manifested all along, but did not act sufficiently candid in that respect." With some sympathy, McPherson noted further that earlier attempts had failed because of the explorer's "groundless dread of the Indians and of starvation, which unfortunately had taken a strong possession of Mr. Campbell's mind and which is more to be pitied than blamed."[22]

Nonetheless, Campbell set out for a third time, and this time succeeded. In September 1848, he reached the confluence of the Yukon and Pelly rivers and built a post, which he named Fort Selkirk. His enthusiasm for exploration boosted by this accomplishment, Campbell now sought permission to continue his explorations, but Governor Simpson was more interested in the successful establishment of the trade, and ordered the trader to stay where he was. Doing so was not easy. Difficulties of supply continued to plague the Frances Lake–Pelly River trade. In both 1849 and 1850, the annual outfit did not arrive intact, and James Stewart, Campbell's able and dedicated assistant, made a series of difficult journeys in an attempt to bring supplies to Fort Selkirk.

The receipt of trading goods did not ensure success. Year after year, Chilcat Indians (a sub-group of the Tlingit) from the Lynn Canal region entered the Fort Selkirk trading zone and carried away most of the prime furs that otherwise would have gone to the Hudson's Bay Company. The Tlingit were trading with the company's s.s. *Beaver*, which paid the higher tariff of the northwest coast rather than the lower one of the interior.

In 1850, Robert Campbell was directed to descend the Lewes to Fort Youcon, exploring the region between his post and Fort Youcon, in order to permit the Fort Selkirk traders to bring their supplies in through that route and allow the abandonment of the Liard River system. The journey, conducted in June 1851, proved an easy one. Little new was discovered, for the Indians had earlier informed the company traders of the course of the river; Campbell had corresponded regularly with Murray at Fort Youcon via Indian travellers. Fort Selkirk was, all believed, about to be placed on a more secure foundation. The enthusiasm was misplaced.

The Tlingit Indians returned *en masse* in 1851, and once more swept the region clean of prime furs, leaving only poor quality pelts for the Fort Selkirk traders. To Campbell's horror, several Mackenzie District officers were arguing for the closure of the unprofitable southern Yukon trade. The issue was resolved the following year. On August 21, 1852, when Campbell had unwisely dispatched almost all of his men on supply and provisioning work, a group of Tlingit ransacked Fort Selkirk, forcing him to flee for his life.[23]

Leaving several of his men with his trusted associate James Stewart, Campbell raced down the river to Fort Youcon and then on to Fort Simpson. There he hoped to convince James Anderson, in charge of the Mackenzie District, to provide the men and arms necessary to punish the Indians. Anderson refused. Unwilling to accept the ignominious loss of "his" district, Campbell set off on an epic snowshoe trek from Fort Simpson to Crow Wing, Minnesota, and on to Governor Simpson's headquarters at Lachine, near Montreal. Campbell travelled over 3,000 miles but Simpson too rejected his pleas for assistance, instead sending him on furlough to England. Robert Campbell's Yukon career was over.

Although Robert Campbell's time in the Yukon was scarcely filled with glory, his name is firmly entrenched in its history. Campbell is remembered and John McLeod is largely ignored because Campbell publicized his activities, particularly in his memoirs.[24] (One account of his explorations in the Yukon was published in the elementary-school textbook, the *Fifth Royal Reader*.) Campbell's account, which emphasizes his role, damns his critics, and paints a picture of commitment, courage, and accomplishment, was widely accepted as the standard interpretation of events. Contemporary records portray Robert Campbell in a less favourable light. He complained constantly about others within the Hudson's Bay Company's service, claiming many times that they were deliberately interfering with his efforts. Campbell also assumed, mistakenly, that he had been specially selected for service within the company and had particular claim to the attention of

Governor Simpson. Responding to Campbell's incessant complaints, Simpson finally wrote with more than a hint of exasperation: "You appear somewhat to have misunderstood the scope of authority I gave you for carrying out your discoveries... I have never hinted that your charge was to be considered separate and independent."[25]

Campbell never reconciled himself to subordinate status within the concern. Faced with difficulties and questions about his efforts, he threatened to resign his commission on several occasions. When, to his surprise, Governor Simpson once agreed to his request, he withdrew it. Over time, Robert Campbell became obsessed with the prospects of the Frances Lake and Fort Selkirk trade, in spite of all the difficulties, his hesitations about the local Indians, and even after evidence mounted against the trade ever being profitable. As James Anderson wrote, "Campbell is a zealous, enterprising man & a really estimable character I understand — but he is mad when he touches on the prospects of Selkirk."[26] Perhaps most surprisingly, Campbell heartily disliked the southern Yukon, an opinion he omitted from his memoirs. His post journals and letters are filled with caustic comments about the weather and the loneliness; he spent little time with the natives living around the post, but pined for companionship, literate discussion, and freedom from the fear of starvation. Though he was ambitious and had great plans for his district, he also hated and feared the north, as the bad poetry he committed to his journal reveals:

> O Solitude, where are the charms
> That sages have seen in thy face?
> Better dwell in the midst of alarms
> Than reign in this horrible place.[27]

He was particularly anguished when his good friend, James Stewart, was away from the post, and found solace in the Bible, his constant companion. He did not, to use the language of later adventurers into the unknown, have the "right stuff."

With the destruction of Fort Selkirk, the Hudson's Bay Company's hopes for a profitable return rested entirely on the success of the Fort Youcon enterprise. Fortunately for the concern, the post, unlike Fort Selkirk, exceeded even the Hudson's Bay Company's optimistic projections. The value of the new post lay, ironically, in a change in the long-established fur trade. Beaver had long been the industry standard, supplying a relatively stable felt hat trade. The introduction and popularity of the inexpensive silk hat in the mid-1840s thoroughly disrupted the beaver markets, forcing the Hudson's Bay Company to sell off huge stocks of beaver pelts at rock-bottom prices. As the beaver trade declined, markets for luxury furs — mink, fox, and especially marten — improved significantly. Fort Youcon, the company was pleased to discover, sat in the centre of one of North America's richest marten areas. For more than twenty years, it became one of the company's most valuable producers of the prime marten pelts so highly prized in Europe.[28]

The Fort Youcon trade was slow to develop, largely because the traders did not have enough trade goods to purchase all the pelts that the Indians brought to the post. As news of the fur wealth of the Yukon filtered back to Governor Simpson, the annual indent was enlarged. Not all company officers supported this initiative into what they knew to be Russian territory. James Anderson, for example, cut back on the Fort Youcon staff in 1852, arguing that in the aftermath of the attack on Fort Selkirk the trans-mountain trade should be cut altogether. The Indians' trade networks quickly re-formed around the new post, with the local Kutchins regulating access to the traders. The post was even free of the problem of food supplies that faced the other Mackenzie District forts. Native hunters and company servants harvested the abundant local resources, including salmon and whitefish, moose, caribou, small game, and the produce from a small garden, ensuring that Fort Youcon remained the envy of other posts.[29]

Trade goods were brought to the Yukon by a route so long and circuitous that it hardly seems possible that the trade it supported could have yielded the Hudson's Bay Company any profit. A glance at a map of Canada shows the staggering logistical feat of bringing trade goods to the Yukon and the furs back to market. Every summer, ships brought trade goods from Britain and York Factory, on the west coast of Hudson Bay. From there they were shipped upriver to Lake Winnipeg and the Red River settlement, the hub of the western fur trade. From what is now Manitoba, the goods went west along the North Saskatchewan River, then over the Methye Portage to the Athabasca River; down that river to Lake Athabasca; across the lake to the Slave River; down the Slave to Great Slave Lake; across that lake to the Mackenzie River; down that river to Peel River; up the Peel to Peel River Post; across the mountains, a long and arduous journey, to the Bell River; and finally down the Bell and Porcupine rivers to the Yukon and Fort Youcon. It sounds — and was — remarkable, especially when it is remembered that except for some sailing on Lake Winnipeg, it was all done with the muscle power of native, Métis, and British labourers.

Because of this enormously long and complicated trade route, the Yukon trade operated on a seven-year cycle. This meant that from the time that trade goods were brought from the manufacturers in England until the furs arrived at auction in England to pay for them, seven years had elapsed. It is a mark of the profitability of the Yukon marten trade that the post was maintained in the face of these impressive logistical and financial difficulties. Until the company was forced to abandon the post in 1869, Fort Youcon served as the centre of European activity in the upper Yukon basin.

The Yukon River Indians welcomed the advance of the fur traders, particularly as it freed them from dependence on the eastern Kutchin bands. The natives moved quickly to exploit the opportunities now available, displaying a sophisticated understanding of the nuances of European trading systems. They sought at every opportunity to exploit the Hudson's Bay Company's concern about Russian expansion. The Fort Youcon Indians repeatedly informed the company traders about Russian plans, prices, and promises, and the company's men had no means of judging the accuracy of the reports. Most often they assumed they were true, and made their plans accordingly.

Behind the vague and uncertain native reports lay an attempt by the Russian American Fur Company to defend their trading interests in the area. Although poorly financed and chronically short of men and boats along the lower Yukon, the Russian American Fur Company traders travelled with some regularity to the Lake Mintokh area at the western end of the Yukon flats. Efforts to expand beyond that point stalled after the communication between Deryabin and Alexander Murray. In 1851, Indians from the Koyukuk River attacked the Nulato post, the Russian company's main establishment in the area, killing Deryabin and several of his employees. The post was immediately re-established, but plans to push upriver had to be postponed. The Russians' inability to challenge the Hudson's Bay Company directly left Fort Youcon secure and profitable.[30]

Frequent native reports about Russian trade served to alert the Hudson's Bay Company traders to the possibility that competition could swiftly alter the commercial balance in the Yukon basin. The company sought other means of controlling Indian trading and trapping activities. They traded only through the natives' "principal men," who were showered with generous gifts in anticipation of their enduring support. But the Indians were difficult to control. If the terms of trade were not sufficiently attractive they simply withheld their furs, traded only low quality pelts, or took their furs downstream to the Russians. The trading chiefs lacked permanent authority within their bands; their advice was ignored if the negotiated conditions were deemed unacceptable.

That the Indians responded so cautiously to the Fort Youcon fur trade underscores their conservative response to European trade goods. Many items — knives, pots, and axes — had been in use among the Indians years before direct contact. They knew in advance which goods they wanted and, like other Indians across the country, did not succumb to a "furs for trinkets" exchange. Initially, they traded primarily for only a few select items, particularly guns, ammunition, tobacco, and beads (which they used as currency). These items were accepted only if they fitted within very rigid specifications; on one occasion, the Indians rejected an entire shipment of beads because they were the wrong colour. Other goods, such as blankets, were "tried out" first. If found to be a useful addition to the Indians' material culture, a process that usually required several years' use, the goods were adopted on a more widespread basis. It was once thought that within a few years, perhaps a generation, of contact with white traders, the Indians lost their traditional skills and became more or less dependent on the traders. More recent research has dispelled this ethnocentric view; certainly the history of the Yukon Indians shows that they took from the trade only what they wanted; the trade was a supplement to their way of life and did not control it. Conversely, the natives exerted considerable influence over the pace and direction of the trade.

The Indians did their best to get the most favourable terms possible from the Hudson's Bay Company traders. The officers had to follow an official price list, or tariff, established for the entire Mackenzie River district. The Yukon tariff compared unfavourably to the prices offered along the north-west coast, but the company refused native demands to raise it. The Hudson's Bay Company really had little choice. If the Fort Youcon tariff was enriched, the company traders believed, the Peel River Indians would carry their furs to the Youcon to trade, forcing the company to transport them back again. Faced with intransigence on price, the natives nonetheless kept the pressure on, demanding goods on credit, expecting more generous "presents," (actually part of the overall exchange), and paying careful attention to the quality of the trade goods. The threat of a boycott was a powerful tool; in 1865, their refusal to trade while Strachan Jones, a company officer who was unbending in his refusal to all native requests, remained at the post led to his removal.

The natives were also very aware of the Europeans' vulnerability. There never were more than twelve company men at Fort Youcon, an island of British influence surrounded by a sea of Indians. From time to time, the Indians were not above hinting that they might attack the post unless conditions of trade improved, threats which took on a new urgency after the destruction of Fort Selkirk. The best the company could do was to point out to the Indians that to destroy Fort Youcon would hurt them economically.

The non-appearance of Russian traders and the Indians' failure to attack the post gradually convinced the Hudson's Bay Company traders that the threats could be taken not too seriously. At no point, however, was the company's confidence such that they could reject out of hand the threats or warnings. The vulnerability of Fort Youcon and the comparative power of the native people ensured at least partial attention to their reports. When, in the early 1860s, the Indians commented that the Russians were again planning an expedition upstream, the Fort Youcon traders asked the Company permission to challenge the Russians on the lower Yukon, thus ensuring the company continued access to the vaunted mid-Yukon marten-producing areas. Their request was initially rejected.

The natives' reports were finally borne out in 1862. After a decade of inactivity in the field of exploration, Ivan Furuhjelm, chief manager of Russia's colonies, demanded greater initiative from the officers of the fur trade. In an attempt to expand business in the Yukon, Ivan Lukin was ordered to travel secretly to Fort Youcon and report on the Hudson's Bay Company operations. Lukin arrived unannounced, stayed for a few days, and then returned downriver. This visit provided concrete proof that the Indian reports, only partially believed over the years, had considerable substance in fact. The Russians *were* coming.[31]

Now that the Russians knew the location of their post, the Hudson's Bay Company could legitimately be expelled at any moment. Faced with the imminent loss of the valuable Yukon River trade, the company decided in 1864 to take the offensive. Boats were dispatched downstream, by-passing middlemen and carrying competition deeper into Russian territory. A Protestant missionary from Alaska later described the episode:

> Long before any steamboats plied these waters, the Hudson Bay voyageurs from Fort Yukon came down through the rapids in large flat-bottomed boats loaded with trade goods, and returned with furs for which these were bartered. Old natives at Tanana still tell with admiration of the Batteaux with six pairs of oars which brought them guns and blankets and powder and shot and tea and tobacco, and gave them better terms than the Russians from Nulato gave.[32]

The Fort Youcon Kutchin, who had so carefully sown the seeds of competition, unexpectedly found themselves done out of a valuable trading position.

While there is no question that the natives welcomed the advance of the fur trade, certain aspects of the arrival of Europeans carried serious, long-term costs. Particularly devastating was the importation of European disease. North American Indians had been biologically separate from Europe and consequently had had no exposure to numerous common diseases, including measles, influenza, chicken pox, smallpox, and whooping cough. The fatal effects of these diseases were felt even before Hudson's Bay Company explorers reached the Yukon River Valley, for the illnesses had been passed inland via native trading networks. Now, with Europeans in their midst, the opportunities for exposure increased. Although the company's officers helped out whenever possible, the Indians had no means of treating the new diseases. Illnesses of the type now being experienced had traditionally been blamed on the sorcery of enemies; shamans, or Indian spiritual leaders, were believed to have great powers to cast spells of this kind. Nothing of this magnitude had ever been visited upon the Yukon Indians. Traditional explanations seemed less than adequate in the face of repeated "virgin soil" epidemics. Anthropologist Shepherd Krech III has estimated that over the first fifty years of contact, close to five-sixths of the Kutchin Indians perished from the many illnesses.[33]

Few outbreaks matched the severity of the 1865 scarlet fever epidemic. Boat crews carrying supplies for the Mackenzie River district contracted the disease and carried it with them into the northland. With no replacements available in the district, the company felt it had no choice but to send them on their way. The infected boat crews continued downstream to Peel's River Post. The disease, which ravaged many bands along the Mackenzie, passed over the mountains with the Fort Youcon supply expedition. Indians died by the dozen; whole families were wiped out in a matter of days. Many of the stricken natives, panicking in the face of the unknown, fled from the trading post, seeking the security of the bush. Unwittingly, they carried the deadly germs to other Indians throughout the Yukon basin. Hudson's Bay Company officers calculated that between 170 and 200 of the Fort Youcon Indians perished, as did countless others far from the view of the traders.

The pattern was repeated many times in the fur trade period, albeit on a smaller scale. It is difficult to assess its demographic consequences. In harsh, biological terms, the loss of the elderly and the very young — the most likely victims of any outbreak — was less serious than the deaths of men and women in their reproductive years. Even so, the population loss was staggering. More difficult to comprehend are the cultural implications of this systematic devastation. The repeated thinning of the native population carried away many of the bands' elders, destroying at the same time much of the oral tradition, local knowledge, and traditional skills so essential to the Indians' cultural survival. The Indians were, if anything, adaptable, but they had to struggle very hard to overcome the personal and communal losses attending the spread of European diseases.

The natives had to deal with more Europeans than just the fur traders; this period also brought the first missionaries and other adventurers interested in unlocking the many mysteries of the upper Yukon River Valley. The Church of England and the Roman Catholic church had raced each other across the northwest, hoping to be the first to place their mark on the "heathens" of the north. By 1858, the Anglican Church Missionary Society and the Catholic Oblates of Mary Immaculate (O.M.I.) had reached the lower Mackenzie. Rev. William West Kirkby made the first move into the Yukon River Valley in 1861. Leaving his post at Fort Simpson for three years, he travelled with the Hudson's Bay Company fur brigades to Fort Youcon, capitalizing on the firm's bias in favour of the Protestant missionary effort. Buoyed by what he felt was an enthusiastic response, Kirkby vowed to return.[35]

When he did, in 1862, his competition followed. Father Seguin of the O.M.I. had been assigned to the Fort Youcon area and had also accompanied the fur traders across the divide. But the Hudson's Bay Company officers spurned Seguin, offering only minimal courtesies and encouraging the natives to remain loyal to Kirkby and the Church Missionary Society.

If Kirkby was pleased with the traders' response, he was distressed by the apparent indifference of the local Kutchin Indians. The excitement attending Kirkby's first visit had faded, raising doubts in the missionary's mind about the chances for success in this isolated charge. But the Church Missionary Society was not easily dissuaded from pursuing a promising field, particularly with the Catholics so close on their heels. Counting on the Hudson's Bay Company–Church Missionary Society alliance to block the O.M.I. from the Yukon, Kirkby directed his efforts towards recruiting a missionary for the Fort Youcon area.[36]

Kirkby's call for assistance was heard by Robert McDonald, a mixed-blood volunteer from Red River. Experienced in native missions and blessed with a facility for Indian languages, McDonald left for Fort Youcon in the summer of 1862. McDonald worked quickly to gain the allegiance of the local Indians, placing particular importance upon learning their language and translating the Bible and other religious documents. The unassuming missionary was perfectly suited for his northern service. He respected the native lifeways, and sought to integrate Christian teachings into Indian culture, rather than demanding an immediate end to age-old traditions. Unfortunately, these promising beginnings faltered in 1864, when the usually robust missionary fell ill with influenza and, for a time, lay near death. He petitioned for permission to abandon his post, and asked his superiors to secure a replacement.[37]

The Church Missionary Society, always hard-pressed to find acceptable candidates for service anywhere in Rupert's Land, reluctantly turned to the task of finding another northern missionary. In 1865 William Carpenter Bompas answered the call. Already thirty-four, and serving as a curate in a small English parish, Bompas was an unlikely missionary. He had attempted several times to secure a place overseas with the Church Missionary Society, but had been turned down due to his unimpressive academic accomplishments and comparatively advanced years. While the C.M.S. would not have sent a man of Bompas's qualifications to such vital fields as China or Africa, the organization agreed to dispatch him to replace Robert McDonald at Fort Youcon.[38]

Bompas — single, uncomfortable in the structured society of England, and desperately anxious to start his work with the Indians — left almost immediately for his northern posting. On Christmas Day 1865, he arrived at Fort Simpson, where to his surprise and dismay he found that McDonald had made an unexpectedly complete recovery from his illness and was ready to return to Fort Youcon. Rev. Kirkby was most anxious that the north not lose the eager Bompas, thus it was agreed that Bompas would work as an itinerant preacher, travelling through the Mackenzie and Yukon regions as season and need dictated. McDonald, who was at Fort Simpson when Bompas arrived, would return to Fort Youcon, thus ensuring that the upper

Top: *William Carpenter Bompas,
first Bishop of Selkirk (later
Yukon) Diocese, devoted his adult
life to missionary work among the
Indians. He was a driven, zealous
man, notable for his inability to get
along with other whites in the
north.* ANGLICAN CHURCH
ARCHIVES

Below: *Tanana Indian, 1865.
Whymper said that the Tananas
reminded him "of the ideal North
American Indian I had read of but
never seen."*

Yukon would remain a Church of England preserve, free from Catholic interference. It was a modest beginning for the missionary enterprise in the Yukon, but the foundations of a much broader effort had clearly been set.

Only later would the missionaries actively publicize their northern adventures outside the confines of the church. For the time being, public knowledge of the far northwest rested on the scanty reports of the fur traders, Robert Campbell's contributions being the most noticeable. In the 1860s, however, a small band of American scientist-adventurers began a more thorough exploration of the Yukon River Valley, at the same time going out of their way to promote their discoveries, publishing popular travelogues as well as scientific articles describing one of North America's last unknown frontiers.

One of the first, and most intriguing, of these adventurers was the young Robert Kennicott. The New Orleans-born Kennicott had become a scientist of some note by the age of twenty. After a short term as the natural history curator at Northwestern University museum, he was recruited by Spencer Fullerton Baird of the Smithsonian Institution to undertake an extended zoological examination of the sub-Arctic. Kennicott's application was well-received by Hudson's Bay Company Governor George Simpson, who offered transportation with the fur brigades and access to the Mackenzie River and Yukon basin posts. He set out in the summer of 1860, travelling from Red River to Fort Resolution. In August he pushed on to Fort Youcon, where he passed the winter. For more than a year he travelled back and forth between Fort Youcon and Peel's River Post, collecting hundreds of specimens of the flora and fauna of the district. When, during a visit to Fort Simpson in 1862, he heard that his father lay near death, Kennicott hurriedly left for Chicago.[39]

Kennicott left a striking legacy in the scientific world, one that extended far beyond his short stay in the north. He was, by all accounts, a remarkable man, blessed with scientific intuition and a gregarious nature. He made numerous friendships with the fur traders, firing their interest in scientific collecting. The H.B.C. officer corps offered excellent material for the Smithsonian's scientific interests. They were, in the main, educated, literate men, often suffering from intellectual starvation in their isolated northern postings. Naturalist William Dall described Kennicott's impact on the traders: "The advent of Kennicott, young, joyous, full of news of the outside world, ready to engage in any of their expeditions or activities and to take hardships without grumbling was an event in their lives. When he taught them how to make birdskins and collect Natural History objects and showed them how, by means of their collections, their names would become known in the civilized world and even printed in books, they seized on the project with enthusiasm."[40]

Kennicott clearly had the Hudson's Bay Company traders on side. At

Fort Youcon he asked James Lockhart to collect animals and birds and requested that Strachan Jones gather fish and insects. James Flett of Lapierre House, an "unadorned brick," according to the scientist, supported the work enthusiastically, however, not leaving matters to chance. Kennicott asked Spencer Baird of the Smithsonian: "Please write to him and set him up a little — not failing to compliment his stepson William for his bird skinning as Flett is pleased with his being noticed. ... Only please remember to write within Flett's comprehension — he is a brick, but, as I've said, an unpolished one and is quite uneducated." The careful cultivation of the traders worked. Lockhart was so anxious to get to collecting that as soon as the spring fur boat departed he rushed into the field. Even before he left the north, Kennicott could write confidently to Baird: "the operations in zoology here are getting quite in earnest and we can now turn the crank and keep the wheels... going from the Smithsonian." For decades to come, Kennicott's many northern friends inundated the Smithsonian Institution and other museums with natural history items, Indian artifacts, reports on northern life, and descriptions of native society.

A later observer noted that Kennicott had "by his travels and collections added directly and indirectly perhaps more than any other to the riches of the Smithsonian collection." His efforts succeeded primarily because of his ability to mobilize the considerable talents and enthusiasms of the fur traders. By demonstrating how men isolated by distance from the comforts and stimulation of European culture could earn respect and admiration in the best intellectual and social circles, Kennicott earned the continued support of dozens of company officers.

Kennicott's interest in the Yukon basin had not been satiated, and when, in 1864, Perry McDonough Collins offered him a chance to return, he leapt at the opportunity. Collins had made his fortune in the California gold rush and, excited about the prospects for investments in Russia, had secured an appointment as American commercial agent on the Amur River. When he returned from this post in 1857, he proposed an overland telegraph line to link the United States with Siberia. After many unsuccessful attempts, he sold the idea to the Western Union Telegraph Company, which had just finished a line across the United States. The project was, for its time, of staggering proportions. The line had to cover hundreds of miles of unsurveyed and almost unpopulated territory. The success of the venture also relied on the Russians' ability to build a connecting line from the Amur to St. Petersburg, no mean feat in itself. Late in 1864, the Overland Telegraph Company, formally organized and with the requisite rights-of-way across the United States, British North America, and Alaska in hand, was ready to start work.[41]

The task of organizing this project fell to Charles Buckley, a military engineer, and Captain Charles Scammon. Buckley, in turn, sought out the highly regarded Robert Kennicott, the only American (and one of the few men outside the employ of the Hudson's Bay Company) who knew anything of the far northwest, to command the exploration work on the Yukon River section of the survey. Kennicott was quick to quit his job at the Smithsonian on the condition that he be permitted to combine scientific collecting with his exploratory work for the telegraph company. Buckley agreed and named the scientist Director of the Scientific Corps in addition to his other duties. Kennicott signed on a number of scientists, including the youthful William Dall, a doctor by training and a naturalist by avocation, to accompany the expedition. He also recruited Victoria artist Frederick Whymper to record the progress of the surveys. Crews set out from San Francisco in the spring of 1865, but even as Buckley's men headed for the northwest, the telegraph project was perilously close to disaster. Other men were at the same time attempting the equally difficult task of laying a telegraph line along the floor of the Atlantic Ocean. When that remarkable exercise succeeded in July 1866, plans for the Overland Telegraph collapsed immediately. However, teams in the field would not learn of this disaster for another year, so the surveys pushed on.

For Robert Kennicott, the assignment answered his fondest wish. Ever since leaving the north three years before, he had longed to return and now, with the necessary financial backing, he could. By May 1865 Kennicott, Frank Ketchum, and Michael Lebarge, two Canadians who were to oversee construction of the telegraph line through the mid-Yukon River Valley, had reached Nulato. Here, tragedy struck. Never a healthy man, Kennicott had suffered a mild stroke before leaving the United States. Still bothered by the affliction, he seemed to have lost the spark and enthusiasm that had so marked his personality. One morning he could not be found in camp. His colleagues set out in search, and found his body on the bank of the nearby Yukon River.

Kennicott's death sent a shock wave through the fur trade posts of the northwest. The H.B.C. officers had lost a treasured friend and the scientific community had lost a man of great potential, only partially realized.

The work of the Collins Overland Telegraph had to continue. William Dall, who had been scheduled to journey to Siberia, took over Kennicott's scientific duties and remained in the Yukon. To Ketchum and Lebarge fell responsibility for supervising the surveys and directing the preliminary work on the telegraph. While Dall and Whymper passed the winter at Nulato, Ketchum and Lebarge, accompanied by the Russian American Fur Company trader, Ivan Lukin (who had first visited Fort Youcon in 1862) journeyed to the Hudson's Bay Company post. After a return trip down the Yukon to secure provisions for further exploration, Ketchum and Lebarge returned to Fort Youcon. Pushing on overland, they reached as far as Fort Selkirk, site of Robert Campbell's ill-fated trading post, before turning back once more. Dall and Whymper, meanwhile, had journeyed up to Fort Youcon, where they were reunited with their colleagues. The telegraph crews now departed, their preliminary explorations completed, Dall's notebooks filled with observations and his bags bulging with specimens of the region's natural history. Whymper had also been active, sketching numerous pictures of the human and physical landscape.

Arrival at Nulato brought unwelcome news of the successful laying of the transatlantic cable and the collapse of Perry Collins' dream of a northern link to Europe. Yet the ambitious telegraph scheme had contributed in ways few had imagined to the opening of the northland. William Dall and Frederick Whymper produced lavishly illustrated travelogues of their journeys, awakening many North Americans to the possibilities of the Yukon River Valley. Frank Ketchum, Michael Lebarge, and several other employees had been struck by the potential of the north and returned to it in the wake of the American purchase of Alaska. Long a private preserve of the Hudson's Bay Company and the Russian American Fur Company, the Yukon basin had now been exposed to the world.

So long as the land west of the 141st meridian lay in Russian hands, however, little was done to develop the region. The Russian government had, at times, urged its fur company to expand its activities in the Alaskan interior and had supported Collins' telegraph project, but in fact it had done little to exploit the potential of its North American holdings. The United States had long shown an interest in the Russian territories. Alaska held resource riches and was strategically placed in the north Pacific. In the passionate era of Manifest Destiny and dreams of a democratic empire, the thought of America leap-frogging across British North America to gain a foothold in the far northwest was attractive in some quarters. Russia, for her part, was anxious to dispense with a disappointing colony.

Negotiations picked up in the wake of the American Civil War. Late in March 1867, Russian and American negotiators, the latter led by Secretary of State William Seward, concluded a deal. The Americans paid $7.2 million for what American critics immediately labelled "Seward's Icebox." The Americans, waiting in anticipation of an announcement, moved in quickly. Hutchinson, Kohl and Company of San Francisco purchased the assets of the Russian American Fur Company and moved into the Yukon River trade. Free traders, a few American missionaries, and a small number of government officials followed the commercial migration into the newly acquired territories.

Increased American activity, first noticeable on the lower reaches of the Yukon, threatened to transform life in the Yukon even more substantially. The H.B.C. soon lost the lower Yukon trade. The annual boat excursions continued, but in 1868 H.B.C. officers met American traders at the mouth of the Tanana River, the usual centre of exchange for the middle Yukon basin.

The Americans demanded an immediate end to British trading on American soil and petitioned their government to intercede. The British and the Hudson's Bay Company officials feigned ignorance, claiming that they had no confirmation that Fort Youcon was actually on United States' territory, and promising to abandon the post if scientific evidence was provided that the site lay outside of Canada. This was a useful tactic, but it did not prevent the H.B.C. from preparing for the inevitable evacuation of Fort Youcon. James McDougall, in charge of the post, warned to expect American orders to vacate, was uneasy with the company's cautious approach and argued that a new post should be opened further downstream to head off any American advance. He was overruled.[42]

American representations at the diplomatic level carried the day. In mid-summer 1869, Governor McTavish of the Hudson's Bay Company sent word that Fort Youcon was to be abandoned forthwith. The men and supplies were to be moved to a new post to be built at the ramparts along the Porcupine River, believed to be on British territory. Hoping to prevent any advantage from passing to the advancing Americans, McDougall was ordered to "set fire to the Fort and destroy everything that he cannot bring away with him." It seemed like an ignoble end to a successful fur-trading venture, but Fort Youcon was not destined for the flames.[43]

In late July of that year, Captain Charles Raymond of the U.S. Navy, travelling aboard the steamer *Yukon* arrived at Fort Youcon, before the instructions to destroy the establishment had reached McDougall. Raymond, after ascertaining that the site was on American soil, immediately occupied the post on behalf of the American government, installed American traders, and ordered the Hudson's Bay Company to cease all trading activities. Due to the lateness of the season, the Hudson's Bay Company men did not have time to move up the Porcupine and so decided to pass the winter at Fort Youcon. McDougall could purchase food supplies from the Indians, but had to turn away all proffered furs.[44]

Despite repeated protestations of friendship and co-operation, the American traders (Captain Raymond having left) and the Hudson's Bay Company men passed an uneasy winter. Barred by the Americans from trading furs to the Hudson's Bay Company, the Indians retaliated by refusing to sell food to the Yankees. The American flag, run up the Fort Youcon flag-pole, disappeared mysteriously one night. The Fort Youcon Indians, who had enjoyed generally favourable relations with the British, resented the intrusion of the Americans into their trading zone, and promised McDougall that they would remain loyal to the company, even after it retreated up the Porcupine.

There was no glory in the company's abandonment of Fort Youcon. When the ice set in the fall, McDougall sent several men up the Porcupine to establish a small post at the foot of the Upper Ramparts, believed erroneously to be on British territory. The rest of the establishment followed the next spring. Although the Hudson's Bay Company head office had decided to sell the buildings at the old post to Hutchinson, Kohl and Company of San Francisco, they had not yet been formally dispensed with. McDougall was ordered to return to Fort Youcon in the summer of 1870 to meet representatives of the American firm and to negotiate the final terms. He arrived early in July and waited in vain until the third of September, when he learned that Hutchinson, Kohl and Company had no intention of purchasing the property and did not even plan to use the fort that year. He removed some supplies left behind during the spring evacuation and returned to Rampart House. Eventually, American traders took over the abandoned post.

The forced removal from Fort Youcon marked the end of an era in the Yukon. The Americans carried a new level of competitive exchange into the trade, altering the economic balance in the region. They also brought the values of the American frontier, including an unsympathetic attitude towards the Indians, and a determination to broaden the economic base into other, non-fur, trade sectors. The Hudson's Bay Company was in full retreat, and would never again have such a presence in the Yukon.[45]

The twenty years between 1847 and 1867 had given the Yukon a place on the maps of the world, but much about this vast, diverse land remained unknown, except to the Indians, who shared their secrets reluctantly. The natives had been brought into the nexus of European commerce and had proven themselves adept at dealing with the new economic and social forces. An even greater change lay in the offing.

DAWSON and THE KLONDIKE

139°30' 139°00' 138°30'W

0   5   10   15 Miles

RIVER

Rock Cr.

DAWSON

KLONDIKE

Hunker creek

Klondike City

64°00' N

64°00' N

YUKON

Cheechako Hill

Bonanza Cr.

⊛ George Carmack's Discovery

Little Skookum ⊛
Big Skookum ⊛

⊙ GRAND FORKS

Gold Bottom Cr.

⊛ Robert Henderson's Claim

RIVER

N

Eldorado Creek

Ready Bullion Cr.

INDIAN

Quartz Creek

RIVER

139°30' 139°00' 138°30'W

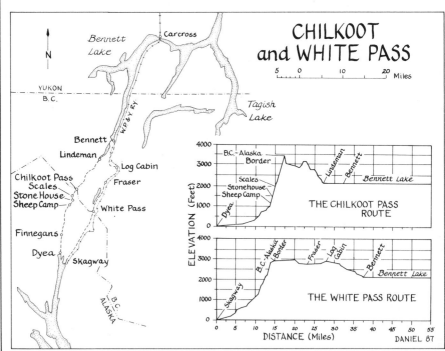

CHILKOOT and WHITE PASS

Bennett Lake

Carcross

5   0   10   20 Miles

YUKON
B.C.

Tagish Lake

W.P.&Y. Ry.

Bennett

Lindeman

Log Cabin

Chilkoot Pass
Scales
Stone House
Sheep Camp

Fraser

White Pass

Finnegans

Dyea

Skagway

B.C.
ALASKA

The Chilkoot Pass Route elevation chart:

ELEVATION (Feet)

4000
3000 BC-Alaska Border
2000 Scales / Stonehouse / Sheep Camp
1000 Dyea
0

Lindeman
Bennett
Bennett Lake

THE CHILKOOT PASS ROUTE

The White Pass Route elevation chart:

4000
3000 B.C.-Alaska Border
2000 Skagway
1000
0

Fraser
Log Cabin
Bennett
Bennett Lake

THE WHITE PASS ROUTE

0   5   10   15   20   25   30   35   40   45   50   55
DISTANCE (Miles)

DANIEL 87

CHAPTER THREE

The Search for Bonanza, 1870–1896

The unceremonious ejection of the Hudson's Bay Company from Fort Youcon marked the end of an era. With Yankee traders now established in the old British post, the contours of the Yukon basin fur trade had been thrown into disarray. The company now faced a difficult choice — to stay in the Porcupine River basin and fight for the remnants of a once profitable trade, or to withdraw to the security of the company's one remaining monopoly zone, the Mackenzie River Valley. The decision was not easily arrived at, for factions within the company held very different visions of the firm's future in the north.

The company was fortunate in its officer in the Yukon. James McDougall was a man of ability, admired in the trade and destined for a long and successful career in the Hudson's Bay Company. Perhaps more important at this juncture, McDougall was well-liked by the local Indians, who respected his honesty, easy-going manner, and openness. They were genuinely distressed when McDougall informed them of the forced evacuation, and spoke earnestly of their determination not to trade with the Yankees. This was more than pure speechifying, although their loyalty was directed more to McDougall than to the Hudson's Bay Company.

Shortly after the Americans arrived, McDougall started construction of a small post at Howling Dog (or Rampart House), below the ramparts on the Porcupine River. Even as the post was being occupied, however, the company decided to abandon the location and re-orient the Yukon trade around the small outpost at Lapierre House. The mistake of the previous year — leaving Fort Youcon standing for the Americans to occupy — was not repeated. McDougall was ordered to burn down the building before he left.

Lapierre House proved to be too isolated to serve the Yukon basin trade properly, and in 1872, the company moved to re-establish Rampart House, this time at the upper end of the ramparts, a point believed to be well within Canadian territory. The manoeuvre served two purposes — offering Yukon Indians an opportunity to continue to trade with the H.B.C. and keeping the

American traders in the Yukon River basin out of the lucrative trade of the Mackenzie River district.[1]

To northern officers, the Yukon fur trade was far from a dead issue. In 1871, the Canadian, British, and American governments negotiated the Treaty of Washington. Among its many terms was a small and seemingly inconsequential provision permitting Canadians freedom of navigation along the Yukon, Porcupine, and Stikine rivers. This concession had been won largely through the intervention of Donald A. Smith, Chief Commissioner of the Hudson's Bay Company, but its importance was not immediately evident. For the company, the right of free navigation held great promise for the northern trade. Until then, supplies for the Mackenzie and Yukon districts had always come overland from Red River, a long and costly journey. Some within the firm believed the transportation system could be turned on its head. Supplies could, they argued, be brought in by way of the Yukon and Porcupine rivers, carried overland to the Mackenzie River basin, and from there could be dispersed to the northern posts. Because this system would use steamers rather than canoes, it promised faster, cheaper, and more efficient transportation. It also held out the opportunity to re-establish a company presence throughout the Yukon River basin.

Not all in the company supported the initiative. The venerable firm had undergone major changes in the 1860s, selling its stock publicly, surrendering its monopoly and land rights to the Canadian government in 1869–70, and undergoing massive internal reorganization. The death of Governor George Simpson in 1860 had resulted in control passing to more cautious administrators.[2] In the midst of the reorganization of the Yukon trade, William Hardisty, chief of the Mackenzie River district, ordered James McDougall to locate an easier route across the Richardson Mountains. The pass then in use, across Stony Creek, was long, arduous, and inefficient. A better route was required if the H.B.C. had any hope of reorienting its transportation route.

McDougall succeeded beyond all expectations. In the summer of 1872, he examined the area north of Peel River Post, and found a low, level pass of some thirty-five miles, half the distance of the pass currently in use. McDougall was ecstatic about the prospects of the new route. With a little work — some swampy land had to be filled, a few hills levelled, and a couple of bridges built — McDougall Pass could, he reported, be converted into a useable passage, joining the East Rat River to the Bell.[3] William Hardisty was similarly excited about the prospects:

> The advantages of the new route discovered by Mr. McDougall are so apparent as to justify us also I think, in looking forward to a bright future for the old District, which has labored so long under the disadvantages, which its isolation and other obstacles have thrown in the way of thorough development of its resources.[4]

Their excitement soon dissolved in the face of corporate intransigence. To purchase the steamers required for the Yukon River and to invest in the road across McDougall Pass required a strong commitment to the northern fur trade. The new Hudson's Bay Company, interested in selling its massive prairie land holdings and moving into the southern retail trade, would make no such commitment. McDougall's Pass sat unused, and would remain so until the Klondike gold rush. For Hardisty, McDougall, and other northern traders, the decision not to proceed was a slap in the face. Having lost the chance to expand and modernize the trade, the northern officers could only do their best to hold on to a shrinking company presence in the northwest.

The discovery of McDougall's Pass raises an interesting question, one that seems not have occurred to the company's officers in the 1870s. The new pass was not that far from the Hudson's Bay Company posts and trails. The eastern Kutchin bands regularly travelled through the area, particularly when hunting caribou. Yet the traders had never been told of the existence of this route. That this knowledge was kept from the Hudson's Bay Company, thus ensuring that the longer Stony Creek Pass remained in use, points once more to the willingness and ability of the natives to influence the direction of the fur trade. The company routinely hired Indians to pack supplies over the mountains, a distance of some seventy miles. Had the Indians told of the easier route, they would have been doing themselves out of work and income. Besides, the Hudson's Bay Company never seemed to have asked the Indians if there was an easier way.

The decision not to develop the new pass left the Porcupine River trade on a very tenuous footing. Americans were making major inroads into the company trade. Native protestations of loyalty dissolved with the discovery that the Yankee traders paid more for furs and made a greater variety of trade goods available. The company continued to believe that "a considerable quantity of Furs will fall into our hands from Indians lower down the Yukon river, who will be induced by the superiority of our goods to continue our traffic with the Indians."[5] The optimism was not entirely misplaced. The company's tobacco and blankets remained much in demand throughout the Yukon River basin, and Indians along the Yukon River either travelled to Rampart House to trade or secured the goods through inter-tribal exchange.

Beyond this modest success, however, the company's trade had fallen on hard times. The Americans proved to be intense competitors, sending native assistants to establish temporary trading posts across the river from Rampart House, escalating prices, and offering generous gifts to Indians who agreed to trade at their stations. The company tried to entice the Indians back, offering employment to particularly talented hunters, providing goods on credit, and trying to match the Americans' gift-giving. John Firth, a trader destined for a long career along the Porcupine and later at Fort McPherson, even walked to the Arctic coast in an attempt to convince

Indians north of the post to bring their furs to the Hudson's Bay Company establishment. But returns continued to plummet. In 1866, Fort Youcon had attracted over £6,000 worth of furs, fully one-third of the returns for the entire Mackenzie River district. By the 1880s, Rampart House was bringing in between £425 and £900, representing a scant 2 to 4 per cent of the Mackenzie River take. Yet the company held on, if only to protect the Mackenzie River district from American advances.[6]

To make matters worse, Rampart House now faced a new challenge. In 1888, Robert McConnell of the Geological Survey of Canada made a brief foray through the Porcupine River Valley. McConnell had planned to survey the Rampart House site, but decided instead to push on to Fort Youcon, where he hoped to meet up with a river steamer. He missed the boat, but his decision to leave without making a survey, believing that was "no object for delay," was about to come back to haunt the Hudson's Bay Company.[7]

The next year, a small American survey team led by J. Henry Turner arrived to locate the Canada–United States boundary along the Porcupine River. A quick examination of the area proved, to Turner's surprise and the Hudson's Bay Company's dismay, that Rampart House was a full thirty-three miles within American territory. Turner stayed two winters at Camp Colonna, his station near the border, as inclement weather through 1889–90 prevented accurate observations. He made a side trip to the Arctic Ocean, accompanied by John Firth, the H.B.C. trader who had earlier walked to the Arctic coast, where he again took sightings of the Canada–United States boundary before leaving in the spring of 1891.[8]

John Firth, incidentally, symbolized the new northern Yukon fur trade. When the trade had had a higher profile and more profitable returns, the company had sent its best, upwardly mobile, traders to the post — Murray, Hardisty, and McDougall. These men were talented and aggressive, and used their northern service as a launching pad for their careers. Firth lacked the formal qualifications of the others. He did not write as well, had few contacts in the company, and lacked the ambitions of his predecessors. In other ways, however, he was perfectly suited for northern service. A gentle manner and quiet demeanor masked his often-noted physical power. He respected the Indians and they in turn thought highly of him. He married a local native woman, and settled permanently in the area. Firth was to spend over fifty years in the region, most of it at Rampart House and Fort McPherson, showing a dedication to the people and the land that exceeded that of his employer.

The discovery that their post was on American territory gave the company pause. Was the expense of moving justified? Staying was no option, for the Americans had repeatedly refused to permit foreigners to operate on their soil. With some reluctance, stakes were pulled up once more and a new Rampart House — the third — was built, this time on the

Anglican Deacon Amos Njootli, a native of the Porcupine River area, and missionary T. H. Canham, are shown with a large wedding party at New Rampart House, c. 1913–17.
YUKON TERRITORIAL ARCHIVES

Canadian side of the border. Almost immediately, the company doubted the wisdom of the move.

As Turner was surveying the region, American whalers were arriving off the Yukon's Arctic coast. Although primarily interested in the whales, the ships' officers immediately recognized the potential of additional profits through the fur trade. The whalers ignored the standard conventions of the interior trade, offering repeating rifles, alcohol, and a variety of other goods not available from either the American traders or the Hudson's Bay Company. The Porcupine Indians quickly learned of these new opportunities and re-oriented their trade around Herschel Island. John Firth, who had fought for years to prop up Rampart House's declining trade, threw up his hands in resignation. As his superior reported, Firth did "not so much mind the opposition from down the River, but it is difficult to oppose the trade from the coast, as they are giving higher prices than ever."[9]

The resignation spread. By 1890–91, company officials freely admitted that Rampart House was nothing more than a "frontier post," designed to keep the Americans at bay and not expected to turn a profit. With the arrival of free traders in the southern Mackenzie and the escalating costs at Rampart House, even this logic seemed indefensible. After giving the Porcupine Indians several months' notice of their plans to quit the area, the Hudson's Bay Company abandoned both Rampart House and Lapierre House in the summer of 1893.

45

The departure of the Hudson's Bay Company marked an inglorious end to a trade that had lasted for almost half a century. The men — Alexander Hunter Murray, John Bell, and Robert Campbell — who had opened the district were now all dead. The once dynamic trading empire had contracted its fur operations while moving on into new, southern directions. The fur trade continued — would even enjoy a major revival in the twentieth century — but the company that had spread the European presence across much of the continent was in retreat.

The Hudson's Bay Company left in the Yukon an Indian population much different than that it had encountered half a century before. The native population had been severely depleted by a seemingly endless series of epidemics. Native society had undergone substantial change, based on the new European technology and the commercial imperatives of the fur trade. The Indians had held their own against everything but disease, from which there was little protection. They had participated eagerly in the fur trade and had influenced the nature of the exchange. The Hudson's Bay Company, which had started it all, was now gone from the Yukon, but the fur trade would continue, sustained by Indian harvesting and the arrival of new traders. For now, however, the Porcupine River district looked deserted, without a substantial European presence and with the Indians pulled to Herschel Island, Fort McPherson, or the Yukon River to trade.

The situation along the Yukon River was much different, for as economic and social activities declined along the Porcupine River, they expanded rapidly upriver from Fort Youcon. Americans had discovered the Yukon. Before the purchase, the Yukon had been the preserve of its native inhabitants, British and Russian fur traders, and a few missionaries, but had been almost totally ignored by the rest of the world. The American purchase of Alaska had changed all that, although people still knew precious little about the far northwest. Because the international boundary was unmarked (and almost irrelevant in the Russian era), and because the entire valley tended to be a single geographical and economic unit, the awakening of interest in Alaska spilled over into the Yukon as well. The telegraph expedition which had preceded the purchase had also resulted in the publication of several books about the region in the United States, where people were curious about this huge and apparently useless land which was now theirs. Kennicott's journals were published in the *Transactions of the Chicago Academy of Sciences* (1869), Dall wrote a book entitled *Alaska and Its Resources* (Boston, 1870), and Frederick Whymper published *Travels in America and on the Yukon* (New York, 1869).

Americans lost no time in seizing the commercial opportunities of the Yukon Valley that the Russians had neglected. As soon as the transfer took place, an American trading company, the Pioneer Company, was formed, made up of ex-Hudson's Bay Company men, Americans who had worked for the telegraph expedition, and even a Russian or two who wanted to stay in the country.[10] The company was not successful, but the Alaska Commercial Company, which took it over in 1869, had better luck. Two French-Canadian brothers, François and Moise Mercier, former employees of the Hudson's Bay Company, provided the energy and enterprise that led to the Alaska Commercial Company's early success. While Moise Mercier took over the trade at Fort Youcon, his brother worked out of St. Michael to establish a trading network, which eventually reached into Canadian territory along the river. Another founder of the company was Michael Lebarge, who had been with Kennicott on the telegraph expedition. For many years this company dominated the commercial life, Canadian as well as American, of the entire valley.

These first American commercial ventures sought to replace the Hudson's Bay Company and to reproduce their fur-trading successes. This they did admirably, fueling even greater interest in the business future of the Yukon River basin. At the same time, however, the advance guard of the North American mining frontier arrived on the scene, setting the Yukon on a markedly different course.

Although the first whites to penetrate the Yukon — the explorers, the fur traders, and the missionaries — had left their mark on the country, it was a gentle and largely unobtrusive one, for they amended but did not radically alter its economy, its appearance, or its racial balance. It was the miners who changed the face of the land irrevocably, bringing it firmly into the orbit of the modern world of development and technology. Perhaps nothing in the history of the western hemisphere has been so disruptive of native societies, or has acted as so powerful a magnet to lure men into new and strange territory, as the possibility of a gold strike. So it was with Mexico in the early sixteenth century, and California in the 1840s, and so it was, to a much milder degree, in late-nineteenth century Yukon.

The great discovery of gold in the Yukon which occurred in 1896 did not occur in a vacuum. It seems simplistic to say so, but gold discoveries are rarely serendipitous; people do not stumble over it while out for a walk. In order for gold to be found, there must be people looking for it. As had happened in California in 1849 and later in British Columbia, gold was discovered in the Yukon because miners knew or had good reason to believe it was there, and had spent years looking for it. If there was gold in the southern and central parts of the western mountain chain, then why should there not be gold in the north as well?[11]

In 1872 three men came to explore the mineral possibilities of the upper Yukon Valley. Leroy Napoleon McQuesten (who understandably preferred the nickname "Jack"), a farm boy from New England, had participated in the California gold rush and had later prospected on the Fraser and Finlay rivers in British Columbia.[12] For a time he had worked in the north for the

Hudson's Bay Company, learning survival and trading skills that were to serve him well in the Yukon. A good-natured, generous man, he later came to be called the "Father of the Yukon." Arthur Harper had emigrated from northern Ireland as a teenager in 1832 and had followed gold rushes in North America for two decades. It was Harper who reasoned that there ought to be gold in the northern part of the Rockies, since there had been plenty of it in the south. Alfred Mayo, a slight wiry man, was a former circus acrobat from Kentucky. A man who liked practical jokes, he was driven, like the other two, by a hunger for discovery and adventure.

While still in the south, the three men heard from a man who had worked at Fort Youcon that there were rumours in the north about gold. Stories had been circulating among the fur traders since the 1850s that there was gold in the tributaries of the Yukon River. One of the employees of the Hudson's Bay Company had written home in 1864 that gold had been found upriver in good quantities, but for some reason he did not investigate this story.[13] Thus when the three men came into the Yukon in 1872 by way of the Bell and Porcupine rivers, the smell of gold was in the air. McQuesten later related a story he had heard about an early find:

> One of the officers [of the Hudson's Bay Company] that came up on the steamer washed out of a jar of dirt near Fort Yukon and he had about a teaspoonful of something yellow in the pan and the officer threw it away remarking that it would not do to let the men see it as they would all leave the steamer... by the way the officer acted trying to hide it from the other men he supposed it must be gold....[14]

In 1873, while Harper was looking for gold in the Tanana region of Alaska, McQuesten and Mayo took jobs with Moise Mercier, of the Alaska Commercial Company, the major company on the American side of the 141st meridian. In the summer of 1874, Mercier and McQuesten travelled from St. Michael aboard the company's steamboat *Yukon* upstream past the company's posts on the river, across into the Canadian part of the valley. Six miles downstream from the confluence of the Klondike and Yukon rivers, near the Indian village of Nuklako, the men built Fort Reliance, the first settlement in what would become the gold country. The purpose of the post was to shorten the journey that the Han Indians had to make to trade at the posts on the lower Yukon. McQuesten and an assistant, Frank Bonfield, hired the local Indians to carry logs for the post, and to hunt and dry meat for the winter. A crude drawing made by a local artist in 1884 shows the buildings — six in all — huddled near the riverbank, their log roofs covered with shingles made of birch bark.

Fort Reliance was an instant success. The traders had plenty of meat, they lived in secure quarters, and before the spring of 1875 they had traded all their goods to the Indians for furs. That year Mayo joined them and they took over the trade of the upper Yukon Valley on behalf of the Alaska Commercial Company, operating it on a commission basis. They eventually established other posts in the region, but Fort Reliance became the centre of activity in the area and the point from which distances to later communities would be reckoned; Fortymile was forty miles downstream and Sixtymile River sixty miles upstream.

But McQuesten, Bonfield, Harper, and Mayo were primarily miners who had turned to trading for a living, and when rumours of gold reached them, they listened eagerly. Although they had not found gold themselves, they had put into place the support network which would sustain the miners who were to come. A main feature of this system was the "grubstake," a system in which the traders gave prospectors supplies and equipment for a season's work on credit. The trust involved in this arrangement was an essential feature of Yukon society in this era.

Their relations with the Indians were generally good, but an incident in 1877 shows the problems that could arise and the rough-and-ready way in which they were solved. In the store at Fort Reliance, Mayo had mixed arsenic with grease and set it out to kill mice. Some Indians broke into the store and three women ate the grease and died. The Indians were furious, and the future of the trade was in question. Jack McQuesten settled the matter:

> I told them that the poison was put in the store to destroy mice and it was out of the way of children and the old people ought to know better and the people that died it was their own fault for breaking into the store and taking things that didn't belong to them. There was one blind girl about sixteen years old that got poisoned — her father said that she was a great help to her mother and he had taken one of our dogs to replace the girl, but if I would pay for the girl he would return the dog. I told him I would think the matter over and let them know later on. Finally I told him the girl's Mother could keep the dog, so that settled the matter and that was the last I ever heard about the poison.[15]

All through the early 1870s tantalizing traces of gold appeared in the Yukon Valley, and stories about finds of gold circulated among the men in the region. McQuesten reported that "Harper & Co. .... had done considerable prospecting...found Gold in all of the streams...but nothing that would pay." Again, "Mr. Rob Bear had about thirty dollars in coarse gold that an Indian by the name of Larieson gave him." In the fall of 1878, McQuesten went to Sixtymile River, and "found Gold on all the bars in small quantities — I found some place where a man could make $6.00 to $8.00 per day but not extensive enough to put on a string of sluices."[16]

The first man who actually found enough gold in the Yukon to cause a degree of interest outside the country was probably George Holt, who in

1878 also had the distinction of being, with his party, the first white man to cross the Chilkoot or the White Pass — it is uncertain which route he took.[17] This required some courage as well as stamina, for the Tlingit (Chilkat) Indians of the region were jealous of their territorial rights; having made a good living for years acting as middlemen between coastal traders and the Indians of the interior, they were not keen to see outsiders exploring their trading routes. Somehow, however, Holt got past them and reached the headwaters of the Yukon River.

The route over the passes became known as the "poor man's route," for it was far shorter, and thus cheaper, than the long steamboat ride upriver from St. Michael or the route over the mountains from Fort McPherson. Beginning with Holt's journey, a small number of men began to use the passes each spring, many of them prospecting in the Yukon Valley only for the summer before drifting on down the river to the outside world. Some, however, did spend more than a summer in the north; it has been estimated that by 1882 about fifty white men were wintering in the region.[18]

In that year another party of miners reached Fort Reliance via the Chilkoot Pass. This one included a French Canadian named Joseph Ladue, who would later play a large role in the gold rush. Ladue and his partners spent the winter of 1882–83 at Fort Reliance, and, to keep themselves busy during the winter, experimented with a new mining technique. During the winter it was impossible to see if the ground was gold-bearing or not, since it was frozen solid. Ladue and the others tried building fires on the ground and scooping out the mud when it thawed. This worked well at first, but after spending three days on a ten-foot hole which promptly filled with water, they gave up.

The little party of miners spent most of their evenings in the store at Fort Reliance, talking and playing cards with Jack McQuesten. At one point, everyone decided that, since there was sure to be a gold rush sooner or later, and since there was no formal authority in the district, they had better make some laws of their own to keep order when the rush occurred. Borrowing from the traditions established in California and elsewhere, they drew up a set of mining laws establishing the size of claims, the rules for staking them, and other matters of interest to miners. McQuesten was selected as the first mining recorder.[18]

The pivotal year in the early mining era was 1885, for in that year a party of prospectors on the Stewart River found a small but tantalizing amount of gold — several thousand dollars' worth — enough to stimulate interest in the region. The technique they used was "bar" mining — panning the sandbars in the rivers and creeks. Within a year there were two hundred men wintering in the upper Yukon Valley. In the summer of 1885, Jack McQuesten, convinced that there was more money to be made supplying the miners than catering to the traditional fur trade, went to San

Francisco to convince the directors of the Alaska Commercial Company to change their retailing policy from trading for furs with the Indians to supplying the miners. He returned to Fort Reliance that fall with fifty tons of mining supplies. In the next year he and Harper moved their post from Fort Reliance to Fort Nelson, at the Stewart River. Now the trade with the Indians was rapidly supplanted by commercial activity revolving around the search for gold; the trading frontier was being pushed into the background, and the mining frontier was beginning to unfold.

After 1885 the number of men searching for gold in the Yukon Valley began to increase. There were a few white women too, for some of the miners brought their wives with them. The two hundred of 1885 grew to about a thousand by 1894, three years before most North Americans had even heard of the place. A majority of these men were veteran miners — men who had gone to earlier rushes in California, Nevada, Colorado, or British Columbia. They were not greenhorns or idealists, and they did not take foolish chances if they could avoid doing so — very few travelled in the winter months, and they wintered close to a trading post whenever possible, to avoid the risk of starvation. Life in the north was not easy, and the chances of real wealth were slight, but life in the factories of the nineteenth-century American industrial revolution was not much easier, and there the chances of real wealth were virtually non-existent. Gold mining, for many of these men, was an alternative to low-paid wage labour, and thus provided an escape from the factories, as pioneering in the west did for others — with the difference that gold miners sometimes struck it rich while farmers rarely did.

These were not the wild-eyed, almost crazed goldseekers of the later Klondike rush, but pragmatic men, weighing their chances, looking out for opportunities, and working patiently while awaiting the arrival of the big strike. They made up a highly mobile population; since they owned nothing but their mining equipment and their personal effects, they could easily move from one location to another. Walter H. Pierce was a typical example. Pierce had worked in the gold fields of Colorado, Idaho, and the Cassiar district of British Columbia before crossing the Chilkoot Pass in 1884. He and his partners built a boat at the headwaters of the Yukon, then spent the summer floating down the river, panning the sandbars at the mouths of the creeks that fed the river. In some places they made as much as $25 a day, more than ten times the average industrial wage for that era. In other places they found only traces. In any case the gold in the sandbars soon gave out, since there was never much in any one place, and the miners were thus constantly on the move. In the fall they retraced their journey and wintered in Juneau. The next year Pierce and his partners came again, this time with enough supplies for eighteen months. Again they spent the summer on the Yukon and its tributaries, testing "favourable looking streams, sometimes staying a week in one place."[19] Where necessary they built canoes or rafts

51

and went up likely tributaries. They travelled light, living off the land, finding traces of gold almost everywhere but no substantial amount. They had a hard winter; during 1885–86 two of the party died of scurvy, and in the spring Pierce and the other survivors went south. One of the early pioneers of the region, Pierce met the fate of a number of men who led the free and irregular life of the miner; back in Juneau in the fall of 1886 he was charged with the murder of a dance-hall girl. He was acquitted, but died four years later of tuberculosis, still in his thirties.[20]

In 1886 the first substantial discovery of gold was made in the region. Harry Madison and Howard Franklin, two of Joe Ladue's original partners of 1882, went down the Yukon River forty miles from Fort Reliance to the mouth of the Fortymile River, then poled their boat twenty-three miles upstream. This took them westward across the 141st meridian into Alaska, though they likely neither knew nor cared that by doing so they had entered the United States. After some searching, they found a rich deposit of coarse placer gold. Again the three traders — McQuesten, Harper, and Mayo — moved their operations, this time from the Stewart River to the mouth of the Fortymile. Though the Stewart post was kept open, the main activity now shifted to the new settlement of Fortymile, which, though the strike up-stream was in the United States, was by accident of geography in Canada. Fortymile became the first fairly permanent town in the Canadian part of the Yukon Valley, remaining as a centre of activity until the strike of 1896, when it was largely abandoned.

News of the strike in the Fortymile district brought more miners to the Yukon, and by the winter of 1886–87 there were perhaps five hundred men wintering there, mostly in the vicinity of the new discovery. It was in this period that sympathetic observers (mostly the local missionaries) began to see what the mining frontier held in store for the Indians of the region. At first the arrival of the miners brought a kind of prosperity to some Indians, for a few were hired as packers or day-labourers. But the long-term impact on them was almost entirely bad.[21] The Hudson's Bay Company had always banned liquor as an item of trade in the area. The miners, however, wanted alcohol, and either imported it or made their own, and had, moreover, no objection to teaching the distillers' art to the native people.

Probably the worst result of the mining activity was that the major economic activity in the region ceased to become fur trading. This had an effect which did not occur to observers at the time: it tended to make the Yukon Indians powerless outsiders in the economic life of their own country. The fur trade could not be carried on successfully without the support of the Indians, and because the fur traders were dependent on them for success, the Indians were able to shape the nature and the flow of the trade to a degree which is only now being recognized. But on the mining frontier the Indians played no role outside of a bit of casual day-labour and some supplying of

Top: *Caribou Crossing, so named for the large migrations of caribou across the river narrows, attracted little interest in the pre-Klondike days. The scenic location would later be a major river crossing for the Skagway to Whitehorse railway.* YUKON TERRITORIAL ARCHIVES

Below: *Miners might spend weeks and months in an often fruitless search for gold. Most tried several creeks, often with different partners, before giving up and heading south.*
YUKON TERRITORIAL ARCHIVES

food, and thus had no control whatever over it; the mining activities proceeded as though the Indians did not exist. Though it is arguable to what degree the miners "corrupted" the Indians (missionaries had many arguments with others on this point), there is no question that the Indians were relegated to the periphery of the mining activity. They could sell their meat and fish to the miners, as they had done to the Hudson's Bay Company, but even if they had wanted to leave their traditional pursuits in favour of full-time wage labour they could not have done so. Most mining operations, then and for some years after, were small ones which did not require a large work force. Furthermore, many of the miners were infected with racial prejudice, believing that Indians were lazy and unreliable, incapable of a day's work. As the mining frontier developed in the late 1880s, the pressing need for day-labour meant that some Indians did find jobs, yet employers hired them only reluctantly and they were paid less than whites.[22] At one point white workers formed a "combination" to exclude native workers from the gold fields.[23] When Indians did work they could earn as much as $8 a day,[24] much more than they could make trapping fur, though less than a white man was paid for doing the same work. But they had to live close to the mining region to get these jobs.[25]

Another aspect of the problem was that after 1885 the trading posts were located with a view to serving the miners' rather than the Indians' needs. The Indians were seriously inconvenienced when their trading posts were shifted suddenly and almost without warning. When Fort Reliance was abandoned in 1887, the Indians who had traded there were compelled to travel the much greater distance to trade at Fortymile. Worse still, there were occasions when whites entered into direct competition with the Indians. Prospectors down on their luck in this early period sometimes tried a bit of trapping or even trading for furs.

It was thus the early gold-mining activities that introduced the industrial sector to the economy of the Yukon region. In the fur trade era little pressure was put on the Yukon's natural resources, and the skills of the native people were an integral part of its economy. With the arrival of the miners, new economic priorities appeared. Now the Indians' skills were increasingly seen as irrelevant, and the focus of economic activity turned to the exploitation of non-renewable resources. Now the skills of the hunter took second or third place to the skills of the geologist.

The men who worked for the Hudson's Bay Company had come north for years at a time and had often become deeply committed to the long-term development and prosperity of the region. Most of the miners were transients, who sought only to strike it rich and make enough money to leave the region forever. For them, and for many others who were to follow them to the north, the Yukon was not a home but an opportunity.

Faced with prejudice and the disruption of their way of life, most Yukon

Indians avoided the mining communities as much as possible, preferring to live in areas distant from the mines. They continued to hunt and trap, to trade with the Hudson's Bay Company and the American traders, even if doing so meant making long journeys. In the late 1880s the Kutchin of the Porcupine River region discovered a new outlet for their furs and their meat in the whaling community which grew up at Herschel Island, off the Yukon's Arctic coast. But this new trade also proved disruptive. The whalers were far more ruthless traders than the Hudson's Bay Company or the Americans; they would do anything to attract the natives to Herschel Island, and were quite prepared to use alcohol and repeating rifles as lures, both of which had been banned for trade by the Canadian government.[26] The social carnival which came to characterize trade at Herschel was in contrast with the sober commercialism of the Hudson's Bay Company in the interior, and the company saw its trade at Rampart House fall off dramatically — a process which further disrupted the existing social and economic structure.

There was innovation as well as disruption in the Yukon in the late 1880s, for it was in this period that the techniques of mining in permafrost were developed. Joe Ladue had experimented with these at Fort Reliance during the winter of 1882-83, and they were perfected five years later during the rush to the Fortymile district.

The gold which lay beneath the ground in the Yukon Valley was locked in the soil for all or part of the year by permafrost. Near the surface the ground thawed in the summer, releasing the gold, but farther down the dirt and the gold it carried were permanently frozen. If the miners were to work their claims for more than a few months out of each year, they would have to find a way to free from the frozen soil the flakes and small nuggets that made up the placer gold. In the early days the technique employed was called "skim digging." This involved working during the summer on the top two feet or so of the surface gravel along the creek beds. Below this depth either water was encountered, which made the work impossible, or permafrost, which made it too difficult to be profitable.[27]

When coarse gold was discovered in the Fortymile district, however, the miners began to look for ways to mine the soil down to bedrock. They assumed that because gold was heavy, the greatest concentrations would be found in the gravels that lay just above the bedrock. This was not always true, as the history of the Klondike discoveries later showed, but there was a bigger problem: how to deal with the permafrost?

In 1887-88, when William Ogilvie was wintering near Fortymile, he suggested to the miners a technique he had seen used in Ottawa to reach broken water mains during the winter: fires should be built to thaw the soil, which would be scraped off, then a new fire built, and so on to bedrock. The thawed soil could be piled beside the shaft until spring freed the creek water which was necessary to wash the gold from the dirt. This suggestion was immediately adopted (some miners, like Joe Ladue, had already experimented with it), and it became the pattern for the early stage of mining in the district. Thus most of the actual mining — the digging part — took place in the winter. An advantage of this technique was that no timbering was necessary in the mining shafts, which often ran horizontally as well as vertically under the ground. The permafrost was as hard as granite, and unless weakened by fire or early thaw, would not collapse.

The payoff occurred after the spring thaw, when the gold, if there was any, was washed from the dirt. This was originally done with a broad shallow metal pan which looked like a cross between a pie tin and a washbasin or a Chinese wok, with a smallish flat bottom and gradually sloping sides. Dirt and water were put in the pan, then the pan was moved in a circular manner so that the water and some of the dirt swished around the pan and then slopped over the side. The water, being lightest, would run over the side first, then the lighter soil, then the sand and gravel; the gold flakes and dust, being much heavier, would stay in the bottom. After this had been done several times, nothing would be left but whatever gold the dirt had contained. Tourists in the Yukon are still invited to try their hands at this simple technique.

Panning was simple and cheap, but not very efficient, as inevitably a certain amount of gold escaped with the water and dirt. It was also time-consuming, and thus came to be used mostly for initial testing of the value of paydirt, or on claims where the dirt was so rich that some loss did not matter. More efficient was the rocker box, which looked like a turn-of-the-century washing machine, and which separated the gold from the dirt by vigorous agitation.

The third method used in the Fortymile district and later in the Klondike was the sluice box. This was a wooden trough, typically six to ten feet long, with little wooden crosspieces about half an inch in height, called "riffles," nailed at intervals to the bottom. The sluice box was fixed at an incline, and water was run in at the higher end. When gold-bearing dirt was shovelled in with the water, the water washed the dirt out the lower end, while the heavier gold sank to the bottom and was caught by the riffles. Every so often the water was diverted from the box, and the gold scraped from the riffles. Sluice boxes were much more efficient than pans or rockers, but they needed a good supply of water — easy enough to come by in the early days, but more difficult later in the Klondike when hundreds of miners competed for the flow of one small creek.

There was an alternative method, which used much less labour, and which enabled the miners to avoid winter mining altogether. This was hydraulic mining, which was developed in California, and which reached the Yukon Valley in 1890. This technique involved directing high-pressure hoses at the banks and beds of creeks. Because the creeks were made up of loose aggregates of rocks, soil, and gravel, they were easily broken up by these hoses, and the resulting solution was directed into sluice boxes. The pressure was created by flumes from neighbouring creeks directed downhill in the manner of a small hydro-electric plant. The first one on the Fortymile, built by Frank Buteau, George Matlock, and their partners, developed twenty-four feet of pressure, and ate the ground away in giant bites.[28] This technique too was to be further developed in the Klondike.

Because of the 1886 discovery of gold, it was Fortymile, not Dawson City, which was the first gold-mining community in the Yukon, and the first settlement which was more than just a trading post. Even though many of the claims were across the border in Alaska, the community itself, located strategically at the confluence of the Fortymile and Yukon rivers, was in Canada, and its residents would have been subject to Canadian law, had there been any in the vicinity. But there was no formal law in Fortymile; it was not until 1894, eight years after its founding, that the first mounted policeman arrived at the community to enforce Canadian law.

Fortymile in its early days was incredibly isolated, dependent for its supplies on wholesalers in San Francisco, 5,000 miles away. Two small steamboats linked the community with St. Michael, 1,800 miles down the Yukon, but if the ships failed to make the trip upriver, as happened in 1889, the community was threatened with starvation. At its largest, Fortymile had about 150 buildings clustered around the store. There were a blacksmith shop, an Anglican mission, a school (some of the miners had their families with them), and ten saloons. Because of the expense and difficulty of getting supplies in, the miners who were there in its early days had to resort to improvisation:

> They made stoves and chimneys out of rocks and mud, using flat rocks for the tops of the stoves. For windows they cut clear pieces of Yukon River ice slightly larger than the window openings and fastened them in place with wooden buttons.[29]

Fortymile reached its zenith in the summer of 1894, when close to a thousand people lived in and near it. That year spawned a rival, for down the Yukon River another strike had been made in the Birch Creek district of Alaska by Sergi Gologoff Chernosky, a Creole[30] interpreter working for Mercier and Harper, and Pitka Pavaloff, his brother-in-law. A new town was founded by Jack McQuesten to supply the miners there. On the Yukon River flats, just across the American side of the 141st meridian, it was named Circle City because of its location on the Arctic Circle.

Circle City, like Fortymile, depended entirely on the success of the local miners. The Birch Creek strike was a rich one, even better than Fortymile, and like the older town spawned a store, saloons (twenty-eight of them), theatres, and even a library. With seven hundred people actually living in the town by 1896, and more in the district, it drained most of the population from its rival, and was described as the largest log-cabin city in the world.[31]

Thus the gold-mining community in the Yukon basin prior to the great discovery of 1896 was an international one, revolving around the communities of Fortymile in the Yukon and Circle City in Alaska. But the fact that the mining districts were split by an international boundary was of no importance to anyone who lived in the region. Miners whose properties lay close to the 141st meridian often did not know in which country they were working. The merchants moved their operations across the border from one community to another without a thought. The point was that it hardly mattered. Until the mid-1890s, the miners were living in a society virtually of their own making. For a number of years there were no government officials on either side of the border. The miners paid no taxes, nor royalties on the gold they found; those on the Canadian side paid no customs duties on the goods they brought in from San Francisco. The only laws they obeyed were those they drafted for themselves.

This was the essential difference between the Yukon in the pre- and post-gold-rush periods. Before the arrival of the North-West Mounted Police, the Yukon was an isolated society of miners — a "community of hermits whose one common bond was their mutual isolation," as Pierre Berton has put it.[32] There were, of course, the colourful characters who seemed to gravitate to gold-mining communities, their nicknames reading like a list of characters from a boys' novel: Salt Water Jack, Big Dick, Squaw Cameron, Jimmy the Pirate, Buckskin Miller, Pete the Pig.[33] But many others were sober citizens (or reasonably so) who were not fleeing from civilization but who had made a conscious decision to come north for a chance at real prosperity, believing that the streets of Fortymile were more likely to be paved with gold than those of the factory cities to the south.

In a sense the miners' society was one of the freest in the hemisphere.[34] The men came and went as they pleased, made their own laws, and depended only on themselves and their partners for survival. The partnerships were highly flexible and informal. Men came together to prospect or work a certain property; if one man decided that the effort was not worthwhile, the partnership broke up with no hard feelings, and each man went his own way to seek his fortune as he saw best. Everyone sought gold, but each as an individual in his own way, joining with others only as it suited him; "for much of his time in the territory a miner never knew whom he might end up associating with, and many of those to whom he became linked in some common enterprise were likely to be strangers to him."[35]

The mobile, casual, almost ephemeral nature of the miners' society is illustrated by the career of a man named Chris Sonnikson, who crossed the coastal mountains in the spring of 1886 with his partners, Charley Braises and Old Solomon.[36] They built a boat at the headwaters of the Yukon, and planned to go downriver to the Stewart. On the way, however, they learned that a veteran prospector named Densmore was prospecting the upper

Yukon; they then changed their plans and joined five other men working in the region.

The new party of eight worked the sandbars of the upper Yukon; several prospected while the others worked the bars where traces of gold had been found. They took turns watching the Densmore party to see if anything valuable turned up there. After a few weeks the Yukon River rose, flooding the most likely sandbars. Sonnikson and Braises decided to go to the Salmon River, where the water had fallen; Old Solomon decided to stay with the others on the Yukon and wait for the water to fall. The two men prospected on the Salmon for a while and then split up; Braises went back to the Yukon, while Sonnikson joined a man they had met in another party, and the two went to prospect the Hootalinqua for a time, after which Sonnikson went back to join Braises on the Yukon. Then the two partners went back to where they had left Old Solomon, but discovered that he and the others had staked the whole sandbar for themselves as soon as the water had fallen. The two then left for another sandbar, but soon broke up, Braises selling his share in the bar to Sonnikson and leaving for the winter, Sonnikson joining yet another party.

All this coming and going, joining and rejoining took place in the five months between April and September 1886, and shows the remarkably fluid and individualistic nature of mining society in the Yukon in the early days. Each miner, although operating on his own, did so by means of a "personal community" of other miners whom he could join or leave as his interests dictated.

As the Yukon mining frontier developed in the late 1880s, the trading and transportation network that held the fragile community together and linked it to the "outside" also became more sophisticated. In 1893 a powerful force appeared at Fortymile to challenge the McQuesten–Harper–Ladue partnership. John J. Healy had been a trader, miner, and a sheriff in the goldfields of Idaho and Montana. In 1886, sensing that a rush was due in the north, he moved to Alaska. He was astute enough to realize that the Chilkoot Pass would someday see heavy traffic, so he opened a store athwart the "poor man's route" to the Yukon, at the head of the Lynn Canal. This store became the nucleus of the town of Dyea. He then persuaded three Chicago financiers to back him in a new trading company which would challenge the Alaska Commercial Company, and in 1892 the North American Trading and Transportation Company was formed. By the fall of that year Healy had steamed up the Yukon River in the *Porteus B. Weare*, a vessel named after one of his backers. In 1893 he arrived at Fortymile, where he built a store called Fort Cudahy (named for another of his backers, a Chicago meat packer) across the Fortymile River from the town and entered into competition with McQuesten's store.

Healy's prices were attractive, but unlike McQuesten he would not grubstake the miners; for this reason and because of his abrasive personality, the miners disliked him. When a woman who worked for him brought a trivial charge against him to a miners' meeting, the miners happily awarded her a year's wages and passage home. Healy paid, but his resentment against the *ad hoc* legality of the proceedings moved him to complain to an old friend of his from his Montana days — Sam Steele of the North-West Mounted Police. The gist of his letter was that Fortymile needed some British justice; this would have important consequences for the mining community.

The miner's meeting which so infuriated Healy was the basic unit of government in the mining communities before the arrival of the Canadian authorities. During this period the miners' society was, in a sense, one of the most democratic in the world. Since there was no formal law in the north, they had invented their own. The basic organization was the "miners' meeting," which as the name suggests was a meeting of all the miners who lived in a certain region. These meetings began as early as 1885, as soon as there were enough miners in the country to justify them, and continued until just after the arrival of the mounted police detachment in 1895. The meeting could be called by anyone, and listened to criminal cases, mining disputes, and personal grievances and quarrels; it then delivered a verdict by a majority vote — often banishment from the community — which was binding on all parties. It could also pass by-laws to regulate any aspect of the community. A witness to these meetings wrote a description of them:

> The powers of the miners' meeting are threefold — legislative, judicial, and executive. No provision is made for a governing officer, the whole fabric resting on the great American principle, "majority rules." Universal suffrage is given, and all have an equal vote. The method of procedure is as follows: If a man has a grievance, he posts a notice to that effect and calls a meeting for a certain date. At the appointed time the miners of the locality assemble, generally in the open air, and a moderator from their number is appointed. Then the prosecutor presents his case; the defendant answers. There is a cross-questioning, speeches pro and con are made, and in the end someone puts a motion, which is either carried or defeated. If carried, the penalty is imposed without delay.[37]

The miners' meeting was more than just a community court, however; it was the basic regulator of mining society, governing not only its legal, but also to a large extent its social relationships. Mining society was so fragmented and individualistic that some means had to be found not only to enforce laws, but also to regulate personal behaviour for the good of the community. This was done by applying various sanctions to people whose behaviour fell too far outside community norms.

Miners in the Yukon lived in a community where each person might have to depend for his success or even his survival on the goodwill or reliability of a stranger. For instance, it was essential that travellers in the country be sure that they could call on anyone at any time for food and shelter; to refuse aid to a stranger in need was unthinkable. Similarly, in a country without police, banks, or secure storage facilities it was necessary that people be able to leave their goods and property untended for long periods without fear of pilferage; thus petty theft was viewed as a serious crime. The selfish man, the loner, the man who pursued his own interests in disregard of others' rights and interest — such a man was not only a nuisance, but a threat to the whole community. For this reason the miners' meeting judged not only offences, but also the character of the accused; not only his past deeds, but what he was likely to do in the future — delivering what has been called "forward-looking" justice.[38]

Other societies have had similar views of behaviour — a Canadian example is Inuit society. The Inuit in the pre-contact period put a high value on good nature, sharing, and helpfulness, qualities that were essential for their survival in a harsh environment. People who were bad-tempered and abusive, if only in words, were sometimes killed before they could express themselves in actions, since an unreliable person was a danger to everyone.[39] The miners' meeting worked on the same principle, though actions rather than words were necessary as proof of guilt, and the punishment was generally banishment rather than death.

The case of Frank Leslie shows the process in action. In 1886 Leslie persuaded four experienced miners in Seattle that he had knowledge of a rich deposit of gold on the Stewart River. The men came up with a grubstake, and the party went over the Chilkoot Pass to the Stewart. It soon proved that the story was a lie, and during the winter of 1886–87, while the men wintered on the Stewart, the four dupes discussed lynching Leslie. Fearing for his life, he waited until it was his week to cook, then dosed a dish of fried beans with powdered arsenic that was kept to poison wild animals. But he misjudged the dose and only made his partners sick. He then tried to shoot them while they slept but was overpowered. The partners then took him sixty miles downriver to the Stewart River post, where a miners' meeting was convened. Leslie's defence was that he had originally acted in good faith, believing the story about the gold to be true, and that he had poisoned and then tried to shoot his partners in self defence. The meeting accepted his story, but nevertheless

he was considered an undesirable citizen, and after much discussion it was decided to banish him, so he was furnished with a sled, provisions enough to get out if he could, was ordered to move up-river at least one hundred and fifty miles from that camp, and assured that if ever he was seen within that distance of it, any one then present would be justified in shooting him on sight. He left to make his way unaided up the Yukon, to and over the Dyea [Chilkoot] Pass, more than five hundred miles, in the inclement weather and spring months, and he succeeded so well that he reached Haines Mission. . . . It was thought he richly deserved punishment, but as they had no prison in which to confine him, nor any way to detain him for any length of time, all they could do was hang him or banish him. His death they did not wish to be directly responsible for, though many of them felt they were condemning him to death in agreeing to the sentence imposed.[40]

The miners' system of justice is further illustrated by the case of a miner on the trail who broke into a cache belonging to another man and took the supplies he needed, an action which no one would have objected to in the Yukon. But he also left the rest of the cache unprotected and animals got at it and destroyed it. When he reached Circle City he told no one what he had done, so that when the owner returned to the cache, it was empty. Without supplies he almost died before getting to town. He had identified the thief by following his trail to town, and, after waiting a few days for the man to confess on his own, he called a miners' meeting. The thief confessed, and was banished from the country. It is significant that the punishment for this offence was the same as for the previous one; indeed, permitting a cache to be destroyed was a form of attempted murder, and in this case the miners likely delivered a fairer justice than a formal court would have.

In both these instances the mining community exercised a notable degree of restraint. The purpose of the meetings was not only to dispense justice, but to prevent conflict. When individuals themselves failed to exercise restraint, the miners' meeting was often able to command it. At Fortymile in the winter of 1893–94, two miners named Wickham and Matlock got into a drunken argument. Wickham stabbed Matlock in the back, but Matlock was able to go to his cabin, get a gun, and return to shoot Wickham through his cabin window. Both men survived, but at a miners' meeting that was called to handle the incident, they were told that if there was further trouble between them, both would be banished. Eventually they became good friends. And at Circle City in 1896 the meeting ruled in the case of two men who had shot at each other that if one killed the other, or even if one died under suspicious circumstances, the other would be hanged without trial.[41]

It is significant that there is very little evidence of homicide on the early mining frontier in the Yukon Valley. There were one or two killings: in Circle City in 1896 a miner threatened to shoot a bartender and was himself shot; the bartender immediately called a miners' meeting which ruled he had acted in self defence. There may have been some unrecorded incidents. But the essential fact was that the miners' meetings and the whole social organization of the mining community militated against violence and were remarkably successful in preventing it.[42]

Considering that the majority of these miners were Americans, it is perhaps surprising that disputes in the Yukon were not generally settled by private rather than public means. Why were there no duels or vendettas in the Yukon? Certainly there were quarrels, and every man in the district had a gun, so both the motivation and means for private violence were there. It has been suggested[43] that one reason is that the miners never really thought of themselves as residents of the Yukon; even those who had been there for years were only transients — men who had come north to strike it rich. They expected some day to return to a home in the south, and were conscious of the reputation they would have there. It would not do for a man who had struck it rich and wished to establish a comfortable bourgeois life in the south to return home marked as a murderer or a desperado. In other words, the Yukon mining frontier was not a land from which people could never hope to return, as Australia had been early in the century, and where thus they could behave as they pleased; rather it was a temporary place from which they hoped to return with reputation as well as wealth. Most men did not wish to be criminals, nor did they wish to be vigilantes. The miners' meeting, by shifting responsibility for punishment to the community as a whole, absolved the individual miners; none of them could be held individually accountable for the community's actions.

The miners did not publicize their northern adventures a great deal, and actually did little to attract attention to the area. There were others, however, drawn by the mystique of the unknown, who would come north to investigate the human and physical secrets of the upper Yukon River basin.

Among the first of these to arrive were a pair of German explorers, Aurel and Arthur Krause, who had previously studied the Siberian Chukotsk Peninsula. They came to the Yukon in 1881 on behalf of the Geographical Society of Bremen. After spending a winter at the head of the Lynn Canal, Arthur Krause crossed the Chilkoot Pass to Lake Lindeman, the first scientist to map the route, while his brother remained on the coast to study the Tlingits.

Americans, drawn by the great debates in the United States about the value of Seward's purchase, were understandably interested in the upper Yukon basin. Their interest, however, was not limited to the American side of the border. The Frederick Schwatka expedition of 1883 resulted from the American army's desire to find out something about Alaska in case it should be called upon to defend it. In particular, General Nelson A. Miles, whose idea the expedition was, wanted to determine what the attitude of the local Indians would be to the arrival of the Americans. Schwatka, a lieutenant in the U.S. Cavalry, was thirty-four when he went to Alaska. He was chosen because of his previous experience in the north; in 1879 he had led an expedition to the central Canadian Arctic to look for traces of the lost Franklin expedition. He had also found time during his military service to earn a medical degree and study enough law to be admitted to the Nebraska bar. Like Robert Peary, a more famous explorer of a generation later, Schwatka was a military man who did not do much soldiering. He spent most of his career either studying or exploring.

There were eight men in the party that left Portland in May 1883, including a doctor, a topographer, a photographer, and an artist — all military men, as well as a miner named J. B. Mitchell, who had prospected in the Yukon Valley and who presumably knew the country. The expedition steamed north past the settlements on the Lynn Canal — by 1883 salmon canneries had been established there — and landed at the future site of Dyea. On June 11, 1883, the men crossed the Chilkoot Pass; Schwatka's description of the journey, aided by Indian packers who charged him $10 to $12 for the trip, is the earliest complete account in English of the route to have circulated widely:

> ...about five o'clock [A.M.] we commenced the toilsome ascent of this coast range pass.... Up banks almost perpendicular they scrambled on their hands and knees, helping themselves by every projecting rock and clump of juniper and dwarf spruce, not even refusing to use their teeth on them at the worst places. Along the steep snow banks and the icy fronts of glaciers steps were cut with knives, while rough alpenstocks from the valley helped them to maintain their footing. In some such places the incline was so steep that those having boxes on their backs cut scratches in the icy crust with the corners as they passed along.... In some of these places a single mis-step, or the caving in of a foothold would have sent the unfortunate traveller many hundred feet headlong to certain destruction. Yet not the slightest accident happened, and about ten o'clock, almost exhausted, we stood on top of the pass....[44]

Schwatka, like most successful explorers, had a strong ego, and he gave names to dozens of the topographical features he passed, ignoring the fact that they already had names given to them by Indians, and in many cases by whites as well. His attempt to rename the Chilkoot Pass after a French geographer failed, but some of his names stuck, including Lake Lindeman, after the secretary of the Bremen Geographical Society; Lake Bennett, after the editor of the New York *Herald*, who was a patron of exploration; and Marsh Lake (the miners had called it Mud Lake), after an American paleontologist. One of his names gave rise to later controversy. He decided that the river which the Hudson's Bay Company men had called the Lewes was actually the upper part of the Yukon, and so marked it on his map. Later, the Canadian government changed the name back to Lewes, but the name did not stick. Despite local support for the original non-native appellation, the name for the entire river system from Marsh Lake to the lower river was changed back to Yukon in the 1950s. Having left his stamp on the maps of northwestern Canada, Schwatka then floated down the Yukon, past the future site of Dawson City, and into American territory.

The American expeditions finally forced a Canadian response. News of the Schwatka expedition roused Ottawa from its total indifference to the Yukon, and seventeen years after it had acquired the region, the Canadian government was moved to send a party north to see what was there. In charge of this party was George M. Dawson, Assistant Director (later Director) of the Geological Survey of Canada. The Survey, founded in 1842, was one of Canada's oldest and most useful government agencies. It was originally designed to assist the mining industry by studying and reporting on the geology of Canada. It also became involved in "economic geology," particularly in providing information to the government to assist in the awarding of railway land grants. It was thus the logical agency to report on the potential riches of the Yukon.

Dawson was born in Pictou, Nova Scotia, in 1849, son of Sir John William Dawson, a geologist and naturalist who later became principal of McGill University. An illness in his youth had left George Dawson dwarfed, with a twisted back, but he had studied geology and natural science in Edinburgh and London, graduating with high honours. When he came to the Yukon he had already done extensive mapping in British Columbia and had written a comprehensive report on the Haida Indians. He had also served with the International Boundary Commission of 1873 which marked the 49th parallel on the prairies. The two other main members of the party were Richard G. McConnell, another geologist, and William Ogilvie, a Dominion Land Surveyor for the government who had played a leading part in the original surveys of the prairie provinces.[45]

The party left for the north in April 1887 and reached the Yukon by different routes, Dawson and McConnell travelling by way of the Stikine River and the old telegraph trail, while Ogilvie went over the Chilkoot Pass. At the end of June 1887, Dawson and his party entered the southern Yukon by way of the Liard River and Frances Lake. They then portaged to the upper Pelly River, canoed down it, and by early August had reached the site of Fort Selkirk. On the way Dawson panned in places for gold, and discovered that "Small 'colours' may be found in almost any suitable locality along the river, and 'heavy colours' in a considerable number."[46] He interviewed the miners that he met in order to be able to assess as accurately as possible the region's mining potential. One man, Thomas Boswell, told Dawson that he had worked a bar on the Ross River that paid $18 per day. There were only two men working the entire Pelly, and they had made only $10 to $20 a day when they found a good location.

Dawson formed an opinion of regions he did not have time to visit by talking to miners who knew the country. From a man named John McCormack he got information on the Big Salmon River, and Thomas Boswell helped him with facts about Teslin Lake and the Nisutlin River. All this material was published as part of the annual report of the Geological Survey of Canada for 1887–88, and was reissued ten years later at the height of the

65

gold rush to satisfy the public demand for information about the Yukon. He also patriotically changed some of Schwatka's names back to their originals, leading to some later confusion in the maps of the Yukon.

Ogilvie's trip into the Yukon over the Chilkoot Pass was an enterprise involving 120 Indian packers, for he brought seven tons of supplies and equipment with him — even then civil servants did not travel light, and the surveys he had been ordered to make required him to carry a number of instruments. On the way he met three men who were soon to become famous in the Yukon as well as outside: George Carmack, Skookum Jim, and Dawson (sometimes Tagish) Charlie. Skookum ("strong") Jim and Dawson Charlie were working as packers, and Skookum Jim carried 156 pounds of bacon over the pass for Ogilivie. Carmack (Ogilvie spells it "Carmac") was living with the Tagish Indians, doing nothing in particular. These three were to make the famous discovery of 1896. Accompanying Ogilvie was William Moore, a man who had made and lost a fortune in the Cassiar gold field. While Ogilvie went over the Chilkoot Pass, Moore persuaded a Chilkoot Indian named Jim to breach the traditional native secrecy about these routes and guide him over a parallel pass, which he named after Thomas White, Minister of the Interior.[47] When Moore met Ogilvie again he was full of the possibilities of this new route:

> Every night during the two months [Moore] remained with us he would picture the tons of yellow dust yet to be found in the Yukon valley. He decided then and there that Skagway would be the entry port to the golden fields of the Yukon, and the pass would reverberate with the rumble of railway trains...[48]

While Dawson and McConnell mapped the Yukon country and made scientific observations, Ogilvie spent most of his time talking to the miners in the Fortymile region. Since he was an official representative of the Canadian government, the miners were anxious to know what Ottawa had in mind for the Yukon; in particular they wanted to know what mining laws were likely to be enforced if and when Ottawa ever asserted its authority in the mining district. Ogilvie informed them that since the Yukon was unique, since there were no placer gold mines anywhere under federal jurisdiction in Canada, no regulations applicable to the Yukon had ever been drawn up, and they should abide by the British Columbia rules, which limited placer claims to 100 square feet. The miners complained that this was far too small for permafrost country; Ogilvie agreed with them that a 500-foot frontage running from the base of the hills on one side of the creek to the base of the hills on the other would be fairer, and this was eventually adopted by Ottawa. The eventual effect of this ruling, of course, was to limit the paydirt to fewer lucky people.

More disturbing to the miners was Ogilvie's news that the Canadian government's policy was to collect a 2½ per cent royalty on gold taken from Crown land; this was "universally condemned."[49] The reason generally given for this condemnation was the expense of mining in the north, but underlying it was the feeling that since government provided absolutely nothing in the way of services to the miners, it had no right to tax them, certainly not without "representation" — such action was simple theft. Since they were mining in a virtual no man's land, as far as constituted authority was concerned, they felt they had the right to keep what they could find. Since Ogilvie was not there to collect taxes, the issue was in any case theoretical.

Ogilvie and his party spent the winter of 1887–88 at Fortymile. Over the winter he made a number of astronomical observations to determine the iongitude of the settlement, and to determine where the 141st meridian crossed the Fortymile River. Ogilvie was compelled to adapt his techniques to northern conditions. First, a base for the astronomical transit had to be found (the tripod, which weighed over four hundred pounds, had been left at the foot of the passes). A tree stump twenty-two inches in diameter had to be found as a substitute; since trees that size were not plentiful in the central Yukon, the search took three days. Observations were taken in temperatures ranging from –30F to –50F (–35C to –46C). He was able to make twenty-two observations between November and February. He marked the position of Fortymile and was able to determine the location of the 141st meridian with a small degree of error — when he returned in 1895 to check his work, he found that his line was 109 feet too far east, perhaps because, as he reported, his tree stump tended to rise and fall slightly with the changes in temperature.

Richard McConnell led a separate expedition to the Yukon by way of Fort McPherson, the Bell River, and Lapierre House. He found this post as well as Rampart House to be in decline — the latter was kept open "as a protection against the encroachment of traders from the west."[50] He went on to Fort Yukon, up the river to Fortymile, where he witnessed a minor stampede:

> A report was brought up by the men on the steamer that a miner had boarded the boat at the mouth of Beaver River, and after talking in a hurried manner to the captain, had suddenly departed, and in his haste had left his purse behind him. The miners reasoned that nothing but a rich find could cause such an excitement, and immediately loaded their boats and started on a wild goose chase down the river only to meet with disappointment at the end of their journey. A few received a passage up again on the steamer, but the greater number drifted on down towards St. Michael's, and left the mining country altogether.[51]

McConnell continued up the Yukon River and left the country in September 1888 by way of the Chilkoot Pass.

When Ogilvie returned to Ottawa in January 1889 he reported at length to A. M. Burgess, Deputy Minister of the Interior. The nut of his recommendations was that the time was not ripe for Ottawa to assert its authority in the Yukon:

> I advised him that . . . until such times as there were more and better means of transport it would be unwise in us to interfere with the affairs of the region . . . that to attempt to collect customs . . . would likely endanger prospecting in our country. Generally my advice was that, as the country was in a very unsettled state, and our mining laws, so far as known, unsatisfactory to the miners, even of our own nationality, any attempt to take charge of affairs on our side of the line would hinder prospecting to the American side, and they would stay there till something very rich was discovered in Canada . . . .[52]

This was welcome news to the Deputy Minister, for the government was looking for an excuse to do nothing in the Yukon so as to avoid the expense that establishing an administration there would involve. Ogilvie's advice was accepted.

After the Dawson expedition, events in the Yukon accelerated towards the great discovery which in retrospect seems inevitable; the more people there were in the country looking for the gold which lay in such tremendous quantities in the river's tributaries, the more likely it was to be discovered. By 1890 the Yukon's potential was beginning to attract the attention of the international press. In that year an American periodical, *Frank Leslie's Illustrated News*, sent a party into the region. It was headed by E. J. Glave, an English journalist and explorer — an associate in Africa of the famous Henry M. Stanley of "Dr. Livingstone, I presume?" fame — but the member who became most famous was a forty-five-year-old Oklahoma-born cowboy and logger named Jack Dalton. The party explored the region between Dezedeash Lake and the Pacific Ocean and travelled over the Chilkat Pass, roughly the path of the modern Haines Road. Dalton returned to Haines Mission in 1894 and built a hotel and a trading post. By 1896 he had blazed the packtrail that bore his name, and was making a fair living from supplying Klondikers who used his route.

Frederick Schwatka returned to the north in 1891, this time working for a group of newspapers anxious to supply their public with colourful news of Alaska. He went north from Juneau and explored extensively in the almost unknown region of the Taku and Teslin rivers.[53] In 1895 William Ogilvie also came to the Yukon for a second time, this time to mark the international boundary from the Yukon River south to the Fortymile, through the middle of what was then the richest gold country. He stayed in the north during the winter of 1895–96 and was on hand when the great discovery took place; he was thus able to play a tremendously useful role in sorting out much of the early confusion about boundaries and claims that accompanied the rush.

While the federal government, represented by George M. Dawson and William Ogilvie, paid scant attention to the Yukon, the Anglican church continued its struggle to bring the Christian gospel to the Yukon Indians. The Anglican missionaries had never had an easy time in the Yukon Valley. Problems with money, with supply, and particularly with manpower had plagued the church from the beginning of its service in the region. The work itself was extremely difficult, for the natives were widely scattered through the region and seldom altered their nomadic habits to suit the needs of northern clergy. Moreover, the Indians were not initially receptive to the Anglicans' message; W. W. Kirkby referred to them as "treacherous, savage and cruel." William C. Bompas, although he dedicated his life to what he viewed as the spiritual advancement of the Yukon Indians, commented, "These mountain Loucheux seem the 'lowest of all people' but I cannot help hoping they are a 'chosen race.'"[54]

Bompas, made Bishop of Athabaska in 1874 (and then appointed Bishop of the new diocese of Selkirk — later the Yukon — in 1891), worked hard to find funds and competent missionaries for northern service. Throughout his long service he was never able really to succeed on either count, at least in part due to his irascible and combative personality and his unwillingness to perform that most vital part of the missionary enterprise, returning to settled areas on speaking and fund-raising tours. The Church Missionary Society in London was more interested in supporting mission fields in Africa and Asia than in Canada, and it was to these places that the bright and ambitious young clergy wanted to go. The Canadian north had to be content with the leftovers. The sad truth, as Bompas himself admitted, was that first-rate men would not come to the Yukon, and second-raters, or those from the lower middle class for whom even the Yukon would be a step up, had to be sought:

> ...it is best not to try to send gentlefolks hither whether male or female, simply because these gentlefolks who undertake pioneer life in the far west, have to come down a peg in their position which is mostly painful to themselves and to those about them. Those of an inferior grade in going to the far west generally rise a peg which is mostly pleasant to themselves and to their neighbours. It is less consequence to me whether he passed a College course or not.[55]

The result was that the Canadian northwest received those missionaries who were "tough but uncultivated . . . suitable for Rupert's Land although not for the more sophisticated fields in Asia."[56]

Those men who chose to stay and make a career in the northern mission field had to be physically hardy, for ministering to the natives of the Yukon Valley required the missionary to itinerate — to cover a huge area, meeting different native groups. Robert McDonald, once recovered from his illness, began to serve the entire Yukon basin from a base at Fort McPherson, crossing the Richardson Mountains every year to visit individual bands. These journeys took him to Fort Youcon and two or three hundred miles past it down the valley, and easily totalled more than a thousand miles of travelling a year. Another missionary, V. C. Sim, who had been recruited to serve in the northern Yukon and had reopened the mission at Rampart House, travelled constantly, attempting to meet each band in his charge at least once a year. Sim's health suffered from the rigours of his long and arduous travels, and he died at Rampart House in 1885 after four years' service.[57] William Bompas, who preferred ministering to Indians rather than to whites, spent weeks travelling along the Porcupine and Yukon rivers; in 1872, he crossed overland from the Porcupine and spent several days at an Inuit camp along the Yukon's Arctic coast.

The arrival of the miners represented a new challenge for the missionaries, who had hoped to bring Christianity to the natives before the society was fouled by the advance of the frontier. The miners brought alcohol and a seemingly insatiable appetite for native women; the missionaries were sure that the Indians would be debauched and demoralized through such contacts. Bompas moved into the middle of the mining field, establishing Buxton Mission at Fortymile in 1892, in an attempt to head off what he feared was the impending corruption of his Indian charges.

The missionaries enjoyed varying degrees of success in their attempts to win the hearts of the natives and the miners. Men who were conscious of their lower-middle-class status might overcompensate for it by putting on airs before the miners, and the class-consciousness of later Victorian society that these men reflected was bound to clash with the rough egalitarianism of the miners' society. J. W. Ellington, who served as a missionary in the region in the 1880s, was so unpopular with the miners that they played pranks on him, "and made his life such a burden, that mind and body both gave way and he had to be taken back to England, where he died in 1892."[58] Others, like T. H. Canham, remained with the native congregations, and had comparatively little contact with the incoming white population.

Bompas and the other missionaries recoiled at the changes wrought by the miners. They were, however, comparatively powerless to influence either the Indians or the miners. The former bent somewhat to the moral pleas of the earnest but pedantic Bompas, whose wife Selina joined him at Fortymile after a five-year separation, but generally followed their own desires in their dealings with whites. The miners wrote the Anglican missionaries and their wives off as whiners and complainers, people who did not understand the traditions of the North American frontier.

Top: *Selina Bompas, wife of Bishop William Carpenter Bompas, came north to work with her husband. She was of particular importance in the management of the small boarding school at Buxton Mission, later moved to Carcross.* ANGLICAN CHURCH ARCHIVES

Centre: *The North West Mounted Police came to the Yukon in 1894, when Inspector Charles Constantine arrived on a reconnaissance mission. His report convinced his superiors of the need for a permanent station in the Fortymile district. This photograph was taken in 1901, after the N.W.M.P. had shifted their operations to Dawson City.* PUBLIC ARCHIVES OF CANADA, PA 17070

Below: *The arrival of the gold miners did not end the natives' harvesting existence. Many Indians did sell meat, fish, and other products to the miners, discovering in the process an alternative to the fur trade.* YUKON TERRITORIAL ARCHIVES

When Indians came to visit Fortymile to trade or just to visit, Bompas took charge of them as much as he could, and gave them a few hours of religious instruction. In the winter, when the miners had plenty of free time, there were many moral snares in Fortymile for the Indians; as Bompas's wife later wrote, "We have every reason to fear that their goings on will be very sad and distressing, and to the ruin of our poor Indians."[59]

Unable by their own efforts to alter the behaviour of the Indians or the miners, the missionaries looked southward for help. Bompas wrote numerous letters to the Church Missionary Society, temperance organizations in Canada and England, the Department of Indian Affairs, the North-West Mounted Police, and the Department of the Interior, demanding attention to the Yukon. In 1893 he wrote on two occasions to Thomas Mayne Daly, Superintendent General of Indian Affairs, complaining that the flow of liquor in Fortymile district was debauching the Indians and endangering relations between the races:

> I think it right to inform you of the danger to which the Indians of the neighbourhood are now exposed for want of any police restraint upon the free and open manufacture and sale of intoxicating liquor among them. About 210 miners have passed the present winter in this vicinity, in British Territory. The Indians have learned from them to make whiskey for themselves, but there has been drunkenness of whites and Indians together with much danger of the use of fire arms.[60]

The following year, he noted,

> My own interest lies principally in the preservation of the Indians who I fear will be finished in a few years unless Government protection is afforded them. Some of them manufacture liquor and it is supplied to them by Whites, and especially to the Indian women for the purposes of debauchery.[61]

The complaints took on an increasingly anguished tone, for Bompas truly believed that the introduction of alcohol and the increase in sexual contact between natives and whites would mark the end of the spiritually and culturally innocent Indians of the Yukon. He made no apologies for his strident and public appeals: "Where the life of an Indian is concerned there appears less occasion to stand upon ceremony." Though at first his warnings made little impression upon southern officials, his appeals could not be ignored forever.[62]

These urgings, combined with those of businessman John Healy and of William Ogilvie, who were also pressing the government to move into the Yukon, finally met with success: in 1894 two members of the North-West Mounted Police were ordered north on a reconnaissance mission. The government's purpose in finally asserting itself in the Yukon was twofold:

...in the interests of the peace and good government of that portion of Canada, in the interest also of the public revenue, it is highly desirable that immediate provision be made for the regulation and control of the traffic in intoxicating liquor, for the administration of lands containing the precious metals, for the collection of customs duties upon the extensive imports being made into that section of Canada from the United States... for the protection of the Indians, and for the administration of justice generally.[63]

Leading this two-man expedition was Inspector Charles Constantine; his companion was S/Sgt. Charles Brown. Born in England in 1849, Constantine had emigrated to Canada with his family as a boy of five. He had served with the Wolseley expedition to Red River in 1870, and had been appointed Chief of the Manitoba Provincial Police in 1880. He had joined the N.W.M.P. in 1886.[64] The two men climbed the Chilkoot Pass and arrived at Fortymile, where they spent the season investigating local conditions. Constantine made an important demonstration of Canada's sovereignty over the Yukon by collecting $3,200 in customs duties from the miners on the Canadian side of the 141st meridian. He reported that there was some grumbling over the matter, but that "better counsels prevailed," and the money was collected without trouble — showing once more that the miners were not disposed to violence.[65] In October he returned south to plan for a larger expedition.

The next year, 1895, the government sent Constantine back to the Yukon, this time in charge of a party of twenty police. Travelling by steamer via St. Michael, the men reached Fortymile in late July, and immediately built a post, Fort Constantine, near Healy's Fort Cudahy, across the river from Fortymile. When the post was finished, Constantine was able to report proudly to Ottawa that he was writing from "the most northerly military or semi-military post in the British Empire."[66]

Constantine's reports to his superiors give an interesting picture of the Yukon in this last period of its pre-gold rush history. He found to his surprise that, contrary to the opinions of Bishop Bompas, there was little drunkenness among the miners. "Many of the miners do not drink at all" he wrote, "and but a few to excess. . . . When they come in from the mines for winter they have a general carouse... [then] the camp settles down...and is-...quiet."[67] Some miners wanted substantial economic development in the Yukon, particularly in mining, and thought that this could best be accomplished by improving navigation on the Yukon River. Others wanted to keep Yukon society closed to outsiders, to prevent an influx of thieves, gamblers, and rival miners.

Constantine had been asked by the government to report on the Yukon Indians and to act as an Indian Agent for the district. At the same time he was told to spend as little as possible on them, since the government had no intention of negotiating a treaty with them. Official policy was to extend the Indian treaties only to areas where long-term economic development and a large white population were expected; since Ottawa believed that the Yukon was a flash in the pan, no treaty was required with the Indians there. Constantine viewed the Indians he met with a marked lack of compassion; they were, he said, "a lazy, shiftless lot and are content to hang around the mining camps. They suffer much from chest trouble, and die young."[68] For Bishop Bompas, who continued to express his concern for the Indians, Constantine had nothing but contempt:

> Bishop Bompas is a disturbing element. He has no use for any person unless he is an Indian. Has the utmost contempt for the whites generally and myself in particular. . . . The Indians are chiefly American ones . . . living on the miners through the prostitution of the squaws. There is a comfortable living for them if they would work which they will not do, preferring to take what they can get so long as they do not starve. During the fish and game season they could procure sufficient of both to keep them comfortably during the winter, but no, they must have a feast and gorge themselves so long as any food lasts. . . .[69]

His main concern, and the government's, was that the Indians cause no trouble, that they not interfere with the development of the mining industry; if they presented no danger, then they could safely be ignored. What he did not realize, or did not care to know, was that these Indians were only a small minority, not typical of the native population of the region. The few who seemed always to be hanging around Fortymile were the people who had been incapacitated by disease and alcohol, and who could not survive in the bush as the majority of their people continued to do.

The Canadian government had invested Constantine with a wide range of powers. Not only was he in charge of the police, he was also the region's magistrate, which made him arresting officer, judge, and jailer in all but the most serious criminal cases. He was also the land agent, the gold commissioner, and the collector of customs. On July 26, 1895, the Canadian government created a new District of Yukon, setting the region apart as a distinct district of the North-West Territories,[70] and giving official recognition to its special character.

A case a year later adjudicated by Constantine marked the change that was taking place in the area's legal system. Under the old system, miners regulated themselves; under the new, law and order was dictated by Ottawa, and on Ottawa's terms. Two men who owned a claim on Glacier Creek leased it to a third man, who hired labourers to work it then defaulted on the payments and left the country. The aggrieved workers called a miners' meeting. The meeting voted to seize the claim, sell it, and give the proceeds to the workers. But when the new owner came to the police post (which was also the recording office for claims) to register his claim, he was refused registration, as the miners' actions were contrary to Canadian law. The man left "breathing defiance." Constantine realized that this was the issue on which his authority would stand or fall; that "this was the turning-point, and should I give them their way or recognize them in any manner, trouble would never cease." He immediately sent Inspector D'Arcy Strickland, his second-in-command, to the disputed claim with ten men, telling him to act circumspectly but firmly, and sent a note to the miners' leaders, warning them to clear off the claim, which they did. One of the men who went to Glacier Creek to evict the miners described what happened there:

> Thereupon a party of twelve of us, armed with Lee-Metfords and prepared for all possible contingencies (for no one could tell how the matter would end, or in what spirit we should be received) went up Forty Mile River in boats and marched across country from Forty Mile to Glacier. I suppose we presented a formidable appearance with our rank and file and our magazine rifles, or perhaps the wrong-doers were beginning to realize that their action had been unjustifiable, for we experienced no resistance of any kind. We warned those in possession off the claim under penalty, and formally handed it to the original owner. We had not to make a single arrest, and after informing every one at the creek that such a proceeding was not legal and must not occur again, we simply marched back to head-quarters, and thus the whole business, which might easily have grown to alarming proportions, closed peacefully and satisfactorily. . . . No ill-will was born us for our share in the proceedings, and I think that every one was in his heart glad to feel that there was a force in the land that would protect his individual rights and those of others.[71]

Thus ended the most serious and practically the only challenge to police and government authority in the Yukon ever posed by an organized group.[72]

It might be wondered why the miners would so easily surrender their authority to the police. The miners' solution to this problem might have been a fairer one than the solution decreed by the police — for the workers were apparently never paid. It was certainly the kind of decision that a miners' meeting was accustomed to make. But as has been pointed out, the miners were disposed to accept and obey law and order, albeit with grumbling.[73]

This incident, combined with Constantine's recommendation that the police force in the Yukon be strengthened, Bompas's pleas, and the bright prospects for the region outlined by Dawson and Ogilvie, eventually persuaded Ottawa that something important was about to happen in the Yukon. An extra twenty men were dispatched to the Yukon, doubling the number of police in the area. By February 1898 the Yukon boasted nearly two hundred police officers. This timely show of authority was fortunate for the Yukon and for Canadian interests there, for the event that would make the Yukon world famous was about to take place.

MAIN ROUTES to THE KLONDIKE

Porcupine R.

YUKON RIVER

Miner R.

Peel R.

MACKENZIE

O DAWSON

Wind R.

Keele River

RIVER

Stewart River

Pelly River

Liard River

CHILKOOT-WHITE PASS

DALTON TRAIL

Teslin R.

Liard R.

Stikine River

DANIEL 87

CHAPTER FOUR

The Gold Rush, 1896–1900

The Yukon, or Klondike, gold rush is one of the few events in Canadian history — perhaps the only one — that has entered into the collective memory of the entire civilized world. The period contained many elements of dime-novel fiction: danger, hardship, harsh climate, challenge, greed, triumph, and despair. It also had to do with wealth and sudden riches, themes of perennial fascination. So absorbed have non-Canadians been by the gold rush that some have actually attempted to appropriate it into the history of their own country. Americans in particular have tended to confuse the Yukon rush with the smaller one in Alaska that followed it; books have appeared which depict the Yukon as part of the American mining frontier, and there is even a "family entertainment park" outside San Francisco which features the Yukon among five "historic American areas."

The timing of the gold rush was perfect. It was the climax of a series of gold discoveries in western North America which began in California in 1849. The first gold rush in Canada's Pacific region took place in the Queen Charlotte Islands in 1842, with a major rush occurring on the Fraser River in 1858. About twenty-five thousand people came to British Columbia during this episode, many of them American veterans of the California gold rush. Two years later gold was found near Cariboo Lake, and in 1861 more gold was discovered on the Stikine River. The trail of gold stretched even farther north when in 1871 there was a rush to the Cassiar district of northern B.C. This path, laid out in successive rushes over fifty years, was like an arrow pointing directly at the basin of the Yukon River.[1]

And the world, particularly the United States, was psychologically ready for a new rush. The American census of 1890 had revealed that although there was still some free land left in the U.S., there was no longer a "frontier" of steadily advancing settlement. This was seen as a turning point in American history, since for the first time since the Pilgrims landed in 1620 it seemed that America had reached its limits. True, there was still space on the Canadian prairies, but homesteading in this region did not appeal to everyone. Where else was a man to go to earn his fortune by the sweat of his brow, away from cities and settled areas? Where could he go for a fresh start, a last chance to make his fortune? The Yukon seemed to offer one last opportunity.

Even economics, that "dismal science," heightened the importance of the gold rush, particularly in the United States. The generation that went to the Yukon had been nurtured on an economic controversy that seems strange to modern ears; an argument over the amount of specie (money in the form of coins rather than paper) that ought to be in circulation. The argument over what was called "free silver" was like the economic program of the Canadian Social Credit Party — so complex that although many people believed in it with the devotion of zealots, few understood how it was supposed to work. At the root of it, however, was the struggle between tight money and inflation; between the capitalists who wanted the amount of money in circulation strictly controlled and the debtors who wanted it increased, so that their debts would be easier to pay off and money for investment and expansion easier to come by.

The ferocity of the fight between these factions in the United States, which reached its peak in the election of 1896, just a few months after the great discovery of gold in the Yukon, was made worse by the fact that there was an economic depression that year which was for a time much worse than that of the 1930s, though it did not last as long. This helps explain why the news of the discovery of gold was greeted with such joy and relief in North America and elsewhere — it was an event the world wanted to happen.

A trivial episode which occurred sixty years after the rush shows how deeply the event penetrated the North American consciousness. In 1955 the Quaker Oats Company, sponsors of a radio show featuring the exploits of Sergeant Preston of the Mounted Police and his dog King, dreamed up a promotional gimmick. The company's advertising agency bought nineteen acres of land near Dawson, printed elaborate deeds to pieces of it, and announced that for a "limited time only," each box of Puffed Wheat would contain a certificate to one square inch of the romantic Klondike gold fields. It proved to be "one of the most successful sales promotions in North American business history."[2] Within a few weeks twenty-one million boxes containing deeds were sold. Though the millions of kids who acquired these certificates actually owned nothing, since the deeds were never registered, and the government repossessed the land for non-payment of taxes in 1965, the promotional stunt had tapped a deep vein of advertising gold — one of the most pervasive of North American folk-memories.

These memories were kindled by the rush itself, but they were kept alive by writers of popular fiction — several of Jack London's grippingly realistic stories are set in the gold rush Yukon — and particularly by the poetry of Robert Service. Generations of schoolchildren recited "The Cremation of

Sam McGee" and his other ballads. It says much for the power of the Yukon legend that Service, though a secondary talent at best, is arguably the best known of all Canadian poets, and certainly the one whose verse has made the most money.

What then *was* this gold rush which so fascinated its own and later generations? In the first place, despite the suddenness with which it occurred, it was not an accident. The men (and women — for a few men brought their wives into the country) who had been prospecting the Yukon River Valley since the 1880s were confident that there would be a big strike eventually. Of course, miners always think that, but in this case there was evidence; small amounts of gold had been found on the Stewart River in 1885, and soon after more was found near Fortymile, which became the centre of mining and trading activities in the region. Not enough gold had been found to make a man rich, but there was enough to lure several hundred men into the country each summer, enough to keep two or three trading posts in business. Because the gold was alluvial, found in flecks and grains and small nuggets in the stream beds, it was evident that at some earlier time it had washed down from somewhere. Where was that somewhere, that mother lode — on a hill, or up another creek? It was evident, given the example of California in 1849 or British Columbia a decade later, that there were rich diggings in the Yukon. It was not a question of *whether* gold would be found in quantity, but *when* and *where*.

The gold was there, and in huge quantities, waiting to be discovered. Because the discovery of August 1896 was in retrospect inevitable — since men knew of the gold and were searching for it everywhere — it hardly seems important *who* made the great discovery. Yet people care passionately about such things, as the story of the discovery of insulin, another Canadian legend, has shown, for to be first is to be famous, as well as merely rich. There is still controversy about who deserves the honour for the Yukon gold rush, but the basic facts are clear enough.

Four men were involved in the discovery, all veterans of the north. George Washington Carmack was an American. Born in California, he had prospected in Alaska for a dozen years before coming to the Yukon. His partners were two Tagish Indian brothers, Skookum Jim and Dawson Charlie.[3] Carmack was unusual among the miners in that he was free of racial prejudice against Indians; in fact he was married to his partners' sister, Kate, and got along with the Indians well enough that the miners called him "Siwash George." The term was an insult; *Siwash* was a derogatory term for an Indian, and Carmack was generally considered to be a "squaw man." The fourth protagonist of the drama was Robert Henderson of Nova Scotia, another experienced miner.

None of these men was a greenhorn, or "cheechako," to use the northern epithet. The two Indians had been born in the country, and the white men had been mining for years — Henderson had been seeking gold in one place or another for twenty-four years by 1896. They were tough, too; Henderson had once fallen off a log while cutting trees to bridge a stream, impaled his calf on the stump of a sapling, hung upside down "like a quarter of beef," for four or five minutes, freed himself, crawled to his tent, and was back at work within two weeks.

In July 1896 Carmack, his family, and his two partners were at the site of what would soon become Dawson, at the junction of the Klondike and Yukon rivers. They were fishing for salmon and drying it for dog-feed when Henderson appeared. He had been prospecting with some other men on the small creeks that fed the Klondike River, and, as the unwritten code of the miners required him to do, he told Carmack that he had found promising traces of gold on Gold Bottom creek. Carmack asked him if there would be a chance for him to stake a claim and get in on the prospects. Henderson replied that Carmack was welcome, but not his brothers-in-law; that there was no place at Gold Bottom for any "damned Siwashes." His prejudice was to cost him dearly, for the brothers heard the remark and resented it.

In early August Carmack, Skookum Jim, and Dawson Charlie poled their boat up the Klondike River for a mile or two, then made their way up Rabbit Creek, through the sand, mud, and fallen stumps which marked its mouth, panning in the shallows as they went. It was perfect weather, the height of a late Yukon summer. Pierre Berton described the scene:

> ...they were struck by the splendour of the scene that lay spread out before them like an intricate Persian carpet: the little streams tumbling down the flanks of the great mountain, the hills crimson, purple, and emerald-green in the warm August sunlight (for already the early frosts were tinting trees and shrubs), the cranberry and salmonberry bushes forming a foreground fringe to the natural tapestry.[5]

Passing a fork where an even smaller creek, or "pup" in miners' parlance, flowed in to Rabbit Creek from the south, the went over the "dome" that separated the creeks, and paid a visit to Henderson's camp at Gold Bottom Creek. Carmack later claimed he asked Henderson to join them at Rabbit Creek and Henderson refused; Henderson denied that, and claimed that Carmack had promised to tell him if he found anything worthwhile. Again Henderson insulted the Indians by refusing to sell them tobacco; "his obstinacy" wrote Carmack late in life, "cost him a fortune."

Back Carmack and his companions went to Rabbit Creek, and there, on August 16, 1896, they became the stuff of legend. Panning up and down the stream, the men found encouraging traces of gold. Then, in a place where the bedrock was exposed, one of the men found a nugget about the size of a dime. They turned over loose pieces of the rock, and saw more gold lying in the cracks, "thick between the flaky slabs, like cheese sandwiches," Carmack related. The men whooped for joy, danced about for a few minutes, then quickly panned enough gold to fill an empty shotgun shell, and made camp for the night.

The next morning Carmack blazed a tree with his axe, and wrote out his notice of claim:

To Whom it May Concern:
I do this day, locate and claim, by right of discovery, five hundred feet, running up stream from this notice. Located this 17th day of August, 1896.   G. W. Carmack.

Under the mining regulations then in force in the Yukon, claims made in creeks were 500 feet wide, running from "rim-rock to rim-rock" of the creek. Carmack, as official discoverer, could make two claims, and his partners one each. With a tape measure the men staked these out: one for Dawson Charlie, one for Skookum Jim, and another for Carmack. The claims were numbered, as on all Klondike creeks, One Above (upstream from) Discovery, One Below, and so forth. (Later, when the three men were no longer friends, and Carmack had deserted his Indian wife for the "respectability" of Dawson society, Skookum Jim said that it was he who had made the discovery but that Carmack had persuaded him to put the extra claim in Carmack's name, since the white miners would not recognize him as a legitimate discoverer. Given the racial attitudes of the time, this is not an implausible story.) After the four claims were measured and staked, Carmack ripped a piece of bark from a birch tree and used it to make a sign on his discovery stake: "I name this creek Bonanza. George Carmack" — and so Rabbit Creek changed its name and became world-famous.

The three men broke camp and headed down the Yukon River to Fortymile to register their claims. On the way they met a number of prospectors and told them the good news. They had no reason to keep it a secret, since they had staked all the claims they were legally entitled to. But they did not walk back over the dome to tell Robert Henderson. The men they met on their way downriver thought that their story was just more prospectors' hot air — Carmack had a reputation for stretching the truth — but when Carmack showed them the shotgun shell full of gold they took off in a hurry for Bonanza Creek. When the discoverers reached Fortymile to register their claims they were again laughed at, but the shell full of gold spoke for itself. It was not the kind of gold that had been found on other creeks — experienced miners could tell where gold came from by its appearance. Soon men began to leave Fortymile for Bonanza Creek, and within a day or two the settlement was all but deserted.

It seemed that every miner in the Yukon had heard the good news and was rushing to the diggings — every one, that is, but Robert Henderson, who, unaware of the discovery over the mountain, continued to prospect on

Eldorado Creek, a branch of the famous Bonanza Creek, was known for a time as the richest piece of real estate in the world. YUKON TERRITORIAL ARCHIVES

Gold Bottom Creek for another three weeks. By then the best locations on Bonanza Creek had been staked. Henderson did stake a claim on nearby Hunker Creek which might well have been profitable, but did not work it, preferring instead to search for another Bonanza. Perhaps, like some miners, he had a psychological will to lose. He left the Yukon with only a thousand dollars in gold, and that was stolen from him before he reached the south. Because he was popular in the north, and because he had in truth pointed the way to the riches even if he had not discovered them, the federal government eventually gave him a pension of $200 a month. He prospected in northwest Canada almost until the day he died, in 1933, but never struck it rich.[6]

That was the first phase of the Klondike gold rush; by Labour Day virtually all the men in the region had converged on Bonanza Creek, the entire creek had been staked, and many of the claims were already producing a rich harvest. Several of these had been staked by greenhorns, for some of the veterans pooh-poohed the discovery, believing that Carmack's find was a flash in the pan and that large amounts of gold would never come out of Bonanza. They were wrong, of course, but there was an even bigger surprise in store. On August 31, 1896, five men decided to try the "pup" flowing into Bonanza Creek from the south. They went half a mile up this nameless tributary and did some panning. To their surprise, there was gold in the stream. They staked claims, and named the creek Eldorado. Each of the original claims eventually produced more than a million dollars, and most of the fifty or so claims that were soon staked there reputedly produced at least half a million before they were worked out — 30 million or so from a creek no more than five miles long. The same amount of gold would be worth about $875 million Canadian or $675 million U.S. in 1988 dollars.[7]

The maddening thing about the claims on the Klondike creeks was the great amount of work necessary to tell whether they contained a lot of gold or hardly any. The gold apparently was once located in a "mother lode," probably on a mountain. Water eroded the mountain, dislodging the gold, grinding it finely, and washing it downhill via the small creeks, where it settled into the sandy creek bottoms. Though most of it was in small grains, there were occasional nuggets, some quite large — one found on Bonanza Creek weighed over sixty-four ounces, worth over $35,000 at 1988 prices. Over the centuries these creeks changed course and built up layers of sediment, so that although some gold was at the surface, like that Carmack and his partners found, most of it was five to twenty feet below the surface, at bedrock. And because of the shifting of the creeks, the miners could never be sure where the original creek had been; it might be right underfoot, or it might be somewhere else. In some cases it was halfway up the banks of the hills that lined the creeks. The only way to find out was to dig down, through the sand and muck, through the permafrost, then haul the dirt to the surface, and wash it out in a pan or a sluicebox. If there was no paydirt in the first few feet, the temptation to sell out and try elsewhere was strong.

Thus the wealth of the Klondike was a matter of chance; some of the great strikes were made by veterans, and others by cheechakos. And the strikes *were* big. There was not as much gold in the Klondike as there had been in California, nor as much as in South Africa, but what there was was concentrated in a small area. Some of the claims had incredibly rich paydirt. Before 1896 ground yielding ten cents a pan was considered well worth working. On Fifteen Above Eldorado three Scotsmen got $400 in two pans of paydirt — more than a year's wages for a working man washed out of the sand and gravel in a couple of minutes. Later some men claimed to have got as much as $1,000 from a single pan.

A famous story which conveys the surreal flavour of the period is the tale of Dick Lowe's "fraction." By the autumn of 1896, there were hundreds of claims up and down Bonanza, Eldorado, and neighbouring creeks. Some of the richest ones had been carelessly or inaccurately measured, and since 500 feet was all a miner could claim, it was vitally important to know the exact boundaries of each one. Fortunately, William Ogilvie was on the scene to perform honest and impartial surveys, and Charles Constantine and his twenty mounted policemen were there to preserve order. When Ogilvie surveyed Two Above Bonanza, he found the claim was wider than the law permitted, and a "fraction," a pie-shaped piece of ground, in this case 86 feet wide at the base, was eligible for claim. Ogilvie, as a civil servant, was barred by law from staking a claim, so Dick Lowe, one of the chainmen on the survey crew, claimed it.

Lowe was an archetype of the Yukon miner. An American by birth, he had found gold in the Black Hills of South Dakota and started a transportation business, only to lose it all in the Indian War. He had been a mule-skinner in the American northwest before coming to Alaska and then the Yukon. His fraction did not look promising, and he first tried to sell it for $900 and then to lease it, but no one would invest in a claim that small. He finally decided to work it himself. His first shaft hit nothing. In the second, he got $46,000 in eight hours. Eventually the fraction yielded over half a million dollars, the richest claim per square foot ever staked in the Yukon. According to Pierre Berton

> Lowe's ground was so rich that a wire had to be strung along the border of his claim to prevent trespassers. Whenever a nugget was found along the boundary line, its ownership was determined by a plumb bob which slid along this invaluable wire.... It was said that as much gold was stolen from Lowe's property as he himself recovered from it, for in some places glittering pieces were visible from a distance of twenty feet.[8]

True to the image of the miner, Lowe became an alcoholic, married a dance-hall girl, threw his money away, and died broke in San Francisco in 1907.

Some, though not many, of the miners who got in on the ground floor of the rush made fortunes and kept them. Clarence Berry, an American who worked with his wife Ethel on Five Above Eldorado, became a millionaire. Perhaps because he had a wife he avoided the temptations of the saloons, held on to his money, and died in San Francisco in 1930 worth several million dollars. Alex McDonald, the "King of the Klondike," on the other hand, made a fortune through investing in other men's mining properties, and lost that fortune the same way, dying broke in the Yukon, still dreaming of new speculations.

In the fall and winter of 1896–97, while men worked and grubbed in the muck of the Klondike tributaries, a new town was growing at the mouth of the Klondike River. Dawson City, named after George M. Dawson of the Geological Survey of Canada, was located on flat, swampy land at the confluence of the Klondike and Yukon rivers, about 10 miles from the site of the discovery on Bonanza Creek. Behind the town rose a steep hill, "the Dome." Though Dawson lies 150 miles south of the Arctic Circle, the midnight sun can be seen from the top of the Dome at the summer solstice, and a picnic there under its glow is a ritual of early summer. The town was ideally located to be the centre of the mining community, since it lay an easy day's journey from the major creeks as well as being on the Yukon River, which was navigable from Dawson upstream to the Whitehorse Rapids, and downstream all the way to its mouth, more than 1,000 miles away on the

Bering Sea. Its physical location was less ideal, as it was flat and prone to flooding.

During the first months after the discovery, the news spread downstream through Alaska, and upstream and south as far as the Alaska panhandle. Hundreds of men began to converge on the new town of Dawson, where Joe Ladue, a Yukon veteran since 1882, had, in 1896, bought land from earlier prospectors at $10 an acre, as well as some cabins from Indians living on the site, and was soon selling town lots at $1,000 each. Ladue built the two essentials of a gold-mining town — a sawmill and a saloon. By the spring of 1897 there were perhaps fifteen hundred people in Dawson. Some of these had come up the Yukon River from mining camps in Alaska, and others had come over the Chilkoot Pass from Juneau and Skagway. These were the men and women who "mined the miners," as the contemporary phrase put it — the saloon-keepers, dry goods merchants, hotel-keepers, laundresses, and all the various townspeople who supplied and made money from the mining activities.

After the ice broke up on the Yukon River in May 1897, more people arrived in the new town, and by mid-summer the population numbered about thirty-five hundred. At the same time, those who had found gold in the initial rush and were anxious to take their wealth south boarded the steamers for St. Michael in the Yukon River delta. There they boarded the Alaska Commercial Company's *Excelsior* for San Francisco, or the North American Transportation Company's *Portland*, bound for Seattle.

These two small ships were the golden armada which brought the news to the attention of the world. On July 14, 1897, the *Excelsior* steamed into San Francisco with over $500,000 in gold and the news went out over the wires. Three days later, when the *Portland* docked at Seattle, with sixty-eight miners carrying over a million dollars in gold, a crowd of over five thousand was waiting at the dock. There was, literally, a ton of gold on the *Portland*; a million dollars' worth weighed well over that when gold sold for $20 per ounce, and since there were no banks in the Yukon then, the metal had to be hauled south by travellers. And there they were, coming down the gang-planks in Seattle and San Francisco, dragging rope-tied, battered suitcases which contained thousands, tens of thousands of dollars' worth of gold.

The news created a sensation. The steamship companies were swamped by enquiries. It seemed as though half the population of North America, together with most of that of Europe, was planning to go to the Klondike, though few people had much idea where it was. Within a few months, thousands of people were headed north. Thousands more were laying schemes to profit from the rush in other ways. It occurred to owners of ships along the Pacific coast that passage could be sold on any old tub, so long as it was Yukon-bound. The dry-goods merchants in Vancouver, Victoria, Portland, Seattle, and other cities realized that all the would-be miners would have to buy supplies somewhere, and there arose a tremendous civic rivalry for the right to the title of main jumping-off point for the Yukon.

Why did they go? For wealth, for adventure, for a change, for a second chance, for a last chance — there were almost as many reasons as there were gold-seekers. Nearly a century later it is difficult to think as these people did, for they lived at the end of the Victorian era, when there were still limitless opportunities in the wilder parts of the "colonies" for a man with the right spirit. It was an age when a phrase like "limits of growth" would have been incomprehensible. Men like Harry Pepper, twenty-one years old in 1897, a ticket clerk in the Winthrop Highlands, Massachusetts, railway station, dreamed of something more exciting than selling train tickets to Boston. One morning he shut his ticket window and took off for the Yukon. There were thousands like him.

In the fight for the Yukon trade, Seattle had a headstart, since it had been supplying the Yukon and Alaska trade since 1891. Now, with the news of the discovery, the Seattle Chamber of Commerce went into high gear, setting up a committee led by Erastus Brainerd to trumpet the city's advantages to the world. Thousands of dollars were collected from local businessmen and spent on advertisements in periodicals and newspapers throughout the United States. Would-be miners arriving in town were urged to write home extolling the virtues of Seattle. In October 1897 the Seattle newspaper printed a special eight-page Klondike edition which was sent to every postmaster and public library in the country, as well as to thousands of businessmen and politicians.[9] Vancouver and Victoria tried the same tactics, but the vociferous boosterism of Seattle overwhelmed its rivals.

There were a number of possible routes to the goldfields. The easiest one was by steamer to St. Michael near the mouth of the Yukon River, then up the Yukon by a smaller steamer to Dawson. This entailed no effort at all on the part of the traveller, but it was expensive, and space on the Yukon River steamers was almost impossible to come by. The shortest route was up the Pacific coast by steamer to the little settlements of Skagway and Dyea at the head of the Lynn Canal, then over the White or Chilkoot passes to Lakes Lindeman and Bennett (the headwaters of the Yukon River), then down the river to Dawson. This route was later called "the trail of '98"; it was the poor man's route, and the one most people used.

But these two routes had a drawback from the point of view of patriotic Canadians; they both required passage through the United States. This was more than just a theoretical problem, since miners' goods brought into the United States were subject to customs duties, which meant that Canadian miners would be better off buying their supplies in American towns than in Canadian ones. Therefore both Canadian patriots and merchants looked for an "all-Canadian route" to the Klondike. There were several of these, but only two important ones. The first involved travelling through central

British Columbia. Travellers left Vancouver and headed for Ashcroft. Heading north through the Cariboo mining district they hit the old trail that had been blazed in the 1860s for the telegraph line to Russia. The line had never been built, but its path, though abandoned for over thirty years, could still be distinguished. Eventually the trail reached Teslin Lake on the B.C.-Yukon boundary, from which passage to Dawson was easy.

This trail, however, was a horror, and of the fifteen hundred or so who started out on it, very few got to Dawson. Those who did arrived much too late to find gold. It was one thing for Indians to move on such a trail; they travelled light, lived off the land, and were in no particular hurry. The gold-seekers were unsure of where they were going, were loaded down with all sorts of junk that the merchants had sold them as indispensible ("cholera belts" to ward off disease were a popular item) and had no time to live off the land. The trail turned to mud, their horses died, and so did some of the men — at least one by suicide.

Even more unlikely were the routes to the Klondike originating from Edmonton. In 1897 Edmonton was a town of little significance on the edge of settlement. It had two advantages, however: energetic civic boosters and the fact that it was the end of steel on a branch line of the c.p.r. Edmonton's business community immediately promoted it as the jumping-off point for an all-Canadian route to the Yukon.

There were three versions of this route: one went via Fort St. John and the Liard and Pelly rivers to the Yukon River; the second went via Fort Nelson to the Pelly — the mounted police sent a party over this one, and it took them fourteen months to get to Dawson; the third, and perhaps the most bizarre, went from Edmonton to the Athabasca River, Lake Athabasca, Great Slave Lake, down the Mackenzie River to Fort McPherson (far to the north of Dawson), then via the Rat, Bell, and Porcupine rivers into Alaska, then back up the Yukon into Canada and Dawson. A variant of this route crossed the northern Yukon via the Wind River Valley from Fort McPherson to Dawson. It is hard to believe that anyone who looked at this route on a map of North America could have attempted it, yet the Hudson's Bay Company had used it successfully for years — but its employees were not amateurs. The wonder is that of the sixteen hundred people who tried these routes, about half actually reached Dawson. Every summer, Edmonton commemorates its rather inglorious part in the gold rush by holding a festival called (to the fury of Yukoners, who would prefer to use the name themselves) "Klondike Days."[10]

Nor were the Americans immune from this kind of foolishness. About a hundred people tried to reach the gold fields via the Malaspina Glacier at the head of Yakutat Bay in Alaska. Nearly half of them died. At the hamlet of Valdez (now a thriving port) three thousand men landed in an attempt to cross the Valdez Glacier and reach the Yukon via the Kluteena River. The result of this absurd, almost criminal idea, was that during the winter of 1898–99 men at Valdez actually died of scurvy, a disease not generally associated with North American society. Episodes such as these were part of what came to be called the Klondike "madness."

But the most famous of the routes, and the one which became fixed in the public mind, was the one which went over the two passes, and particularly the Chilkoot trail — the so-called trail of '98. It is a short trail. A remarkable fact of geography is that the end of the trail at Lake Lindeman, from which it is possible to go by boat to Dawson (and right past it more than a thousand miles to Bering Strait) is only about thirty miles from salt water at Skagway. All through the summer and autumn of 1897, boats loaded to the gunwales with would-be miners, and those who hoped to live off their labours, steamed north from the west coast ports, up the inside passage off the coast of British Columbia, into the Lynn Canal, a long, narrow fiord that pointed like a finger at the gold fields. At the head of this inlet lay two towns, Skagway and Dyea. Skagway was the bigger of the two, a roaring frontier town which by late 1898 had a transient population of 10,000. Today it has about 750 people, and survives off the tourist trade, while Dyea is not even a ghost town.

But in 1897 both towns were alive and boisterous. Skagway was like a town out of western American fiction. Though it had a sheriff and a U.S. marshal, it was in fact ruled by a thug in the classic American cowtown mould — a man named Jefferson "Soapy" Smith. Smith was a small-time crook who organized a gang which held Skagway and Dyea in an iron grip. His agents preyed on the greenhorns, offering them advice and then robbing them, steering them into gambling halls where they were fleeced, buying them drugged drinks, or simply knocking them out and picking their pockets. Sam Steele, who commanded the mounted police in the Yukon at the height of the rush, described Skagway as it was when he passed through there in the early months of 1898:

> Robbery and murder were daily occurrences. . . . Shots were exchanged on the streets in broad daylight. . . . At night the crash of bands, shouts of "Murder!" cries for help, mingled with the cracked voices of the singer in the variety halls; and the wily "box rushers" [variety actresses] cheated the tenderfeet . . . in the White Pass above the town the shell game expert plied his trade, and occasionally some poor fellow was found lying lifeless on his sled where he had sat down to rest, the powder marks on his back and his pockets inside out.[11]

In July 1898 Smith was killed by vigilante Frank Reid in a Skagway street shoot-out. Reid "died for the honour of Skagway," but Smith's fame lingers on; in that strange way in which western towns transform their villains, he is no longer a vicious thug, but a "character" from Skagway's colourful past. The two graves lie near each other in the Skagway cemetery, but it is Smith's which has had to be fenced off to discourage souvenir hunters from cutting away pieces of it.

Having survived Skagway, the traveller who wanted the shortest route would trek around the spit of land that separates that town and the smaller, though equally corrupt community of Dyea, which was the beginning of the Chilkoot trail. The first few miles of the trail were deceptively easy; a pleasant walk through spruce woods bordered in the summer with wildflowers, marred only by the men, horses, and mules which clogged the path. Soon, however, the trail began to steepen, and small glaciers could be seen hanging from the mountains which crowded in on it. The path became swampy, a mixture of dirt, mud, and snow, depending on the season, with great round boulders, dead horses and mules to skirt, and increasingly, piles of goods and supplies cast off by men who were beginning to have second thoughts about carrying them over the pass.[12]

The trail slowly became steeper; then, at the timber line, there was a widening, where a community named Sheep Camp had grown up to provide crude meals and lodging for travellers. This was a tent community which at its height had a floating population of more than a thousand. One of the main occupations of the denizens of Sheep Camp was packing goods for miners at high rates (some men made $50 a day carrying supplies — twenty times the industrial wage in the south). The local Indians, for instance, had made good livings as packers for several years before the rush, and were conditioned to the work. The other occupation was crime, for this was the last chance before the Canadian border for the crooks to fleece the travellers. In some ways Sheep Camp was worse than Skagway, for there was an urgency about the place; a short distance further on was the Canadian border, past which the crooks could not operate. Steele described the place:

> Neither law nor order prevailed, honest persons had no protection from the gang of rascals who plied their nefarious trade. Might was right; murder, robbery and petty theft were common occurrences. The shell game was there likewise, the operators could be met with on every turn of the trail, pushing the business to the utmost limit so as not to lose the golden opportunity which could not be found on the other side of the pass, where life and property were safe.[13]

And there were dangers of other kinds on the trail. In early April 1898 an avalanche crashed down on the trail above Sheep Camp, killing more than sixty people. Some of the victims were taken to Dyea, where Soapy Smith's men robbed the corpses. Today the wooden markers of their graves stand in a fenced enclosure, with grass neatly trimmed. Outside the fence is second-growth forest, the tall spruces, ferns, and grass hiding the few collapsed buildings which are the rotting remains of Dyea. Other than the graves,

Top: *When the stampeders disembarked in Skagway or, here, in Dyea, they found their supplies engulfed in a jungle along the shore. Having located their goods, their next task was to find some way of wrestling them over the mountains and into the Yukon.* YUKON TERRITORIAL ARCHIVES

Centre: *From the foot of Chilkoot Pass, the scene appeared, and was, daunting. And yet, the stampeders struggled on, shouldering their heavy packs and heading up the mountain side.* YUKON TERRITORIAL ARCHIVES

Below: *Each stampeder was required to carry one ton of supplies into the Yukon. Carrying the bulky packs over the Chilkoot Pass was back-breaking work.* PUBLIC ARCHIVES OF CANADA there is nothing to indicate the location of this once-turbulent town.

A few miles beyond Sheep Camp was a rock formation known as Stone House, and then came the final climb to the summit. Here, ironically in American territory, took place one of the epic events of Canadian history, commemorated in photographs almost as famous as the one taken of driving the C.P.R.'s last spike thirteen years earlier. The final climb to the summit of the Chilkoot Pass was only a few hundred yards long, but it rose at nearly a forty-degree angle. The only way to get over the pass was on foot, carrying everything, and in the winter of 1897–98, when the trail was at its busiest, steps for that purpose were cut in the snow. An enterprising businessman had built an aerial tramway, rather like a primitive ski-lift, to carry goods over the pass, but it was too expensive for most people. Thus day after day, for months, men (and some women) trudged up the path, step by step, in an unending line. Those who left the path for a rest might wait for hours to get back on, for the line was unbroken and unending.

If it had been a question of a single climb, with perhaps a packsack containing a bedroll and some food, it would not have been such a torment. In fact for a single trip it is an easier climb in the winter than in the summer, when the absence of snow uncovers huge boulders which block the trail. But the mounted police who guarded the summit of the pass would not let anyone into the country without enough money or supplies to last six months, and for most people that meant packing as much as a ton of goods over the pass. A man could manage a hundred pounds, which meant that the average miner would have to make the trip perhaps twenty times. The ordeal could take weeks, unless the travellers were rich enough to afford to hire the professional packers, many of them Indians, who charged what the traffic would bear — as much as a dollar a pound — to take goods over the pass. And they were not dressed in modern synthetic clothes which weighed little while keeping them warm. They were wrapped in heavy wool serge or canvas duck, which became wet with snow and sweat, chafing their skin and weighing them down. Yet up the summit steps they went, gasping, sobbing for breath, the last steps on their hands and knees. They were less than twenty miles from Dyea and they had climbed 3,500 feet, most of it in the last few miles.

Some members of what the Victorians called the "frailer sex" went over the Chilkoot Pass, though they were generally not burdened with heavy packs. Like the men, they were all types: miner's wives, prostitutes, women out for change and adventure. A member of this last category was Martha Black, one of the most vivid personalities in Yukon history.

Martha Black was born into a wealthy Chicago family in 1866 and was married at nineteen to a young railway executive. In 1897, bored with middle-class life, the two decided to seek adventure in the Yukon. When her husband changed his mind and decided to go to Hawaii, she left him (she never said why she preferred Dawson to Honolulu), and went north with her brother. Martha, pregnant at the time, walked the Chilkoot trail in July of 1898 and forty years later wrote:

> In my memory it will ever remain a hideous nightmare. The trail led through a scrub pine forest where we tripped over bare roots of trees that curled over and around rocks and boulders like great devilfishes. Rocks! Rocks! Rocks! Tearing boots to pieces. Hands bleeding with scratches. I can bear it no longer. In my agony, I beg the men to leave me — to let me lie in my tracks.[14]

But she was a tough woman. She survived the journey, reared the child of her broken marriage alone, went into the lumber business, married a Yukon lawyer who was eventually appointed Commissioner of the Territory, followed her husband to England during the First World War, and in 1935, when she was almost seventy, was the second woman in Canadian history to be elected to the House of Commons. She died in 1957, at the age of ninety-one, virtually the personification of the self-reliant northern woman. Like so many others who went over the pass, her feelings about the experience were mixed. Would she do it again, she asked herself? "Not for all the gold in the Klondyke... And yet, knowing now what it meant, would I miss it?... No, never!... Not even for all the gold in the world!"[15]

Once Martha Black and the thousands of other travellers reached the top of the Chilkoot Pass they were in Canada — not in the Yukon, but in a small corner of British Columbia which separated the Territory from Alaska. Just where the Canada-American boundary was in this part of North America was a matter of dispute in 1897, and the issue was not resolved until the Alaska boundary controversy was settled in 1903.[16] But when the rush began, Ottawa had ordered the mounted police to establish posts at the summit of the Chilkoot and White passes, and there the boundary remained, and remains to this day. At the summit, the miners cached their goods and returned for another load, sliding down the hill on the seats of their pants like children. Once all their goods were over the top, they checked in with the police (who also acted as customs officers), submitted to the mandatory search for forbidden liquor, paid what duty was necessary, and trekked their supplies to the shore of Lake Lindeman, ten miles from the summit, from where they hoped to build boats and float downriver to Dawson.

The other trail, which ran from Skagway over the White Pass to Lake Bennett was not so steep and was 600 feet lower, so that horses could be taken across it — but it was longer, stretching about forty-five miles. It was also muddier, so that in wet weather, which occurred often, it became congested. By the fall of 1897 it was impassible and traffic on it all but ceased. The horror of the White Pass Trail was the fate of the horses, mules, and oxen who were driven along it. Nearly everyone who wrote reminiscences of the

Top: *The North-West Mounted Police had a commanding presence during the Klondike Gold Rush. Each person entering by way of the Chilkoot Pass, shown here, or the White Pass was required to report to the* N.W.M.P. *station. The rules of Canadian law, the stampeders quickly discovered, were going to be enforced.* PUBLIC ARCHIVES OF CANADA PA 16151

Centre: *Women soon discovered that their domestic talents — as cooks, seamstresses, laundresses — were in very short supply in the Klondike. A handsome return awaited the female entrepreneur who was prepared to turn her traditional training into a commercial venture.* YUKON TERRITORIAL ARCHIVES

Below: *Having conquered the Pass, the stampeders stopped along the shores of Lake Lindeman and Lake Bennett and built makeshift craft — to call them boats is being too generous — to carry them down river to Dawson City.* YUKON TERRITORIAL ARCHIVES

Top: *The stampeders' first glimpse of Dawson City, a panorama of a jumbled and disorganized waterfront, could hardly have been cause for optimism. They discovered that Dawson's streets were not paved with gold; instead, they were knee-deep in mud.* YUKON TERRITORIAL ARCHIVES

Top left: *The North-West Mounted Police insisted that all boats heading for the Klondike stop at Tagish and register before continuing downstream. At the peak of the rush, the police had great difficulty keeping up with the massive migration.* YUKON TERRITORIAL ARCHIVES

Centre left: *The stampeders' boats, which had enough trouble on the rivers, proved particularly ineffective on the lakes encountered en route to the Klondike, including Bennett, Tagish, and this one, Marsh Lake. Most of the members of the amateur flotilla made it to Dawson City.* PUBLIC ARCHIVES OF CANADA PA 22486

Below left: *Miles Canyon and nearby Whitehorse Rapids were the most treacherous segments of the Yukon River. Having witnessed a series of drowning as unskilled boatsmen tried to make their way through the canyon, the North-West Mounted Police ordered the use of guides to navigate the crafts past the danger zone.* PUBLIC ARCHIVES OF CANADA C 15022

trail included a gruesome description of the section of the trail called Dead Horse Gulch. Here is that of Jack London, who went over the trail in the fall of 1897:

> The horses died like mosquitoes in the first frost and from Skagway to Bennett they rotted in heaps. They died at the rocks, they were poisoned at the summit, and they starved at the lakes; they fell off the trail, what there was of it, and they went through it; in the river they drowned under their loads or were smashed to pieces against the boulders; they snapped their legs in the crevices and broke their backs falling backwards with their packs; in the sloughs they sank from fright or smothered in the slime; and they were disembowelled in the bogs where the corduroy logs turned end up in the mud; men shot them, worked them to death and when they were gone, went back to the beach and bought more.[17]

95

Of the many thousands who left the south for the goldfields in the summer of 1897, only a handful actually made it to Dawson before the Yukon River froze in late October. Most of those who went over the White and Chilkoot passes spent the winter on the shores of Lakes Lindeman and Bennett. For the thousands of men living under canvas at Bennett, the main community on the lakes, the winter was not a time for relaxation, for the only way to Dawson, 500 miles down the Yukon River, was by boat, and the boats had to be built on site. Thus the collection of greenhorns from the south who had left their clerking jobs, their classrooms, workshops, offices — these men who had been turned into beasts of burden on the passes now had to become boat builders.

Photographs of Bennett taken in the winter of 1897–98 show a community that looked as though it was having a gigantic garage sale. Thousands of tents, not only small ones, but large ones that served as saloons, hotels, and businesses, were surrounded by all the gear that had been carried over the pass: sleds, stoves, canned food, furniture, and mining supplies of every description. Alongside were piles of rough-sawn boards. Thousands of boats were being built, and the surrounding hills were rapidly stripped of trees for lumber. Nails and caulking had been hauled over the passes. The planks were produced in saw-pits; platforms on which one man would stand pulling up on a six-foot saw while his partner stood underneath, covered in sawdust, cutting the wood on the downstroke. It was bitterly hard work, and the suspicion that a man was shirking his part of the job led to the breakup of more than one partnership; one pair whose friendship had snapped under the strain bitterly divided all their goods, including the completed boat, down the middle. Then, on May 29, 1898, the ice on the lakes went out, and over seven thousand boats began the race for Dawson. Some did not get far, sinking in the short river that linked Lakes Lindeman and Bennett.[18]

Every aspect of the Klondike gold rush invites superlatives, and the trip downriver to Dawson was no exception. Contemporaries used words like *armada* and *argonauts* to describe the fleet and the crews that drifted, poled, and sailed with jury-rigged masts down the river. It was not all clear sailing, for the turbulent Miles Canyon lay in their path, and Whitehorse Rapids after that. The canyon, though still an impressive sight, has now been tamed by the Whitehorse hydro-electric dam, which has partly filled it, but it was a fearsome obstacle in the spring of 1898, with its sheer cliffs narrowing the river to a third of its normal width. The rush of water through the canyon wrecked over a hundred boats and drowned five men before the mounted police realized that a catastrophe was in the making, and arrived to avert it. The police ordered that boats be inspected and registered, that no boat judged unsafe could carry men through the canyon, and that women and children must walk around it. An entrepreneur named Macaulay built a tramway with wooden logs as rails to haul boats around the obstacle, and made a fortune that spring. Once past the canyon and the Whitehorse

Rapids, then downriver past the less dangerous Five Finger and Rink rapids, it was virtually clear sailing the rest of the way to Dawson.

The picture of a police corporal at Miles Canyon laying down regulations for thousands of miners raises another icon of the gold rush era. The miners are a famous symbol of the Klondike gold rush, but equally so is the North-West Mounted Police constable — braving danger, holding the passes, facing down bad characters, helping the unfortunate, demonstrating to the world that the Yukon was an outpost of British-Canadian law and justice; that the writ of the Yankee desperado would not run there.

At the beginning of 1896, there were 20 mounted police in the Yukon. Now their reputation, already rebounding in southern Canada from the controversy over their role in the 1885 Riel Rebellion, was about to be tremendously enhanced. After the discovery, the strength of the force was increased, to 40 in May 1897 and to 196 by February 1898; eventually it reached over 300. Commanding the police in the Yukon was Sam Steele, a veteran of the 1866 Fenian Raids in Ontario and the Red River Rebellion of 1870, the man who had single-handedly outfaced prairie Indians and striking C.P.R. workers. Steele was one of the most impressive figures of the gold rush, the quintessential example of the anglo-Canadian imperial spirit of the late nineteenth century, and a man determined to prevent disorder in the Territory.[19]

The mounted police adopted a policy of flexibility in establishing their detachments in the Yukon. Whenever a discovery was made, a new community sprang up almost overnight, and the police were among its first citizens. If it looked as though the settlement might be permanent (which in gold rush terms meant a year or so), the police built a log cabin as a detachment; if not, they put up a tent. Most of the smaller detachments were manned by only one or two men. By the end of the rush there were thirty-three of these detachments in the Yukon and adjacent parts of British Columbia.[20]

Because they were for several months the only representatives of government in the Yukon, the mounted police were compelled to provide a tremendous range of services beyond simply enforcing the law. They collected customs duties at the border until Ottawa sent up civilians to take over; for several months they carried the mail in and out of the Territory and ran the local post offices. They were the original recorders of mining claims and of land titles, and they acted as coroners, Indian agents, health officers, tax collectors, jailers, magistrates, guards for the Dawson banks, and later as returning officers at elections. There was little going on in the Yukon that they did not know about. Sam Steele, whose headquarters were in Dawson at the height of the rush, described his working day:

My working hours were at least nineteen. I returned to rest about 2 A.M. or later, rose at six, was out of doors at seven, walked five miles up the Klondyke on the ice and back over the mountain, visited every institution under me each day, sat on boards and committees until midnight, attended to the routine of the Yukon command without an adjutant, saw every prisoner daily, and was in the town station at midnight to see how things were going.[21]

The mounted police had a definite idea of what a gold rush society should be like, and it bore no resemblance to the kind of community that had developed in the California and other American gold rushes. The police were appalled by the traditions of the small frontier democracies that had developed in the American mining communities, where lack of public order had led to the rise to power of villains like Soapy Smith, and the ensuing disorder and vigilante justice. They and their superiors in Ottawa were determined that nothing of the sort should happen in the Yukon.

They were particularly alarmed by the fact that the majority of people coming in to the gold fields were Americans. As representatives of the eastern Canadian establishment view of what the ideal society should be, they were deeply suspicious of Americans, particularly the lower-class types who seemed to be crowding into the Yukon. As one officer of the force put it, "a considerable number of the people coming in from the Sound cities appear to be the sweepings of the slums and the result of a general jail delivery."[22] Skagway was exactly what the police and the government wanted to avoid in the Yukon.

In order to make sure that the Yukon remained orderly, the police did not hesitate to invent law to fit the unusual circumstances they encountered. When Steele laid down regulations for navigating Miles Canyon, he prefaced them by a speech to the miners which began "There are many of your countrymen who have said that the Mounted Police make up the laws as they go along, and I am going to do so now, for your own good."[23] There are many instances of law invented *ad hoc* by the police in the Yukon. Barring people from entering the country without adequate provisions was illegal. So was the common police practice of warning bad characters to get out of the country while the getting was good.

In these actions the police were fully backed by the Laurier government in Ottawa. To reinforce the police, the government detached a force of 200 men of the Canadian Army — a quarter of the entire army — called the Yukon Field Force, and sent it north in the summer of 1898.[24] The existence of this body of men is one of the lesser-known aspects of the gold rush, but it played an important part. The Field Force was designed not only to assist the N.W.M.P. in such duties as guarding the banks and the shipments of gold out of the country (another of the many duties shouldered by the police), but also to demonstrate to the world, and particularly the United States, that Canada was determined to enforce its sovereignty in the Yukon. It was no coincidence that the Yukon Field Force was sent north at a time when Canada and the United States were quarrelling over the location of the international

98

boundary, and over the question of customs duties collected on the routes to the goldfields. The United States had four companies of the regular army stationed in Alaska, and the Canadian government felt compelled to make some demonstration of potential force.[25]

And there was some reason for a display of firmness and resolution, for there were a few moments of international tension in the Yukon during this period. A group of Americans organized themselves as the "Order of the Midnight Sun," and it was rumoured that they and their supporters in Skagway were planning to liberate the Yukon from British tyranny. But it was all bar-room bravado, and nothing came of it. There was alarm in Dawson when someone hauled down the Union Jack at the summit of the White Pass, but the culprit turned out to be a drunken railway navvy in need of a blanket. Most of the alarms were of this sort.

The Yukon Field Force was commanded by Lieutenant-Colonel T. D. B. Evans of the Royal Canadian Dragoons, and consisted of officers and men of the Royal Canadian Artillery and the Royal Regiment of Canadian Infantry. Because they were military men in uniform, they could not travel through American territory without permission, which it was considered politic not to seek. They thus used an all-Canadian route. Travelling from eastern Canada to Vancouver, they went by steamer up the west coast to Glenora on the Stikine River, then marched up the old telegraph trail to the headwaters of the Yukon River. With them they carried two Maxim machine guns with 12,500 rounds each, 300 rounds for each man's rifle, and nearly 200,000 pounds of food. All this gear, and 200 men, were landed at the muddy hamlet of Glenora in May 1898.

Although the Field Force went over the same telegraph trail that had defeated so many civilian gold-seekers, it had little real difficulty in achieving its goal, and reached Teslin Lake in early July. The reason for this was that the force had what others lacked: good organization and money. The government was able to hire over three hundred pack animals to haul the supplies, and the members of the force, instead of adopting the "every man for himself" philosophy which characterized the civilian effort, were under strict discipline. Of course, it was a hard trip, particularly for the four members of the Victorian Order of Nurses who were attached to the expedition at the urging of Lady Aberdeen, the Governor General's wife. Nurse Georgia Powell wrote a description of the trail:

> Through deep forest we went, where the trail was narrow and the branches of trees threatened our eyes or tore our [anti-mosquito] veils disastrously, through tracts of burnt and blackened country, in some cases the ashes still hot . . . through forests of wind-fallen, upturned trees, whose gnarled roots and tangled branches made insecure and often painful footing; over sharp and jagged rocks where slipping would be dangerous . . . a strain that only the strongest and most sinewy woman could bear.[26]

The force built its headquarters at Fort Selkirk, and fifty men were sent to help the police in Dawson. Half the force returned south in the fall of 1899, and in the spring of 1900 the rest went home; most of them were soon in South Africa as part of the Canadian contingent serving in the Boer War.

The experience of the Yukon Field Force's trip to the Yukon points out another fact about the trail of '98: its rigors depended very much on the wealth, experience, and common sense of the individual. Some of the people who went to the Yukon had lots of money, and for them the journey was a pleasant adventure. Such a person was Nevill A. D. Armstrong, age twenty, son of an English baronet, who in 1898 was sent to the Klondike as assistant manager of the Yukon Goldfields Mining Company, an English concern. He took the roundabout route by steamer from San Francisco to St. Michael and up the Yukon River. He had the price of a steamer ticket — the steamship companies, knowing a good thing when they saw it, were charging $1,000 for the fare to St. Michael by the fall of 1897 — and for him it was all colour and adventure. Tales of hardship and privation meant nothing to him: "The enthusiasm of youth is not easily quashed," he wrote. "Besides I was luckily not in the position of thousands of these men who had flocked here without proper provision and nothing to fall back upon...I was the accredited representative of a substantial firm to buy what holdings I thought promising." Armstrong must have been an unusually reliable young man — he had already worked for three years on farms in the American southwest — and in fact he was able to buy Yukon properties which brought his backers substantial profits. It was he who found the giant nugget on Bonanza Creek.[27]

When the flotilla of boats reached Dawson in the late spring of 1898, the great gold discovery was nearly two years in the past. There was still gold to be discovered, but the irony of the trail of '98 was that most of the people who participated in it did not get rich, for the best locations had long since been staked. Dawson City was still a young town that spring, only twenty months old, but it had already seen two hard winters. In the first of these, the winter of 1896–97, about a thousand people lived in the new city. They were almost all veterans of the north, since this was the winter before the news got out. During the winter there was feverish activity both in Dawson and on the creeks nearby. In town the sawmills ran non-stop, and saloons, hotels, and dance-halls were quickly built by those who had come in from Circle City and Fortymile to profit from the rush. Small houses began to line the streets stretching back from the river.[28]

The town was built almost entirely of lumber, most of it green, and fires were an ever-present menace. Three great blazes, in the autumns of 1897 and 1898, and in April of 1899, swept Dawson; the last one, which was the worst, destroyed 117 buildings and more than a million dollars' worth of property.

At the height of its glory, in the summer of 1898, Dawson was full of the frenetic bustle typical of boom towns. Front Street, the main thoroughfare of business and entertainment, was crowded with men, gossiping, discussing business, or simply walking around the town — for many men, having successfully reached the Klondike, had no idea what to do once they discovered that not only were the streets of Dawson not paved with gold (though some enterprising men sifted gold dust from beneath the floors and foundations of the saloons), but that the gold-bearing creeks were fully staked. Some men left almost as soon as they reached Dawson, while others took labouring jobs to earn enough money to get home. Dawson's population, like that of most boom towns, was extremely fluid; men left the Territory on the same kind of sudden whim that had brought them there in the first place.

On the creeks, men built fires on the frozen ground, then dug up the thawed muck and piled it in preparation for the spring work of sluicing. There was a tremendous element of suspense in this, for unless the muck was studded with nuggets, it was difficult to tell how rich the ground was until it could be sluiced. This meant that a huge pile would be built up over six months of winter; in the spring it could yield a fortune, or almost nothing. On the other hand, some of the diggings were so rich that every shovelful thawed over a stove yielded gold. It was mostly a matter of luck.

Perhaps the greatest surprise of the gold rush came in the fall of 1897, after all the good locations on the creeks had been staked. It occurred to a few cheechakos, relative newcomers to the Territory, that perhaps not all the gold had settled at the bottoms of the gulches; that perhaps higher up the sides of the creek beds, where the ground level had been thousands of years before, they might find old gold-bearing beds. It was an inspired guess, though the veterans scoffed at it, and when Oliver Millett of Lunenburg, Nova Scotia, tested the theory by prospecting on a hill far above George Carmack's claim on Bonanza Creek, he staked a claim that produced a half million dollars worth of gold. The place was called Cheechako Hill. Soon every hill in the region was covered with claims, making the terrain even more like a moonscape as trees were cut down for fuel and sluice boxes, and the dirt and muck was heaped up everywhere.

In town and on the creeks, there was a great deal of gold, but little to spend it on. Dawson was woefully undersupplied, for by the time the discovery occurred in August 1896 it was too late to place orders with wholesale merchants in the south. There was lots of liquor in the town, for that was a commodity which always found a path to a mining community, but there was a shortage of clothing, food, and consumer goods of practically every kind. The result was, as an economist could have predicted, inflation. Salt cost $25 a pound. Eggs were a dollar each — in the south, less than a penny. Men gambled for huge sums in gold because there was nothing else to do.

Next winter, 1897–98, saw more of the same. This was still before any appreciable number of people from the outside had got to Dawson, and again

Klondike gold, despite stories circulating in the south at the time, was not lying on the surface, to be scooped up by the shovelfull. The gold was buried deep beneath the surface, along bedrock. Extracting the gold-bearing dirt — and one prayed that there was gold in the gravel — was an arduous, dirty business. YUKON TERRITORIAL ARCHIVES

there was a shortage of everything. Charles Constantine, commanding the N.W.M.P. in Dawson, made an effort in the fall of 1897 to convince people not to stay in the town over the winter, as supplies of food were so low that he feared scurvy or actual starvation. Though no one did actually starve that year, there was certainly some malnutrition among the miners, and even the police had to go on short rations for a time.

The exaggerated rumours of starvation which reached the outside world were so harrowing that the United States Congress authorized the expenditure of $200,000 to have a herd of 539 reindeer shipped from Norway via New York, by train to Seattle, and by ship to Haines, Alaska, from where Lapp and Norwegian herders drove the unlucky beasts over Dalton's trail. The trip from Haines to Dawson lasted from May 1898 to January 1899, and when the 114 surviving animals reaching their destination it was they, not the miners, who were starving. The episode was one more monument to the ignorance and hysteria which marked the world's reaction to the rush.

This period spawned some of the great legends of the gold rush era. Legends seem to need nicknames, like Bill Gates, who was named "Swiftwater" when he boasted once too often about his career as a boatman in Idaho. Gates had been one of life's losers until a strike on Eldorado Creek made him fabulously wealthy. He was short and homely, with a straggling moustache, and had been reduced to washing dishes in Circle City before his luck changed. Now he dressed like a lord and spent like a drunken sailor — he was reputed to have bathed in wine on more than one occasion. Swiftwater Bill, according to Pierre Berton, had a crush on Gussie Lamore, one of the prostitutes from the mining towns downriver who flocked to Dawson when news of the rush got out. Gussie was fond of eggs, a luxury item in Dawson, and one day, probably in the winter of 1896–97, Swiftwater Bill saw her in a restaurant on the arm of a gambler, eating fried eggs. He retaliated for the snub by paying two coffee tins full of gold for all the eggs in Dawson, and, depending on the account, frying them one by one and feeding them to stray dogs, presenting them to Gussie as a present, or feeding them to other dance-hall girls as revenge. Of course Swiftwater Bill died poor, but not until he had survived the rush by nearly forty turbulent years which saw him involved in bigamy, fraud, and mining swindles in South America.

During the twelve months that followed the spring of 1898, the gold frenzy reached its height, and the population of the Yukon peaked at about thirty thousand — no one is sure of the exact numbers because people came and went ceaselessly, and an exact census was not taken until 1901. On June 13, 1898, the Yukon was made a Territory,[29] partly in response to the demand of the citizens, who wanted some measure of local self-government, and partly to forestall the desire of the government of the North-West Territories in Regina to make money by selling liquor licences in Dawson. The Commissioner of the Yukon was appointed by the federal government in Ottawa, and the members of the Council were appointed by the Commissioner. The first man to hold the office was James Morrow Walsh, one of the great figures of the early pioneering days on the prairies. He was not a success as Commissioner, quarrelling with the police and others, and soon resigned, to be replaced by William Ogilvie, who knew the country, was popular among the miners, and had good political connections (he was the uncle by marriage of Clifford Sifton, Minister of the Interior).[30]

The members of the first Territorial Council were all government administrators, including Sam Steele of the N.W.M.P. Council meetings were at first not even open to the public. Ottawa had no intention of permitting any kind of local self-government in a turbulent community which had a strong American element. Only later were local citizens appointed to the Council, and only after the rush had ended were Council elections permitted.

Thus Dawson was not a democratic town in the American frontier tradition. On the other hand, it was an amazingly peaceful community, in the sense that there were few crimes of violence. The Yukon was not a good country for murderers, since the police were, as one commentator put it, "rapid, simple and severe" in their methods. And there was virtually nowhere to hide. Very few men had the native skills necessary to live off the land, and there was at least one mounted policeman in every community to watch for bad characters. There were only a few practical ways to leave the Yukon, all of them closely guarded by the police. The physical geography of the Yukon thus made it much easier to police.

Methods of justice in the Yukon may have been rough-and-ready, but they were effective. Sam Steele was presiding as a police magistrate one day when a blustering American came up before him on a charge. When Steele found him guilty and fined him $50, he said "Fifty dollars — is that all? I've got that in my vest pocket." Steele added "and sixty days on the woodpile. Have you got that in your vest pocket?"[31] The woodpile was behind the police barracks. The government offices consumed a thousand cords of wood each winter, and this was sawn and split by prisoners working ten-hour days on the huge woodpile, which, Steele noted with satisfaction, was "the terror of evil-doers."

In 1898 Dawson became the largest city in Canada west of Winnipeg. This, the last great year of the rush, was the year in which all the excitement and razzle-dazzle which made Dawson City famous reached a peak. Along with the miner panning gold and the upright Mountie, the image that comes to most people's mind at the words *gold rush* is the dance-hall. In some ways, these dance-halls stood at the centre of Dawson life, at least for the miners, for they were a combination of saloon, gambling hall, and theatre.

The first theatre was the Opera House, built in 1897, a building with a saloon and gambling tables in the front and a theatre in the rear, with a stage, benches on the floor, and boxes at the side — all the theatres in Dawson followed this pattern. It was lit by candles, and the stage curtain was made of blue denim.[32] The Opera House was followed by the Monte Carlo, the Novelty, the Pavilion, and others, but the largest and most famous was the Palace Grand, which was opened in 1899. Built by Arizona Charlie Meadows, a hustler from the United States who had made his fortune with a souvenir newspaper extolling the virtues of wealthy Yukoners, the Palace Grand held 2,200 people, and, like its rivals, its theatrical fare was a combination of the absurd and what passed for "high-class" entertainment. On the opening night at the Palace Grand, an actress dressed as the Fairy Queen alighted gracefully from her carriage and sang "All Coons Look Alike to Me."

The theatres became the social centres for the miners who could afford to patronize them, and those which did not burn down proved highly profitable. The clientele was almost exclusively male. A man could drink in the saloon at the front of the house and then watch the show at the back. If he was flush with gold and wanted to show off, he could rent a box and treat the dancers and actresses who worked in the establishment to champagne at $50 a bottle (the women made a 10 per cent commission on each bottle). If he was really rich he might treat the whole house.

Most of the actresses and performers who played Dawson were second-rate at best, since it was not worth the effort of a real star to go so far for a week's engagement, and the Dawson newspapers frequently complained that the actresses could not act nor could the singers sing. However, those who did have some talent, or whose personality appealed in some way to the crowd, could have a tremendous success in the town. Cad Wilson, a redhead who played the Orpheum and the Tivoli, had something about her that made the miners want to lavish money on her; she had the biggest belt of nuggets in

Top: *This was, as the caption says, "One of the Girls," a prostitute drawn to Dawson City to "mine the miners."* NATIONAL MUSEUMS OF CANADA

Centre: *Although the Klondike Gold Rush was primarily a man's event, some women made the trek to Dawson City. Most noticeable among them were the dance-hall girls and the prostitutes — this photo was captioned "Goddesses of Liberty Enlightening Dawson, Y.T." There were, however, also a number of women involved in other lines of work, often with their husbands, who ventured north in search of gold.* PUBLIC ARCHIVES OF CANADA C 18642

Below: *Dawson was, in 1897 and 1898, a makeshift town. There was little lumber available, and too many people for the overcrowded facilities. Tent encampments, like this one along Bowery Street in 1898, were commonplace.* YUKON TERRITORIAL ARCHIVES the Yukon, and was reported to have persuaded a man known as the Sawdust King to spend $1,700 on champagne in one evening. She eventually left town with $26,000 in earnings. Maggie Newman, billed as the "Princess of the Klondike," reduced the homesick miners to tears with her sentimental songs sung in a childish voice. Weeping into their moustaches, they threw coins and nuggets at her, and she left the Yukon with a fortune.

While they were not actually on stage, the actresses were expected to hustle the miners for drinks and this led to more than one evening's memorable entertainment. On one occasion, an actress named Nellie Lewis, cast as Madame Prudence in *Camille*, had been drinking with some miners in a box while waiting for her cue. The actress playing Marguerite called her several times from the stage, but got no reply. Eventually, Nellie's head, considerably dishevelled, appeared between the curtains of the box, yelling, "Madame Prudence ain't a-comin' tonight. Don't you think she's a-comin' to-night." Although dragged from the box, she was as good as her word, and the play had to finish without her. The crowd loved it.

But immorality in the theatres was not tolerated — not for Dawson the strip-tease exhibitions of Circle City. When Freda Maloof, a "seductive Greek damsel," did a belly-dance at the Novelty Theatre she was fined $25 for indecency, despite her plea that she was performing a Mohammedan religious dance which was educational rather than pornographic.

The authorities did tolerate gambling and prostitution in Dawson — so long as they were orderly. After an initial period of confusion, in which there was uncertainty as to who had the right to regulate the sale of liquor in the Yukon,[20] the police and Commissioner Ogilvie took firm control of the situation. Saloons were ordered to close from midnight Saturday until midnight Sunday, and women were forbidden to drink in them. The prostitutes were herded into a specified section of town (much to the rage of the citizens who were there already) and were later forced to move across the Klondike River to Klondike City, or "Lousetown," as it was popularly called.[33]

Prostitution was, of course, illegal in every jurisdiction in Canada in 1898. It was tolerated in Dawson for the same reason it was tolerated in most cities on the Canadian prairies in the early days: the authorities concluded that it was too prevalent and too popular, and probably too necessary to public order to suppress it in a community in which the population was made up of a high proportion of single young men. For a time the prostitutes were arrested and fined, but since that made it seem that they were being licenced, the police adopted the policy of ignoring them unless they made public nuisances of themselves, in which case they were told to leave the country. Eventually both prostitution and gambling were outlawed in the Territory, but this did not occur until 1901, when the rush was over, and Dawson had become a more settled community.[34]

It is as common today as it was in the 1890s to romanticize the gaudier aspects of gold rush history. The prostitutes of Lousetown did not, as a rule, have hearts of gold, nor did they all end by marrying rich miners. When as a girl, Pierre Berton's mother Laura and her friend crept out one day to spy on them from the hill above Lousetown, she was charmed by what seemed to be their gay manner, their chatter, and their colourful clothes. But this was a middle-class fantasy, which bore slight resemblance to the reality. Some led miserable lives, abused by pimps or succumbing to alcohol. At least one committed suicide. But in the main, these were women of sturdy stock — they had to be to have survived the trek over the Chilkoot Pass. And if photographs of women like Snake-hips Lulu are accurate, a touch of *embonpoint* was no impediment to a successful career as a prostitute.

Of course not all the women in the Yukon during the gold rush were actresses, prostitutes, or dance-hall girls, but it was these colourful ones that the contemporary journalists and the later legend-spinners focused on. It is not always easy to separate fact from fiction. This is particularly true when the lives and behaviour of these women actually did deviate so spectacularly from the lives and behaviour of "decent" women in southern Canada. Some of these lady legends did eventually achieve "respectability." Lulu Mae Eads, for instance, worked the Floradora and the other hotels in company with Diamond-Tooth Gertie, Babe Wallace, the Oregon Mare, and others, but she married the hotel's owner, and stayed in Dawson after the rush to become a mainstay of the community.

The fantasies about life in the Yukon nurtured in the rest of the world were fed by the poetry of Robert Service, who made a fortune by telling readers what they expected to hear about the gold rush. The fact that he did not arrive in Dawson until several years after the rush made it easier for him to shade the truth, for by that time even the residents of the Yukon were gilding some of the harsher realities of gold rush life. His first poem to achieve success, "The Shooting of Dan McGrew," was written in 1906 while he was working in a bank in Whitehorse, far from the site of the events he described. Like so much of his poetry, it depicts a gold rush which is part truth and part fantasy. The first stanza is accurate enough:

A bunch of the boys were whooping it up in the Malamute saloon,
The kid that handles the music-box was hitting a jag-time tune;
Back of the bar, in a solo game, sat Dangerous Dan McGrew
And watching his luck was his light-o'love, the lady that's known as Lou.

Where Service goes wrong is when he gets to the violence:

Then I ducked my head, and the lights went out, and two guns blazed in
    the dark;
And a woman screamed, and the lights went up, and two men lay stiff
    and stark;

Pitched on his head, and pumped full of lead, was Dangerous Dan
   McGrew,
While the man from the creeks lay clutched to the breast of the lady that's
   known as Lou.

Miners found themselves lying on the floors of Dawson saloons often
enough, but not because they were full of lead. L. E. Karp, in an article
about Service in *North* magazine, remarks that his poetry is a "fresh,
imaginative, and vivid portrayal of a unique phase of North American
history, the fabulous gold rush."[35] Whether it is fresh or not is for the literary
critics to decide, though it seems that Service borrowed heavily for form and
inspiration from Kipling. Vivid his verse is, and also highly imaginative. In
fact, since it sold so widely, it was a major influence in shaping the English-
speaking world's perception of the gold rush. (It is worth noting that Karp,
in his article, thought of the rush as a "North American" rather than a
Canadian phenomenon.) But Robert Service's Dawson City, with shots
ringing out and bullet-riddled miners lying on the floors of saloons simply
did not exist. In fact, it was illegal to carry a handgun in Dawson.

Nonetheless, the Territory was by no means free of crime. In fact, at the
time, more charges were laid per capita in the Yukon than in any other part
of Canada. This was particularly true for offences like theft, fraud, larceny,
and assault — the kinds of crimes one would expect in a community where
there was much loose money lying around in the form of gold. The rate for
larceny was five times that of Ontario, and for fraud sixteen times. For
assault and battery it was eight times Ontario's, though only marginally
higher than that of B.C. and the North-West Territories (which then
included present-day Alberta and Saskatchewan).

Interestingly, however, once arrested, an accused person's chances of
being convicted were lower in the Yukon than anywhere else in Canada.
Though the "crime rate" was high, the conviction rate was low. The
conviction rate for assault and battery in the Yukon was a sixth that of
Ontario, for fraud about half, and for larceny two-thirds. This surprising
fact was a result of police methods used in the Territory. One technique the
mounted police found effective during the gold rush was to bring charges
against petty criminals, bad characters, and those who offended in other
ways, and to tell them that if they left the Territory forthwith the charges
would be dropped.[36] This practice was referred to as "getting a blue ticket."
Of course, it was quite illegal; it amounted to a kind of deportation, and
neither the police nor anyone else had the right to deport citizens or aliens
without due process. Nonetheless, the order to leave seems to have been
widely obeyed, since the alternative was likely a conviction and many weeks
on the woodpile.

An example of the process in action was given by Sam Steele. Interestingly, the offender, presumably one of the sort of Yankees the police

disapproved of, had not even broken the law; he had spoken disrespectfully of Queen Victoria.

> Some of the people objected to Royalty in general, did not like monarchs, and would speak slightingly of ours. One of those was an actor in the theatres in Dawson, and when his conduct was reported by the sergeant he was given an opportunity to say he would sin no more or take his ticket for the outside. This had the desired effect.[37]

In this case the man was given a chance to repent, but the incident illustrates how the social order was preserved in the Yukon at the expense of what today would be considered ordinary civil rights. As the American anthropologist Thomas Stone has pointed out, the police did more than merely enforce the law in the Territory; they also performed the function of "symbolizing class dominance" — that is, they made sure that the Yukon was not only peaceful, but conformed as much as possible to eastern Canadian middle-class social norms of that era.[38]

Before the rush the federal government had virtually ignored the Yukon, but once the scale of the Klondike discovery became apparent, it sought a means of extracting revenue out of the miners' good luck. This money was not intended for the development of the Territory or to invest in its future, but to enrich Ottawa's coffers. Clifford Sifton expressed the official policy when he observed that "The Yukon is not the same as any other gold mining country in the world, and the difference consists in the fact that it is good for nothing except mining, which in all probability will be temporary."[39] In accordance with this attitude he several times raised the royalty schedule on gold extracted from the creeks, but each time his efforts to increase Ottawa's share of the riches ran into violent opposition from the miners and the Yukon business community, who shared Sifton's view of the region's future and wanted to maximize returns before the gold ran out, and he was forced to withdraw the regulations. Sifton wanted a larger share of the region's wealth for Canada, but he did not get it.

On a more positive note, Sifton did plan to integrate the Yukon into the nation through an all-Canadian rail link between the northern interior of British Columbia and the Yukon Valley; this scheme, hatched in response to pressure from the Canadian business community, was aimed at diverting the Yukon trade from Seattle to Vancouver and Victoria. The proposed route was by steamship from those cities to the Stikine River (where Canada had right of passage under the Treaty of Washington), up the river into British Columbia, then north to the Yukon. He had personally investigated the feasibility of the route on a trip to the region in the autumn of 1897, in which his party went over the Chilkoot Pass to Lake Lindeman, back over the White Pass, and visited Taku Inlet and the Stikine River, both possible routes for a railway.

Sifton entered into negotiations with the entrepreneurs William Mackenzie and Donald Mann, but the plans fell through under the weight of American obstructionism and Canadian political wrangling. The death of this railway scheme and the subsequent construction of the White Pass and Yukon Railway cemented the transportation link between Skagway and the Yukon and dealt a mortal blow to Sifton's goal of capturing the Klondike trade for Canadian business — the cornerstone of his Yukon policy.

It is clear from Sifton's actions that the federal government viewed the region as a potential source of short-term profits for Canadian business. The Yukon was an annoyance rather than a source of pride to Sifton and the government. Charges of political corruption levelled at the Yukon civil service (some of them well-founded), battles over railways, royalties, and mining concessions, dissipated what interest Sifton had in the region. Eventually he was to hand the economic destiny of the territory over to large corporations who were more efficient than individual miners, and complained less.

As often happened in North America when an event like the gold rush took place, the native people of the area were considered peripheral to the event, and some were overwhelmed or pushed aside by the rush of white settlement. Though common enough in the history of North America, this was particularly ironic in the Yukon, given the fact that natives were the co-discoverers of the great treasure on Bonanza Creek. Nor did the Canadian government concern itself much with the fate of the Yukon Indians before, during, or for many years after the gold rush. The Indians of the Territory were not even encouraged to sign a treaty or to establish themselves on reserves.[40]

The reason why the government of Canada did not sign a treaty with the Yukon Indians, of whom there was a declining population of about two thousand in 1898 (government population figures for the northern Indians were notoriously inexact) was that Ottawa did not want to have the Indians choose land for a reservation on which gold might later be found. Nor did they want the Indians to move into the communities. The government felt that they were ''best left as Indians'' — that they should continue as nomadic hunter-gatherers, as far away from the settlements as possible.[41] Ottawa believed that the Yukon gold rush was destined to be a transitory event, and that the Territory would never sustain a large white population. There was thus no need to be concerned about the welfare of the Indians, who, rather than make demands on the government, could simply go on being Indians.

The majority of Yukon Indians did exactly that. A few, weakened by disease or trapped by alcohol, did gravitate to the settlements, where they lived a precarious existence on the fringe of white society. A few turned to begging, but even those native women who had prostituted themselves to the miners before the rush were put out of work by the numerous white prostitutes who swarmed to the north after 1897. The majority of Indians,

Top: *The Indians found themselves pushed to the background during the Klondike gold rush. While the stampeders provided a large market for their furs, fish, and meat, they also brought disease and dislocation for the Indians living in the Dawson area. At the insistence of Bishop Bompas, the government created a small reserve downstream from Dawson City, at Moosehide, where the Indians were expected to live.* YUKON TERRITORIAL ARCHIVES

Centre: *The Klondike Gold Rush was as much an American phenomenon as a Canadian one. Most of the stampeders came north from the western states of the U.S.A. As a result, celebrations of American holidays, like this one on the fourth of July, 1899, attracted great attention.* PUBLIC ARCHIVES OF CANADA C 14258

Below: *The tent city of Bennett is shown in 1898. Thousands of stampeders, desperate to continue the trip to Dawson City, waited at Bennett for the ice to leave the lake and the Yukon River system.*

111

however, continued in their traditional way of life. What they gained from the gold rush was the opportunity to sell food to the miners; moose meat and other game could always be sold at the mining camps. In some cases they found seasonal wage employment as wood-cutters for the steamboats on the Yukon River, or occasionally as day labourers on the creeks (though there was reluctance to hire them in many cases). But such jobs were an overlay to their way of life — an additional way to earn money for food and supplies for a few weeks or months before going back on the land.[42]

Although the native population of the Yukon was reduced to an extent by introduced diseases — the Han Indians, who lived in the area of the Klondike, were all but wiped out by illness — the gold rush did not have as catastrophic an effect as might be expected. The miners did not really take up much space in the Territory; Dawson City and the other communities occupied only a minuscule fraction of its land area, and the rest was left relatively undisturbed. A combination of race prejudice on the part of whites and the Indians' own desire to retain their way of life meant that many Indians took from the gold rush only what they wanted, yet avoided being completely overwhelmed by it. Nearly half a century was to pass before the welfare state tied them to white society with unbreakable bonds.

Though the gold rush was a spectacular manifestation of human preoccupation with material wealth, there were those among the population of the Yukon who served God instead of Mammon. There were a number of missionaries of various denominations active in Dawson by 1898; the most notable of these was Father William Judge, a Jesuit missionary to the Indians at Nulato, downriver in Alaska, who was ordered by his superior to Fortymile in 1894, and who followed the rush to Dawson in 1897. He built a church and a hospital, staffed with nuns and lay nurses (some of them male). He devoted himself to the care of the sick and injured, to the detriment of his own health. When he died in January 1899, worn out by his labours but known throughout the Territory as the "saint of the Yukon," he was not yet forty-six.[43]

Bishop W. C. Bompas, the other great religious figure of the period, pursued a different goal during the rush. His main concern continued to be the Indians, who were by 1898 not only ignored by the government, but were largely neglected by the traders who had once eagerly sought their business. Bompas moved his mission from Fortymile to Dawson, justifying his action not on the grounds that the miners needed him, but that the Indians of the locality did. He was not popular with the authorities, and the police hierarchy in particular disliked him, accusing him of being more interested in the welfare of the Indians than of the general population. As one government official noted:

> My complaint with regard to the missionaries is that instead of teaching the Indians self-reliance and independence they aid most strongly in

making them mendicants. I am daily in receipt of letters from Indians, written by a missionary, asking for all sorts of favours.[44]

In 1901 Bompas moved again, to Caribou Crossing (Carcross), where he died in 1906, still lamenting the events which had made his Indian charges only bit players in the great drama being played out in the Yukon.

The population of the Yukon reached its peak in 1898–99, but by the end of that year the notorious Chilkoot Pass was all but deserted, for a modern and far easier method of reaching the gold fields had become available. Early in 1898 a group of British financiers, expanding on an earlier idea, had decided to build a railway from Skagway over the White Pass to the head of navigation on the Yukon River, and in April of that year the White Pass and Yukon Railway Company was organized. Construction began immediately. With the thousands of travellers and tens of thousands of tons of goods destined for the north, it appeared to be a project which was bound to be profitable. There were all sorts of logistical difficulties. As many as two thousand men were needed to labour on the project, and since most men in the area were intent on finding gold, the company had to employ those down on their luck, or men from Skagway who had been robbed by Soapy Smith and needed work to get another grubstake.

The engineering difficulties were even more immense. The line rose from sea level to 2,880 feet in just twenty-one miles, winding through canyons and hanging on the sides of sheer cliffs. The decision to build a narrow-gauge line of 3 feet instead of the North American standard of 4 feet 8½ inches made the task easier. A 250-foot tunnel was blasted out of the granite, and a steel cantilever bridge was built 215 feet above Dead Horse Gulch; for a time it was the highest railroad bridge in the world.

In contrast to earlier North American railway projects, the men who built the Yukon and White Pass do not seem to have been exploited and mistreated, probably because labour was hard to come by in the region. And there was always the alternative of getting a labouring job on the creeks; on one occasion the navvies all downed tools and left work at the news of a new strike at Atlin. There were few serious accidents on the projects, and the men were paid $3 for a ten-hour day and given free lodging, though they had to pay for their meals. The project was a resounding success. The first train ran to Carcross on Lake Bennett in July 1899, and the line was finished to Whitehorse, 110 miles from Skagway, a year later.[45]

The White Pass and Yukon Railway laid the foundation for a significant change in the Yukon, since it was the basis for the growth of the new town of Whitehorse. Whitehorse was ideally suited as a transportation centre. Located downstream from the treacherous Miles Canyon and Whitehorse Rapids, it was the head of safe navigation on the Yukon River. From the railway station which sat on the riverbank, dominating the town, it was only a few steps to one of the steamers, many also owned by the railroad company,

which took freight and passengers to the goldfields. From the very beginning, Whitehorse contained the seeds of future growth. But it remained only
a transfer point until the defence exigencies of the Second World War made it
the Territory's focal point.[46]

In the summer of 1899 the Klondike rush ended when a discovery of gold
was made on the beaches of Nome, Alaska. Because very few of the people
who had come to the Yukon after 1897 had found enough gold to make their
trip worthwhile, there was a large floating population in Dawson and
elsewhere in the Territory anxious to participate in another rush. When the
strike at Nome was announced, many of these people left for Alaska. Others
left for the south. But this did not mean that Dawson turned into a ghost
town, simply that there was no gold for newcomers. Those who had good
properties continued to work them. The year of greatest gold production in
the Yukon, in fact, was 1900, when over $22 million worth was taken out of
the creeks (in 1897 the figure was $2.5 million; in 1898 $10 million). After
1900, production began to decrease, but very slowly, so that up to the end of
1911 $140 million in gold had been taken out of the ground. The population
of the Yukon declined from about thirty thousand at the height of the rush in
late 1898 to just over four thousand in 1921, of whom nearly half were
Indians. Gold was still being taken out of the creeks more than sixty years
after the rush, and with the sharp increase in world gold prices in the 1970s,
there was another flurry of activity.

The most dramatic change in gold mining at the end of the rush was not
the loss of population but the change in mining methods. There was an
almost incredible concentration of gold on some of the claims, where, it was
said, hundreds of dollars' worth — literally, two pounds of gold or more —
could be taken from the ground in one shovelful. This could not last. Soon
the concentration of gold in the ground began to decline, so that it became
uneconomical to work the claims in the old, wasteful, labour-intensive way.
For a time, more efficient methods helped to reduce the cost of labour.
Thawing frozen ground by means of fires was supplanted by steam-points,
which were driven into the permafrost. Then hydraulic mining was introduced; water was pumped under high pressure through hoses which were
directed at the banks and hillsides, washing away large amounts of dirt and
gravel in a short time.

The final phase of the transformation of mining was the introduction of
the dredges. These giant machines were so efficient that they could make a
profit processing as little as a few cents' worth of gold in a cubic yard. They
were enormous floating machines; launched on the creeks, which were
dammed up to float them, they chewed their way up the creeks, reworking
the claims (which had wasted a considerable proportion of their gold in the
comparatively inefficient sluicing process), leaving the serpentine trails of
tailings — like the castings of some monster worm — that are a striking
feature of the landscape in the vicinity of Dawson.

In order to make the dredging process feasible, the original claims had to be consolidated. Shortly after the gold rush, large mining corporations became interested in acquiring gold properties. Clifford Sifton was originally opposed to the idea of consolidation, writing that there was "no possibility of any mining companies getting a group of claims. A policy of that kind would simply blanket the whole country and stop development." As early as January 1898, however, he changed his mind and presented new regulations that permitted corporate control of large stretches of gold-bearing ground.[47] Twenty-year dredging leases extending up to five miles each along the creeks were now authorized. Some claims were bought from their owners, who were no longer making a profit, or wished to sell out, and many were acquired from the territorial government after having been abandoned. Large corporations, or "concessions" as they were called — the Treadgold, the Guggenheim — came to dominate the economy of the Yukon, and day labour began to replace grubstaking on the creeks. Of course, prospecting continued, as it does to this day, in hundreds of creeks all over the Territory, but near Dawson, where most of the gold was located, corporate capitalism had replaced the individualism of the mining frontier. It was when this happened that the rush could truly be said to be over.

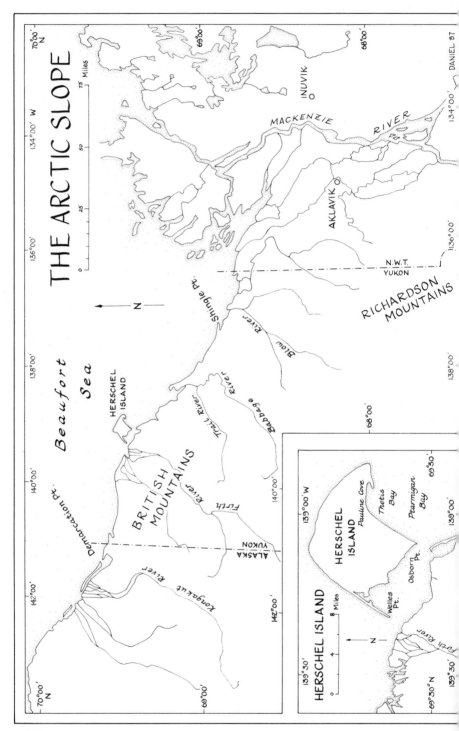

THE ARCTIC SLOPE

DANIEL 87

CHAPTER FIVE

Herschel Island: the Unknown Yukon

The first part of the present-day Yukon to be reached by Europeans was a region far away from the modern communities of Dawson and Whitehorse; it was in fact a part of the Territory that most southerners have never heard of. In the Beaufort Sea, a mile off the northern coast of the Yukon and thirty miles east of the Yukon-Alaska boundary, lies Herschel Island, a rectangular piece of land about eight miles by six in area. Most of the island is flat, but at one point it rises to an elevation of 600 feet. It is timberless, almost featureless, but it has one advantage that made it attractive to Europeans — it possesses the best harbour along that part of the Arctic coast.

Before the Europeans arrived, a number of Inuit lived on the island, and others crossed over periodically from the mainland to hunt caribou and to fish in the waters which surrounded it. Then and later the local waters teemed with fish and with whales, and it was easy to keep warm by burning the driftwood which floated down the Mackenzie in large quantities and fetched up on the island's low, flat beaches. In the year 1800 there were perhaps as many as 2,500 Inuit living on the island and the adjoining stretch of coastline between the Alaska boundary at the 141st meridian and the Mackenzie Delta, a hundred miles to the east of the island.[1]

The coastal Inuit knew of the existence of the Kabloona, the white man, for Russians had been trading with the native people of Alaska since the middle of the eighteenth century, and news of these traders — and some trade goods — had circulated as far as the Beaufort Sea region by way of Indian middlemen. But none of these new people had actually visited the Inuit before the second quarter of the nineteenth century.

Herschel Island appeared on the map of the known world as a result of the twists of European power politics of that era. After the British victory in the Napoleonic Wars was capped by the triumph at Waterloo in 1815, Great Britain became for a time the most powerful country in the world. At the same time, as a result of a general downscaling of the British armed forces, there were hundreds of unemployed and underemployed British naval officers available to establish Britain's glory in peacetime exploits. Fully 80 per cent of naval officers had neither ships to command nor duties to perform. In the early nineteenth century the Canadian Arctic played the same role as outer space did in the mid-twentieth: it was a field of adventure, rivalry, and scientific discovery for the great powers of the world. By this time there was no longer a commercial rationale for finding the Northwest Passage; in the words of John Barrow, Second Secretary to the Admiralty, the search was "one of the most liberal and disinterested that was ever undertaken . . . having for its primary object that of the advancement of science, for its own sake, without any selfish or interested views.[2] In the field of scientific exploration, as in industry, Britain was determined to be paramount.

Thus, in 1825, John Franklin, a forty-three-year-old veteran of the British navy, was sent to map North America's Arctic coastline. It was his third northern expedition. In 1818 he had been second-in-command on a voyage to Spitsbergen, and in 1819–21 he had led an expedition to the mouth of the Coppermine River which had resulted in the deaths of ten of his men from exposure and starvation, mostly due to bad planning. On the 1826 expedition he was better prepared. He descended the Mackenzie River in two boats, following the path pioneered by Alexander Mackenzie thirty-three years earlier. Passing through the delta he sent one of his boats east to map the coast to the Coppermine River, and took the other boat west along the Arctic coast, the first European to do so. Shortly after reaching the open sea he met a large group of Inuit camped on the shore. He had previously determined to open "communication with the Esquimaux by landing amongst them, accompanied only by Augustus, his interpreter." The Inuit, however, realizing that Franklin's boat contained objects of great value to them, pressed forward in a manner he found menacing.

> At no time did they appear to have hostile intentions, but the Inuit pressed close around the stranded sailors, carrying off supplies, trade items, even a pistol, anything that the beleaguered seamen could not preserve . . . as the looting became more intense a violent conclusion seemed likely, until suddenly the boats were released by a rising tide and the expedition scurried away down the coast.[3]

The name Pillage Point commemorates the incident. Franklin later claimed that another group of Inuit told him that the first group had intended to murder his party, something that is difficult to judge, given the cultural gap between the two races. Certainly there were what one student calls "fundamental misunderstandings" present in these early contacts between the Yukon Inuit and Europeans. James Richardson, in charge of another part of the expedition, reported that the Inuit followed the boats in amazement; only women rowed, yet here were people with beards bending at the oars.

On July 17, 1826, Franklin sighted a low island just off the coast, and named it after the well-known British chemist and astronomer Sir John Herschel, the son of the even more famous Sir William Herschel, discoverer of the planet Uranus and Astronomer Royal to King George III. Perhaps to his surprise, Franklin found that the island and the Arctic coast nearby did not constitute a kind of uninhabited northern desert. There were many Inuit on the island, and more along the coast. At one point a fleet of Inuit boats set out from the coast to meet him, and Franklin's men counted seventy-three kayaks and five umiaks before they lost count.[4]

Franklin found the Inuit of the region to be a friendly people, in contrast to those at the mouth of the Mackenzie. Though these people had never before seen a European, they were carrying steel-tipped arrows; Franklin learned through an interpreter that these had come from Inuit living farther to the west, who had got them from Russian traders. He gave them presents, and continued his mapping of the region. He did not quite succeed in his mission, which was to rendezvous with a British ship west of Point Barrow. Plagued by ice and bad weather, he turned back in mid-August 1826, 150 miles short of his goal. He returned to his base at Great Bear Lake, and the next year went home to England.

A decade later two more Europeans came along the northern coast of the Yukon, this time as part of an expedition commissioned by the Hudson's Bay Company to complete the survey of the coast that Franklin had left blank. The company was a surprising participant in "scientific" exploration, for its earlier exploratory thrusts had all had a singular commercial purpose. There was a connection, however. Its monopoly in Rupert's Land was under review; the company, in fact, wanted to press for an early renewal of its licence. Company Governor Sir George Simpson sponsored a major Arctic expedition, a sure-fire technique of winning public support. In command was Peter Warren Dease, an employee of the company who had spent many years in the Athabasca and Mackenzie districts. His companion was Thomas Simpson, cousin of Sir George, who had worked for some years as a clerk for the company. In the summer of 1837 the two men came down the Mackenzie with fourteen men and two boats, turned west, and headed for Point Barrow. Like Franklin they had problems with ice, wind, and fog, but they persevered, and reached their destination; the whole of the Arctic coast west of the Mackenzie had now been explored.

Also like Franklin, Dease and Simpson found that the Inuit of the western Arctic were friendly but inclined to pilfer. In the account he published of the expedition, Simpson had few good words to say about them; even their friendliness he called "deceitful good-humour,"[5] and warned that when they got guns, white men would not be safe in the Arctic. Simpson seems to have been mentally unstable; not only a racist (he disliked Indians and Métis as much as he did the Inuit), but subject to periods of depression, he hungered for glory. On a trip back east to press his case for a new expedition, he was shot to death south of the Red River colony, under circumstances which have never been fully explained.[6]

For the next fifty years the Inuit of the Herschel Island region remained relatively undisturbed. In 1840 the Hudson's Bay Company established Fort McPherson at the edge of the Mackenzie Delta, providing a closer alternative to Russian traders for the supply of European trade goods. But the main theatre of European activity in the north in this era was in the central and eastern Arctic, where the search for the lost expedition led into the region by Sir John Franklin in the 1840s absorbed the energies of the British and the attention of the entire world. In 1867 Alaska was purchased by the United States, and in 1870 and 1880 Canada acquired formal title to the Northwest Territories and the Arctic, making the Inuit officially Canadians — but this meant no more to them than it did to the Canadian government, which neither knew nor cared about the region. In the 1880s, however, a series of events occurred which were to change forever the lives of the people of Herschel Island.

Though the Inuit of the Herschel Island region had little material wealth as white people reckoned it, their country possessed a resource that aroused the acquisitive instincts of nineteenth-century southerners in much the same way that gas and oil do today to their twentieth-century counterparts. A century ago the lure was also oil — whale oil, as well as other products of the bowhead whales that teemed in the Beaufort Sea.[7]

Whaling was a centuries-old industry; in the United States, the New England ports had been centres for the whaling fleet since the beginning of the Republic. By the mid-nineteenth century the industry had spread to the Pacific coast, and hundreds of whaling ships were operating out of San Francisco and other ports. There was a booming market for the products of the hunt: whale oil was used for lubrication and lighting, particularly before the development of the distillation process for petroleum. But an even bigger prize was baleen — the tough, flexible cartilage-like substance that hangs from the top of the whale's mouth, filtering out large fish and enabling the animal to swallow large quantities of the shrimp-sized krill that is the mainstay of its diet. From the baleen were made fishing rods, buggy whips, and particularly stays for the corsets that were a necessity for women who wished to follow the dictates of Victorian fashion. In order to as nearly as possible achieve the desired twelve-inch waist (some managed it, to the detriment of their health), something flexible yet strong was needed — baleen was perfect.

There was a lot of money in whaling, at least for the captains and the owners of the ships. Around 1900 whale oil sold for $15 a barrel and baleen $6 a pound. A bowhead whale could yield a hundred barrels of oil and two thousand pounds of baleen, making the whale worth up to $15,000 — this in an age when the average worker counted himself fortunate to make $400 a year. A lucky ship could catch $400,000 worth of whales on one voyage.

Whales were caught by shooting a kind of small grenade at them that exploded deep inside the animal — the days of hand-held harpoons were decades in the past. A special darting gun was developed for the Arctic whaling industry which permitted the whalemen to harpoon and shoot the whales in one action; previously, wounded whales had often escaped into the ice pack, dragging the gear with them. The animals were taken as fast as they could be hauled aboard and stripped of their baleen and blubber.

Naturally scores of entrepreneurs entered the trade, and by the 1880s they had thinned out the whales of the northern Pacific region considerably. By that time the whaling ships were passing through the Bering Strait and hunting off the north shore of Alaska. They hesitated to go east of Point Barrow (the northern-most point in Alaska), however, for fear of being trapped in the ice over winter, but eventually some of the whaling captains decided to risk the trip, to see if the rumours they had heard from the Inuit about the fabulously rich whaling grounds east of the point were true.

Thus, in the summer of 1888, the manager of the Pacific Steam Whaling Company's station at Point Barrow sent one of his harpooners, Joe Tuck-field, and a small Inuit crew hired for the journey, five hundred miles east in an open whaleboat to scout the region and report whether it was worth the whaling fleet's trouble to risk conditions east of Point Barrow. Tuckfield spent the winter of 1888–89 with the Inuit near the Mackenzie Delta. He returned the next summer with the sensational news that bowhead whales were "as thick as bees" in the region — bees that were worth $10,000 to $15,000 each. Furthermore, there was a first-rate harbour at Herschel Island. The news stimulated tremendous interest; the government agent at Point Barrow wrote to a friend in the south that Tuckfield had "returned with accounts that made almost everybody crazy, of the great amounts of whales down there. . . . The beaches are lined with driftwood so there be no danger of freezing and there is plenty of game."[8] It is worthy of note that there was a U.S. government agent at Point Barrow; there was no permanent representative of the Canadian government at Herschel Island, nor within a thousand miles of it.

As soon as the news broke, the *Thetis*, an American revenue cutter on duty in the region, steamed to Herschel Island to determine if the story was true, and if perhaps the island might be in American waters. Commander C. H. Stockton, captain of the *Thetis*, found to his disappointment that it was part of Canada, but named the natural harbour Pauline Cove. It is significant that the Americans were very much on the spot as the new opportunities opened up. The fact that Herschel Island was part of Canada mattered not at all to the whalers, nor to the Canadian government. It was the *Thetis* that took the soundings and the observations on land which made possible the publication in 1890 of the first chart of the island, wherein it was dutifully noted that Herschel Island was part of the Dominion of Canada.

In the summer of 1890, two American ships arrived at Herschel Island. The island was so far from the ships' home port, San Francisco, that it was impossible to go north, hunt, and return home in one short season. Thus from the beginning it was planned to have the whaling ships remain in the north for at least one winter. This was why Pauline Cove, at the south-east corner of Herschel Island, became the centre of whaling operations: the ships had to find a safe anchorage for the winter; in the open sea they could be crushed by ice. This had happened on more than one occasion to vessels which lingered late in the season in open waters: thirty-two ships were crushed by ice off the Alaska coast in 1871, and five years later twelve more met the same fate.[9]

The first ships to exploit the whales in Canadian waters were the schooners *Mary D. Hume* and *Grampus*. Because they were the smallest ships in the Pacific Steam Whaling Company's fleet — the *Mary D. Hume* was only ninety feet long — it was considered that they would be best suited for operations in the shallow waters of the Beaufort Sea near the Mackenzie Delta. The two vessels arrived at the island on August 20, 1890, unloaded their supplies, and built a warehouse on the sandspit at Pauline Cove. The ships were frozen in by September 15, and the crews began to prepare for the long winter ahead. Over a hundred cords of driftwood were collected and stacked near the warehouse. Emergency supplies and the ships' boats were put on shore for use in case fire broke out on the ships. The ship's decks were roofed over with lumber and canvas, then insulated with blocks of sod cut from the tundra. Later in the season, blocks of snow were banked up against the ships, and ice from a nearby pond was cut and put on racks to provide fresh water. Periodically the ice was cut from around the rudders and propellers of the two ships to prevent damage.

In addition to the food which the ships brought with them, supplies of fresh meat were obtained through trade with the sixty or so Inuit who camped near the ships, and sometimes with Indians from the Old Crow region, who crossed the mountains south of the coast to trade. The meat — caribou, goose, and ptarmigan — was stored in cellars blasted out of the permafrost and roofed with sod. It gave variety to the men's diet and also helped prevent scurvy.

Though the crews were well housed and well fed, they had problems with the climate, particularly with frostbite, as they were unprepared for living in conditions where the temperature went to −40°C. Hartson H. Bodfish, first mate on the *Mary D. Hume*, became quite skilled at performing surgical operations, especially the amputation of frozen toes. His first operation was on one of his own, crushed by a falling piece of rigging:

122

Pauline Cove, Herschel Island, is the best natural harbour between Point Barrow and the Mackenzie River Delta. As a result, it became the logical wintering site for the whaling fleet.
ROYAL CANADIAN MOUNTED POLICE PHOTOGRAPH

I sent the steward for the captain to do the job, but he was busy at the time and asked me to wait. I thought rather fast. My foot was numb from the accident. I knew that the longer I waited, the more painful the amputation would be, so, with the steward and cabin boy looking on and groaning, I whetted up my knife and cut it off myself. The way it was injured made it necessary for me to unjoint the bone from the foot, too, but I did it, and there was considerable satisfaction in having performed my first surgical operation.[10]

The crew also suffered from boredom, and in mid-winter, six of them deserted, and headed for the Hudson's Bay Company post at Rampart House, more than three hundred miles away. The ships' officers went after them to recover the goods they had stolen and found them about seven hours' travel from the ship, badly frozen, and glad to be caught.

The whalemen soon found that Tuckfield had told the truth — the Beaufort Sea was a whalers' paradise. In July 1891, as soon as the ships were freed from the ice, they headed eastward, and the *Mary D. Hume* found a treasure in whales near Cape Bathurst; in less than two months her crew took twenty-seven whales. During the same time the *Grampus* took over twenty-one.

The *Grampus* stayed one winter at Herschel Island, and the *Mary D. Hume* two. In the winter of 1891–92 the first death occurred among the crew, when John Meyers, a sixty-year-old black seaman from Baltimore, died of "inflammatory rheumatism." His body was covered with snow and logs until the ground thawed enough to permit a proper burial.[11] His was the first of many deaths which over the years filled a small cemetery on the island with

123

plain wooden markers. By the middle of the second winter the crew of the *Mary D. Hume* were starved for news from the outside world, so William Mogg, the ship's third mate, walked the three hundred miles to the Hudson's Bay Post at Rampart House for news. But the Hudson's Bay men and the local Anglican missionaries knew little more than he did, and were able to tell him only that Queen Victoria was alive and Lord Salisbury was still prime minister. When Mogg got back to his ship after another three-hundred-mile walk, Hartson Bodfish wrote that this was "wonderful news for a bunch of New England Yankees who had received no mail for over twenty-six months!" And Mogg was reported as saying as he left Rampart House that "he needed [the missionaries'] prayers to protect him from damnation from profanity on the return trip."[12]

Both of the two pioneering ships made a fortune; the *Mary D. Hume* returned to San Francisco in 1892 with $400,000 worth of baleen and whale oil aboard, one of the most profitable whaling voyages in American history. It is difficult to appreciate the size of this sum in today's sadly depreciated currency, but it was more than a thousand times the average annual wage of a factory worker. When the *Mary D. Hume* docked at San Francisco in September 1892 her crew looked as though they had been marooned, as in a sense they had:

> The sailors looked like a lot of wild men when they came ashore; they had long hair, longer beards and clothing that was patched and tattered beyond recognition of the original hue and texture of the garments. There were only three pairs of shoes in the party, the remainder of the crew being shod with deerskin and rubbers.[13]

Mary D. Hume was a tough as well as a lucky ship, for in the late 1970s she was still afloat, working as a tug in Puget Sound, her hull nearly a hundred years old.

News of the wealth to be found in the Beaufort Sea drew other ships north, and during the winter of 1894–95, fifteen ships wintered at Pauline Cove. The community became a virtual boom town, with about five hundred whalemen living there, as well as a number of Inuit families; in 1896 it was reported that twelve hundred people were at the island, living either on the ships or in buildings erected on shore.[14] Herschel Island became an economic magnet that drew native people from a wide area. Vast quantities of food were required — a naturalist has estimated that each ship at the island consumed more than ten thousand pounds of caribou meat a year — and meat had to be brought in from as much as two hundred miles away. The bulk of the meat was provided by the Nunatarmas, the Inuit of the northern Alaskan interior, who came east to exchange meat for trade goods at the island.

The whaling ships had a reputation for being filthy and stinking, since the process of rendering whale blubber into oil, which took place in large iron kettles on deck, produced clouds of greasy black smoke. Other sailors claimed that they could be smelled twenty miles to leeward. But the ships had a certain amount of style, and between hunts were carefully cleaned.

The captain's quarters on the *North Star* were certainly handsomely appointed, "the wood being of curly and birdseye maple, the door panels of French laurel, pilasters of mahogany, coving of rosewood, and other parts inlaid with black walnut and gilt, and the ceiling is painted white. The furniture is in harmony with the general fittings, and on the floor is a tapestry carpet of subdued hues." Even the pantry "was finished in black walnut." The crew's quarters were, admittedly, considerably more modest.[15]

For a dozen years — from 1891 to 1903 — the whaling crews operated as if Herschel Island were a no man's land, which in a sense it was. Until 1894, when the first member of the North-West Mounted Police arrived in the Yukon, there was no official representative of the Canadian government within a thousand miles of the island, and even after the discovery of gold in the Yukon in 1896 brought the police to the Territory in force, they were still hundreds of miles away and had no effect on the whalers. Ottawa simply balked at the expenditure that would be involved in sending government officials north, and in any case, believing that the rumours that began to filter south about what was happening to the Inuit were exaggerated, saw no need for action.

The barter economy at Herschel Island involved more than trading for food. The crews needed their clothes mended, and Inuit women were paid in trade goods for that service. Away from home for a year or two, the men were also lonely and felt the need of other services from the women. Some captains solved this problem by arranging to have Inuit women live with them in dwellings on the land. (Beginning in 1894, other captains brought their wives with them; presumably these women pretended not to notice their husbands' friends' companions.) The arrangements usually involved some sort of barter with the husbands or male relatives of the women, and the Inuit did not object to this; in fact the women involved felt honoured, and were envied by their friends.

For the members of the crew it was a different story. In the first place they had little money. Many of them were deadbeats of one sort or another who had signed on the ships in a kind of desperation. Some were

not sailors at all, and have never been to sea before signing on, some are men who have come to sea to get away from the drinking habit, and a few...have done time for some offence in the United States....Altogether they are rather a rough lot.[16]

125

These men were forbidden to have regular Inuit companions, and could not have afforded this luxury in any case. The arrangement under which these men signed on for the trip was known as the "lay" system. The lay was a percentage of the take — captains got $1/12$ to $1/15$, cooks and engineers $1/25$, and ordinary seamen as little as $1/35$. What was really inequitable was that the value of the lay was calculated differently according to a man's rank. The officers' lays were based on a price for whalebone of $5 per pound; those of the mates of $2.50 per pound, and those of the remainder of the crew of $1.50 per pound. The crew members were often charged exorbitant prices for their supplies, and since these could easily amount to the whole of their share of the profits, they often arrived home as poor as they had left, or even in debt.[17]

The combination of sexual frustration and the knowledge that they were not going to strike it rich, combined with the harsh climate and hard work, and the fact that many of the crew were bad characters from the west coast waterfronts, led to periodic outbursts of violence. This was especially true after 1896, when word filtered north that gold had been struck near Dawson. On more than one occasion whalers' crews deserted and tried to hike overland to the diggings — a journey of more than four hundred miles that few of them could have made alive. Some had to be dragged back to the ships by force; others froze to death on the way to Dawson. On January 21, 1896, seventeen men deserted the ships, and twelve more on March 12. A party of ships' officers and Inuit were sent after them, for "as long as any number of deserters remained at large, it was a temptation to other men to desert and join them." The episode ended with a confrontation straight out of a Hollywood western:

> In March... a pursuit party was again dispatched and again "held up" by the deserters, who this time took two sleds and dog teams as well as supplies from their pursuers. A few days later a pursuit party of officers again reached the deserters, but were driven back twice in attempts to shoot it out with them. ... Ten days after the initial desertion, natives reported being robbed by the deserting crewmen, and a third party was sent out. ... A pitched battle again took place when the party reached the deserters' camp; this time the officers returned with six of the deserters, one of them shot to death in the gun battle and another badly wounded. The survivors were put in irons and chained to the decks for a month.[18]

A recent study which has analysed the isolated society which existed at Herschel Island during this period has concluded that much of the violence and discontent among the crews was rooted in the fact that the officers and men were separated by a profound social gap.[19] Part of the problem lay with the method used for recruiting the ships' crews. Men were often more or less shanghaied from among the waterfront drifters of San Francisco, Honolulu, or other Pacific port cities, and were considered by most captains to be scum not worth much consideration. They could be a violent lot, and the whaling captains had to be handy with their fists. Hartson Bodfish of the *Mary D. Hume* later became captain of the *Beluga*. He encountered a typical incident:

In 1896 the second mate of the *Beluga* "had trouble" with a crewman and hit him. The crewman responded by seizing a handspike and attacking while others in the crew urged him to go ahead and kill the officer. The mate escaped, and reported the incident to the captain . . . who immediately went after the crewman in question, "laying him out without any delay," but the affray escalated when one of the crewman's supporters jumped in and stabbed Bodfish. Bodfish, undeterred by his wound, grabbed a squeegee and continued the fight, decking his attackers and some others before the fight ended. Bodfish had his attacker put in irons and "triced up" in the rigging for twenty minutes, by which time "he had experienced genuine contrition and promised to behave himself."[20]

Crew members wreaked even greater havoc among themselves. In 1894 there was a "knifing affair" on the *Newport*, and in 1895 one man stabbed another in an argument over laying out a baseball diamond. In 1896 the second mate of the *Jeanette* got drunk and shot a sailor through the leg; in the same year Captain Bodfish noted that he had "kicked the cook this morning for threatening the Steward with a cleaver." In 1903 a crew member on Bodfish's vessel was so tormented by his mates that he took a knife to one of them, delivering "eight cuts on his body, one near the collar bone and another in the upper arm being very serious," and another "along his lower ribs that was ten inches long." In 1905 a member of the *Karluk*'s crew named Nugent stabbed another man in a quarrel over loading ice from a pond. He was put in irons, and after he had been so confined for two months, the crew petitioned the captain to keep him in irons indefinitely, as he had threatened the lives of several of them.[21]

Not everything at Herschel Island was darkness and violence, especially after some of the senior officers began bringing their wives and children north with them. Herschel Island saw amateur theatrical productions and minstrel shows, performed either on stages built on the ships' decks or in a large frame storehouse which contained a billiard and games room. This building, constructed by the ships' crews in 1893, was still standing over eighty years later, the oldest frame building in the Yukon. There was also a baseball league in the summer with four teams: the Herschels, Northern Lights, Arctics, and Pick-ups. The officers' wives organized elaborate dinner parties (the crew members were not invited to these), and ornate hand-written invitations to New Year's Eve and other parties still exist in private collections.[22] Each week there was at least one social gathering — dinner, dance, birthday party, whist party — and most weeks there were several. The Fourth of July saw a universal celebration, not the least because it was the approximate date on which the ships could be freed from the sea-ice.

But despite diversions, the picture of life for the crews of the whalers was one of overwhelming misery and hardship. They were not invited to the fancy dress balls held by the officers; instead they had to resort to "cards, whiskey and visits to an Eskimo house when nature demanded the company of women."[23] And the loneliness and discontent among the crews had a bad effect on the Inuit as well. The men tried to get around the ban on cohabitation with Inuit women by teaching the natives how to make home-brew out of molasses, raisins, and potatoes, with a view to seducing the women. In this they were frequently successful, and the drunken parties that resulted led to the rumours of "orgies" that trickled south even as far as Ottawa.

But as usual, the worst effect of the whalers on the Inuit was the diseases that they introduced. Because very few whites had visited the western Arctic before 1888, the Inuit had not built up immunity to common European illnesses. When the whalemen infected them, not only with venereal diseases, but also with measles and influenza, the Inuit had no resistance, and died in appalling numbers. By the mid 1890s the local population had shrunk to such an extent that the whalers had to import Inuit from Alaska to work for them. Diamond Jenness, the great Canadian anthropologist, estimated that by 1930 only a dozen of the original two thousand to twenty-five hundred Inuit population of the western Arctic remained, the rest having succumbed to imported diseases.[24]

The trading activity at Herschel Island attracted Indians as well as Inuit. Because trading was a secondary activity to whaling, which bore the overhead costs of the voyages, the whalers could trade goods with the natives at a cost considerably below that of the Hudson's Bay Company at Fort McPherson and Rampart House to the south. As one captain wrote:

> Arctic whalers were trading ships as well as whalers, and it was quite on the cards that a good profit might be made in trade even if very few whales were taken. There had always been some trading, but I think the trading developed to a new high level at about this time, owing to the increased knowledge among the whalers and likewise among the natives.[25]

Because these men were not "traditional" traders, they did not limit themselves to the traditional trade goods: muzzle-loaders, tobacco, tea, and blankets. Instead they offered new trade goods: repeating rifles, alcohol, and canned goods, which attracted Indians from a wide area.

There was also a "respectable" element on the island, for missionaries reached it as early as 1893, not long after the whalers did. In 1891 Bishop W. C. Bompas, whose vast northern diocese included the northern Yukon, wrote to the Anglican Church Missionary Society, warning that Americans had penetrated the region, and were "inclined to offer them [the natives] liquor." He asked for men and money to establish a mission on the island, and the Society acceded to his request.

The man sent to open the new mission was Isaac O. Stringer, who arrived in 1893 having spent the previous winter at Fort McPherson, getting used to the country and learning something of its customs and languages. Stringer was later to become famous as the "bishop who ate his boots" when his food ran out during a long sled trip across the Richardson Mountains in 1909. In 1893 he was at the beginning of his career, twenty-seven years old and straight out of Wycliffe College in Toronto, full of enthusiasm for his task.[26]

Stringer had been recruited for northern work by Bishop William Reeve of the diocese of Mackenzie River, and from 1893 to 1897 he divided his time between Herschel Island, the mission post at Peel River, and other Inuit settlements in the region, such as the summer camp at Kittigazuit. After four years of periodic visits to Herschel Island, Stringer returned in the summer of 1897 to establish a permanent mission. Accompanying him was his wife Sadie, whom he had married in 1895, and her uncle, W. D. Young, who was to assist him in running the new mission.

To Stringer's surprise, on his first arrival at the island in 1893 the whaling captains welcomed the missionary, made him comfortable, and even provided quarters for him. "I was doubtful as to how I would be received," he wrote, "and I thought I would be very satisfied if they would let me stop with the Indians [who had accompanied him] in their quarters. But I was invited at once into the Captain's cabin and received a hearty welcome."[27] He found himself in a rather awkward and ambivalent position. On one hand he was anxious to cultivate good relations with the whaling captains, and he welcomed the opportunity to socialize with men of his own class, or closer to it than were the crewmen. On the other hand he was personally and officially opposed to the trade in liquor with the Inuit. He wrote of this dilemma:

> I could not have been much better used under the circumstances if I had been the President of the United States. But I can't help feel that a little indiscretion on my part or some undue circumstances might cause just as hearty an opposition. Why should they be friendly to a lonely mission-ary, who, if he says all he thinks, would condemn some of their darling sins? . . . I know that many of them would do a great deal for me or anyone else in my place under the circumstances in this country. But this winter I got a better insight into their life and manner of living — and seven ships instead of four does not make matters any better.[28]

Despite his opposition to the spread of liquor and promiscuity among the Inuit, Stringer was wise enough to be discreet in his criticism of the whalemen. He did preach at least one sermon on the evils of drink, but the

Top: *The Inuit population indigenous to Herschel Island and the surrounding area had been all but wiped out by the early twentieth century. The combination of European diseases and the dislocation associated with the arrival of the whalers destroyed a society that had survived for generations.* ANGLICAN CHURCH ARCHIVES

Below: *Isaac O. Stringer (the O. did not stand for anything) was the first Anglican missionary at Herschel Island. Famous for an expedition across the Richardson Mountains that earned him the nickname, "The Bishop Who Ate His Boots," Stringer succeeded William C. Bompas as Bishop of the Yukon. He is shown here with an Inuit wedding party.* ANGLICAN CHURCH ARCHIVES

ships' officers did not take offence, probably because the sermon had little practical effect. The captains were glad to have an educated man to talk to in the long winter days, and the captains agreed with the missionary that drunkenness and disorder were bad things. When reason did not work, Stringer threatened to complain to Ottawa, and the captains signed an agreement to put an end to the liquor traffic — an agreement which was very loosely honoured.

The Stringers' primary purpose was to bring Christianity to the Inuit, and to this end the missionary began to preach weekly sermons, which were interpreted by an Inuit named David Copperfield. The couple also provided more practical services. They ran a school, which was attended by Inuit and whalemen, and Mrs. Stringer gave lessons in shorthand to several crew members who longed for a steady job once they got back to San Francisco. She also bore two children in that lonely spot.

When the couple left the island in 1901 to return south, they were replaced by Rev C. E. Whittaker and his wife. Whittaker had a rougher time with the crews, as he was not as tolerant as Stringer. Moreover, he suffered personal tragedy on the island; one of his children died there — the explorer Roald Amundsen, visiting the island in 1906, recorded the sad sight of the Whittakers leaving the island for ever, dragging their daughter's body with them on a sledge.[29] Whittaker's difficulties in his post seem to have been the result of his personality, which was acerbic and inflexible. Unlike Stringer, he was not popular with the whaling fleet, and in turn complained of them on numerous occasions to the government. The mounted police officer in charge of the Herschel detachment wrote of him in 1903:

> This man is so much disliked by the whalers that some of them tried to make the natives believe that Mr. Whittaker was the cause of Leviauke [a local Inuit] being arrested.[30]

Oddly enough, the Inuit seemed not to have objected to the state of affairs at Herschel Island. They were all there of their own free will, and they seem to have thought of it as a wonderful place, where there were parties and games all the time, and where fascinating and useful goods could be acquired. Such, at any rate, is the impression given in the memoirs of a man who spent several years of his youth at Herschel Island. Nuligak was a Mackenzie Delta Inuit; born in 1895, he lived there throughout the later part of the whaling period, and as an old man dictated his memoirs, which have been translated into English. These clearly reflect the delight that the Inuit found in the food and gadgets that the whalers brought:

> When summer came Uncle Kralogark took us west to Herschel Island. . . . Crowds of Eskimos came there. That fall I saw some very large ships. The sailors we met always had something in their mouths; something they chewed. It so intrigued me that I kept staring at their jaws. One certain day that "thing" was given to me. I chewed — it was delicious. It was chewing gum. From that day I was able to recognize some of these white men's things.[31]

Though the Inuit do not seem to have minded the state of affairs at Herschel Island, the missionaries did, and complaints from Stringer and Whittaker found their way to Bishop Bompas at Fortymile. He in turn complained to the police when they first arrived in the Yukon in 1894, and the police forwarded the stories to Ottawa. In 1895 Inspector Charles

131

Constantine reported from the Yukon the evil rumours that had reached him via a ship's engineer who had deserted and made his way south to the police post at Fortymile:

> The carryings-on of the officers and crews of the whalers there was such that no one would believe... large quantities of whiskey are taken up in the ships... as long as the liquor lasts, the natives neither fish nor hunt, and die of starvation in consequence. .... The captains and mates of these vessels purchase for their own use girls from nine years and upwards.[32]

This was probably a bit over-stated — Inuit died, but seldom from starvation — but the tone was accurate enough. Bishop Bompas echoed these complaints, and for a number of years nagged the government to take some action before the violence and debauchery at the island led to the "utter ruin" of the Inuit. Earlier, in 1894, Stringer had described a similar scene:

> As I write some geese are passing and they [the Inuit] were banging away with their rifles. It is a wonder some are not killed with all the rifles and rum. Almost every man has a rifle. Now Kokhiks wife comes in and takes the drum telling me its all right not to be afraid and now she drums away and sings as if mad. .... Outside many are dancing and staggering and swaggering around after the manner of drunkards in general. .... At times they were very wild in their demonstrations one or two began crying for children they had lost.[33]

In fact, it is difficult to give an accurate assessment of the nature of Herschel Island society in the 1890s, since perceptions of it varied so widely from one observer to another. Was it an "outpost of civilization," as the explorer Stefansson described it, or, as the Nome press called it, "the Sodom of the Arctic"? It seems to have depended on the moral standards of the reporter. The Reverend Whittaker, a stickler for morality, said that "the scenes of riotous drunkenness and lust which this island has witnessed have probably never been surpassed,"[34] which seems a bit strong; perhaps Whittaker during his English education had never read Edward Gibbon's description of the Roman Empire, which made Herschel Island seem tame by comparison.

Certainly the authorities thought that the missionaries' tales of immorality were exaggerated. The comptroller of the mounted police complained that it was difficult "to convince the goody-goody people that in the development and settlement of a new country allowances must be made for the excesses of human nature."[35] Many of the tales of debauchery and "bacchanalian orgies which beggared description" that were breathlessly retailed in the south were exaggerations. According to one excited author:

> Down the gangplanks surged a motley horde of mixed humanity till the sand[s]pit was overrun with a drunken mob of dark-visaged kanakas, bearded Russians, ebony-faced Negroes, and the off-scouring of the

Barbary Coast. Rum flowed like water. Fighting, drinking, and debauchery became the order of the day.[36]

But as one expert noted, if this picture was literally true, few whaling masters would have wintered at Herschel, and certainly none would have brought their wives along.

The Canadian government was initially reluctant to move to assert its authority in the western Arctic, particularly since they discounted the missionaries' tales of horror. After 1894 Ottawa had asserted its authority in the central Yukon, but the northern part of the Territory continued to be ignored. What finally moved the government to action in the northern Yukon was the question of sovereignty. The presence of American whalers operating in the Beaufort Sea contravened a number of Canadian laws, including a ban on trading alcohol with natives and selling them repeating rifles. No royalty was paid on whales taken, which by the First World War amounted to over $13 million in total value, nor was duty paid on goods traded with the Inuit, which came to another $1.5 million.[37]

Worse still, because there was no official Canadian presence in the region, and no Canadian laws enforced, the possibility existed that Canada's claim to sovereignty over the region might be placed in doubt. As an official in the Department of the Interior commented:

> It is feared that if American citizens are permitted to land and pursue the industries of whaling, fishing and trading with the Indians without complying with the revenue laws of Canada and without any assertion of sovereignty on the part of Canada, unfounded and troublesome claims may hereafter be set up.[38]

The law came to Herschel Island in 1903. By then the government had, in the mounted police, a force with wide experience in Yukon service. It was also the year of the settlement of the Alaska boundary dispute — an agreement which disappointed and infuriated Canada, and made Ottawa determined not to let more of the north go to foreigners by default. The fact that American whaling ships were operating in the same way in Hudson Bay as in the west lent urgency to the government's desire to assert its northern sovereignty.

Two mounted police detachments were set up in the western Arctic in the summer of 1903; the main one was at Fort McPherson, and the satellite one at Herschel Island. The detachment at the island consisted of Sergeant Francis J. Fitzgerald and Constable F. D. Sutherland. Fitzgerald, born in Halifax in 1869, was a veteran of fourteen years' service in the N.W.M.P., and had served in the Yukon during the gold rush. He exemplified the qualities that were expected of a mounted police officer: he was fit, resourceful, fair, firm, and unmarried (which freed him for lengthy periods of northern service).

Top: *The police maintained control of the Herschel Island region through a regular series of patrols, most conducted in the dead of winter. This patrol, photographed shortly after Christmas in 1909, was travelling from Dawson City to Herschel Island.* PUBLIC ARCHIVES OF CANADA PA 29622

Below: *Sergeant F. J. Fitzgerald established the first North-West Mounted Police detachment at Herschel Island in 1903. He died in the ill-fated Lost Patrol of 1911.* ROYAL CANADIAN MOUNTED POLICE PHOTOGRAPH

When Fitzgerald and Sutherland arrived at Herschel Island after a 200-mile trip in an open boat, they were practically destitute, for the government had sent the expedition north woefully undersupplied, expecting the police to improvise according to conditions. The two men had little food, no fuel, and nowhere to live, and had to borrow a sod house and coal from the whalers. They were expected to enforce compliance with Canadian laws among a foreign population which might naturally be expected to be hostile to their mission. Their only assets were the force of their personalities and the tenuous authority of the Canadian government, thousands of miles away.

But the police at Herschel Island had other, less obvious factors favouring their mission. In the first place, they and the whaling captains were not necessarily antagonists. The captains also feared the disorder which could be caused by unruly crew members, and were glad to have officials on the scene to help keep them under control. After Fitzgerald had subdued a drunken sailor or two, hauling them back to ship to be placed in irons, the captains realized that the police were as much allies as enemies.

More important still was the fact that the police had no drastic effect on the operations of the whaling ships. By 1903 the whaling industry was in decline, the whales in the Beaufort Sea were beginning to thin out, and some ships were wintering at Baillie Island, 250 miles to the east of Herschel Island. The most practical demonstration of Canadian sovereignty in the region was the collection of duties on whales caught and goods traded with the Inuit, but if captains wished to avoid payment, they simply did not call at Herschel Island. The police had no ship of their own, and could not patrol the coast to bring the law to ships which avoided their post. Nor could they insist on a thorough search of all the ships that came their way, particularly when they were under obligation to the whalers for fuel and housing.[39]

The result was that Sergeant Fitzgerald was reduced to a certain amount of bluffing in his operations. He asked the captains for a list of the goods brought in for trade, and required them to pay duty according to these lists. They complied, and produced the lists, accurate or not, and Fitzgerald collected a small sum based on them. In international law, it was the demonstration of Canada's authority that counted as proof of Canadian sovereignty in the region; the actual sum collected was immaterial. As far as the liquor traffic was concerned, Fitzgerald reported that he had checked the flow — but to what extent it is difficult to judge. Certainly those who wanted liquor could still get it, but the presence of the police compelled a certain amount of discretion.

There was in fact a fair degree of harmony among the residents of Herschel Island in its days of glory, with the possible exception of the Reverend Whittaker, who seemed to have a talent for alienating people — a considerable liability in a remote northern post. In 1907 he ran afoul of the police when he interfered in their internal affairs. The episode casts light on an aspect of life in the Arctic that for obvious reasons received little publicity — sexual relations between whites and Inuit. Again, it concerned Francis Fitzgerald. As did many white men stationed in the north for years at a time, Fitzgerald had taken an Inuit woman, named Unalina, as a common-law wife. Eventually he decided to legally marry Unalina, and applied to his superiors for permission to marry, as all mounted policemen in that era were required to do. Whittaker, who as a clergyman was keen on "proper" marriages, also wrote to the police urging them to grant permission. But at that time, and for many years thereafter, it was unthinkable that a police officer should marry a native woman. Fitzgerald's immediate superior rebuffed Whittaker in no uncertain terms, writing that "he would prefer reporting to Ottawa that Fitzgerald had blown his brains out rather than that he had married a native woman."[40]

Herschel Island did not die with the end of the whaling industry in the western Arctic. It remained the centre of government activities and the major supply depot for fur traders working in the area. The schooner Arctic *is shown at Herschel Island in 1923.*

This story had a sad ending. Unalina and Francis Fitzgerald had a daughter, Annie, who was crippled in an accident while a child. In 1926, long after Fitzgerald's death, Annie surfaced at the Hay River Residential School, where the principal tried to get the Royal Canadian Mounted Police to assume responsibility for her. She was in a "pitiable" condition — a hunchback — but the Commissioner of the R.C.M.P., while expressing concern (and surprise), refused to provide funding for her. Eventually the government provided an annual grant of $145 for three years for her to continue at school so she could be trained for housework, but she died soon after, at the age of eighteen.

By the time the First World War broke out in 1914, the whaling industry in the western Arctic was dead, and so was Francis Fitzgerald. Whaling was killed by the invention of synthetic substitutes for baleen; Fitzgerald was killed by overconfidence and bad luck. As leader of the four-man 1910–11 winter mail patrol between Fort McPherson and Dawson, Fitzgerald, then an inspector, had tried to set a speed record, and had the misfortune to get lost in the Richardson Mountains during particularly severe winter. He kept trying to find his way to Dawson until it was too late to return to Fort McPherson, and in February 1911 he and his companions died, three of starvation and exposure, and one of suicide.

On the occasion of this tragedy, the Reverend Whittaker made another gaffe. When the bodies of the four men from the "Lost Patrol" were brought to Fort McPherson, Whittaker somehow got hold of Fitzgerald's diary, and based on its contents, wrote a sharply critical letter about the patrol, accusing Fitzgerald of setting out ill-prepared, ill-guided, and with poor dogs. The mounted police were extremely sensitive about their public image, which was damaged by this episode, and the fact that Whittaker's comments were partly true did not help matters. They reacted with huffy denials of his allegations.[41]

Despite the decline of the whaling industry, however, Herschel Island continued to be a trading and administrative centre for the western Arctic. Inuit who could no longer earn trade goods by working for the whalers turned to hunting fur, particularly muskrat and fox. By 1915 the fur trade had grown to the extent that it partially replaced whaling as a source of income for the Inuit. The trade was intensely competitive, with the Hudson's Bay Company, some San Francisco firms, and both Canadian and American independents competing with each other. In 1915 the Hudson's Bay Company opened a post on the island. Three other posts operated on the Yukon's north coast in this period. The Hudson's Bay Company ran a post at Demarcation Point between 1921 and 1924, and another at Shingle Point from 1920 to 1928. H. Liebes and Co. also operated at Shingle Point between 1917 and 1921. By 1923 the Hudson's Bay Company had established posts eastward along the Arctic coast from Herschel Island as far as King William Island.[42] But the company never made much money from the trade in that part of the north, even when fur prices were high. The Herschel Island post was kept open primarily to deter competition from other traders, and as a regional transportation depot to assist in the shipment of supplies from ports such as Vancouver to company posts to the east of the Mackenzie Delta. In the 1920s silver fox pelts sold for $50 each, and some Inuit made enough money to buy large motor schooners and other materials goods; one trapper made nearly $15,000 in a year — a fortune in those days. White trappers also came north, lured by the high fur prices. The Inuit hunter Nuligak remembered this era as a happy, prosperous time:

> From Christmas to New Year's the dancing drums never stopped. . . . On Christmas Day we were all invited by the minister to dinner. On New Year's it was the H.B.C.'s turn to entertain us with all kinds of good things to eat. The R.C.M.P. also gave us a day, in between these two. We had all kinds of games, and we returned home only when we felt like it.[43]

A number of explorers visited the region in this period and used its harbours as a base or a stopping place. Roald Amundsen navigated the Northwest Passage between 1903 and 1906. In 1905, nearing the end of his journey, Amundsen's ship, *Gjoa*, was beset in ice for the winter at King's Point. The crew built two small houses of driftwood and erected a small observatory (which later became a crypt for one of Amundsen's men who died during the winter). The explorer visited Herschel Island several times that year and, in late October, decided to travel overland to Fort Yukon to spread the news of his successful voyage. Amundsen was disappointed to discover that there was no telegraph station at the trading post, so he pushed on to Eagle City, where he dispatched word of his Arctic adventures. He then returned to King's Point for the winter. In July 1906, the last season of his famous expedition, he cast off from his northern Yukon harbour and headed west. His tumultuous welcome at Nome was a foretaste of the enthusiastic reception awaiting him throughout the world.[44]

Yet another explorer/adventurer, Vilhjalmur Stefansson, similarly focused public attention on the Canadian Arctic. Stefansson made several highly publicized expeditions to the western Arctic, stopping often at Herschel Island for supplies. Stefansson recognized few boundaries between promotion and science; some of his discoveries, such as the alleged "Blond Eskimos" of Victoria Island, brought hoots of derision from traditional scientists, but earned the explorer much public acclaim. He had, however, become a figure of considerable note, and when he approached the Canadian government for financial support for a major Arctic expedition, they could not turn him down.

This Canadian Arctic Expedition (1913–18) Canada's most ambitious northern undertaking, was under the direction of Stefansson and R. M. Anderson. The venture floundered from the beginning. The *Karluk*, carrying Stefansson's Northern Division, was caught in floe ice in September 1913 and, after drifting westward for three months, sank off Wrangel Island with the loss of eight lives. Stefansson had left the ship long before the sinking, so anxious was he to push on with the explorations.[45]

The work continued in an atmosphere of recrimination and anger. Stefansson, always the loner, put his own needs ahead of those of his colleagues. He routinely angered the mounted police and the missionaries with his carping criticism, publicity-seeking activities, and his unrelenting self-promotion. Stefansson fell seriously ill at Herschel Island. After more than a month in the police barracks, he was sent south for medical care. A special police patrol carried him as far as Rampart House; from there, he secured Indian guides to take him down the Porcupine River to Fort Yukon.

Stefansson left a legacy of bitterness, but he focused North American attention on the Canadian Arctic. He was, in the words of his best biographer, "less of a scientist, in the strict sense, and more of a publicist and promoter."[46] The police officers disliked the pretentious explorer, and feared that his naïve notions of the "Friendly Arctic" would attract unprepared adventurers to the north. As Sergeant Fitzgerald noted of Stefansson:

> Such men as Stefansson claim they can live on the country: they can by some one else supplying the food. All those people are a drain on our supplies[.] [I]t is impossible to refuse a white man if he is short of food.[47]

When Stefansson publicly deprecated the efforts of Arctic missionaries, they responded with bitter denunciations of their own. His fellow scientists protested Stefansson's lack of attention to research. One later wrote:

138

Mr. Stefansson has persistently misquoted, libelled or ignored the work of every scientist member of the late Canadian Arctic expedition, so that instead of feeling an honest pride in having been engaged in more or less valuable work in the North, most of us feel inclined to apologize for having been Arctic explorers rather than be connected in any way with Mr. Stefansson or his schemes. He had made a laughing-stock and a byword of the name of explorer. [48]

Another crew member was even more direct:

I learn here [Herschel Island] that V.S. completely succeeded in "getting the goat" of everybody here and at Fort McPherson. It is strange, but no one seems to have a good word for him; seldom have I seen a man for whom there were fewer good words than is the case with V.S. along the coast. It may be due to the climate or the men here, but some or rather most of it must be due to V.S. himself. [49]

The work of Stefansson and the other explorers did have an impact. Members of the Canadian Arctic Expedition surveyed the Arctic coastline of the Yukon and explored several of the rivers flowing into the ocean. They also conducted extensive surveys of the natural history of the region. Perhaps their greatest contribution, highlighted by Stefansson's promotional efforts, was to keep Herschel Island and the Arctic slope in the public eye in the years after the demise of the whaling industry.

The explorers could use Herschel Island as a base because the mounted police maintained their detachment at Herschel Island throughout this period. When the whaling stopped there was not a great deal for the police to do except to survive, which in that environment seemed to take up most of their time. The entries in the Herschel Island detachment diary for the autumn of 1906 give the flavour of police life there:

Sept. 29th — Saturday. 24 [F] above, strong wind. Scrubbed out quarters.
Sept. 30th — Sunday. 24 above. Very strong gale.
Oct. 1st — Monday. 25 above, fine. Hauling wood to storehouse.
Oct. 2nd — Tuesday. 27 above, strong wind. Hauling wood to store-house.
Oct. 3rd — Wednesday. 24 above, strong wind. Hauling wood to storehouse.
Oct. 4th — Thursday. 22 above, foggy. Cleaning up storehouse.
Oct. 5th — Friday. 25 above, fine and calm. Repairing dog harness.
Oct. 6th — Saturday. 21 above, fine and calm. Cleaning stove pipe and scrubbing out quarters. [50]

When in 1928 the R.C.M.P. (as the force was called after 1920) finally

As the administrative centre for the western Arctic, Herschel Island was the headquarters for the regional police detachment and was the obvious site for a series of heavily publicized court cases involving Inuit defendants. This photograph was taken on July 16, 1923. ROYAL CANADIAN MOUNTED POLICE PHOTOGRAPH

acquired the *St. Roch*, a seaworthy patrol vessel of their own, the ship, commanded by Henry Larsen, called regularly at the island and sometimes wintered there.[51]

Still, by 1920 probably not one Canadian in ten thousand had ever heard of Herschel Island. What brought it to public attention in southern Canada was a sensational criminal case tried on the island in the summer of 1923.

Alikomiak and Tatimagana, two men from the Coppermine region, were charged with the murder of a Hudson's Bay Company trader. Alikomiak, while under arrest at the Tree River detachment, east of Herschel on the Arctic coast, shot and killed Corporal W. A. Doak of the R.C.M.P. A judicial party went north from Edmonton to hear the case, and the two Inuit were convicted and sentenced to death. The case aroused great public interest, and a lively debate took place in the press as to whether the sentences should be commuted. This was not the first time that Inuit had killed whites in the western Arctic, however, and the government was determined to make an example of the two men. Thus on February 1, 1924, the two were hanged in an abandoned whaling shed — the first Inuit executed for murder under Canadian law.[52]

What killed Herschel Island as a community was the Great Depression of the 1930s. The 1929 stock market crash put a stop to luxury consumption, sending prices for furs plummeting. Inuit hunters like Nuligak who had been called "plutocrats" in the 1920s were now practically reduced to starvation. Because of its isolation, Herschel Island had always been expensive to supply, and pressed by the harsh economic realities of the Depression, government and private industries alike tried to economize on their northern operations as much as possible. In 1937 the Hudson's Bay Company trader at the island noted that there was "No Fur this year. Mostly cash sales."[53] The company moved its post to Tuktoyaktuk, and the R.C.M.P. moved its western Arctic headquarters to Aklavik and eventually closed the detachment at the island. A government official commented that:

> the new routing of the Western Arctic freight by way of Mackenzie River has meant the desertion of Herschel Island as there is no longer any shipping by Point Barrow. The Hudson's Bay Company and the R.C.M.P. have left there. Captain Pedersen, who had brought in supplies around by Alaska for the past 42 years has this year shipped everything by the H.B.C. boats down the Mackenzie.[54]

With the government and the traders gone there seemed little reason for the Inuit to stay. Occasional Inuit trappers from the Mackenzie Delta would come into the region for a season of hunting, but when the Inuit left the area, there was no permanent trapping base left to sustain trade. By the Second World War the island was deserted.

The shift towards the Mackenzie Delta was a gradual one. The Anglican missionaries had been trying for years to establish schools among the Inuit, but a shortage of teachers and money reduced their effort to occasional classes taught by clergy and their wives. In 1922 a mission was established at Shingle Point, on the coast midway between Herschel Island and the Mackenzie Delta, in response to the growing local Inuit population at this favoured fishing and trading site. When the Roman Catholics opened a residential school at Aklavik in 1924, the Anglicans felt compelled to respond in kind. They feared that they would otherwise lose the attention of the Inuit of the western Arctic, who were opposed to the church's procedure of removing the children from the district and shipping them south to Hay River for years at a time.

Such an undertaking promised to be expensive, however, and the church could not proceed without federal government assistance. The Anglicans' Arctic Mission, established to co-ordinate work in the far north, decided to proceed with a temporary school, to gauge the Inuit response. They settled on Shingle Point as the site and, in 1929, welcomed the first children into their humble establishment. The Inuit responded enthusiastically to the new school, so much so that many children had to be turned away. As was the pattern with northern residential schools, the teachers sought, more successfully here than elsewhere, to integrate a Canadian curriculum, teaching in English, Christian education, and training in traditional skills:

> The boys are taught to hunt the caribou, the birds, white whales, etc., as well as to make nets, catch the fish, dry them, etc. The girls are taught cooking, how best to utilize everything that comes to them, and in many other ways to become suitable citizens in Eskimo settlements in days to

come. The fact that we have two Eskimo hunters at the school who take the boys hunting and fishing, etc., and two Eskimo women who teach the girls to sew boots, clothes, etc., is sufficient proof of the seriousness of our intention regarding these matters.[55]

The Arctic Mission was convinced that the Shingle Point school had demonstrated its usefulness, but they were not wedded to that site. Problems with sea-ice and food had interfered with the work of the school, and when the Anglican church looked for a permanent location, they turned away from the Arctic coast. The Department of Indian Affairs built a new facility for the church at Aklavik, a Mackenzie Delta community that was emerging as the administrative centre of the western Arctic. Shingle Point was closed and, in August 1936, the staff and students, almost fifty in total, moved to their new quarters.

It is difficult to assess the effectiveness of the missionary activities in the Herschel Island region. Many whites had little use for them, either personally, as in the case of Whittaker, or on philosophical grounds. Vilhjalmur Stefansson despised them, believing that they taught the Inuit useless lessons and customs and interfered with their ability to survive in their environment. K. G. Chipman of the Canadian Arctic Expedition accused the missionaries of Herschel Island of saving souls for profit:

> Most of the natives have what is known as a "fox skin" name, Pete, Harry, Elias, Carry, Tommy, etc. These names they are proud of and consider them as a mark of distinction. It seems that Bishop Stringer and Mr. Whittaker christened the natives, big and little, and gave to them names. For this service they received a fox skin for each person. That is a good business.[56]

The missionaries defended themselves vigorously, Stringer writing in 1927,

> Gradually they [the Inuit] were brought to a knowledge of God in spite of all the severest kinds of temptations through the whalers and other white people along the Arctic coast. Now the majority of the Eskimos along five hundred miles of the Arctic coast from the Alaska boundary have been baptized, and most of the adults confirmed.[57]

Of course both men could have been right; it depends on one's personal view of the value of Christianity to native people.

The police returned to Herschel Island in 1948, using it for a number of years as a dog-breeding station, but the day of patrolling by dog-sled was drawing to a close, and the detachment closed in 1964. From time to time the island was visited by hunting parties; in 1962–63 eight Inuit trapping licences were issued for the area, and the following year, four.[58] Inuit families on occasion used the old buildings (in the 1980s there was one family living there), but for the most part it was left to a slow process of decay. The wooden headboards marking the graves of the whalemen who died there in the 1890s were blown flat in the 1970s, but the names on them can still be read. At least one is a child's grave — that of George Edson, son of a whaling captain, who died at Herschel Island in February 1898, ten days before his first birthday.

The government of the Yukon had always ignored this northernmost part of its jurisdiction. Since communications between Herschel Island and the Mackenzie River were far easier than between the island and Dawson, it seemed only sensible to let it become *de facto* a part of the Northwest Territories. Indeed, for a time there was some confusion as to whether the island was part of the Yukon or the Northwest Territories. There was even a proposal in 1928 to transfer it to the Northwest Territories on the grounds that it could be better served by access to the Mackenzie River than via Dawson. One government official wrote:

> I think if the present boundary is changed to cut off all that area within the watershed of the Beaufort Sea, together with the islands in the Beaufort Sea, north of the Yukon, and to add this area to the Mackenzie District, it would not greatly concern the people of the Yukon.[59]

He was right about Yukoners' indifference; but because of apathy and the gradual disappearance of the Herschel Island community, nothing was done about the matter.

With the energy crisis of the 1970s, however, the island assumed new importance. Discoveries of gas and oil deposits in the Beaufort Sea, and talk of constructing a modern port at Pauline Cove impelled the Yukon government to take action to demonstrate its authority over the island. In June 1972 Commissioner James Smith of the Yukon Territory flew with some reporters and members of the Territorial Council to raise the flag of the Yukon for the first time above Herschel Island.

Oil exploration off the north coast of the Yukon began in 1973, and since that year the stupendous sum of $6.5 billion has been spent by oil companies exploring and drilling for gas and oil in the Beaufort Sea. Some very substantial finds have been made, notably in the Amauligak field forty-five miles northwest of Tuktoyaktuk, where in 1986 Gulf Canada announced a find of 700 to 800 million barrels.[60]

Herschel Island and the Yukon's Arctic slopes, all but ignored from the 1930s to the 1940s, have become the focus of considerable debate in the last decade. The Berger Commission recommended that the northern Yukon, home of the massive Porcupine River caribou herd, be set aside as a wilderness park. At the same time, the Committee for Original Peoples' Entitlement (C.O.P.E.), representing the Inuit of the western Arctic, laid claim to aboriginal land rights in the region, as did the Council of Yukon Indians, representing the claims of the natives of Old Crow. The competing demands, further clouded by corporate plans for port developments at

Once the busiest community in the western Arctic, Herschel Island is now all but abandoned. Recent oil and gas exploration in the region has led to renewed interest in the island and its natural harbour. YUKON GOVERNMENT PHOTO

Herschel Island or Shingle Point, made the region a focus for the conflicting native, business, and government interpretations of the future of the Arctic.[61] In July 1978, the federal government announced that the northern Yukon, including Herschel Island, had been closed to development, pending the establishment of a national park. There was, once more, little consultation on this decision, although it did ensure that native needs and rights in the area would not quickly be ignored in favour of short-term commercial interests. Controversy surrounding the area did not soon end. In the mid-1980s, the United States government announced that it was granting oil exploration permits for the Alaskan lands contiguous to the Northern Yukon, even though that area was on the migratory path of the Porcupine caribou herd. When the issuing of permits was extended to the off-shore, the Reagan administration challenged Canada's long-standing, but unofficial, boundary in the western Arctic — the northward extension of the 141st meridian to the 200-mile limit. Perhaps the most significant change, however, was in the new Yukon attitude to the north slope. In 1987, the Yukon government announced the establishment of the Herschel Island Territorial Park, the first such park in the Yukon, a fitting symbol of the renewed interest in this long-ignored region.

CHAPTER SIX

After the Gold Rush, 1900-1918

The Klondike gold rush was too rich, too frantic, to last long; there was not enough gold in the world, let alone in the Yukon, to satisfy the hunger for wealth of the tens of thousands who had rushed north to find it. At first there had been gold to spare and even to waste. Ripped out of the earth, washed by crude and inefficient methods, gold worth untold thousands of dollars was lost to the Yukon's streams and rivers. The gold never ran out completely, of course, and it was mined with reasonable profits for the next six decades — it is still mined when the world price goes high enough to justify the expense — but within a year or two the rich diggings were played out. There was still work in and near Dawson, but the era when a couple of men with picks and shovels could make a fortune was over, and the age of the machines had begun.

The Yukon did not die after the rush, but as early as the end of 1898 its population began to shrink, as men began to look elsewhere for the big strike. In that year the discovery of gold at Atlin, B.C., just across the border from the southern Yukon, drew some miners away. During the Atlin rush two astute businessmen saw a different opportunity. Isaac Taylor and his partner, Bill Drury, saw that many of the prospectors, having carried a ton or more of supplies over the coastal mountain passes, were quitting the north shortly after their arrival. Taylor and Drury bought up the supplies for a fraction of their worth, and used the outfits as the basis for a successful retail operation. The men then moved into the fur trade, opening their first post at Little Salmon. From this beginning was to grow the Yukon's largest retailing operation, with posts scattered throughout the territory.[1]

But Atlin was a side-show; the first great blow to the Klondike came from Alaska, where in the winter of 1898 gold was discovered in paying quantities on the beaches of Nome. In Dawson, a city overflowing with unemployed stampeders, many of whom had come far to discover little, the news rekindled an old excitement. Although the police warned the miners about the dangers of winter travel, hundreds set off down the frozen Yukon River, hoping to beat other prospectors to the new find and to avoid coming in second once more. When the ice broke in the spring, the human trickle out of Dawson turned into a flood. The first steamers to leave town were jammed with prospectors; the river was once more filled with makeshift rafts, although this time they were leaving Dawson, not arriving. Thousands had abandoned Dawson; the gold rush, which had never stayed in one place for long, had moved on once more.[2]

Dawsonites did not despair, however. In 1898–99 the Klondike fields were still producing well, stampeders from the south continued to arrive, though fewer every month, and soon some of the Nome adventurers retreated to Dawson City, discouraged by the slim pickings of the new strike and the violence and disorder that attended it. In the spring of 1900, Dawson City and the Klondike enjoyed a modest recovery. The boom-times were gone, but many believed that a stable, lasting community would now emerge from the turmoil of the gold rush. William Ogilvie predicted that Dawson would stabilize at around ten thousand people and that the rich Klondike deposits would sustain a prosperous community for at least twenty years[3].

The next blow caused more damage. In the summer of 1902 an Italian immigrant, Felix Pedro, struck gold near a makeshift trading post opened the year before near Alaska's Tanana River. Additional strikes on Cleary, Fairbanks, and Ester creeks confirmed the richness of the Tanana gold field. The rush would centre on the new community of Fairbanks, soon to challenge Dawson City as the cornerstone of the Yukon basin gold frontier.[4] The Klondike once more emptied in response to the new discovery, but this time most of the miners did not return. Tanana had much more to offer than Nome, and the miners and workers who rushed downstream in 1903 found opportunities long since gone in Dawson. As Fairbanks grew, and Dawson's slide picked up speed, a number of businessmen joined the exodus. On the frontier, national boundaries had little meaning; the people went where the gold, and the opportunities, were to be found. The lemming-like impulse which drew people to the gold rush also worked in reverse; when enough people began to believe that Dawson was doomed, the prophecy became self-fulfilling. It was Fairbanks' turn for glory now, and Dawson would have to wait and see if this blow would be fatal.[5]

By the summer of 1904, the writing was on the wall for Dawson. It was no longer the brightest hope for the northwest, and many original Dawsonites had left for the new field. Experienced miners in the Klondike fields could see that the high-grade deposits had already been worked over, and that new mining techniques were required to sustain gold production. Faced with the harsh realities and the high costs of modernization, many simply sold out to the companies consolidating claims in the Klondike, and headed for Fairbanks, where the story was that individual prospectors still had a chance.

There were social as well as economic changes in Dawson. The rowdy, boisterous community of the first years of the gold rush was becoming "civilized." Dawson was beginning to look respectable, as the reform efforts of the middle-class residents, particularly the Women's Vigilance Committee, challenged the gambling halls, brothels, and dance halls that had once made the city seem so sinful. The new morality in Dawson, however, owed as much to depopulation as to moral crusades, for by 1901, Dawson's population had fallen to half of the gold rush peak. There was less sin partly because there were far fewer sinners.

It was ironic that as the economy of Dawson began to collapse, it gained an outward appearance of permanence and stability. Responding to Commissioner Ogilvie's optimistic forecasts about the Yukon, the federal government had authorized the construction of an elaborate administration building, a new courthouse, a new post office, and an imposing Commissioner's residence which became Dawson's social focus. As the population declined, the new civil service buildings proclaimed it as the administrative, legal, and commercial centre for the upper Yukon River basin. This was, in the words of Hal Guest, author of a history of Dawson City, "Dawson's golden age," an age of elegance which masked a valiant but losing battle to maintain the status and prosperity of the Klondike gold rush.[6]

The numbers told a sad tale. No census had been taken of the Yukon at its height in 1898, since the next regular census was not due until 1901; the best estimate of the Territory's maximum population was forty thousand. It fell to slightly over twenty-seven thousand in 1901, of whom over nine thousand lived in Dawson City, with most of the rest on the Klondike creeks. Ten years later, the Yukon had only eighty-five hundred people, more than a third of whom lived in Dawson. The city's collapse continued, and in 1921 it could claim fewer than a thousand residents. Dawson City would never regain the energy and excitement of the gold rush days, nor would it again enjoy the status and authority of the first years of the twentieth century. The city was clearly on the skids, but it was not to go down without a fight.

One way in which Dawsonites reacted to the decay of their community was by attempting to prove that it was indeed a going concern — that it was just as vital and "civilized" as any town in southern Canada. In particular, there was a strong desire on the part of middle-class citizens to make Dawson a "moral" place; if Ontario's capital in this era was known as "Toronto the Good," then Dawsonites aspired to make their town "Dawson the Better." Southern Canadians and some federal officials had always thought of Dawson as a sinful place, so there was both public and private support for the campaign to clean it up, to make it the kind of place where decent folk could live without being confronted daily in the streets by gamblers and harlots. Since in the first decade of the century there were still hundreds of single young men in Dawson, the campaign for moral purity was bound to produce a certain amount of civic tension.

147

The restructuring of Klondike society began in 1901. In short order the government put restrictions on gambling, the sale of alcohol, and prostitution. These actions did not, however, satisfy the reformers. Reverend J. Pringle, the Presbyterian minister in Dawson, continued to use his seat on the Territorial Council to wage further battles against immorality.[7] The mounted police supported these battles, even though their own men often succumbed to the temptations of the flesh. Sam Steele had been particularly anxious to control the "fast women and 'tin horn gamblers' galore" who made a profitable living off the miners' weaknesses.[8] But Steele and the police were concerned more with order than morality, and concentrated mostly on harassing gamblers. Steele did not try to close the saloons, so long as they were orderly, and after he left the Yukon, Commissioner James Ross proceeded slowly with new measures, always being careful to consult the business community.

At times, efforts to regulate the saloons ran afoul of administrative manoeuvring. Commissioner F. T. Congdon, a passionately partisan Liberal, used liquor licences to reward his supporters, undercutting the effort of several years to regulate drinking. When Congdon left office in 1904, the police moved quickly to eliminate the practice of paying women a percentage for drinks they solicited, and imposed further regulations on gambling. Under the next Commissioner, Alexander Henderson, the forces of morality found a new and powerful backer. Like many of the church people and social leaders, Henderson saw no justification for the remnants of the frontier lifestyle in Dawson City, and ordered an immediate clamp-down on the saloons, hotels, and brothels. But as he soon discovered, there was a substantial demand for the services of these establishments, and many people, particularly men from the creeks, who scoffed at the moralizing of the Dawson elite. Their protests, plus the fact that the taxes paid by these establishments were crucial to the municipality, forced a hasty retreat. Morality in the Yukon had to be tempered by a little common sense and an eye on municipal revenues.[9]

The battle against prostitutes was similarly clouded. Several of the women who crossed the passes in 1898 to mine the miners had married wealthy men; they were no longer "langorous lilies of soulless love," but now moved in comparatively respectable circles. Nor could those who were still in their original business be ignored, for Dawson was a small place, and these women were only too evident when they appeared in public. Early in 1901 Major Z. T. Wood of the mounted police announced that prostitutes were banned from Dawson City. Many left the Yukon for Nome or Tanana; others left for the south. Some simply moved across the Yukon River to West Dawson, or across the Klondike River to Klondike City, known locally as Lousetown. This cut into business considerably, for Lousetown was connected to Dawson by an open bridge, and the parade to the brothels required an exposure that many men, at least those who cared for their public reputation, did not care to undergo. The moral crusade continued, for prostitutes still came into town to shop, and their very presence offended some good citizens. Some even dared to continue their business in Dawson, flouting public authority, but doing a land-office business. Civic officials and the police harassed them constantly.

The government, led by Commissioner Henderson, broadened the attack to include the dance-halls, on the principle that cleaning them up would eradicate most of Dawson's immorality. This effort was ultimately successful, leading Mayor Wood to claim that Dawson City was "as free from immorality as any Eastern City, and much more so than any mining camp that has hitherto been known."[10] The saloons remained, as did the prostitutes, but by 1905 the reformers' protests had been largely satisfied. Brothels were forced to operate discreetly, as in southern cities, and the saloons had to obey a lengthy series of regulations. The police kept a close eye on all operations, and moved quickly to stamp out any expansion of vice. The battles themselves represented Dawson's struggle for social respectability and the community's intense sensitivity to comments in the national press and in the House of Commons about immorality on the northern frontier. Dawsonites wanted to prove that civilization could flourish in the far northwest, and that social stability had followed the heady and chaotic days of the gold rush.

The increasingly middle-class nature of Dawson society in the new century showed itself in ways other than the anti-vice crusade. The civil servants, businessmen, police officers, and professionals who made up this class — and more particularly, their wives — struggled to erase the frontier nature of the community. Access to this group was strictly controlled; only those of suitable social and economic background were admitted. The arbiters of correct behaviour were the women, who made strenuous efforts to reproduce the upper-middle-class social life of the southern communities. Each woman had a "day," for which she produced elaborate invitations and hosted an "at home." Callers, dressed in their best, were fêted with a fancy tea and refined conversation. Laura Berton, whose day fell on the second Tuesday of the month, described the process:

On one's day, one was at home to the entire town during the hours of the late afternoon and early evening. One spent many days before *the* day salting the almonds, preparing the olives, churning the sherbet in the freezer, preparing trays of home-made candies. One made sure the proper people were honoured by being allowed to "pour" or "pass," and the coefficient of success was calculated in direct ratio to the number of people who turned up. Thus it was possible to compute mathematically the social standing of the entire upper crust of Dawson City.[11]

The ritual was comical and rather sad in its artificiality — the irony was that Laura Berton, as an elementary school teacher, would not have been included in such a circle in Toronto or Vancouver, but in Dawson the definition of what constituted the "upper crust" had to be loosened considerably. In the winter the social set went snowshoeing, on sleighing and dog-sled trips, or to one of the town's many evening dinners and dances. Fancy-dress balls, which sent men and women scurrying to buy, make, or send outside for elaborate costumes, were held throughout the year — St. Andrew's Day, New Year's, Washington's Birthday, Easter, Discovery Day, and others.[12] This, clearly, was a class-conscious society, fighting to eliminate the stigma of the town's frontier heritage and trying to be as modern and fashionable as their counterparts in the south. In this, Dawsonites were only doing as people have always done in similar situations, struggling to put a good face on their isolation and distance from the centres of society and anxious to make as few concessions as possible to their isolation. Dawson was, at least in its pretensions, a society that could well have been plucked from southern Ontario and recreated on the banks of the Yukon River.

A society which aspires to elite status must of course have people to exclude, and the ones left out of Dawson's upper crust tended to be the colourful characters of the gold rush days who had given the community its unique character in the first place. According to Laura Berton, three of the richest and most influential businessmen in the Yukon — pioneer Big Alex McDonald; one-time sailor, boxer, and promoter-extraordinaire Joe Boyle; and mine developer A. N. C. Treadgold — were not welcome in the homes of select society. The former dance-hall girls, no matter who they had married, were beyond the pale, as were the miners, labourers, and transients who continued to make up a large percentage of Yukon society.[13]

The Yukon social pyramid was small after 1900, but it had sharply defined lines, in contrast to the rough egalitarianism of the years preceding the strike. At the top stood the Commissioner and judges, the officers of the North-West Mounted Police, the top civil servants, clergy (particularly the Anglican Bishop), lawyers, bankers, leading businessmen, and single women from respectable professions — nursing and teaching, who, though not of the financial elite, were welcome at the top as women who would balance the sex ratio somewhat. Below them, and occasionally welcomed into their ranks, was the "downtown crowd," less prosperous merchants and small businessmen. Lower on the social ladder were the labourers, mine workers, and the constables of the North-West Mounted Police (who did not, in this period, come from the best of social backgrounds, and were, moreover, miserably paid). At the bottom of the social heap were the white men with native wives, mixed bloods, dance-hall girls, and prostitutes. Below them all were the Indians, most of whom stayed on the tiny Moosehide reserve downstream from Dawson City.[14]

Robert Service, bank clerk, poet, and "Bard of the Klondike," worked out of this modest cabin in Dawson City. He is shown here in 1909. YUKON TERRITORIAL ARCHIVES

There was another line that sharply divided Dawson society: politics. Patronage was, of course, a deeply entrenched Canadian tradition at this time, and when Laura Berton arrived in Dawson City, the community was highly politicized: "Dawson at this time was a predominantly Liberal town. The Liberals held all the Government jobs and as a result most of the prominent socialites were Liberals."[15] While territorial Conservatives complained about the blatant favouritism, solidly Liberal newspapers carried the government's advertising, party supporters received preferential treatment on the awarding of the controversial mining concessions, and loyal Liberals received the lion's share of construction and supply contracts.

The federal election of 1911, which returned a majority Conservative government for the first time in fifteen years, demonstrated the strength of political influence in town. Dawson Tories went wild with delight, for the patronage plums were now theirs for the picking. Liberals, who held their government jobs primarily as a result of their political allegiances, skulked out of the territory, some not even waiting for official notice of their firing. Many Conservatives who had long since left the Territory rushed back to take their places, notably George Black, long one of the city's dominant Tories, who claimed the prize of Commissioner of the Yukon Territory. Political loyalties overlay all other divisions of the community, which owed so much of its existence to government patronage.[16]

Not everyone in Dawson conformed to the divisions of class, politics, and race. Bishop Stringer and his wife, Sadie, who moved the headquarters of the Yukon diocese to Dawson City in 1906, paid less attention to the social conventions than did most others. Sadie, in particular, welcomed native people to her home, referring to them as "the roses around my door," and often had the wives of Indian missionaries staying there. The wife of Julius

151

Kendi, a native minister from Mayo, visited several times, and was included in Mrs. Stringer's social gatherings. Although the other ladies were clearly upset with this breach of social convention — as she well knew — she continued the practice.[17] But few followed her lead, for most members of the social elite found the social code to be a comfort and a barrier separating them from the harsher realities of life in the north.

It was within this social world that Robert Service, the "Bard of the Klondike," operated. He wrote his first gold rush poems while a bank clerk in Whitehorse, before he had even visited the Klondike region. Service published his first volume, *Songs of a Sourdough*, shortly before he was transferred to the Dawson City bank. He became a familiar, if shadowy, figure on the social landscape, a loner who avoided social occasions and seldom sought companionship. At first he was a poet without honour in his own country; most Yukoners had never heard of him, and when Governor General Earl Grey asked to meet him during his visit to Dawson, Service had to be rounded up and produced, as no one had thought to invite him to the official reception. Eventually, he became the most famous Yukoner, and to his obvious discomfort, his attendance at social functions became almost mandatory.

When the royalty cheques started rolling in, Service quit his job with the bank, but remained in the north for a few years. He became even more reclusive and thought little of his own work; in a conversation with Laura Berton, he commented of his poetry, "That's the stuff the public wants. That's what they pay for. And I mean to give it to them." And, sensibly, he continued to profit by doing so. Eventually he left the Yukon for southern France, where he continued to write, turning away from the Klondike to deal with other themes, but his inability to reproduce the magic of his gold rush poetry darkened his later years.[18]

By the time Service reached Dawson City, the appearance of the gold fields had changed tremendously. Just as Dawson society struggled to overcome isolation and gain some measure of stability, so the Klondike fields were undergoing major transformations. The days of the individual prospector and the mining methods that had produced the gold rush were finished as an important economic force, though a few loners still continued to work the more distant creeks. Now the symbol of the gold fields was not the pan but the dredge — the enormous, mechanical beast that slowly chewed its way like a dinosaur along the river beds. Dredges processed tons of gold-bearing gravel each day, and could make a profit on a trace of gold in each cubic yard — paydirt that could not support a miner working with simpler techniques. The first dredge arrived in the Yukon in 1900, and was moved to Bonanza Creek after a short, but unsuccessful trial on the Yukon River. The second test was a success, and demonstrated that the Klondike had life after the prospectors. High-tech mining was obviously the way of the future.[19]

The mining regulations of the early Klondike were, of course, not suited to new technology, which required a consolidation of the old claims. The regulations had to be changed, with the backing of the federal government. Ignoring the recommendations originating in the north, which called for the preservation of the existing system, Clifford Sifton, Minister of the Interior, had decided that the future of the Klondike field lay in the introduction of these modern mining techniques. The Yukon had long caused Sifton problems, particularly when Governor General Lord Minto had visited the Territory in 1900 and lent his considerable political weight to local complaints against the federal government. Sifton chose James H. Ross as Commissioner to undertake the difficult task of steering the new mineral regulations into operation.[20]

The basis of the new system was the "concession" — a grant from the government permitting the concessionaire to buy up existing and lapsed claims, control water rights, and otherwise manage large areas of the goldfields. Although concessions had been granted as early as 1898, the system did not pick up steam until after the turn of the century. Sifton had introduced new regulations in 1900 permitting the consolidation of claims and regulating the potential conflict between the needs of placer mining and the much larger concessions. By 1904, some forty-four concessions had been granted, some of them comprising as much as five miles of creek bed. The concessions were controversial from the beginning, not the least because of charges of political favouritism in granting them — it was almost mandatory for an applicant for a concession to be a contributor to the Liberal Party.[21]

The most famous of the concessionaires was A. N. C. Treadgold, a former British public schoolmaster who had come to the Yukon in 1898 as correspondent for the *Mining Journal* and the *Manchester Guardian*. Treadgold, a short, energetic, gnome-like man, who in old age looked rather like the late Lord Beaverbrook, had an audacious vision of the new Klondike. He began to buy up claims, purchased an interest in other concessions, sought backing in England for his schemes, and came to Sifton with a plan for a massive reorganization of the Klondike creeks in one giant concession. To make it work, Treadgold asked the government for a virtual monopoly over water resources, the essential element in placer mining, plus large amounts of land, tax exemptions, and other privileges. Sifton was enthusiastic: "It is the chance of a lifetime to have the country put upon an enduring basis and development started upon a scale hitherto unknown in mining in Canada. Too much hypercriticism will wreck the whole plan."[22]

Despite some resistance in the Liberal cabinet, Treadgold was given a concession in 1901, though some of the more extreme elements of the original plan were modified. The concession gave Treadgold and his partners exclusive rights to a large part of the Klondike goldfields, including water and timber rights, for a period of thirty years.

The news was greeted with horror in the north, and Yukoners rallied against Ottawa's initiative, which threatened to destroy the Klondike as they knew it. Public meetings, editorial protests, and dozens of letters to the government spelled out the general hostility to the scheme. The Dawson Board of Trade complained of the "Monopoly of [the] Treadgold Octopus," and demanded that the entire concession scheme be scrapped.[23] Although the protests were vehement and widespread throughout the Territory, Sifton persisted.

But in 1903, in the minister's absence, the government agreed to the establishment of a royal commission, under Justice B. M. Britton, to be dispatched to the Yukon that summer to investigate the Treadgold affair. The commission's report was inconclusive, but the federal government, bowing to the storm, cancelled the concession in 1904.

Sifton levelled the blame for this debacle squarely on Treadgold's "stubborn narrowness & complete incapacity for business of a large scale."[24] Sifton himself remained convinced that large-scale mining was the only possible future for the Klondike fields, an opinion echoed in the Britton Report. However, he was losing interest in the Yukon, which he now held responsible for its own economic distress. Gold production had been falling precipitously, from over a million fine ounces in 1900, worth $24 million, to slightly over 420,000 ounces in 1905. Consolidation was already underway, as miners banded together to operate their claims more efficiently. To make matters worse, the gold discoveries at Nome and Tanana had drained much of the entrepreneurial vitality from the region. Change was coming, but not on the scale the government wanted. Mechanized mining offered the Territory a stable future, Sifton believed, but the violent reaction to the Treadgold proposal had probably deterred potential investors. Sifton had other struggles to tend to, including the political battle that would soon lead to his resignation from the Liberal Party.

The immediate future of the Yukon looked gloomy. James Ross, although still well-respected in the north, had fizzled in Ottawa, seldom attending the Commons and unable to defend Yukon interests adequately. As the *Dawson News* editorialized, Ross had been "as impotent as a katydid in a simoon."[25] With the cancellation of the Treadgold concession and the report of the Britton Commission, the Yukon was left without a plan for its economy. The old methods were failing to sustain the Territory, the new proposals had been rejected, and the future was unclear.

Treadgold's dream of consolidation had not yet died, nor had the concessions been completely eliminated. Something obviously had to update or replace the old placer mining system, and efforts to modernize the operations continued. The Klondike Mines Railway was under construction from Dawson to the creeks — it passed over one of Treadgold's Bonanza Creek claims — and was completed to the creeks in 1906. Construction of the line led to an incident which showed that there was still something unique about life in the Yukon:

> Treadgold did not like the fact that the railway crossed one of his claims...so he proceeded to the claim...and removed a rail from the track....Jerome Chute, railway contractor, politely picked up Mr. Treadgold and lifted him off the track and deposited him some feet from the track. Treadgold in the meantime made an effort to free himself, but not until the more skookum Mr. Chute deposited him beside the track as aforesaid. The railway crew relaid the track, while Contractor Chute held Mr. Treadgold. Treadgold afterwards returned to the middle of the track and refused to get off to let the engine pass onto his claims. Dave Curry, foreman, took Mr. Treadgold in charge, and knelt upon the chest of Mr. Treadgold until the engine passed. The story of the incident...was the subject of considerable talk.[26]

But the railway never showed a profit, and closed in 1914.

In 1905 Treadgold still continued to lay financial plans, flitting about the Yukon, then leaving in the fall in constant pursuit of financial backers. The following year, a construction team arrived with orders from Treadgold to build a water ditch seventy miles long, stretching by means of ditch, flume, pipe, and inverted siphon from Twelve Mile River to Bonanza Creek. Thus did Treadgold hope to get around the contentious matter of water supplies, the issue that had stalled his earlier grandiose scheme to corner the Klondike fields.

Treadgold continued to buy up properties, picking up small claims and some of the remaining concessions, adding to an impressive list of holdings in the Klondike. Word also leaked out that the promoter had the financial backing of the wealthy Guggenheim family. When two of the Guggenheims visited the Klondike in 1906, it seemed as though the dreams about a revitalized gold-mining operation were about to come true. Work continued on the water ditches, additional dredges were built, and a power plant to supply the electric dredges was begun. In October 1906, the registering of a large block of claims surrounding Bonanza, Eldorado, and Hunker creeks under the Yukon Consolidated Goldfields Company and Northwest Hydraulic Mining Company provided final confirmation of the scale of the Guggenheim interest. The consolidation process was well underway.

By 1907 the results of the new investments were apparent. A sawmill at Twelve Mile Creek, water ditches, the Twelve Mile power plant and the new dredges — each weighing close to eight hundred tons — were all in service. New steam-thawing techniques were used to loosen the permanently frozen gravel. Through the summer, work also started on the construction of four new dredges from parts brought in over the previous year from the south. Operations were streamlined under the newly formed Yukon Gold Com-

Top: *This flume, six feet wide and 4 feet deep, was part of the Yukon Gold Company's Yukon Ditch, which carried water for over 70 miles. The water was used for the company's Grand Forks hydraulic operations, 1908.* YUKON TERRITORIAL ARCHIVES

Centre: *The Klondike dredges were massive structures. These men were building a dredge at Bonanza Basin.* YUKON TERRITORIAL ARCHIVES

Below: *The dredging and hydraulic operations of the large mining companies were impressive, capital-intensive affairs. This photograph shows the Yukon Gold operation at Guggieville, near the mouth of Bonanza Creek, c. 1918–20.*

pany, still controlled by the Guggs, as the family was known in the Yukon. A. N. C. Treadgold sat on the company's board of directors, but was not as active as before in the Yukon operations. So dominant was the new enterprise that many of the remaining operators worked over their richest ground and then sold their holdings to Yukon Gold.

These developments brought the Yukon squarely into the mainstream of the world economy, a process which raised new problems. In the old days the Yukon mines succeeded or failed on the initiative of individual miners and the richness of the ground. Now the mines were at the mercy of distant stock exchanges and the vagaries of international capitalism. In 1908 a stock market collapse in the United States raised questions about the Yukon Gold Company's strength. Some questionable promotion of its stock by a financier named Thomas Lawson resulted in bad publicity for the company and some difficulty in continuing with the work in the Yukon. There was a public outcry when the company tried to bring in low-paid contract labour from Vancouver. Eventually, however, Yukon Gold put its operations in order and began mining. When the Twelve Mile Ditch opened in 1909 there was a major expansion of hydraulic and dredging operations; the company continued to buy up gold properties, and although gold production remained far below its level of a decade earlier, the company continued to show a profit.

But Yukon Gold and the Guggenheims had little commitment to the Yukon. Profits from the operation were, after the first years, transferred to southern investors through dividend payments. There was little re-investment and no real attempt to diversify. As Yukon returns dipped during the First World War, with labour in short supply and costs high, the company began to shift its operations to new goldfields, in such places as Alaska, Idaho, and Malaya. One by one, the dredges were shut down and dismantled. By the middle of the war, the Guggenheims had lost interest in the Yukon and abandoned any hope of long-term profits. According to one estimate, the company took over $31 million in gold from its Klondike properties during this period, delivering over $9.8 million in dividends to its shareholders. In that day, few asked what Yukon Gold delivered to the Yukon in return.

Despite its size and dominance, Yukon Gold was not alone in the goldfields. Joe Boyle, the tough and aggressive owner of the Canadian Klondyke Mining Company, was a formidable competitor. Boyle had been involved with the Klondike since 1897, when he bought into a large concession near Hunker and Bonanza creeks. He and his partner Frank Slavin were boxers who, with some others, had applied for a large concession and later discussed selling it to A. N. C. Treadgold. Some preliminary work was done on the project, but the concession was soon embroiled in the leasing controversy that ended with the establishment of the Britton Commission. [27]

Boyle could do little more than cut wood on the property, trying in vain

Top: *Hydraulic mining extracted a considerable toll from the environment. In addition to diverting water supplies, the mining method involved the systematic stripping of dirt and gravel off gold-bearing hills, like this one at Lovett Gulch, 1911.* YUKON TERRITORIAL ARCHIVES

Centre: *Even as the famed Klondike prospectors were scouring the creeks for gold, more sophisticated developers were introducing new technology to northern mining. These hydraulic operations at Hunker Creek, c. 1900, were among the first in the Yukon.* PUBLIC ARCHIVES OF CANADA

Below: *Within a few years of the strike at Bonanza Creek, the small holders were gone, and their properties had passed into the hands of large scale developers. Very quickly, they moved dredges onto the creeks, like this one on Bonanza, and began to process the still-rich Yukon gravels.* PUBLIC ARCHIVES OF CANADA to raise enough money to start full-scale mining. Facing considerable opposition within the Yukon, Boyle headed outside in an attempt to raise money. In 1904 he found supporters in the Detroit Yukon Mining Company, a small concession already active in the Klondike fields and building a railway to help with mining operations. Boyle negotiated a deal with the group, which led to the formation of the Canadian Klondyke Mining Company. The new company began work in 1905, establishing a power plant on Bear Creek and constructing a new dredge. The other principals, particularly the Rothschild family, took an active interest in the property, visiting the Yukon several times to oversee mining operations.

In 1907 Boyle found himself embroiled in a legal controversy with his fellow investors. The Detroit group had agreed to sell the Guggenheim interests, a move that Boyle protested vehemently. The court case was initially decided in Boyle's favour, but the struggle continued. In 1909, Boyle and his former partners finally settled the matter in a deal which permitted him to buy out the outstanding shares in the company, leaving him in full control of Canadian Klondyke, with the financial resources necessary to keep his mining operation in the field. Always anxious to outstrip Yukon Gold and A. N. C. Treadgold, and ever the optimist, Boyle announced in 1910 that he was building the world's largest dredge — Canadian No. 2 — a behemoth costing over $300,000 and capable of handling over ten thousand cubic yards of gravel each day. Boyle, his finances secure, now represented a formidable challenge to Treadgold's plans for control of the Klondike.

Although A. N. C. Treadgold had helped create the Guggenheim empire in the Klondike, he disliked working for others. He eventually decided to sell out his holdings in Yukon Gold and go it alone. Work on his properties began in earnest in 1909–10, marked by the construction of a substantial power plant on the Klondike River. Treadgold split his time between supervising construction and mining crews in the Yukon and floating deals in the financial centres of North America and England. His new company, Granville Mining Company (which included a future American president, Herbert Hoover, among its partners), now moved to dominate the Klondike.

Key to the scheme was an amalgamation with Joe Boyle. A complex stock deal, which allowed both Treadgold and Boyle to control their operations while permitting joint ventures on projects of mutual importance, was struck in 1912. Boyle appears to have gotten the better of the deal, and gained considerable control over the goldfields as a result. The two men did not work well together, for Treadgold's regal demeanour was at odds with Boyle's more confrontive and abrasive style. Both sought to be "King of the Klondike"; neither was comfortable sharing the spotlight. The men tried to unravel their complex affairs, trading stock, forming new companies, adopting new technology, and expanding mining operations in new directions. Treadgold's gamble did not pay off. His supporters tired of his endless

Canadian No. 4, the Canadian Klondike Mining Company's dredge, is shown working along the Klondike River. Yukon Gold Company's operation is visible in the background. YUKON TERRITORIAL ARCHIVES

promises and began to pull out of the Granville Mining Company. By the middle of the First World War he had lost control of the gold-mining empire he had built; by 1920 he was bankrupt, and his dream of controlling the Klondike seemed dead.

Treadgold's loss was, however, Joe Boyle's gain. Under his direction Canadian Klondyke continued to expand operations, its balance sheet showing a healthy profit. The paper machinations also continued, as Boyle created a new entity, Boyle Concessions, to combine his various holdings. Assets were shifted back and forth between his various corporate shells. Boyle was now truly the "King of the Klondike." His trains ran regularly between Dawson City and the creeks, new dredges were brought in-stream, gold production expanded, and, in 1913, he purchased the Northern Light, Power and Coal Company, which supplied electricity to Dawson City. Boyle was a "hands-on" administrator, routinely involved with the field operations of his Klondike holdings. It was not all clear sailing, for Boyle found himself embroiled in numerous court cases, several involving Yukon Gold. The companies' properties were so close that Boyle's dredging operations threatened the physical stability of the Guggenheim facilities.

The two companies were dramatically different. Boyle was a Yukon booster, revelling in his stature as the local magnate. He was active in community affairs, including a bizarre scheme to take a Yukon team to compete for the 1905 Stanley Cup that ended in ignominious failure. The Guggenheims, in contrast, were outsiders, exploiting the Territory's resources, doing most of their purchasing and hiring in the south, only marginally committed to the stability and future of the Yukon. Boyle made numerous investments in the Territory, some of which (his ownership of the

Dawson utilities for instance) brought him much grief and controversy.

Boyle's operation ran into difficulty during the First World War. Like Yukon Gold, Canadian Klondyke had trouble finding enough workers, and faced constantly rising prices. Through the war, the company ran into financial problems, and at times had trouble meeting the payroll. Boyle's credit dried up, and his legal troubles — an ever more complex web of corporate and personal entanglements — continued. When in 1916 he left for Europe and his strange, dramatic future, he left his son, Joe Boyle Jr., a training mining engineer, in charge of his company. But Joe Jr. could not pull the company out of its financial and legal morass, and in January 1918, Canadian Klondyke passed into receivership. The short-term reign of the King was over; the pretender to the throne was in the wings and would return shortly.

While Boyle's struggle for the Klondike had captured the Territory's attention, other miners had turned their eyes to other parts of the Yukon. The transition from Dawson to other regions was difficult and painful, hampered by fears that the Yukon's wealth was played out. As economist Kenneth Rea has written, "By 1914 the public conception of the Yukon as a land of quick wealth had been transformed into a growing conviction that the Territory was not worth the expense associated with maintaining it."[28] Nonetheless, the ever-optimistic prospectors were determined to put life back into the Yukon economy. It would not be easy, and the returns would be slow in coming.

Before the gold rush, miners had found promising traces of gold on Livingstone Creek, and there had been a modest rush to the district. Joseph Peters, in partnership with George Black, developed a good deposit of placer gold. A small community sprang up with the usual dance-hall, saloon, stores, roadhouse, and mounted police detachment. But the creek was hard to reach — forty miles by a twisting winter trail from Lake Laberge — and the gold was limited. Nonetheless, the original claims produced an estimated $1 million by 1920.[29]

Early in the century, gold had been discovered on creeks emptying onto the west side of Kluane Lake. Prospectors and speculators once more raced to the strike, set amidst the towering mountains and emerald lakes of the southwest. The stampede, like so many others, lasted a year or two. A couple of the prospectors, Eugene and Louis Jacquot, stayed on, their imagination captured by the dramatic potential of the Kluane district. The Jacquots established a trading and shipping company, and were among the first to recognize the opportunities for big-game hunting in the Territory. Their hopes of reproducing the success of Joe Ladue, the fast-moving businessman who capitalized on the Klondike rush, had been dashed by the inconsequential gold discoveries. Captivated by the beauty of the region, however, the brothers married local Indian women and settled in the Kluane district.[30]

The search for a new Bonanza reached to all corners of the Territory.

The completion of the White Pass and Yukon Route, linking Skagway and Whitehorse, eased travel in the southern Yukon. The completion of the bridge at Carcross, shown here in July 1900, permitted continuous travel between the Pacific coast and the head of navigation on the Yukon River. YUKON TERRITORIAL ARCHIVES

Small gleanings of gold had been taken before 1900 from the Firth River, which flows northward into the Arctic Ocean, but little development had ensued. Excitement soared when Ben Smith and Jujiro Wada, a Japanese adventurer and prospector, made a promising strike in March 1908. Ten groups of prospectors headed into the isolated zone the next summer, scouring the Firth and Old Crow regions for further evidence of major deposits. They failed, although a few hopeful adventurers continued their explorations. By 1913, most of the prospectors had abandoned the field, yet another illusory "Eldorado" that kept alive dreams of a second Klondike.[31]

Only slowly did Yukoners begin to consider the possibility that their future might not lie in gold. The rapid improvement of transportation, stimulated by the opening of the White Pass and Yukon Railway and the expansion of steamship service, made it reasonable to think of exporting other ores of greater bulk but lower value.

Miners had been active along the Stewart River for decades; there had been sporadic strikes and prospectors pushed up the river, hoping that the many creeks and rivers held another great gold deposit. The arrival in 1901 of some two hundred miners led to the development of a small community at Mayo and the construction of a road to the lower Stewart River. New gold discoveries followed in subsequent years, enough to maintain enthusiasm, but not sufficient to set off a full-scale rush.[27] Mayo developed into a minor regional centre, the terminus of steamboat travel along the Stewart River, connected by winter stage to Dawson City. In July 1903 Jacob Davidson had uncovered a rich deposit of silver and lead near Galena Creek, a small pup some twenty miles from Mayo. The claim was permitted to lapse, but Davidson's partner, H. W. McWhorter, regained control of the property and arranged for a trial shipment of ore to Consolidated Mining and Smelting Company's smelter in Trail, British Columbia. Shipping costs were steep, but the high-grade ore paid for them and provided a healthy return besides. The Silver King claim was sold to Thomas Aitken and Henry Munroe, who once more tested the waters with a shipment of a thousand tons of ore to a San Francisco smelter. Shipping costs continued to plague the enterprise. It cost over sixty dollars a ton to transport and process the ore, a third of the expense coming on the short journey from the mine to Mayo. Shipments continued but only of the highest grade ore, for the owners simply could not support a larger operation. The richness of the original strike was, however, sufficient to encourage other prospectors to continue the search for additional silver and lead deposits. They would find their new "Bonanza," although not until after the First World War.[32]

Copper was also added to the Yukon's short list of marketable resources. During the gold rush, prospectors had discovered a massive copper deposit surrounding Whitehorse. Although the deposit was large and rich, low prices for the metal and the high cost of transporting ore to the railhead by road kept excitement in check. In 1900, two prospectors named McIntyre and Granger developed their Copper King deposit and made a trial shipment. But copper prices were extremely volatile, and the Whitehorse mines were subject to the fluctuations of the international market. In 1906, prices skyrocketed, leading to preliminary construction of a railway spur line toward the mines. When prices fell by half the following year, work stopped, not to pick up again for another three years.

After 1912 copper prices stabilized, and under pressure from Ottawa the White Pass and Yukon Railway reduced their rates. With the start of the First World War, demand picked up and the copper mines became profitable. Atlas Mining dominated the field, operating such rich properties as Pueblo, Arctic Chief, War Eagle, and Grafter. Production rose from 286,000 pounds in 1910 to over 1.8 million pounds in 1913, and peaked in 1916, when over 2.8 million pounds of copper ore left the Territory. The mines, operating on the temporary wartime profitability, did not last long. Water seepage, forcing costly pumping operations, combined with high transportation costs and unreliable markets to doom them. Operations ceased in 1920, to be revived temporarily late in the decade. Only in the 1960s did copper mining again form a major part of the territorial economy.[33]

Here and there throughout the Territory there were other hopeful signs. For a couple of years a silver mine operated at Conrad, on Tagish Lake, and the Engineer Mine, a major gold operation on the lake, was based on a discovery by Captain Alexander, an English Boer War veteran who had been active in the region since 1903.

Despite the widespread perception that mining was the Yukon's sole economic activity, the fur trade remained very much alive in this period.

Top: *The British Yukon Navigation Company dry-docked its fleet each winter. The Whitehorse shipyards, shown here in 1901, were the headquarters of the company's steamer operations.* YUKON TERRITORIAL ARCHIVES

Top left: *Conrad City, a small mining community on Windy Arm, Tagish Lake, enjoyed a brief life in the 1910s. The ore deposit, worked off and on over the years, was neither large nor rich enough to support a permanent settlement.*

Centre left: *Rampart House enjoyed renewed life in the early twentieth century, as a revitalized fur trade brought traders back into the Porcupine River valley. Dan Cadzow, the most prominent of the traders, established a profitable trade at Rampart House.* YUKON TERRITORIAL ARCHIVES

Below left: *Whitehorse was the major entrepot for river and rail traffic along the Yukon River. The community grew little in this period, because of the seasonal nature of river navigation and the control exerted by the British Yukon Navigation Company, which owned much of the land in the town.* YUKON TERRITORIAL ARCHIVES

High prices, improved transportation, and the opportunity to combine prospecting with trading led to a rapid expansion in the number of independent traders active in the field. Many had little attachment to the area, and exploited the trade for a quick profit. But in contrast with the general northern experience, a number of reputable, reliable, and trustworthy traders also opened shop in this period. Taylor and Drury quickly expanded throughout the Territory and Eugene and Louis Jacquot put down roots at Burwash Landing. In the far north, Dan Cadzow moved into the void left by the departure of the Hudson's Bay Company. Like many of the Yukon traders, Cadzow planned to stay for a long time, and treated the Indians with respect and honesty. Thomas Riggs, who visited Rampart House in 1911, described Cadzow's operation: "The place is run as closely to old Hudson's Bay practice as possible. Practically all material was traditional Hudson's Bay, such as the old-time axe shapes, the Assomption sashes, blankets, etc. I think Dan liked to think of himself as a Hudson's Bay factor."[34]

While the Yukon escaped some of the abuses that plagued the northern fur trade, there were still many problems. Prospectors, desperate to get a grubstake for future exploration, joined the hunt for furs, often paying little attention to the long-term future of the resource. As Frederick Congdon wrote in 1910:

> One difference between hunting by trappers and by Indians is that, while the Indian always leaves a stock of all fur bearing animals in a district to continue the species, the white man does not. He goes into a "creek" and absolutely extinguishes all the individuals in it and therefore makes it impossible that it should be restocked from any animals left in the district.[35]

The territorial government did little to regulate the fur trade, which was considered to be of minor importance to the Yukon economy. Because there were no export taxes, the government did not keep track of the thousands of pelts leaving the Yukon each year, most of which found their way to American markets. Not until 1919 did the territorial government begin to extract some revenue from the resource and start to take note of the substantial contribution the fur trade made to the regional economy.

While officials paid little attention to Yukon furs, international dealers had long noted the quality of the region's production. This was particularly true of fox skins, among the most valuable pelts in the early twentieth century. The demand for Yukon foxes was such that trappers and traders did a substantial business in live-trapping the animals for shipment to southern fox farms. In time, Yukon entrepreneurs saw the wisdom of establishing their own fur farms. The territorial council began to regulate the trade in 1914, requiring licences to operate fur farms and limiting the live-trapping operations. Within two years, seventeen fox farms, most small in size, were in operation. Fox-farming seemed to offer greater stability than the hunt for wild animals, but it too was vulnerable to the fluctuations of international markets. Fox-farming fell off dramatically in the next decade, and many operators went out of business while others shifted to the trickier task of raising mink.[36]

That the Yukon economy kept afloat at all reflected the continued improvement of territorial transportation. Construction projects undertaken during the Klondike gold rush reached fruition only after the Klondike fields had gone into decline. As the economy declined, regional transportation actually improved, a reflection of the White Pass and Yukon Railway's commitment to the area and the technological advances in navigation.

The completion of the White Pass and Yukon Railway to Whitehorse in 1900 was the major turning point. The railway did not replace river travel — since Whitehorse was more than three hundred miles from Dawson, the stern-wheelers remained very much in use — but with access from Skagway to Whitehorse now assured, the pattern of bringing supplies and people in by way of Bering Strait and the lower Yukon was quickly altered. The upper

Yukon, and hence the Skagway, Carcross, Whitehorse, and Dawson City corridor, would dominate the regional transportation system in the twentieth century.[37]

As the dominant force in Yukon transportation and anxious for the advantages of controlling the entire transportation system, the W.P.Y.R. quickly began to diversify into river operations. A subsidiary company, the British Yukon Navigation Company, was created, and shipyards were built in Whitehorse and Dawson. The B.Y.N.C. began to build stern-wheelers and buy out its competitors. Others could not compete with the co-ordinated rail and river system, and by 1904 the B.Y.N.C. had all but eliminated the competition on the upper Yukon. On the lower Yukon, a similar consolidation of American carriers ensued, a reaction to the rapidly contracting economy in the area. By 1910 it was clear that the Yukon basin could not support two separate transportation systems — either the upper or the lower river networks would have to go. After a battle made brief by the fact that neither side was financially strong, the American-owned Northern Navigation Company surrendered. A new White Pass subsidiary, the American Yukon Navigation Company, was formed in 1914 to operate the lower Yukon boats in co-operation with the upper river service. The upper Yukon had wrested control of the Yukon River from Alaska, thus ensuring the continued viability of the railway and the Whitehorse-based steamers.

The resolution of the transportation battle also ensured, for a time, the continuation of the unique international community in the Yukon and Alaska. Many of those who had pressed to the new goldfields in Nome and Tanana or to later strikes in Ruby and Iditarod had originally lived in Dawson City. Klondike experience became a link between the peoples of the Yukon basin, as they followed the careers of pioneers who had moved elsewhere in the north. The revised transportation system required that almost anyone entering or leaving the northwest had to pass through Skagway, Whitehorse, and Dawson. National boundaries meant little to a people so tied together by history, common surroundings, and now a single transportation route linking them to the south.[38]

The economic condition of the region was such that transport companies did little to extend the riverboat network. Traders in isolated areas either operated their own boats, as Taylor and Drury did, or contracted with small operators to carry supplies up the Porcupine, Pelly, or other rivers. Where possible, government steamers, particularly those operated by the mounted police, were made available to the public. The government even provided modest subsidies for companies such as Side Streams Navigation, founded in 1909, which were willing to operate along the Stewart, a shallow, rock-filled river that required special shallow-draft stern-wheelers.

The British Yukon Navigation Company's triumph over its rival gave it tremendous influence over the Territory. Its freight rates would determine the survival of businesses in the Territory, as the Whitehorse copper miners and the Mayo developers discovered to their chagrin. The same was true of Whitehorse, the Yukon's first real company town. Businesses had watched the construction of the railway carefully. When the railhead neared Whitehorse, Yukon retailers Whitney and Pedlar and their rivals Taylor and Drury rushed into town. It was soon evident that the land holdings, freight yards, and boat docks of the railway would dominate the community. By 1910, most of the people in town worked for the W.P.Y.R. or its subsidiary, the B.Y.N.C. Those who did not were wise enough to realize that the fate of their community rested on the success of the rail and river system.[39]

The White Pass and Yukon Railway, despite its power, was not omnipotent. High freight rates, seen by the company as essential for corporate survival but by most customers as exploitation, led to a series of confrontations. Businesses struggling to survive in a rapidly declining economy pleaded with the W.P.Y.R. to keep rates low. At times, freight rates to the Yukon exceeded the wholesale value of the goods carried. The company was clearly putting its investors' needs first:

> The directors of the White Pass and Yukon Route recognized that the days of the "fast buck" in the Yukon were over and they followed a conscious policy of "getting all that they could, while the getting was good." The shareholders extracted every last possible profit from the operation, oblivious to the needs of the Yukon and to the detriment of the physical facilities of the railway.[40]

It was a familiar corporate tale, one too often repeated in Yukon history.

For those Yukoners struggling to make a home in the north and to establish some measure of stability, what they perceived as the transportation companies' exorbitant prices were a tremendous affront, one which they protested often and loudly to Ottawa. In 1911 the White Pass and Yukon Route agreed to a voluntary reduction in the tariffs.[41]

Elsewhere in the Territory the progress of transportation was more clouded. The Klondike Mines Railway was never a success, despite government subsidies. The Overland Trail, linking Dawson to Whitehorse during the winter months, suffered a similar fate. The Canadian Development Company had secured a contract to deliver the mail — one of the few secure sources of revenue around — and used this as a basis for their overland operations. The White Pass and Yukon Railway, continuing its efforts to control all aspects of Yukon transportation, bought out the C.D.C. in 1901. The following year, the government awarded W.P.Y.R. a contract to build a winter trail between Whitehorse and Dawson. The route, some 330 miles long, was open by November 1902, permitting regular movement between Whitehorse and Dawson City for all but a few weeks each year. The journey averaged about five days, with meals and overnight stays at some of the many roadhouses built along the route, a rough, jarring expedition that tested the endurance of travellers.

Beyond this, little was done to improve transportation in the Yukon. The gradual introduction of automobiles — the first car arrived on the Overland Trail in 1912 — encouraged improvements to the main trails and the construction of short roads near the communities. But the small population and the paucity of automobiles convinced the government not to spend the money necessary to build a proper road system. The Dawson area received most of the road-building grants, as befitted its needs and political clout. Continued activity across the river from Dawson City led to the construction of a cable ferry across the Yukon River, providing for regular and inexpensive transit throughout the area.

While roads, a railway, and riverboats moved people and supplies more expeditiously around the Territory than had been the case before the discovery of gold, the Territory before the First World War remained very much an outpost of Canadian civilization. Communication with the south, particularly with the federal government in Ottawa, was painfully slow at first, leaving Yukoners with an uneasy feeling of isolation, and adding to their well-founded sense of being ignored by other North Americans. In 1899, the Department of Public Works opened a telegraph link from Dawson to Skagway. By sending telegrams on the coastal steamers to Vancouver, messages could reach Ottawa in four to five days. The Department of Public Works then began construction of an all-Canadian telegraph line, linking the Yukon with the British Columbia telegraph grid. The new system, opened in 1901, cut the delivery time in half and made Yukoners more a part of the North American mainstream.[42]

The federal government was not interested in investing in the economic future of the Yukon, but it was not prepared to let the Yukon manage its own economic destiny. The country's hold on its northland was too weak and too recent to permit the largely American frontier community to determine its own future. Fortunately for Ottawa, there was a ready means of reconciling parsimony and the responsibilities of token sovereignty — the North-West Mounted Police.

The police had been a fixture of northern life from before the Klondike discovery and had carefully managed all aspects of the rush to ensure that the rowdy, anarchistic traditions of the American frontier were not carried into the Yukon River Valley. Renamed the Royal North-West Mounted Police in 1904, the force found itself with even more duties in the wake of the Klondike collapse. When the government began laying off civil servants early in the twentieth century and decided in 1904 to disincorporate the city of Dawson, additional duties fell to the police. New posts were established in the southern Yukon, at Teslin and at Dalton Post, in an attempt to regulate the flow of liquor from British Columbia and Alaska to the Indians there. These posts were largely ineffective, since Indians could cross the border into Alaska to drink, but the government felt that the gesture had to be made. When new communities opened up — Mayo, Livingstone Creek,

Conrad, and Burwash — the police were there almost as soon as the prospectors. The force also moved into the fur-trade districts, providing some measure of control and support for the largely Indian population along the Pelly and Porcupine.[43]

The R.N.W.M.P. did not ignore the thousands of square miles and hundreds of Yukoners not served directly by the permanent settlements. Before the day of extended radio service and the airplane, routine police patrols carried the mail, made scheduled visits to trappers or settlers in the back-country, registered mining claims in a new district, carried supplies, and checked on local game conditions. Foot patrols were usually undertaken in the dead of winter; at other times river navigation provided faster and more reliable access. There were also many special patrols to search for criminals, investigate complaints of overhunting, search for lost prospectors or hunters, carry sick people to hospital, or conduct surveys of previously unexplored territory. Although many Mounties were stationed in the Territory only a short time, others stayed for many years and made a sustained effort to integrate themselves and the law they represented into their communities.

The churches were another post-rush aspect of the Yukon. Most retained at least some presence after 1900. The Church of England predominated, largely because of its strong presence in the Yukon before the gold rush. But it, like the other denominations, had difficulties. Bishop Bompas, whose sponsor the Church Missionary Society supported only native missions and was not particularly interested in spiritual work among the mining population, had trouble attracting enough clergy and paying those who came. The church did send a few men — Isaac Stringer (who had left Herschel Island on leave in 1903) was followed by the Reverend H. A. Cody, a novelist, who arrived in 1904. Some southern clergy came north because they had been infected by an ecclesiastical variant of gold rush fever. E. P. Purdy, Rector of St. Matthew's Cathedral in Brandon, Manitoba, succumbed to the disease, left his charge and came north to Dawson to work with the miners. Like that of many of the stampeders, Purdy's interest in the Territory quickly waned, and he left after two years. Attempts to secure more men ran afoul of a national church more interested in international missions than northern work. Bompas, in his usual undiplomatic style, condemned the lack of support:

> We in the west have [allowed] ourselves to be completely mastered by the east. They use us as they like, give us what small modicum of help they like and assume control of our work and expenditures & restrict us from our efforts to raise funds. The MSCC [Missionary Society of the Canadian Church] is I think a failure. Our connection with it should be dissolved and the west be independent. The future belongs to the west & it may soon control the east.[44]

Bompas, never comfortable with whites, retreated to the security of a native pastorate in Carcross, where he remained until he relinquished the control of the Yukon church to Bishop Stringer in 1905. Stringer returned from his leave to Dawson City, where he and his wife became popular members of the community.

Stringer quickly moved to raise the church's profile. He organized a Territory-wide synod for 1907, which resulted in a strongly worded series of resolutions calling for protection of Indian harvesting rights, better housing for natives, and government grants for day and residential schools. Stringer was well-suited to his task. He had enough of the social graces to be accepted by Dawson society, but was also able to relate to the native people and working men who belonged to his church. A careful and practical administrator rather than a mystic, Stringer was a welcome change from Bompas.[45]

The other denominations were also active during the post-gold rush period, particularly around Dawson. The Presbyterians had the fiery reformer John Pringle. Roman Catholic work fell under the control of Reverend Bunoz of the Oblates, who oversaw a series of mission stations around the Territory, and the Sisters of St. Ann continued to operate their school and hospital in the gold rush capital.[41] While the Yukon was not a conventionally religious society, the number and variety of churches in Dawson and the existence of clergy in Whitehorse, Mayo, and Conrad added a civilizing touch to the area.[46]

While most denominations worked with the miners, the Church of England tried to balance service to the white population with a large native mission field. Even though Stringer had moved to Dawson, largely to re-establish a few bridges to the white community, the church remained active in the back-country. In 1911, for example, the church supported stations at Moosehide, Fortymile, Selkirk, Whitehorse, Teslin, Champagne, Carcross, and Rampart House. Filling the missions was not easy. Whereas Bompas had found most of his recruits in Britain, Stringer enjoyed greater success with recent graduates from Canadian theological schools. A few of the missionaries served lengthy terms, but most stayed only a few years, working up the ecclesiastical ladder from Indian mission to a non-native congregation to a placement outside. Cecil Swanson, whose career followed such a path, thought little of the process: "I felt that I should have been left there [Little Salmon] for at least seven years. It takes time to develop a trusting relationship with the Indians, and a lifetime to learn and use the language. . . . Short-term missionaries are useless."[47]

Stringer solved the manpower shortage, at least in part, by hiring native clergy. Bompas, though fond of Indians as people, had had little confidence in them as clerics, but the new Bishop was more sanguine. A number of Indian lay readers, including Julius Kendi, Richard Martin, Amos Njootli, and John Tizya, were ordained and sent to serve native congregations in the northern half of the Territory. Native clergy required greater supervision than their academically trained white counterparts, but their Christian determination, willingness to stay in the north, and much lower salaries justified their employment. Although the Anglican church was slow to recognize it, the widespread use of native lay readers and clergy played a major role in the long-term allegiance of the Indians of the Yukon to that denomination.[48]

The church was determined to prepare the Indians for a modern, industrial future. The cornerstone to this plan was a modest day-school program and an aggressive campaign to secure government funding for a residential school. Day-school classes were run by missionaries, white church members, and, in a few cases, native lay readers. Parents seldom kept their children in classes for long; the dictates of harvesting almost always won out over the protests of the teachers. The quality of the staff varied widely. Bishop Stringer defended the hiring of Jacob Kendi, a native man, at Rampart House in 1916 in a rather back-handed fashion: "He is perhaps not as well qualified to teach as most of our teachers, but he was the best man available. Again, at this place the Indians have to go off for weeks and months to hunt and fish, so that school can be held only when they come to the Post for a few weeks." Under such conditions little could be expected. T. G. Bragg, Superintendent of Education for the Yukon, bemoaned the effort, "The ordinary day schools are practically useless, and the energy and money expended in maintaining them are comparatively barren of results." Not surprisingly, the Anglican clergy felt that a residential school would show better results.[49]

Residential schools had been in place in the south for several decades, but the results had been disappointing. By 1905, both the national church and the federal government were questioning their usefulness. When approached on the topic by the Yukon clergy, Frank Oliver, Minister of the Interior, commented,

> My belief is that attempt to elevate the Indian by separating the child from his parents and educating him as a white man has turned out to be a deplorable failure. . . . The mutual love between parent and child is the strongest influence for the betterment of the world, and when that influence is absolutely cut apart or is deliberately intended to be cut apart as in the education of Indian children in industrial schools the means taken defeats itself. . . . To teach an Indian child that his parents are degraded beyond measure and that whatever they did or thought was wrong could only result in the child becoming, as the ex-pupils of the industrial schools have become, admittedly and unquestionably a very much less desirable element of society than their parents who never saw the schools.[50]

But such opinions were unfashionable in that era, and political considerations soon forced Oliver to ignore his own advice.

Bishop Bompas had moved his small, church-funded boarding school — an orphanage, really — when he shifted the centre of church operations from Fortymile to Carcross in 1904. He and his successor were anxious to expand the school, and repeatedly petitioned the government for the necessary funding. But Bompas would not live to see his dream fulfilled; he died in June 1906, his passing much mourned by his native friends, although by few whites. In 1908 Ottawa agreed to send two educational inspectors to assess the schooling needs of the Yukon Indians. They reported favourably on the Anglicans' efforts and encouraged the government to fund the school. The new facility, built at a cost of more than $10,000, opened in Carcross in 1911, the jewel of the Anglican plans for the moral and cultural improvement of the Yukon Indians. It would take a decade or more for the first children to work their way through the school. For now, Stringer and his clergy turned to the difficult task of convincing Indian parents to part with their children to send them to the new residential school.[51] While the government responded favourably to this program for native people, it was far less generous in its treatment of the Territory as a whole.

Led by an active and vocal Dawson City press, Yukoners voiced their displeasure over planned mining regulations, new royalties, government services, and alleged corruption within government ranks. They had much to complain about, from the lack of elected representation at the local and federal level, to misguided or ill-timed federal attempts to regulate the placer-mining sector. The tremendous furor over the concession system had only added to regional resentment.

Improvements came slowly. As the gold rush continued through 1896 and 1897, the government could delay no longer. Money started to trickle north for roads, bridges, wharves, more civil servants to handle the deluge of government business, an expanded police force to supervise the swarming mob of prospectors, and an improved mail service — a constant concern of isolated northerners. That the progress was so slow reflected both Ottawa's determination not to offer provincial status to this isolated, transient society and a fear that the largely American population might, if given the political power, move in directions contrary to Canadian interests in the north.

A general description of federal legislation in the Yukon would actually tell little about the nature of the evolution of government structures. The handling of administrative matters — the point of contact between citizens and government — reveals the extent of Ottawa's apathy more clearly. Under federal legislation, the appointed Commissioner had — and was expected to exercise — sweeping power over local administration. Through his four senior associates, the Gold Commissioner, the Crown Timber and Land Agent, the Legal Advisor, and the Comptroller, he had effective control of the Territory. Significantly, the legislative separation of federal and territorial jurisdictions was more apparent than real. J. T. Lithgow, for example, was both Comptroller and Territorial Treasurer, and was paid by both the federal and the territorial governments. Before 1908, the top civil servants usually filled the appointed positions on the Territorial Council.[52]

Even after the council was elected, however, councillors had only limited control over expenditures, which remained the bailiwick of the Commissioner and his staff. Nor did they have the authority to hire the civil servants, a prerogative that belonged to the Commissioner. Attempts to increase the council's power failed. The awarding of the electoral principle proved an empty victory, for real power did not accompany the right to select political representatives. This was in part a result of the decline of the Yukon. As people departed, leaving political and administrative structures intact, a smaller and smaller elite found itself wearing more and more hats, increasingly unable to separate their functions as territorial councillors from their other duties and positions.

The collapse of municipal government in Dawson City illustrates the failure of political development in the Yukon. After much debate and consideration, Dawson City was incorporated as a city in December 1901. Another debate ensued over the nature of civic government. The business community preferred an appointed council, while others wanted an elected mayor and council. The latter option prevailed, a municipal election was held, and, early in 1902, the council began its work. But as the population declined, many political leaders departed for the outside, leaving holes in the political fabric, while simultaneously eating into the tax base. As the hastily built and poorly planned city aged, the expenses of maintaining its services mounted. Faced with rising costs, a number of citizens began in 1904 to circulate petitions calling for the disincorporation of the city. By September of that year the city council was dissolved and Dawson City lost its charter. From 1904 on, the complex and expensive issues of municipal administration would be dealt with by the territorial government. Taxpayers had saved themselves some money, but in doing so had edged the city one step closer to its grave.[53]

The dismantling of the government and administration continued throughout the federal and territorial administration. The Territorial Court had been established in 1897, with the arrival of Judge T. H. McGuire. He was replaced by Judge C. A. Dugas the next year, and Dugas was joined two years later by Judge J. A. Craig. The two men, Craig rigid and formal, Dugas more light-hearted and not as hard-working, had much work to do. The two justices were joined in 1901 by C. A. Macaulay as Police Magistrate, an appointment which made possible the hearing of appeals within the Territory.

There were endless difficulties with the administration of justice in the Yukon. The law required that jurors be British subjects, a major problem given the high percentage of Americans in the population. The movement of people out of the Territory caused numerous delays in cases and resulted in

174

the dismissal of many charges. Also, within a decade of the establishment of the court system, it was obvious that the three judges did not have enough work to do. Dugas and Craig, like many Yukoners, routinely took extended vacations in the south. In 1912, both were pensioned off, with the provision, never enforced, that they had to return to the Yukon if the court required their services. Judge Macaulay was left to act as Justice of the Peace, Police Magistrate, and Territorial Judge. Any challenge to his decisions had to be taken to the Court of Appeals of British Columbia. As was the case elsewhere in the administrative structure, the Yukon received the full services of government but then faced the steady bleeding away of political rights and government offices. The wholly elected council remained, but that too would go in time.[54]

The citizens' meetings of the pre-gold rush era, which had been suppressed by the mounted police, resurfaced as the principal forum for registering displeasure with government policies in February 1900 when a gathering of British subjects loudly proclaimed their opposition to the lack of elected institutions. Out of this meeting came the Citizens' Committee and a formal petition. Other meetings followed, and the protest gained force when the census reported that there were more than four thousand British subjects in the Territory. The first battle was won — two territorial councillors were to be elected in 1900.[55]

When Governor General Lord Minto visited the Territory that same summer, the Citizen's Committee presented a petition calling for a fully elected council, representation in the House of Commons, and changes to liquor and mining regulations. The same committee steered two candidates to victory in the territorial election, issuing a stinging rebuke to the Liberal Party in the process.

In the aftermath of the election loss, and still smarting from wide-ranging antagonism to the federal administration in the Yukon, Clifford Sifton reluctantly conceded that William Ogilvie was ineffectual as Commissioner. With little notice, Sifton arranged for Ogilvie's removal (he was officially permitted to resign) and his replacement by James Hamilton Ross, a former politician and administrator from the North-West Territories. Ross was a perfect choice, and managed to calm matters in the Yukon. Well-versed in the politics of the periphery, Ross sided with the Yukoners and carried their protests into the inner sanctums of power in Ottawa. By 1902, he had secured three additional elected seats on territorial council and, his greatest coup, the right of citizens to elect a representative to the federal parliament.

Little did James Ross know that he would be the one taking up that seat. While Ross was away negotiating a better deal for the Yukon, and singing the praises of a Territory making major strides towards self-government, the catastrophic Treadgold Concession scandal hit. Sifton found himself under unrelenting attack in the House of Commons, hounded by an opposition that loved to see the arrogant minister on the defensive. In the midst of the scandal, the by-election for the new House of Commons seat loomed. Fearful of having an opposition member from the Yukon in the seat, Sifton was desperate for a Liberal win. He urged Ross to resign as Commissioner and accept the Liberal nomination. In the face of personal disaster, Ross did so. His wife and daughter had recently died in a boating accident, and, on his way back to the Yukon, Ross suffered a stroke. He still agreed to stand for office, offering only his widely admired name to a campaign that he left entirely to his supporters.

Ross was aided, ironically, by the Citizens' Committee's choice of candidate. They selected Joe Clarke, a combative, intemperate politician, who often flirted with libel and slander. The contest saw both the vituperative Clarke and the more dignified Ross campaigning strongly against the Treadgold Concession. Ross won by a narrow margin. Sifton could breath more easily, but only temporarily, for another Yukon politician soon began to cause him grief. Seeking Ross's replacement as Commissioner, he accepted Yukoners' advice and appointed F. T. Congdon, an active Yukon protest leader.

Congdon, a newspaperman-turned-lawyer who had worked hard on behalf of the Yukon Liberal Association, had strong political and administrative credentials. He also had intense ambition and the sense of direction of a loose cannon on a slippery deck. The new Commissioner used his office and the strings of patronage to build an impressive political machine, one tied more to him than to the Liberal Party. The actions of "King Congdon" quickly aroused public discontent, but the Commissioner had widely co-opted many potential opponents into his group of cronies. The battle started within the Liberal Party — between the "Tabs" (Congdonites) and the "Steam Beers," led by a Liberal brewer — and provided an opening for the Conservative Party in the Territory. While Congdon tried to oil his machine, the Territory's Tories went about building their own opposition force.

Congdon's partisanship quickly divided the Yukon. The next federal election, slated for December 1904, provided a test of his strength. The Commissioner secured the "Tab" nomination and resigned his position. His opponents rallied around Dr. Alfred Thompson, a well-respected Yukon figure. The campaign was corrupt even by the standards of the time. Patronage positions were offered, threats issued, bribes given, newspaper columns controlled, voters added illegally to the lists of electors, and election officials given strict orders to aid Congdon's campaign. Even with the manipulation, Congdon lost by a sizeable margin. Thompson would take the opposition Tory message to Liberal Ottawa. Supporters of the former Commissioner lobbied in an attempt to get his old job back, but the government had had enough scandals from the Yukon, and British Columbia politician W. W. B. McInnes was appointed to the position.

By 1905 the political landscape had been completely transformed. Sifton was gone, at odds with his own party over the question of separate schools on the prairies. Ross had resigned, soon to be rewarded with elevation to early oblivion in the Senate. Congdon, too, was gone, his patronage machine in tatters. Their replacements, Thompson and McInnes, proved well-suited to the task of pressing for political reform. And Frank Oliver, Sifton's replacement, was sympathetic to the north and supported their efforts. After years of acrimony, the discovery that federal and territorial politicians and administrators could work together toward a common end was reassuring to the few Yukoners who remained in the north.

There were still problems. Congdon resurfaced in territorial politics as Legal Advisor, and began to toss darts at his replacement and his political foes. Commissioner W. W. B. McInnes, facing criticism from within the Liberal Party about conduct of his administration, resigned to return to the less tumultuous world of British Columbia politics. Eventually Congdon, too, had had enough. He resigned his position and left for Ottawa, where he hoped his organizational and political skills would be more appreciated. The struggles that Congdon had initiated would live on in bitterly contested territorial contests and a general distrust of elected and appointed officials. Such was the legacy of the man who wanted to be the political "King of the Klondike." The federal government was again inundated with suggestions for a new Commissioner, but this time advice from the Yukon was over-ruled and Alexander Henderson, former B.C. Attorney General, was recruited for the post.

The Yukon was, by now, reeling from economic collapse and the steady decline of Dawson and the creeks. Ironically, in 1908 the federal government finally acceded to the long-standing request that the Territorial Council be made wholly elected. The new council would actually have little real power and, with the Territory suffering from the post-gold rush depression, people invested little emotional energy in the legislative process, except for the distribution of patronage. In the winter of 1908, following Alfred Thompson's resignation, a federal by-election was called for January 1909. Yukon cold did little to quell the political steam, for the combatants included none other than the boisterous Joe Clarke, staunch Tory George Black, breakaway Liberal Robert Lowe, and, most remarkably, the once-disgraced F. T. Congdon, seeking a last hurrah. Political rhetoric flew wildly, most of it focusing on the personal, professional, or moral failings of the candidates. Congdon won the January 1909 vote by a healthy margin and returned to Ottawa in triumph.

The 1908 by-election campaign was the last real political battle in the Yukon for many years. As the Territory continued to decline, the federal government reduced its expenditures there and regional revenues shrivelled.

Through a quirk of the electoral system, the Territory was in a unique political position. Federal elections in the Yukon took place well after the elections in the south — a full month after in 1911. Although Congdon's excesses had forced a break in the tradition, Yukoners, as a rule, wisely voted for the governing power. When the results of the 1911 election revealed a Conservative victory, Tory hopes in the Territory were immediately revived. As Laura Berton described it, party faithful were quick to see the opening:

> What celebrating there was that night among the Dawson Conservatives. Within an hour of victory the Tories had every possible party worker (and some impossible ones) slated for the coveted jobs so long held by the enemy. . . . The next stage (or so it seemed to me) was jammed with Conservatives pouring back into the country. John Black, George Black and all the others who had left with me more than year before on the last boat, ostensibly for ever, were now preparing to return in triumph.[56]

The plums, what few remained, now went to the Conservatives. George Black got the first prize, the job of Commissioner. The Tories wanted to add the Yukon seat to the government benches in Ottawa. Those veterans of the 1904 election, Alfred Thompson and F. T. Congdon went head to head in yet another bitterly fought personal campaign. The Conservatives won handily, aided in no small measure by the Yukoners' realization that the support of the government was crucial to the territorial economy.

The two men faced each other for the last time early in 1918. That year the Yukon voted after the Unionist victory of the previous year. Both Thompson and Congdon tried to present themselves as non-partisan Unionist candidates, the latter on the slimmest and most creative of pretences. When Yukoners voted, they gave a majority of their votes to Congdon, but the weird confrontation was not yet over:

> Alfred Thompson was declared their Member of Parliament by a vote on division in the Canadian House of Commons. That odd turn of events occurred as a result of the rather difficult problem of distributing the votes of Yukon soldiers for and against Borden's government between two men who both claimed to be Unionist candidates. After an initial period of confusion, the Commons, by a majority decision, chose to assign Thompson the Unionist ballots and Congdon the Liberal ones, thereby turning the doctor's defeat of 110 into a victory of 10.[57]

It was a suitably bizarre ending to the Yukon career of Congdon, the man who had done so much to sour the political atmosphere in the Territory, diverting a potentially powerful, regionally based protest movement into a mud-slinging political environment in which the only constant losers were the long-term interests of Yukoners and the political stability of the Territory. The Yukon was, in the final analysis, ill-served by its politicians. But perhaps they were only reflecting the society from which they had emerged. Like most miners, workers, businessmen, and corporate investors in the

Top: *In the early years of the century, there were signs that the Yukon was maturing politically. The establishment of a completely elected Territorial Council, pictured here, proved to be only a temporary victory. By the First World War, the federal government had already started to dismantle the Yukon's political and administrative apparatus.* YUKON TERRITORIAL ARCHIVES

Below: *Hundreds of Yukoners volunteered for overseas service during World War I, including the members of the 17th Yukon Machine Gun Company, and those who could not serve in the military found other ways of showing their support for Canada's battles in Europe. Most of the young men who served never returned to the Yukon.* YUKON TERRITORIAL ARCHIVES

Yukon, the politicians placed personal gain ahead of regional needs. They could not, in fact, see the underlying problems in their society, seeking instead to respond to the short-term demands of their supporters and to use public office to reward those who put them there. In power, the Conservatives were no different from the Liberals. The Yukon was one of the country's most unusual patronage pots, used by both parties to pay off partisans; in the face of this unrelenting self-interest, there were few standing up for the Yukon. The Territory could only lose as a result.

In the midst of this period of gloom, partisanship, and retrenchment, the First World War provided an interval of unity and a feeling of shared purpose. Despite the Territory's feelings of isolation and neglect, or perhaps in part because of them, Yukoners responded to the war with an enthusiasm matching or exceeding that of all other parts of Canada. The Yukon's per capita rate of enlistment was the highest in the country, as was the rate of purchase of war savings bonds. Although the Yukon newspapers carried a good deal of international news, the outbreak of war in August 1914 was unexpected; it "fell like a bombshell" on the residents.[58] The response was instantaneous and enthusiastic; Martha Black, the Commissioner's wife, described the effect of the news on a theatre party:

> As though answering an overwhelming urge, they stood in unison and commenced to sing "God Save the King." The effect was electrical. With one move, the audience was on its feet, and never in the world, I dare say, was our national anthem sung with greater fervour or more depth of feeling than in that moving picture house in that little town on the rim of the Arctic. Although eight thousand miles of mountain, land and sea separated us from London, the heart of the Empire, yet England's King was our King, and England's Empire was our Empire.[59]

During the war, Yukon women played their usual strong role in shaping the community's response to external events. They took an active role in supporting the war effort, not confining themselves to rolling bandages, knitting socks, or supplying tobacco and other "comforts" to the troops, but actively moulding opinion in the Territory. The women's organization most in the forefront was the Imperial Order Daughters of the Empire, which founded several chapters in the Territory during the war to promote the war effort and loyalty to Britain. Through the I.O.D.E., women served as tireless propagandists for the Allied cause. The minutes of the monthly meetings of the I.O.D.E. record the presentation of books to the schools as prizes for student essays on patriotic themes, and the disbursement of large sums for Belgian relief, presents for the troops at Christmas, and the like. The December 1915 meeting of the Whitehorse chapter of the order opened with the reading of a patriotic verse:

> So that tyranny will fall
> Canada will give her all;
> With her dearest she will part
> For the cause that stirs her heart.
> Take this message to the Huns,
> Canada's behind the guns.

The chapter then received one hundred copies of a pamphlet entitled "Why Don't You Wear a Uniform?" to be sold and distributed locally. The Whitehorse chapter was asked by Commissioner Black if it would like to contribute money to buy a machine gun for the Yukon Machine Gun detachment. The government employees had already bought one, at a cost of $1,000. The ladies of the I.O.D.E. gladly complied, and raised another $1,000 for a second gun.[60]

One unfortunate result of the Yukon's patriotism was an increase in the drift of population out of the Territory. A number of Yukoners were members of militia units in southern Canada, and they quickly left to join their regiments. Between a hundred and two hundred men volunteered for service in the first days of the war, and by the end of 1914 several hundred more went outside to enlist.[61] Since the population of the Yukon in 1914 was only about seven thousand, the departure of so many healthy men in their twenties and thirties would obviously have a depressing effect on the Territory's economy. Indeed, all through the war the operators of mining concerns in the Yukon complained of labour shortages, and some had to curtail their operations.

Most Yukoners enlisted quietly, for there was little hoopla associated with recruiting in the Territory, no "inspiring sounds of marching bands nor the thrilling sight of magnificent battalions marching past," as Martha Black put it.[62] An exception to this rule was Joe Boyle's Yukon Detachment of the 2nd Regiment, Canadian Mounted Rifles. He was probably the richest resident in the Territory in 1914, and as soon as hostilities broke out he organized a machine gun company of fifty-four men at a personal cost of $50,000.[63] The regiment was accepted into the Canadian Expeditionary Force by Colonel Sam Hughes, Minister of Militia and Defence, and left Dawson by steamer on October 10 to a tremendous ovation: "Under the blaze of lights and with the band playing and the populace shouting, the boys of the Boyle-Yukon detachment got away for war."[64] Boyle became famous in the later stages of the war as the "saviour of Roumania" from the Bolsheviks, and the supposed lover of the glamorous Queen Marie. After his European exploits he did not return to the Yukon to repair his ruined empire. Instead, he turned his energies to promoting oil deals in eastern Europe. He died in England in 1923.

The patriotic enthusiasm for a distinctively Yukon contribution to the war effort continued when Commissioner George Black organized another Yukon contingent. Black, in his forties when the war broke out, resigned his post, enlisted in the army, and was given permission in August 1916 to organize a company of infantry, which later became the 17th Machine Gun Company. That the rush to the colours was not quite as spontaneous in 1916 as it had been in 1914 is suggested by the recruiting letter Black wrote and circulated in the Territory:

You cannot fail to realize that it is the duty of every able-bodied man in Canada, who is not supporting helpless dependents, to offer his services to fight for the Empire in this great crisis. That Yukon has done well, that many of her Men have gone, that Yukon women are doing their duty, does not relieve you. It is a matter of individual manhood. Each must decide for himself whether or not he will play the part of a man. We have remained at home in safety while others have been fighting our battles for over two years, although no more obligated to do so than you or I have been. They have, for us, in many cases, made the supreme sacrifice. They are calling to you and to me for help. Are we going to fail them, or will you come with us?[65]

In 1916 Black led his men to England, and the formidable Martha bullied politicians until she was permitted to go with him, the only woman on the troop ship with several thousand men. The fact that she had just turned fifty made this devotion to the cause (and to her husband) all the more remarkable; of course, Martha always liked adventure.

While the men were, in the words of the popular war song, ''somewhere in France,'' patriotic activity continued at home. Support for the war effort in the Yukon did not seem to dim even as the dreadful casualty statistics mounted. Though the ladies of the I.O.D.E. prayed at every meeting that the war might end, they fulminated against the Hun right up to Armistice Day. Virtually every social, political, cultural, and athletic event held in the Yukon throughout the war became a fund-raising event, and the Yukoners' efforts continued at a high level until the end of the war. It was a matter of intense pride to Yukoners that their per capita contributions far exceeded those for Canada as a whole. The Canadian Patriotic Fund, one of the more important of the numerous war relief organizations, reported in June 1916 that the Yukon, with a population of eight thousand, had contributed $62,000, or nearly $8 per capita. The average for Canada was about $1.[66]

Some forms of patriotic self-denial, however, the Yukoners shunned. The First World War saw the triumph of prohibition in much of the rest of Canada, as patriotic Canadians, anxious to share if only vicariously the suffering of the troops, voted to deny themselves the pleasures of the cup. Not so the Yukon; although the Territory was intensely patriotic, the use of alcohol was too thoroughly ingrained in the fabric of its society to be uprooted even in the cause of thrashing the Kaiser. A plebiscite held in August 1916 on the question of territorial prohibition saw the anti-prohibitionist ''wets'' win by three votes out of over seventeen hundred cast.[67]

The Territory's contributions of manpower and wealth to the war effort only accelerated the Yukon's decline. Each year more and more people packed their bags and left Dawson and Whitehorse for the last time. Even those who still retained some measure of commitment to the Yukon had fallen into a pattern of spending as much as half the year outside. For those in the north, the annual leave-takings of fall had become a mournful symbol of the Yukon's decay:

> The last boat's departure was a considerable rite in Dawson City, for it effectively marked the beginning of winter. It was invariably a sad and sentimental occasion. The dock was jammed with people, for the entire town turned out for the ceremony of leave-taking. The last boat was always packed with the wealthy going out for the winter, the fortunate going out forever, and the sick going out to die. The atmosphere was electric with brave untruths. Every last soul on the boat pretended to be returning the following spring, but in point of fact few ever did so. The last boat had a curious and depressing finality about it. For some reason those people who were quitting the country for good always waited for the last boat, and the last moment, before they did so. Thus it became more than just another boat leaving town; it became a symbol of the town's decay. There was always a forced joviality among those on the dock who called "see you next spring" to those on the deck, but when the final whistle sounded everybody on dock and deck began quite openly to weep. Then the boat pulled out into the river and turned its prow towards the south, leaving a little crowd of people standing on an empty wharf, looking cold and miserable and quite forlorn.[68]

In the fall of 1918, this ritual of leave-taking turned into an unthinkable tragedy which in a sense, tore the heart out of the Yukon. That year the last boat from Dawson was crowded with the usual mix of seasonal transients — Yukoners, Alaskans, and others — leaving the north forever. Lulu Mae Eads, the former dance-hall queen, was leaving, as was Captain Alexander of the Engineer Mine, the O'Brien family of Dawson, and too many other citizens of the Territory. They were all heading south, up the Yukon River by steamer, across the White Pass on the railway to the docks at Skagway. There they waited, celebrating their liberation from the northern winter, for steamship passage south.

At the end of October, close to three hundred of them found passage aboard the s.s. *Princess Sophia*. Commanded by Captain Locke on its regular run down the Lynn Canal from Skagway to Vancouver, its cabins jammed to overflowing with a cross-section of northern society, the ship ran onto Vanderbilt Reef in a blinding snowstorm. It sat on the reef for a day and a half, while the captain and would-be rescuers in ships hovering nearby debated the wisdom of attempting to take the passengers off across a low reef swept by a heavy swell. Then, on the night of October 25, the wind increased. Changing direction, it blew the ship off the reef, splitting her plates. The *Princess Sophia* sank quickly; there were no survivors. All of the passengers and crew died of drowning, suffocation by bunker oil, or exposure. Close to 10 per cent of the Territory's white population had perished in less than half an hour.[69]

With the Yukon weakened by the ravages of a far distant war and the decimation of the *Princess Sophia* disaster, regional politicians had little fight left for the series of body blows delivered in 1918 by Arthur Meighen, the Minister of the Interior. With little warning, Meighen announced the abolition of the position of Commissioner, the dismantling of the elected Territorial Council, a slashing of the federal budget for the Territory by almost half, and the closure of several government offices. Protests were registered, and for a time it seemed that the energy and commitment of the early reform drive had re-emerged, but the federal government and the House of Commons paid virtually no attention to cries of distress from the frontier, and the proposals passed with little debate. The evisceration of Yukon government and politics met with indifference in the rest of the country. Later representations to Meighen and the government succeeded in reversing some of the measures, and re-establishing the Territorial Council, but at a weakened level.[70]

In twenty years the Yukon had gone from fame to obscurity. Having gained, after a concerted fight, some significant political reforms, Yukoners suffered the ignominy of having the federal government declare to the country that the Territory no longer deserved the financial and political resources it had come to count on. There could be no greater symbol of how far the Yukon had fallen from the heady days of the Klondike gold rush than the sight of territorial representatives scurrying off to Ottawa to beg for political rights only slightly greater than those of a large city and to plead with authorities to keep a few government buildings in Dawson City open. The gold rush was surely over. Could the future hold more bad news? The few Yukoners who remained could be excused for wondering if worse was to come.

CHAPTER SEVEN

The Lean Years, 1918–1939

At the end of the First World War the Yukon was in a sorry state. An economic recession, war losses, and finally the *Princess Sophia* disaster had pushed the Territory into the doldrums. Ignored by the federal government, with a transient population, it seemed to many Yukoners almost as if the gold rush had never happened. In 1921 there were only 4,157 people in the Yukon Territory, less than half the population of ten years earlier. Dawson had shrunk to one-third of its size in 1911, a twentieth of that of 1898. Even Whitehorse, whose population usually grew in the summer months with the increase in transportation activity, held only 331 people in 1921, down from 727 in the last census. Close to fifteen hundred of the Yukoners were native people — the major constant in the region — who continued to live off the land, and could be found in the isolated seasonal camps of the fur trade districts. Most whites, except for some missionaries, a small number of fur traders, and the Royal North-West Mounted Police officers, lived in the towns.

Before the war it had seemed that the Yukon was headed toward social stability. There was an increasing ratio of families to single men in the Territory, and the ratio between males and females had become more nearly even. But the war had reversed that promising trend. In 1921 there were about twice as many males as females. The gold rush pattern of a Territory dominated by young single males on the move had been re-established.

Most of the prospectors who had given the Territory so much of its character had left. Gone, too, were many of the businessmen and promoters who had swarmed north during the gold rush. Most Yukon communities seemed to be constantly saying good-bye to someone, either at the steamboat dock or, increasingly, at the funeral parlour.

The demographic slide was, of course, the result of the implosion of the Yukon economy. Gold production declined steadily in the aftermath of the war, falling as low as 26,000 fine ounces of gold in 1926, a shocking collapse from a high of over 1 million ounces in 1900. The fabulously rich Klondike goldfields had, it seemed, finally been picked clean. At war's end, there was little to replace the decaying gold-mining sector. Promising gold returns from the Mayo-Keno area — the post-rush hope for the Yukon — in the war years, aided by temporarily high prices, had turned sharply downward in the early 1920s, with production declining from 360,000 fine ounces in 1916 to only 19,000 fine ounces four years later.[1]

Other minerals were hit equally hard. The copper mines, primarily in the Whitehorse copper belt, demonstrated the continued vulnerability of Yukon mining to world market forces. High wartime prices had fueled a major expansion, enabling producers to overcome the otherwise prohibitive production and transportation costs. The end of military purchasing forced prices down to pre-war levels, and tore the heart out of the Yukon copper sector. Yukon mines had shipped more than 2.8 million pounds of copper in 1916, the peak year of production. Shipments fell to only 165,000 pounds in 1919, and stopped altogether in 1921. Trial shipments were sent outside in 1928 and again in 1930, but low prices and high transportation costs made the exercise unprofitable.

From time to time there was a glimmer of hope, but each one seemed eventually to flicker and die. The Silver King mine near Galena Creek had seemed to be one such glimmer. Trial shipments of silver ore had been sent to smelters in Trail, B.C., and San Francisco, but transportation costs were so high that only the highest-grade deposits could be developed profitably, and within two years the mine closed. The closure of the Silver King property in particular made the glory of the Klondike years seem a rapidly fading dream.[2]

Interest had, however, been spurred in the district, and prospectors continued to scour the hills for other minerals. On July 10, 1919, Louis Beauvette staked a claim, which he named Roulette, atop Keno Hill. News of the strike reached A. K. Schellinger, a mining engineer with the Yukon Gold Company, who interested his superiors in the new prospects for silver and lead. The company quickly invested in the property, and a small rush to Keno Hill followed. Over six hundred claims were filed in the next year, and by the summer of 1920, some one hundred men were at work on the property.

But the Keno Hill mines, although rich, were hard to reach, since the swift and shallow waters of the Stewart River made navigation difficult. The Yukon River steamers could not ascend this tributary; even the shallow-draught vessels used on the river could go no further than Mayo. Carrying the tons of ore from the mines, located some thirty miles away, was almost prohibitively expensive. Through much of the 1920s, it cost more to move the silver and lead from Keno to Mayo than it did to ship the supplies from Mayo to markets in the south. Only the fact that the deposits on Keno Hill were extraordinarily rich made working them worthwhile. The company

Silver-lead ore, mined from the Elsa-Keno area, was stock-piled along the Mayo riverfront awaiting shipment to refineries in the south. YUKON TERRITORIAL ARCHIVES

held back from expensive investments in the property, preferring to develop only silver-rich veins, which permitted the ore to be shipped directly to market. The Yukon Gold Company exploited its properties until 1924, at which time it leased its claims to Treadwell Yukon Company.

The Keno Hill properties were given a future by the work of Livingston Wernecke, a geologist working for Alaska Treadwell. A shy, intense man, who ran his mining camps with a firm hand and a strong sense for minerals, Wernecke started work on a property close to the Y.G.C. mine. Unlike the Yukon Gold Company, the newly formed Treadwell Yukon Company was prepared to make long-term commitments to the Keno Hill property. Well-informed as a result of Wernecke's thorough work and careful observations, Treadwell looked for ways of making their mine more cost-efficient. Transportation, of course, remained the major barrier. In the winter of 1922–23, Treadwell brought in a caterpillar tractor train to move supplies and ore, which radically changed the economics of mining on Keno Hill. It also constructed a concentrating mill in 1924, further reducing transportation costs, and permitting the development of the less valuable milling-grade ores.

The Yukon Gold Company and Treadwell Yukon Company controlled the Keno field. They poured large amounts of money into the venture, gambling that as yet uncovered deposits would pay off their investments. Smaller operators, unable to raise enough investment capital, had no option but to sell to the two dominant firms. The purchase of the assets of the United Keno Hill Company in 1924 allowed Treadwell to rationalize its mining operations. This corporate concentration forced many small developers out of business or required them to rely on Treadwell transportation and milling facilities. Treadwell Yukon Company had made major strides in adapting mining and transportation technology to the conditions of the Mayo-Keno region, and had enabled the silver-lead mines to take over the lead in the territorial economy. The project was not large — Treadwell directly employed only one hundred men in 1924 — but by the middle of the 1920s the Keno mines were clearly carrying the Yukon economy.

With Treadwell Yukon Company in the forefront, lead production reached almost 8.9 million pounds by 1930; silver output also reached a new peak that year, topping 3.7 million fine ounces, 14 per cent of all Canadian production. Most importantly, the Keno deposits were rich enough and the Treadwell operations sufficiently stable and well-financed to survive fluctuations in world prices. Exploratory efforts, now aided by the use of airplanes, continued as Treadwell attempted to expand its reserve base. Even the best planning, however, could not offset the chaos that befell the Treadwell operations in the early 1930s. The onset of the world depression, declining world prices, and the final exhaustion of the principal Keno Hill deposits threatened the demise of the industry. In the fall of 1932, the concentrating mill on Keno Hill was closed; after carrying the Yukon for a decade, it looked as though the Keno mines were about to collapse. After several unprofitable attempts to develop new properties, Treadwell closed its Yukon operations in 1934.

The expansion of mining activity had changed Keno from a transient tent village to a permanent settlement. A townsite had been set aside in 1922, cabins, a liquor store, and a stable were built. The seeming stability and richness of the Keno Hill strikes had encouraged a small number of miners to bring their wives and families into the town. Now they found themselves faced with upheaval.

But then, to the delight and surprise of corporate investors and labourers alike, work on Galena Hill uncovered several new rich veins, and major United States government purchases of silver ore following the passage of the Silver Purchase Act of 1935 pushed the price back up. A concentrating mill was built on site and, in the midst of general economic chaos, Treadwell Yukon Company announced that the firm was about to expand. The development of new mines, like Calumet, offset the closure of worked-over properties such as Silver King. In 1937, Yukon mines produced almost 4 million fine ounces of silver, a record for the Territory, and over 6 million pounds of lead, with most of the ore coming from Treadwell properties.

The Keno operation demonstrated the radically different approaches to northern mining. The Yukon Gold Company had high-graded its properties, taking the best ore out as quickly as possible, investing minimal amounts in local infrastructure and abandoning the mines at the first hints of unprofitability, a common pattern in the Yukon. Treadwell Yukon, which invested heavily in roads, equipment, mills, and other facilities, took a longer-term view. Its activities sustained the local and territorial economy, encouraged the growth of Mayo and the development of a new community at Keno. Both the Y.G.C. and Treadwell Yukon made money on their investments; according to one estimate, the companies earned a profit of approximately 20 per cent on the $23 million worth of silver and lead taken from the area between 1919 and 1942. Even Treadwell, however, fell into the pattern of removing corporate profits from the Territory. Wernecke attempted to expand company exploration activities, but had to defer to company officials who wanted the Keno profits for operations outside the Yukon.

From the beginning, miners and companies had petitioned the territorial and federal governments for assistance with roads and river transportation. But the Territory did not have much money at its disposal, and the federal government provided only modest aid. Even in the provision of roads, for example, private enterprise in the form of Treadwell Yukon was compelled to contribute close to a third of the cost of road construction in the Mayo to Keno area. The Territorial Council also assisted with bridges, subsidized the Side Streams Navigation Company (a subsidiary of the White Pass and Yukon Route), provided an airfield, and moved the territorial assay office to Keno City for the convenience of the miners. Political representation came more slowly; the Mayo district lacked a voice in the Territorial Council until 1926, when it was permitted to elect one of the four members.[3]

The Keno Hill mining development lacked the drama and excitement of the Klondike gold rush: Louis Beauvette is not as well-remembered as Carmack, Skookum Jim, and Dawson Charlie; Treadwell investing in concentrating mills and access roads was not as colourful as the stampeders straining up the Chilkoot Pass; silver and lead, for all their value, lacked the mystique of gold — there was no Robert Service at Keno to immortalize "the men who moil for lead." In the 1920s and 1930s, however, Yukoners were grateful for the Keno Hill mines, for they played a major role in sustaining the Territory. Only the silver and lead operations of the Yukon Gold Company and particularly the Treadwell Yukon Company prevented a total economic collapse in the lean years after the First World War.

The importance of the silver-lead mines also emphasized the continued deterioration of the Klondike goldfields. Territorial gold production had started to decline during the First World War but during the 1920s it dropped precipitously. In 1900, the Yukon had produced almost 80 per cent of Canada's gold; by 1926 only 1.5 per cent. Canadians could almost be forgiven for believing that the Klondike had disappeared.[4]

Gold-mining did continue, of course, but not in a way that Klondike stampeders would recognize. By the end of the war the once-prominent dredging companies were facing bankruptcy. Granville Mining, North West Corporation, and Canadian Klondyke were all in receivership, and the situation at the other companies was no better. Three companies, Yukon Gold Corporation, New Northwest Corporation, and Burrall and Baird Company, accounted for three-quarters of the territorial production. About eighty small operators, some still using the techniques of the gold rush era, could be found in the goldfields, but their returns continued to decline. The once-rich gravels of the Klondike Valley had been all but picked clean. New techniques and machinery capable of handling vast quantities of material quickly and efficiently were required to produce a profit. The development of new ground-thawing techniques, for example, enabled dredges to move more quickly through the gravels. Despite such advances, however, the companies were not in a strong financial position.[5]

During this period the federal government continued to support the concentration of ownership and production in the Klondike goldfields. Despite the loud protests from the small operators, the government again amended mining regulations to permit even larger concessions in the Klondike fields. In 1923, a number of investors created the Yukon Consolidated Gold Corporation out of the existing firms, including the three largest: Burrall and Baird, New North West, and Canadian Klondyke. The transition reflected the stagnation in gold production. It was a sign of the times that in 1929, the year of the great consolidation, placer gold operations produced less than 30 per cent of the Yukon's total mineral production. Gold was no longer king in the Yukon.

But there were still vivid characters in the goldfields, notably the ever-controversial A. N. C. Treadgold. Although his financial affairs were tangled, Treadgold now controlled the Yukon Consolidated Gold Corporation. He and his rival Joe Boyle had once been the Klondike's great gold entrepreneurs, and he made a triumphant return — a symbol of the Yukon's past optimism, and perhaps Dawson's last hope for a prosperous future. Lewis Green described Treadgold's re-entry into Yukon life:

Gold mining continued well after the end of the Gold Rush. The once dynamic and vibrant creek communities had become, by the 1920s, company towns, occupied on a seasonal basis. These buildings and dredge tailings were located near the mouth of Bonanza Creek, 1922.
PUBLIC ARCHIVES OF CANADA

He was bubbling over with enthusiasm for his new dreams, and the local people, having watched the struggle of the operating companies under receivership, were certain that better days lay ahead. At Bear Creek, he recognized all the old-timers who had worked with him in the past and greeted each one by name as if only a few days had lapsed since he left the Klondike of 1912.[6]

Behind Treadgold's confident exterior, however, lay only half-formed plans for the troubled Klondike mining operations. Treadgold paid little attention to the dredges, thus leaving the most profitable side of his operation starved for cash, while spending great sums on experimentation, bringing in electric shovels in 1925 to excavate the gravels. His financial position, based on intricate financial dealings in England, remained shaky. He was away from the Yukon for long stretches, and had to depend on managers like Andrew Baird and W. J. Rendell to handle the day-to-day operations of the Y.C.G.C. His constant stream of instructions from London was too much for the strong-willed Baird, who was eventually fired.

Treadgold paid little attention to shareholders, ignoring the advice of his employees and dealing ruthlessly with anyone who questioned or challenged his authority. Lack of planning brought on numerous crises; in the spring of 1929, uncertainties about the solvency of the Treadgold operations forced a number of suppliers to withhold their goods and convinced many employees to seek work elsewhere.

Not surprisingly, Treadgold eventually faced a major challenge to his control of the goldfields. Insiders, led by Yukon pioneer Tom Patton, campaigned to unseat him. The protest group, labelled "The Conspiracy" by Treadgold supporters, attempted a shareholders' revolt, over the determined opposition of their target. By 1930, they had wrested control of the day-to-day operations from Treadgold, but the speculator kept his grip on the financial strings. They also petitioned the Secretary of State to investigate Yukon Consolidated Gold Corporation's internal affairs; Ottawa accountant G. T. Clarkson was appointed to conduct the inquiry. Clarkson's report, issued in the midst of the shareholders' struggle, offered a damning critique of Treadgold's administration and provided fuel for a court challenge to his control of the company.

The judgement of the court, issued in the spring of 1932, contained a strong denunciation of Treadgold's affairs, focusing particularly on his secretiveness. The judge ordered a cancellation of Treadgold's shares in the Y.C.G.C. While Treadgold sulked — his friends thought him near-suicidal — his opponents moved to take over the company. Andrew Baird managed the Klondike operations, while Tom Patton took over Treadgold's role as president. But Treadgold was not finished. While company affairs in the Yukon staggered on, under-financed and without long-term direction, Treadgold received a new hearing in Toronto in 1933. He lost again, the judge once more agreeing that he had acted improperly in promoting the company. A. N. C. Treadgold had devoted much of his adult life to the Klondike mines; the decisions stripped him of all shares and involvement with his creation, the Y.C.G.C. He continued his appeals to the Canadian courts and later tried his luck in front of British judges. These failed as well, but Treadgold persevered, obsessed with regaining control over his Yukon company. In the end, separated from his wife and bankrupt, he borrowed money from anyone who would lend it to him, promising them a share of the Y.C.G.C. when he finally won his case. He died in 1951, very much a Yukon promoter of the old style, still pursuing the dream of regaining his crown as King of the Klondike.

The Treadgold controversy had drawn much attention away from the practical problems of mining in the Yukon. As Treadgold himself had demonstrated, only large, well-capitalized companies could continue in this increasingly marginal industry and region. To exploit the resource efficiently and quickly, a complex organization, including expensive and complex dredges and hydraulic facilities, work camps, miles of roads, and power plants was essential.

Ironically, the onset of world-wide economic calamity in 1929 led to a return of some prosperity for the Yukon goldfields. The price of gold, locked at around $20 an ounce for decades, was officially raised to $35 in 1933, making many operations in the Yukon suddenly profitable. Much of the credit for reversing the tattered fortunes of the Y.C.G.C. belonged to its manager, W. H. S. McFarland, who straightened out the mess left by Treadgold's quixotic administration. Dredging and stripping operations were reorganized and expanded, and the company returned to profitability. By the middle of the 1930s, gold production had reversed its downward trend. In 1939, Yukon producers delivered over 88,000 fine ounces of gold worth over $3 million to market, the highest level in twenty years, and prospectors returned to the field in large numbers, particularly in the Carmacks district.

The improved economic picture did not come without problems. The Yukon Consolidated Gold Corporation faced numerous complaints, particularly from its employees. Workers demanded better wages and complained bitterly about their working and housing conditions, particularly as long as Andrew Baird remained in charge. He was, nonetheless, a better employer than Treadgold had been. As the wife of one employee commented in 1931, "I admit that you are a tightwad and a skinflint but as long as you are in charge the employees know that their wages will be paid promptly."[7] Workers' complaints were, of course, limited by the high levels of unemployment outside and the comparative stability of work in the Yukon. With McFarland in charge, and with company shareholders looking with enthusiasm toward the future of the industry, working conditions improved and the industry gained a measure of stability it had not known for years. The revitalization of the Klondike fields came as a pleasant surprise, for most had written the industry off as an aging relic of the gold rush. Collapse had been close at hand, but survival now seemed assured, at least for the short term.

In the midst of the economic uncertainty of the post-war period, the Yukon fur trade remained stable. The international demand for furs had picked up appreciably in the last years of the war, and escalated even more quickly in the 1920s. The territorial government had previously paid little attention to this seemingly minor component of the regional economy, but surging prices and demand, expanded competition, and the prospect of widespread over-hunting forced the government to consider measures to regulate the industry.[8]

Initially, the natives had much of the Yukon trade to themselves, although prospectors and miners occasionally brought furs to market. Once the stability and profitability of the Yukon trade had been well-established, however, white trappers were attracted in increasing numbers. Fur prices remained high through most of the 1920s and 1930s. As Louis Levy, a San Francisco fur merchant wrote in 1927:

> Lynx, Red Fox, Cross Fox and Mink are in very strong demand and in fact all furs from the Yukon are bringing around 25% more than last year at this time....I handle all Shorty Chambers' furs, and have Johnny Johns the native buying furs around Carcross country. Am handling Thayer's furs from Carmacks. These traders are up against Taylor and Drury's who are hard competitors, and we can pay more than they do, as I get better prices and can pay more....Business has been

very good for the past four months and all indications point to a good season.[9]

The territorial government left traders and trappers alone to establish their own rules of exchange, counting on the Royal Canadian Mounted Police to control any abuse of the game resources. The trapping of individual species, particularly beaver and marten, was suspended on several occasions when over-hunting threatened the long-term stability of the resource, but these regulations were imposed cautiously in order to prevent hardship on the largely native hunting population. The Yukon remained out of step with southern conservation concerns, its comparative lack of regulations in contrast to the more heavily controlled conditions elsewhere in Canada. A major redrafting of the Yukon Game Ordinance in 1938 brought Yukon practices closer to national norms, but throughout most of the Territory, trappers continued to do much as they pleased.

The fur industry contributed thousands of dollars to the territorial economy, making up nearly 10 per cent of its revenue. Returns on the trade fluctuated from a low of $78,000 in 1920–21 to a high of over $600,000 in 1927–28, an exceptionally good year in which furs almost matched the value of gold produced. The industry required limited capital investment, except by the largest fur-trading companies, and provided a regular source of income for several hundred Indians and whites throughout the Territory. For these reasons, it quickly expanded through the Yukon. In 1921, there were twenty-seven licensed fur traders in the Territory working out of eighteen locations; nine years later, there were forty-six posts in operation, owned by thirty different operators.

The fur trade was an industry unlike the other main sectors of the economy. The trappers were independent workers, not wage labourers, and were not tied by contract to a particular trading company. Most of the trappers were Indians; almost none of the traders were. Dominating the trade was the locally-owned Taylor and Drury Company, run by Isaac Taylor and William Drury. They operated their own supply steamer, freeing them from dependence on the White Pass and Yukon Route ships, a necessity given the eleven widely scattered posts operated by the company in 1930.

The trading system, like the pre-gold rush mining economy, operated largely on credit. Reliable and skillful traders had no difficulty securing a winter's outfit from one of the many traders operating in the Territory, the loan or "jawbone" to be repaid with the returns from the winter's harvest. Indians, of course, knew the intricacies of the fur trade well by this time, and readily exploited competitive situations when they worked to their advantage. Those in isolated areas, like Ross River, often had to travel long distances if they wished to benefit from competitive bidding, but in periods of intense competition small independent traders carried their wares

Away from the Whitehorse-Dawson corridor, the fur trade remained the dominant form of economic activity. Taylor and Drury Company, a Yukon-based company had posts around the territory, including one here at Teslin, 1921. YUKON TERRITORIAL ARCHIVES

Claude Tidd, an R.C.M.P. officer and a talented photographer who left a remarkable set of images of his northern activities, is shown outside a wall tent with a native family, near Rampart House, 1920. YUKON TERRITORIAL ARCHIVES

throughout the Territory. The traders, of course, sought to tie the Indian trappers to their post. Taylor and Drury accomplished this by paying the trappers for their furs with company tokens, usable only at the firm's outposts. But the Yukon escaped the corporate concentration that had overtaken much of the northern fur trade. In the neighbouring Northwest Territories, the competitive traders drawn to the region during the 1920s sold out one by one to the powerful and well-financed Hudson's Bay Company, which controlled much of the industry to the east by the 1930s. The H.B.C. did return to the Yukon, re-establishing its long-abandoned post at Fort Selkirk in 1937, but did not expand much from that base.[10]

In general, native people benefited from the prosperous fur trade of the 1920s and 1930s. Because of their ability to live off the land, they were able to wait out temporary declines in fur production and short-term fluctuations in fur prices; white trappers, in contrast, arrived when prices were high and usually left when returns fell off. There were occasional problems between native and white trappers over the latter's use of poison, as well as complaints against each other for over-hunting. A number of white men who entered the trade, like Dan Cadzow at Rampart House, Poole Field at Ross River, and Eugene Jacquot at Burwash, married native women and stayed in the Yukon with their families.[11]

The vitality of the fur trade rested on the persistence of Indian harvesting. So long as natives continued to live off the land, and away from the mining communities, the fur trade flourished. Through the 1920s and 1930s, when the mining economy struggled for stability and offered few openings for any Yukoners, the native people continued to stay away from it, preferring the harvesting lifestyle to the dubious benefits of mining. Sustained by native participation and steady international demand for northern furs, the Yukon trade remained a vital element of the regional economy.

While the Indians played a crucial role in the stability of the Yukon's oldest commercial activity, they also participated in the Territory's newest industry — big-game hunting. Yukoners, natives and many whites, still depended on wild animals for sustenance. That rich Americans were prepared to pay hundreds of dollars to hunt for big-game trophies on the last frontier seemed rather odd to people who still regularly hunted for food, but it brought in money, so no one laughed openly at the Yankee hunters.[12]

Big-game hunters had come north before the First World War, but their numbers increased steadily in the 1920s. The Yukon had a good reputation for the quality and size of its animals; the White River area, the southern lakes, and the Mayo area in particular attracted considerable attention from hunters, around thirty of whom came to the Territory each year through the 1920s, a number that dropped off quite sharply during the Depression. Many of the Yukon's most prominant long-term residents — the Jacquot brothers, Shorty Austin, Charlie Baxter, and Indian guides Paddy Smith and Jimmy Kane among others — participated in the new industry. Most of the guides operated on a part-time basis only, for there was not enough business to sustain them all full-time. Only a few, the Jacquots, Baxter, and the most famous, Johnny Johns, achieved much stability in their operations.

Native people, who did much of the actual guiding and thus ensured the successful reputation of the Yukon industry, had limits placed on their participation in it. Under a 1923 regulation, Indians were barred from serving as chief guides. That regulation was later eased, giving the Commissioner wide discretionary powers to determine if the Indians were capable of handling the financial and administrative tasks associated with guiding.

Johnny Johns, a Carcross Indian, got around the regulations by becoming enfranchised. Others, like Billy Hall and George Johnson of Teslin, had their applications turned down and were forced to hire on with white guides if they wished to work in the industry. Pressure for such racism clearly came from the desire of white guides to eliminate competition. Upon learning that Johnny Johns had received a licence, one government agent claimed, "It really means the taking away of the livelihood of guiding from the white men if any more Indians are granted the privilege of acting as Chief Guides."[13]

Big-game hunting earned the Yukon much favourable publicity, for the hunters wrote widely and enthusiastically about their frontier experiences. But though the territorial government exacted its toll through large non-resident licence fees, and though the hunters spent freely during their short stay in the Yukon, their numbers were so small that the overall economic impact on the region was comparatively slight.

There was, however, another side to the tourism industry in the Yukon. The mystique of the Klondike gold rush had grown rather than diminished over time. During the rush, dozens of travelogues, diaries, and novels had been written about it. Newspaper articles by the hundreds had helped fuel widespread interest in all aspects of the Klondike, and in the 1910s and 1920s, publication of Robert Service's poetry and Jack London's short stories strengthened a growing North American fascination with the far northwest. Migration to the last frontier was a possibility for the young and adventurous, and the passion to see the Yukon was still there.

The costs and difficulties of access to the northwest seemed an unavoidable barrier to regular tourist traffic, and yet, each summer a number of people made their arrangements and ventured north to see the land they had read so much about. But Yukon business leaders did little to encourage or exploit this southern fascination with their Territory. There were many hotels still standing, remnants of the gold rush days, but most stood abandoned and decaying. In the busy summer months, when business travel on the trains and steamboats peaked, room for casual travellers was often scarce. A few saw the potential, however, and following the example of the big-game guides, began to organize for annual migrations of tourists.

The Territory had much to offer tourists — the dramatic mountains and lakes of the southern Yukon, the historic Yukon River journey aboard the fascinating and well-appointed river boats, and of course the many attractions of the Dawson area. The White Pass and Yukon Route did its utmost to develop the business, for it was desperate to find passengers and cargo for their under-utilized train and stern-wheeler service. Coastal steamship firms, including the Alaska Steamship Company, the Pacific Steamship Company and the Canadian Pacific Steamship Company, were persuaded to arrange two-day stop-overs at Skagway, giving the travellers time to ride the train to Carcross, with longer trips possible. Special excursions were organized out of Carcross, taking travellers on a beautiful journey along Tagish Lake and through "Canada's Alps." The highlight of the trip was Ben-My-Chree, a gardener's oasis on the edge of the frontier established by a retired English couple, Mr. and Mrs. Otto Partridge, at the south end of Tagish Lake. The trip continued from there to Brooks Inlet, where tourists travelled a tiny railroad that joined Tagish and Atlin lakes. Another boat carried them across the lake to the old gold-mining town of Atlin. Altogether, it was a wonderful journey, marked by signs of the famous Klondike rush and some of Canada's most striking scenery. Those who made the journey spoke enthusiastically of the expedition, but were not able to convince southerners in sufficient numbers to make the southern Yukon a major tourist destination.[14]

In the inter-war years, access to the Yukon continued to be a major problem. In an era when most major investments were put on hold pending a major economic revival, emphasis was placed on maintaining existing transportation facilities and lowering the still excessive costs of moving about the Territory. The Yukon's modest road system became increasingly important after the war, serving as an off-season adjunct to the river steamers. This was particularly true in the Mayo district, where unnavigable rivers forced developers to construct roads to the mines. Yukoners, however, ran into strong resistance from the federal government on this score, for road construction in the north was costly and the returns to the nation slight. Thus, repeated territorial requests for assistance failed to sway a federal government which still doubted that there would be permanent development in the Territory. Through most of the 1920s, the Yukon government could do little more than maintain existing roads and assist with the construction of trails to promising mining areas. Even the Yukon's main land route, the winter Overland Trail from Whitehorse to Dawson City, had fallen into serious disrepair, and declining traffic had forced many of the roadhouses to close. Laura Berton described the new order of things:

> Many of the roadhouses which in the old days had been spotted every twenty-two miles along the winter road were closed. Passengers now had to provide their own lunches and these were eaten in the open after being thawed out by a bon-fire on the side of the trail. In the old days we had made the journey in less than a week. Now the stage only made a post a day and, if the trail was bad, the trip often took longer than a fortnight.[15]

The White Pass and Yukon Route cancelled its overland service in 1921, no longer needing the route to maintain control of the lucrative summer mail contract. Various small operators tried to keep the trail in operation, but with little financial success. Dawsonites lost out further when the trail was diverted towards Mayo, which now generated the bulk of the winter traffic. Northerners asked for more; George Black wrote, "What my constituents are more interested in are roads, for in so vast a country transport is a vast problem." The government was not listening.

River transport was more stable, but even here the corporate concentration and declining service that characterized the entire Yukon economy was evident. The collapse of Side Streams Navigation a year before the end of the war had removed the only major competitor to the British and Yukon Navigation Company upstream of Dawson, and it moved into the void left on the Mayo route. With the exception of Taylor and Drury's pup steamer, *Thistle* (later replaced by *Yukon Rose*), which supplied the firm's widely scattered posts, B.Y.N.C. had the Yukon rivers almost to itself.

For the first few years of the 1920s, Dawson City maintained its central role in river transport. Ore from Mayo was shipped via Dawson, where it was loaded aboard American Yukon Navigation Company steamers (owned by a W.P.Y.R. subsidiary) and sent downstream to the Bering Strait. Improvements on upstream navigation, particularly the development of a new, shallow-draft barge, permitted the W.P.Y.R. to reverse this pattern, moving the ore to Whitehorse where it was loaded on the train for Skagway. When the Alaska Railroad reached Fairbanks in 1922, the American Yukon Navigation Company was pulled off the lower Yukon, cutting the commercial link which for fifty years had linked the two territories of the Yukon River Valley. Although few noticed the change immediately, the shift represented the first major barrier between Alaska and the Yukon, an early brick in what would later become a solid wall.

A transportation development that attracted more attention at the time was the struggle to improve river navigation along the treacherous and shallow Stewart River. The construction of the SS *Keno* in 1922, specially designed for low-water service, helped, but the addition of lining cables and the removal of rocks in the waterway were also required to ease transit on the river. Attempts to open navigation upstream from Mayo proved less successful, leaving transportation in the area to the roads and winter tractor-trains.

Among the many problems of sub-Arctic transportation was the short season. The late break-up of the ice along the Yukon River, and the shallow water of Lake Laberge routinely delayed the opening of navigation and cut into the shipping company's ability to move supplies in and out of the Yukon. Several attempts were made to extend the season. In 1925, the W.P.Y.R. constructed a dam across the Yukon River between Miles Canyon and Marsh Lake. By holding water back during the winter, the company could create a flood in the spring to force the ice out of Lake Laberge, extending the season by as much as three weeks.

Environmentalists of a later day would have shuddered at the W.P.Y.R.'s second method of improving water transportation. Late each winter, company trucks discharged gallons of oil, diesel fuel, and carbon black on the lake ice. If the weather co-operated, the enhanced heating action could eat

199

Winter may have stopped the riverboats, but Yukoners nonetheless found ways to get around. This train of an automobile and two sleds was on Lake Laberge in 1922. YUKON
TERRITORIAL ARCHIVES

through several feet of ice and permit ships to get through the lake to the open river below. In conjunction with the government, the company also undertook minor dredging operations in an attempt to improve river navigation, but grants were so small that little work of substance could be undertaken.[16]

That the ships continued to run on a regular schedule at all provided further evidence of the impact of the Mayo-Keno mines. The shipment of supplies into the mines and the removal of ore and concentrate kept the White Pass and Yukon Route steamers on the river during the Yukon's lean years. But the cost of rebuilding the *Klondike* and *Casca*, both of which ran aground in 1936, bit deeply into company profits and stalled additional efforts to improve river navigation. The steamers, like much else in the Yukon, were holding on and waiting for better times. The combination of tourist traffic and mine-related cargo kept the company afloat, but just barely. For all its monopoly control of Yukon River transport, the company had trouble paying its bills in the troubled 1920s and 1930s. Cargoes had fallen off dramatically from the pre-war period; in 1928, the firm carried about half the tonnage it had in 1914. Company officials sometimes spent their own money to keep ships on the river, and commercial customers were often required to pay in advance in order to keep operations moving. There were no great corporate profits drawn from the White Pass and Yukon Route operations; no dividends were paid between 1912 and the 1950s. This, perhaps, explains the absence of sustained criticism from Yukoners dependent upon the W.P.Y.R. monopoly. In these doldrum years, the company's ships and other operations were among the Yukon's only economic constants.

While the familiar river steamers served as the foundation for the Yukon economy, the development of air transport in this period held out the prospect of a more promising future. Surplus airplanes and demobilized pilots looking for work were peculiarly well-suited for the transport needs of the far north. The first planes, part of the First Alaska Air Expedition, reached Whitehorse in August 1920, moving on to Dawson City and then to Nome. The Yukon Airways and Exploration Company, owned by a small group of Whitehorse and Mayo businessmen, started operation in 1926. Although within three years the firm fell victim to weak management, insufficient capital, and a series of crashes, it made many think about the potential for air transport in the Yukon.[17] Treadwell Yukon also got into the business, purchasing two planes to transport prospectors around Mayo and to deliver mail from Whitehorse to Dawson when the Overland Trail was closed.

The early Yukon pilots were a courageous lot. There were few landing strips; wheeled planes usually landed on sandbars. The region's many lakes and rivers provided relatively safe landing for planes equipped with pontoons or skis, depending on the season. Pilots had treacherous winter conditions to deal with, and few roads or other landmarks to indicate routes. Crashes were frequent and often fatal. Although the need for air travel was obvious, it is not surprising that the industry had to struggle to succeed in the Yukon.

Northern air service came into its own in the 1930s. Within the space of a few years, Canadian Airways, Northern Airways, and United Air Transport began operations in the Territory. Not to be outdone, the White Pass and Yukon Route established its own airline, British Yukon Aviation, in 1934. Regularly scheduled service was now available to Whitehorse, Mayo, and Dawson City. The highly skilled pilots and engineers who manned the northern planes paid particular attention to the special needs of sub-Arctic navigation and devised ways of dealing with the vagaries of the northern climate. The federal and territorial governments joined with private companies to build, expand, and maintain a rapidly growing network of Yukon airfields.

The introduction of air travel brought sweeping changes to the north. Airmail service began in 1927, when Andy Cruikshank, aboard the *Queen of the Yukon* (owned by Yukon Airways) flew a plane-load of mail from Whitehorse to Dawson and Mayo. It was not an official flight — people mailing letters had to affix a special Yukon Airways stamp issued for the service. The pilot's wife actually delivered the mail, in a unique fashion. The plane did not land at Dawson. Instead, Mrs. Cruikshank simply threw the mail bag out the window as they flew over Dawson, after which the plane continued on to Mayo. Soon mail delivery by plane became more routine, bringing previously isolated communities back into the mainstream of regular communication.

As with any technological advance, the change from surface to airmail service gradually but inevitably brought old traditions and techniques to an end. Percy DeWolfe, widely hailed as the "Iron Man of the Yukon," had

It is hard to convey the extreme cold of a Yukon winter in a photograph, but this picture of a Dawson street, 1915, at 60 degrees (F) below zero comes close. YUKON TERRITORIAL ARCHIVES

been a '98 stampeder, but unlike many, he had stayed after the rush. After years of freighting, fishing, hunting, wood-cutting, and other ventures, DeWolfe landed a contract to deliver the mail between Dawson City and Eagle, Alaska. His initial contract called for a lump-sum payment of $125 per round trip, 204 miles by dog-sled in the winter. The journey, challenging at the best of times, was particularly dangerous in the weeks before break-up and after freeze-up. His exploits were legend in the north, his stamina, reliability, and good humour the stuff of which northern folk heroes were made. By the mid-1930s, however, DeWolfe's work had lost its lustre, replaced by the more daring and even more dangerous flights of the early Yukon pilots. Percy DeWolfe remained a fixture on the Yukon landscape with his Dawson-to-Eagle run until 1950. Long before that date, however, planes had largely replaced the Percy DeWolfes of the Yukon with the faster (but no more reliable), airmail service.[18]

The availability of air transport brought other benefits. Supplies could be flown into remote mining camps, allowing industrial operations to continue where in the past they would have had to close for weeks while supplies came overland. Fur trappers no longer had to transport their supplies hundreds of tortuous miles upstream to their traplines; now, bush-planes could drop them near their outposts and retrieve them again at the end of the season. Seriously ill patients, once doomed for want of a doctor, could be delivered to hospital by plane. Yukon pilots regularly risked death themselves on their many flights of mercy.

The addition of air service, and improvements in internal transportation brought Yukoners closer to the mainstream of North American society. They could now keep in touch with changing developments on the outside, and maintain closer contact with friends, family, and associates within the Territory. But this represented one of the few improvements in Yukon society. The souring of the gold-mining sector (though offset in part by the new silver-lead mines), sapped much of the vitality from a community already weakened by war and the disaster at Vanderbilt Reef.

The signs of decline were particularly evident in Dawson City. Once the gem of the Klondike, and famed throughout the world, Dawson now had the appearance of an overgrown graveyard. Dozens of dilapidated and crumbling buildings lined the streets. As Laura Berton wrote, "Those people who were left in the town had by this time taken on some of the qualities of Dawson's aging buildings."[19] There was room for several thousand residents, but by 1921, only 975 remained in town; ten years later, the number had fallen to 819. Dawson rebounded somewhat during the depression years, and in 1941 the local population had grown to 1,043 people. As Laura Berton sadly noted, funerals had become the major social event in the Dawson of the 1920s. Symbols of decline could be seen everywhere. The United States government removed its consulate in 1918, the *Dawson Daily News* stopped daily publication in 1920, more businesses closed each year, old-timers moved "outside" (or into the hospital), and commercial life slowed to a crawl. The town seemed in its death throes.

The revitalization of the goldfields after Treadgold's disastrous consolidation attempt provided a much-needed respite, and to a degree put Dawson back on its feet. But it was now little more than a standard company town, though corporate control was offset somewhat by the presence of the territorial government, and could no longer even claim economic pre-eminence, since the centre of mining had moved to the Mayo district. Still, Dawson City was avoiding the long-expected total collapse.

Old traditions died hard, and Dawsonites clung to the rituals of the past. The familiar social whirl — fancy bridge parties, engraved calling cards, and elaborate dances — remained in evidence, although for lack of people the strict class barriers of the past had to be relaxed somewhat. Royal Canadian Mounted Police constables, formerly considered too plebeian for the town's top social events, were now welcome in the winter round of soirées. "Scarlet fever," an affliction of the heart affecting many of the town's single women, still struck with some regularity in town, though the prize was now a constable rather than an inspector.[20] There were lingering signs of the old pretensions. Literary clubs, well-attended church services, the dances and receptions, and a stratified society that kept government officials and business leaders distinct from the mine workers and other wage labourers offered faint reflections of the "sophistication" and "culture" that community leaders so anxiously sought. Outsiders, however, were far from impressed with the shrivelled and form-ridden community on the banks of the Yukon River.

Dawson was no longer the frontier town of old. There were a few old-timers still around, as witnessed by continued attendance at Yukon Order of Pioneers meetings, but the glitter of their earlier dreams for Dawson had worn dull by years of hard news. Most of the townsfolk were short-timers from outside, who stayed a year, perhaps two, before trying their luck in the promising places in the south. For those struggling to make a go of life in the north, the constant movement of people in and out of the Territory was a bitter sign of the Yukon's greatest failing — the lack of commitment by the very people making a living from her once-famous resources.

Whitehorse, on the other hand, had changed little since the gold rush years. It remained under the thumb of the White Pass and Yukon Route, which controlled the local economy and owned much of the land around the townsite. The city lived by the seasons of the river, flourishing in the spring when workers arrived to lower the dry-docked steamers into the river and falling into somnolence each fall as the same workers departed for winter jobs and better weather in the south. The town had few ambitions, and even the episodic development of the local copper belt did little to fuel dreams of its future.[21]

Although the transportation hub of the Territory, and hence vital to the Yukon's economic health, Whitehorse felt ignored. Federal officials paid little attention to the town, which was perhaps to be expected, but the territorial government similarly dismissed the town's repeated claims for financial assistance. Dawsonites looked down their noses at the seasonal town, which they saw as little more than a train station, docks, and a few hotels. Whitehorse was, as a result, a quiet town, well-controlled by the police, where everyone seemed to be passing through. Evidence of White Pass and Yukon Route domination was everywhere to be found. Company officials and local businessmen lived in a small enclave to the southwest of the Main Street business district. The skilled workers, most of them employed on the W.P.Y.R. trains, in the boatyards, or on the steamers, lived in less modest homes in the adjacent districts. Transient workers, who made up the bulk of the town's summer workforce, put up makeshift dwellings near the railyards. There were a few Indians in the community, despite attempts to keep them out, but they lived to the north, on the small residential reserve set aside for them. The Indians, too, were transient, moving back to the traplines and hunting grounds as seasons dictated.

The entire community lived on the rhythms of the White Pass and Yukon Route transportation steamers. The trains, however, operated all year, providing the one reliable contact with the outside world. The arrival of the trains, although routine, was an important ritual:

Train day was an event in Whitehorse. It meant mail, fresh milk and green vegetables, strangers in town....It was considered no more than a patriotic duty for every true Whitehorse booster to swell the crowd at the station or dockside. As one socialite explained to me, "I think it's our duty to show the tourists that we're not all Indians and Eskimos and that we know how to dress decently."[22]

For all its modest appearances, Whitehorse was the Yukon's third community, the transportation entrepot that stood behind Mayo's mines and Dawson City's gold mines and administrative offices. That this small, seasonal, company town would hold such an important place in the territorial scheme of things reflected the modest pace of Yukon development, and the collapse of the glorious dreams of the Klondike era.

There were a few Yukoners — like Isaac Drury and William Taylor — who dedicated themselves to the commercial future of the north and re-invested in the Yukon. Most people however, from unskilled workmen to the investors in the Treadwell Yukon Company, viewed the north in a different light. For them the Yukon was a place to make money in and then to escape from. The companies took their profits out of the Territory and re-invested them in other ventures; the Yukon lost the benefits of any spin-off spending. Most workers were little different, migrating like the geese with the change of the seasons, taking much of their pay-packets with them to their families and homes in the south. The Yukon paid the price of instability, marginal business opportunities, and the absence of enough committed Yukoners to sustain pressure on the federal and territorial governments to change the status quo. It seemed that the Yukon was destined to be forever a land of yesterdays and tomorrows, whose best days lay far in the past or well in the future.

The Yukon Indians viewed the region differently. For them, as for their ancestors, this was home. The Indians were not particularly noticeable in the 1930s. They could be seen in towns, but under controlled circumstances; their cabins and camps lined the Yukon's rivers, and they often worked as wood-cutters and packers for the river steamers. But they were not to be found in the mines or in the service industries, nor did they have a political presence.[23]

In the back country, away from tourists and government officials, natives and whites mixed freely and easily. Fur traders like Dan Cadzow, Shorty Chambers, Poole Field, Eugene Jacquot, and Del Vangorder were their friends, business partners, and often their relatives by marriage. Other men, attracted by the high fur prices of the 1920s, came only temporarily and did not seek to make their relationships with Indian women permanent. Missionary doctor Grafton Burke, writing of the white men of the Porcupine River area, claimed that "traders in these isolated places vie with each other as to who can 'swell the population.'"[24] Those who did take Indian wives often found themselves shunned by white society in the Yukon. Laura Berton gives a poignant example:

> She was a pretty little thing, bright and neat, and I think could have made him a good wife, but the parents were so shocked they would neither see nor speak with him. This attitude drove him from the town and back into the bush, where his life was spent among the Indians, hunting and cutting wood for a living. Now here he was, standing by the river with his dark, wiry children clustered about him, the fish wheel in the background turning slowly with the current, the salmon smoking under the trees. In all intents and purposes he was a native.[25]

Away from the towns, the numerical dominance of the Indian population ensured that natives and whites would get along well. The process was aided by the presence of the Royal Canadian Mounted Police, who maintained a number of posts in outlying areas, and controlled relations between the two groups. There were only a few flare-ups, very seldom violent, a testament to the accommodation reached between the races away from the mining camps and river ports. It was clear, however, that the native traders and trappers were not free to shift their families to the mostly white towns, where a different reception awaited them.

Whitehorse, Dawson, and Mayo, in contrast, were white enclaves. Natives were permitted inside the communities only under very specific conditions. They came as temporary labourers, to fill a void caused by a lack of white workers, to buy goods in the stores, and, on occasion, to participate in parades and festivals. They came also to visit the missionaries, to seek help from the doctors, the hospital, the Indian agent, or the mounties. Although welcome for such short visits, provided they stayed sober, Indians were not encouraged to stay.

The communities, working through the police and the federal government, had various ways of controlling native settlement. Special residential reserves were established for the Indians; the Mayo reserve, a particularly symbolic example, was located two miles downstream from the main settlement, and on the opposite side of the river. Thus, the Indians could live close to the towns, as many did on a temporary basis each year, but not so close as to annoy local citizens. Faced with protests from whites, the government established a curfew restricting Indian access to Dawson and, in 1933, invoked a permit system for any native wishing to move into Dawson City. Although such measures were privately acknowledged to be illegal, they served their purpose. There were many such examples. The Mayo hospital, financially supported by the Treadwell Yukon Company, refused to admit Indians into the general wards; they were treated in a tent attached to the outside of the building. Indians and whites did not often mingle in

Whitehorse, Dawson, and Mayo. Police officers and men such as Yukon Indian Agent John Hawksley, a former missionary, implemented such measures as were necessary to placate white protests and to control native incursions into the white enclaves. This discrimination was justified on the grounds that Indians had to be protected from the baneful influence of white society until they were ready for full assimilation. However specious that argument, it was widely accepted by whites involved with Indian affairs.[26]

While the government and police concentrated on keeping the Indians out of town (and the natives were more interested in hunting and trapping anyway), the task of preparing them for assimilation fell to the churches. The Anglican church in particular had deep roots in the Territory, and served both native and white congregations. The other denominations had fallen on hard times after the gold rush, and many clergy had left the Territory.

The Anglican church had always had difficulty attracting suitable candidates for northern service. The problems were magnified by the poverty of the Yukon Diocese and limited support for Canadian missions by the national church. Bishop Stringer struggled with the problem of having his many overtures to potential recruits rejected by people who felt that God had called them to work in the pleasanter surroundings of a middle-class urban parish in southern Canada. Unable to attract suitable full-time candidates, Stringer turned in the 1920s to student preachers at the Anglican Theological College in Vancouver. The government provided small salaries and expenses for Indian day-school teachers. By offering to have his missionaries run a day school while the Indians were in camp, Stringer was able to get the government to subsidize Anglican missionary efforts in the Yukon. The summer students were an earnest, energetic bunch, who took to their work with the enthusiasm of youth and Christian commitment. They knew little, however, about the realities of northern missionary work, could seldom speak the native languages, and did not stay long enough to make an appreciable impact.[27]

Much the same could be said for the full-time missionaries that Stringer recruited. By the 1920s, almost all of the new members were Canadians, a change from the largely British missionary corps of the previous century. They were an upwardly mobile group, many of whom used their Yukon service as a stepping stone to a more fashionable parish in the south. Even those of long service were moved about so frequently that their work was hampered. The redoubtable A. C. McCullum, a quiet, modest man, worked at five different stations during his seventeen years in the Yukon. Cecil Swanson, who had served for four years among the Carmacks and Little Salmon Indians, was moved to Whitehorse, and from there he moved south. Swanson, like a number of other missionaries, was convinced that the missionaries' mobility was undercutting their impact on the Indians. As he succinctly put it: "Short-term missionaries are useless."[28]

To discover that many Anglican clergy used the Yukon as a stepping stone to a middle-class career in the south should be no surprise. Why should the missionaries be any different than other whites in their approach to the Yukon? There were a number, of course, who saw the missionary enterprise differently and dedicated their lives, in the manner of the Roman Catholic priests, to their Indian congregations, but such people were clearly the exception among the Protestant clergy in the Yukon.

There were alternatives to bringing white missionaries north, one of them being the recruitment of native clergy. Although the training of Indian catechists had long been an Anglican objective, Bishop Bompas had had little faith in their ability to spread the gospel. Bishop Stringer, more flexible and open and without the manpower to staff his widely scattered missions, took a different tack. During his tenure, which ended in 1932, Stringer recruited seven natives — Julius Kendi, K. Kunizzi, Richard Martin, John Martin, Amos Njootli, J. Pelisse, and John Tizya — as priests, and others as lay readers. Adapting the church to the presence of native spiritual leaders was not always easy; they often expected more freedom, status, and salary than the church was prepared to give. Some whites within the church were troubled by the Indians' lack of formal education; their concerns were heightened when several of the Indian priests ran afoul of the church administration over financial and personal matters.

The church had other troubles. When John Machray, the financial officer of the Ecclesiastical Province of Rupert's Land (and the University of Manitoba) absconded in 1932 with several hundred thousand dollars of trust funds, the northern missions faced a serious crisis. Bishop of the Yukon, A. H. Sovereign, was transferred to the Diocese of Athabasca; Bishop Geddes of Mackenzie River was given charge of the Yukon in addition to his other duties. In 1939, the Diocese of the Yukon was transferred to the Ecclesiastical Province of British Columbia, severing a connection with Red River and Winnipeg that had originated in the 1860s with the work of W. W. Kirkby and Robert McDonald.[29] Despite these struggles with finances and personnel, the Anglican church pushed on with its missionary program for the Yukon Indians. The cornerstones of this effort were the church's two residential schools, the Carcross (Chooutla) school for Indians and St. Paul's Hostel, which housed mixed-blood children not eligible for entry into the Indian school.

The Carcross school, financed by the federal government, had opened in new quarters in 1911. The schooling program ran into numerous difficulties, not the least of which was the reluctance of most parents to part with their children for long periods of time. The devastation wrought by disease took its toll on the students, many of whom came to school already suffering from tuberculosis, and the tragic incidence of children dying while in Carcross eroded public confidence in the school. Through the years, the Anglicans would have great difficulty keeping the school filled, and strug-

The Anglican Church had long sought federal assistance for an Indian residential school. The government finally provided the money for this facility, built at Carcross in 1911. The building burned to the ground in 1939. ANGLICAN CHURCH ARCHIVES

gled constantly with the Indians' concern about the facility. The school's academic program was limited to basic writing and arithmetic, and promoted loyalty to Christianity and the British Empire. Particular emphasis was placed on practical skills; native boys were taught carpentry, hunting, gardening, and, for a time, how to run a printing press. The girls were trained in domestic service and were expected to assist with the kitchen and cleaning work in the school. The teachers hoped that their students would leave their school as missionaries in their own right, carrying to their communities a reverence for God, middle-class morality, southern standards of hygiene, and the Protestant work ethic. If properly prepared, the argument went, these young Indian adults would become the guiding lights for their villages, leading the native population toward Christianity and the mainstream of Canadian culture.[30]

As the first graduates emerged from the school in the 1920s and 1930s, the missionaries had their hopes in most cases dashed. The shift from the rigidly controlled surroundings of the school dormitory to the more open lifestyle of the hunting camp required a sweeping transformation for which most students, after years in the school, were not prepared. In 1926, an Anglican from the Porcupine River area pleaded with Bishop Stringer not to send a girl back home:

If C____ M____ girl comes back, she is going into the filthiest hovel in the country....A dirt floor, two tiny windows which cannot be seen for the flies, stinking meat and fish being all over the cabin, the stench unspeakable, six people already there, and now a seventh, and under the willows on the dirt floor, all the filth of a long winter throwing off a deadly effluvia, in a stifling heat...Bishop, I plead with you not for humanity's sake, but for the sake of the Dear Lord who redeemed us, not to send a decent girl back to untold misery and evil, where she cannot help but curse the very day she was born.[31]

While whites seldom saw much value in Indian lifeways — hence the almost hysterical tone in letters such as this — there was some reason for this concern. Children raised in the residential school under strict church discipline and in an environment totally unlike that of the Indian village, would undoubtedly have difficulty readjusting to the old way of life. Moreover, the mission school specifically and systematically taught the children that village customs and traditions had no place in twentieth-century Canada.

There were a few "successes," as the church called young adults like James Wood, Jacob Njootli, Johnny Johns, and Maggie Daniels, who became models of what the Anglican teachers hoped to produce, but for every success there were many who did not make the adaptation required, and who found themselves struggling between the expectations raised by their education and the realities of life in the Yukon. A summer missionary at Carmacks in 1934 offered a succinct and accurate assessment of the issue; graduates, he noted, "are potential outcasts of their own people and are not quite up to the standards of the white intellect. In other words, they are 'betwixt and between' — a condition of pitiful helplessness."[32]

The mission school was, from the beginning, a complex and disruptive force in the life of the Yukon Indians. No one familiar with the school doubted the zeal and commitment of the educators. The missionaries truly cared about the Indians, fervently believing that they were doomed unless they made an accommodation with the new literate and industrial order. However, their methods — their way of showing their love — left an indelible scar that ran through native society in the Territory, a scar that would deepen and fester to become one of the most contentious points in native-white relations in the Yukon.

The Anglican church followed a different policy with its school for mixed-blood children, St. Paul's Hostel, which opened in Dawson City in 1920 and moved to the old Good Samaritan Hospital in 1923. The federal government made a special concession for this institution, providing financial support even though it was not legally required to do so. The school, supported initially by the Anglican Forward Movement, was under the control of Miss E. J. Naftel, formerly of Carcross. She was replaced in 1923 by C. F. Johnson, an old-time pioneer who, while on his way to the Klondike, had been convinced to join the missionary corps in the Mackenzie River district.[33] The hostel provided housing and close supervision for about thirty mixed-blood children, who attended regular classes in the Dawson Public School. Out of school hours, they received additional instruction in practical skills. Here there was no attempt to change completely the lives of the mixed-bloods. To the church and the government, the fact that these children had at least half non-native parentage meant that they were closer to the norms of white society. As Bishop Geddes later commented, the hostel wanted only to allow each child "to fit himself to take his place in the community as a white man."[34] Most of the children had fairly regular contact with their parents, many of who supported the school financially. St. Paul's Hostel was far less intrusive, and hence less disruptive, than the Carcross Residential School. Still, the facility stirred its fair share of controversy. Some parents protested the inclusion of mixed-blood children in the regular school system. The *Mayo-Keno Bulletin* in its September 1925 editorial bluntly stated the views of at least part of the community:

> Why should the people's money be used to house, feed and clothe the somewhat prolific progeny of able bodied men who have mated with native women? . . . Does the Federal Government realize that the result of its misplaced generosity is to encourage a certain class known as "squaw-men" to shift their parental responsibilities on the shoulders of an unwilling public?[35]

In an era of general restraint, the government seldom initiated programs specifically for the Yukon Indians. John Hawksley, the Yukon Indian Agent, did look after the specific and local needs of the natives. But he did not travel around the Yukon a great deal, and seldom sought out work for his office. He saw his job as one of mediating between Indians and whites, and responded swiftly to any particular native request, but he was not a strong or vocal advocate of Indian rights in the Yukon. Even this modest protection was lost, however, when Hawksley retired in 1933. No replacement was appointed. Instead, the government assigned responsibility for Indian affairs to the Royal Canadian Mounted Police, who in turn made it a part-time responsibility for one of their officers, on a rotation basis. For their part, the Indians placed few demands on the government. Indians suffering from illness and able to get to a doctor or hospital received medical attention. Relief was available for Indians facing privation, with the provision that able-bodied men and women were expected to work for their supplies. Few natives, mostly widows and the elderly, availed themselves of such charity.[36]

Despite government expectations to the contrary, the Indians did not provide much work for the police. In the 1920s, the Old Crow Indians repeatedly ignored government regulations against gambling and drinking. They were confident that they would not be arrested, for the nearest court was hundreds of miles away in Dawson City. The government moved with glacial slowness in response to frequent police requests for the power to deal with the problem. Local missionary A. C. McCullum was appointed Justice of the Peace in 1928, but the commission arrived after the reverend had already moved away. Although the police continued to have problems imposing their will on the Indians, few serious crimes in this period involved them. For instance, a 1921 rumour that the White River Indians were planning a raid on a neighbouring band proved on police investigation to be groundless.

For both the Indians and the government, the issues of greatest concern had to do with land and harvesting rights. When natives faced competition for resources in Old Crow in 1929 and at Little Atlin in 1932, the government stepped in and offered protection. Both Indians and Indian Agents supported more sweeping measures to assist native interests, and to prevent the over-hunting that accompanied the revitalization of the fur trade in the 1920s, but these were not often implemented. When in 1932 Joe Squam requested ownership of his family's "traditional" lands around Wolf Lake, his application was rejected. Several years later, Harper Reed, Indian Agent from the Stikine River Agency, proposed that a native-only hunting reserve be established in the southern Yukon. Mounted police reports failed to substantiate Reed's claims that the land was being seriously over-hunted. Charles Camsell, Deputy Minister for the Department of Mines, offered a more general reason for turning the proposal down:

> If we are not going to reserve our northern regions exclusively for the use of the natives but are looking to encourage the opening of these regions to the people of Canada generally, then I think we must limit the extent of these preserves to meet the pressing needs of the natives but no more.[37]

While the federal government had clearly decided that the Yukon was not to be retained as a native preserve, it had no clear idea of how the Territory might develop. In the wake of the collapse of the Klondike goldfields, the government had all but given up on the Yukon, content to spend minimal sums maintaining a formal administrative presence. Because it retained control of natural resources, Ottawa had the power to set the pace for regional development. The Territorial Council, in contrast, was the focal point for demands for government assistance, but lacked the money and authority to assist or encourage expanded economic activity. The Yukon was not alone in this. The prairie provinces similarly lacked control of natural resources before 1930, and devoted little attention to their northern lands until they had the rivers, lakes, minerals, land, and timber under their jurisdiction.

The federal government had a rationale for not expending more resources on the north. To expand too rapidly, it was argued, would upset the balance of native life, forcing hundreds of Indians to depend on government support to survive. And a country as large as Canada had many demands on its meagre resources. Through the 1920s, much energy and capital was expended on readjusting to the post-war world, completing the settlement of the southern plains and building up the country's still limited industrial

George and Martha Black were the "first family" of the Yukon for much of the 1920s and 1930s. Both represented the Yukon in the federal House of Commons; George Black also served as Speaker of the House. PUBLIC ARCHIVES OF CANADA

capacity. In the next decade, while governments across the country struggled with the Great Depression, even less attention was directed to the Canadian north. In the past, government-supported ventures, particularly railways and canals, had fueled the country's economic expansion. The collapse of the national railway system during the First World War had taken the bloom off the Canadian tradition of mixed government and private investment.[38]

For these reasons, northern development was left to the marketplace and the investment patterns of southern corporations. Treadwell Yukon, A. N. C. Treadgold's Yukon Consolidated Gold Corporation, and the White Pass and Yukon Route made the decisions that shaped the future of the Yukon. These decisions naturally rested on the concern for profits. By removing itself from the development game, the federal government lost the right and the ability to regulate the economic development of the Yukon Territory. Since most of the corporations, with the notable exception of the White Pass and Yukon Route, acted with little concern for the long-term interests of the Territory, the boom-and-bust pattern of the past was almost certain to continue.

Throughout these years the Yukon did, somewhat surprisingly, retain its single Member of Parliament. For much of that time, that member was George Black, ably aided by his formidable wife Martha. George was an old-time Conservative and an unabashed partisan, and his wife was, if anything, even more so. She dominated Dawson and Yukon society, assuming the British and Canadian mannerisms appropriate to her position as the wife of a leading lawyer and the Territorial Commissioner from 1912 to 1916. George Black's wartime service, his solid Tory contacts, and his following throughout the Yukon brought him victory in the 1921 federal election. He was re-elected in 1925, 1926, and 1930, and during the government of R. B. Bennett he was made Speaker of the House. In 1935, when he was stricken with a serious illness, Martha ran in his stead, appealing to Yukoners to elect her to office as a reward for her years of service to the Territory. The unabashed appeal to sentiment succeeded, but just barely, and Martha squeaked into office. George regained the seat in the next election and remained in office until 1949.[39]

George Black was a Tory of some note, but he was not a regional booster, and he did little to generate support for Yukon government. Black made the obligatory back-room moves but was unable to staunch the continued shrinkage of federal funding for the Yukon Territory. Perhaps no one could have stirred up much national interest in the Yukon's problems between the wars, but at a time when the Territory required a vigorous and unabashed defender, it sent south a man with good political connections and personal ambition but not a great deal of fire.

Black's last years in office were somewhat troubled. He became a bit of a character, notorious for taking pot-shots at rabbits on Parliament Hill, and he had serious trouble with the prime minister, who refused him the usual prize of appointment to the Privy Council, an honour finally accorded to him by Prime Minister Louis St. Laurent. He died in 1965 at the age of ninety-two; Martha predeceased him in 1957 aged ninety-one, still the *grande dame* of Yukon society.

Having decided to stay out of territorial development, the federal government also continued to dismantle the territorial administration. The process had begun in the wake of the gold rush, but intensified under Arthur Meighen, Minister of the Interior in the Borden government. In 1918 Ottawa gave itself the power to disband the elected ten-member Territorial Council, planning to replace it with an appointed council of two. The territorial subsidy was slashed in half, forcing many civil servants out of their jobs and out of the Territory. Yukoners protested, hoping to ward off yet another body-blow to a society on the verge of total collapse. The government relented, and decided to maintain an elected three-member council, with representatives from Dawson, the Klondike (shifted in 1926 to Mayo), and Whitehorse. While it was a far cry from the large representative council of earlier years, the preservation of at least some local democracy was greeted enthusiastically in the region.

But the council had little effective power. The appointed Commissioner controlled it and could veto its legislative and budgetary decisions. As official representative of the federal government in the Yukon, the Commissioner also controlled federal expenditures. He was like a British governor dominating unsophisticated colonials. The council and its small civil service found themselves constantly deferring to federal administrators. The major federal departments, particularly the Post Office, the R.C.M.P., and the Department of Public Works, controlled most of the money and thus much of the Yukon.

The territorial government, in contrast, had little money. Its revenue came from federal grants and a variety of sources, particularly liquor but also hunting licences, fur export taxes, municipal levies, and registration fees. These sources provided some $200,000 in 1927, but the money was never enough to maintain the schools, libraries, health programs, roads, and bridges. Even more costly, as the pioneers of '98 aged and became infirm, were the hospitals and welfare programs; Dawson's aging population was particularly expensive and, in government terms, non-productive. The regular addition of old-timers to the welfare rolls or their entry into hospital represented yet another drain on an already strained budget, and further confirmation of the continuing collapse of the Yukon economy and society.

Eventually the Yukon government turned into a single person. As funding dried up, civil servants were laid off, and government work was curtailed, George Jeckell emerged as the dominant administrative force in the Yukon. A solid, if unadventurous man who adhered closely to his superiors' instructions, Jeckell, like the mounted police in the 1890s, wore an unusual variety of hats and titles. He had been named Controller in 1913, and later became Public Works Agent, Income Tax Inspector, Mayor of Dawson (ex officio), Registrar of Land Titles, and Senior Territorial Executive Officer, the latter following the abolition of the office of Gold Commissioner in 1932. It was, as Jim Lotz observed, "a withering away of the state in a way which Marx never envisaged. One man wore many hats, and the Commissioner was a virtual dictator, ruling the Territory on behalf of the federal government."[40]

The Yukon's political impotence was emphasized by the re-emergence in the late 1930s of the proposal that British Columbia should annex it. The instigator was T. Duff Pattullo, elected premier of British Columbia in 1933. Pattullo, who had been a civil servant and businessman in the Klondike at the turn of the century, was enthusiastic about the prospect for northern development. After a term in office, his province suffering through the Depression, Pattullo linked the annexation of the Yukon to his plans for the construction of a highway to Alaska. The road, to be built as a public work, would open up the north, stimulate tourist traffic, and help offset the economic distress of the 1930s. The federal government, anxious to be rid of a financial burden, had by April 1937 tentatively agreed to the transfer. Nobody asked what Yukoners thought; Ottawa had no constitutional duty to do so. Responding to organized complaints from the Territory, Pattullo remarked "It does not seem reasonable that the destiny of a territory as large as the Yukon should be finally determined by the few residents living there." The proposed annexation, announced with such fanfare and seemingly inevitable, failed over the question of continuing a territorial grant to St. Mary's Catholic School, which at the time had only fifteen students. Prime Minister Mackenzie King, remembering what a political hot potato the funding of separate schools had been on the prairies, skipped deftly away from the issue, and the project fell through. The Yukon had been saved, not because Ottawa cared about it, but through sectarian prejudice and political cowardice. The lack of concern in southern Canada for the integrity of the Yukon Territory was a cruel blow for those fighting to maintain a semblance of stability there.[41]

By the end of the 1930s, the Yukon had adjusted resignedly to its new condition, one much similar to its situation before the Klondike gold rush. The population was small, Ottawa's interest negligible, and economic returns modest, but for a few, hopes lived on. With the Klondike goldfields back in operation and the Mayo-Keno mines carrying the Territory, its future looked promising, if not bright. There were, however, two Yukons by the end of the 1930s. In the mining corridor — Skagway to Whitehorse to Mayo to Dawson — the imperatives of the industrial age dominated. Here whites dominated the communities, and Indians were generally not welcome. Buttressed by government offices, seasonal transportation activities, and a modest tourist trade, this sector of Yukon society clung to the legacy of the gold rush, living off the faded dreams of the Klondike and the belief that persistence would be rewarded in yet another boom. Many, however, saw the Yukon only as a place to make money, and whether labourer, skilled worker, entrepreneur, or industrialist, they invested their time and money and took their returns with them to the south. It was not much of a basis upon which to build stability.

The more stable part of Yukon society lay away from the mining corridor, along the streams and in the hills that made up so much of the Territory's land mass. There was little here to excite the politicians, or to fuel dreams of empire. But it was here that the Indians lived, almost alone in their commitment to the Yukon. There were a few whites in the "always afternoon years"[42] who shared the Indians' dedication to the people and land of the Yukon and who sought a better future for the north. But it was the Indians who had the deepest and most enduring connection to the Yukon, past and present. They were not like their ancestors of a century before — technology, schools, missions, disease, and economic change had altered much of their pattern of life — but they remained uniquely adapted to the contemporary realities of life in the north. They were there for the long haul, and were determined to be around when the goldfields ran bare and the silver and lead veins had been picked clean.

The irony was that to the observer the Indians no longer seemed to be part of the Yukon. Visitors saw the decaying remnants of the Klondike rush and the modern machinery of the mining frontier. They saw white settlements and the signs of technological progress. In these surroundings, the Indians seemed anachronistic, their hunting and trapping ways already outdated by the advance of western civilization. But the Yukon remained, in many ways, theirs. No treaties had been signed, the Indians moved freely about the land, ignoring the seasonal migrations of other Yukon workers. In the winter months, when whites had left the Territory or else stayed close to their communities, the Yukon seemed to have reverted back to the days of the fur trade.

The 1920s and 1930s were, perhaps, the Yukon's "winter years." For Yukon boosters, these were hard, bad times, for the population had fallen, business was down, and productivity had dipped dangerously low. There was some hope that the next decade would bring a return to prosperity and a revitalization of the Yukon. It would come, but not in a way anyone could have guessed, and not in a fashion that would please the long-term residents of the Yukon. For in the next decade the Yukon Territory would be caught in a flood-tide not its own making, and would be swept up in the forces of world power politics and another great war.

YUKON 1942~1946

PIPELINES •—•—•
AIRFIELDS ▲

0   100   200 Miles

DANIEL 87

CHAPTER EIGHT

War and Upheaval, 1939–1946

By 1939, the Yukon seemed to have disappeared from the national consciousness. Tourist interest in the Territory had dwindled to almost nothing during the Depression, as had its general economic vitality. The Yukon had returned to its pre-gold rush roots, sustained only by the fur trade and a relatively stable dredge-mining sector based in the Klondike. But by 1943 that pattern had been overturned, as tens of thousands of people once more flooded into the Yukon, upsetting the economic and social structure and setting the Territory once more on a new course.

Yukoners in 1939 were not expecting a boom. Like other Canadians, they acknowledged the outbreak of war in Europe with resignation. The young men, many of whom had been without jobs for years, went off to recruitment centres and training camps. Klondike mining operations faced serious dislocations. The Yukon Consolidated Gold Corporation was the Yukon's largest employer, hiring as many as 700 men a year to keep its dredges and subsidiary operations functioning. The wartime manpower shortage made it difficult to keep operating. While the Y.C.G.C.'s frustrations mounted — the gold was there but profits could be made only if the men could be found — there was little they could do. The company kept going as best it could. In 1940, ten dredges were in operation, 625 men hired and over $2.6 million worth of gold recovered.

Bigger troubles lay ahead. Through the 1920s and 1930s, the Y.C.G.C. had capitalized on the workers' need for employment by keeping wages relatively low and avoiding making improvements in the workplace. Lewis Green offers a dismal picture of the life of Klondike placer miners:

> The working conditions were often difficult. Despite protective clothing, the men on the stripping and thawing crews would be wet much of the day in temperatures that were often close to zero Fahrenheit towards the end of the season. Most shifts were ten hours long, seven days a week, all paid at the going hourly rate without overtime. All employees were

required to produce. Any unable to meet the company's expectations, whether for physical or other reasons, were replaced immediately. The camps were spread out along the creeks, up to fifty miles from Dawson. Even though new buildings had been added, the camps were often crowded and lacked many amenities, such as adequate washing facilities. There were many complaints over the food.[1]

Before the Second World War workers in the north had little option but to accept these terms, if only for one season before they could leave for the outside. Now, with a great demand for skilled industrial workers throughout the country, Klondike miners were in a sellers' market. In July 1941, at the height of the mining season, Y.C.G.C. workers demanded a $1-a-day cost-of-living bonus. When the company refused to negotiate, the men dropped their tools and walked to Dawson City. The arrival of close to five hundred men worried the townsfolk. What were their intentions? Would the local economy collapse? The protest leaders kept the men in close check and prevented any violence, and waited for the company to act. The company offered to meet the workers half-way, but the men held out for more. Finally, after nine days on the streets of Dawson, discussions between the labour leaders, company officials, and a federal negotiator, flown in specially to deal with the crisis, resolved the impasse. The workers received a substantial wage boost — sixty-two cents per shift — and also gained recognition of their "employee's council," a major concession from the anti-union Y.C.G.C.

Although improved wage rates and some modest improvements in living conditions stabilized the work force temporarily, opportunities on the outside were too attractive for many Klondike miners. From a pre-war level of over 700 men each season, the Y.C.G.C. could put only 400 men in the field in 1942, only 172 two years later, and 186 the following year. The company had no choice but to close down dredges; in 1944, only three of the massive machines remained in operation. Eventually Yukon Consolidated took the unprecedented step of hiring native workers. The experiment did not work, although the Indian men were "dependable," because the natives continued to follow the seasonal cycles of the harvesting economy and were not prepared to alter their patterns to suit the gold-mining industry's requirements.[2]

The work force returned at the end of the war, but in the interim Y.C.G.C.'s production fell precipitously. From a high of $2.8 million in 1942, returns fell to slightly over $610,000 in 1944. The problem did not lie with the resource, for the gold was there for the taking, and the price of gold rose from $36 to $38.50 an ounce in the early 1940s. There was little the company could do but wait for the end of the war, hoping for a return to prosperity in peacetime. The dislocation of gold-mining operations knocked out one of the cornerstones of the territorial economy; it was not the only foundation to be eroded.

Treadwell Yukon Company had carried the Yukon through much of the 1920s. The company had explored extensively through the mountains in the Mayo-Keno-Elsa area, seeking out new deposits in an attempt to keep operations alive. Throughout the 1930s, the firm maintained a high level of production and profits, while rapidly depleting known resources. Returns fell off dramatically in the late 1930s. The Silver King property went out of production in 1939, followed by the Elsa mine and processing mill. When the United States government stopped the purchase of foreign silver during the Second World War, Treadwell Yukon lost its principal market. The combination of closed markets, lower prices, and the near exhaustion of the major ore bodies was too much for the company. In its 1941 Annual Report, Treadwell Yukon announced that it would be unable to continue operating. In May 1942, the Treadwell Yukon Company was formally dissolved. The company had few regrets. It had re-invested in the Yukon only those sums necessary to increase the productivity and profitability of its operations; the profits were exported and invested outside the Yukon. According to one conservative estimate, Treadwell Yukon profits reached $4.6 million, or 20 per cent of the total value of the mineral production from the area. Now the mines that had carried the Yukon were closed.[3]

In other circumstances, the closure of the Treadwell properties would have devastated the Yukon Territory. The territorial government had invested heavily in public services and transportation facilities for the Mayo region; that money, and the people working for the government, were now redundant. The White Pass and Yukon Route Company relied heavily on the silver and lead mines; close to 40 per cent of the company's earnings came from this single region, permitting the W.P.Y.R. to maintain its full Yukon operations. The ripple effects would, in normal times, have ruined the territorial economy. But these were far from normal times, and the closure of the Treadwell Yukon properties seemed scarcely important in the hyper-inflated wartime economy of the Yukon Territory.

During the First World War, Yukoners had struggled to show their interest and involvement in the international confrontation. They would face no such challenge in the Second World War, for the war came to them, in a way that few had anticipated. Between 1942 and 1946, thousands of American soldiers and civilians poured into the Territory, preparing the way for the defence of the far northwest. In a fashion reminiscent of the Klondike gold rush, the Yukon was transformed, while once more attracting attention across North America. The Yukon had been rediscovered, and would never be the same again.

The story begins back in the days before the war. For years, the politicians of Alaska and the Yukon had been lobbying unsuccessfully for a highway link to the south. They had, at different times, received support from fellow promoters in British Columbia, the Pacific northwestern states, Alberta, and other provinces and states that hoped to capitalize on the future

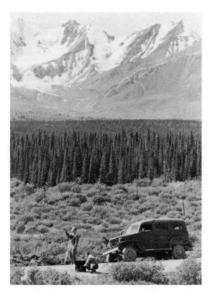

U.S. Army photographers worked alongside the construction crews during the building of the Alaska highway, leaving a tremendous photographic legacy of the first northern megaproject. PUBLIC ARCHIVES OF CANADA

development of the far northwest. The fate of these proposals reveals much about the nature of northern isolation and southern interest in the Yukon and Alaska.[4]

The most highly publicized venture originated with T. Duff Pattullo, premier of British Columbia in the 1930s. Pattullo had joined the Klondike gold rush, a Liberal patronage appointee assigned to assist the Commissioner of the Yukon. From the first, Pattullo was captivated by the prospects for the north, and recognized the need for an all-Canadian overland link to the Klondike. Pattullo's predecessor, Simon Fraser Tolmie, also dreamed of a highway to the north, and even convinced the United States to sponsor a joint commission to investigate the prospects for such a road. Partisan concerns forced Pattullo to oppose this venture, but when he was elected premier in 1933, he quickly revived his own dreams for the north.

Pattullo took office in the midst of a severe depression and found the provincial treasury bare. Nonetheless, he believed that government spending on major public works such as bridges, hospitals, and highways could lead the provincial economy out of the economic collapse. Pattullo's problem was that he had no money for such ventures. When the United States Congress voted $2 million in 1935 for a highway to Alaska, the idea that had simmered in Pattullo's mind for many years came to the fore.

The Alaska Highway took on special life in 1937. Pattullo turned to the Liberal prime minister, William Lyon Mackenzie King, for support, but King, as usual, was cautious about anything that smacked of innovation or expenditure. American President Franklin D. Roosevelt, on the other hand, supported the plan and encouraged Pattullo to continue his efforts. The federal government resented the British Columbia premier's intervention in what was clearly a matter for the diplomatic service. King was particularly incensed, confiding to his diary that Pattullo, "like a fool, has been telling the Americans what to do to get under way with public works in Canada." The British Columbia initiative had, however, forced the federal government's hand. More formal planning would have to follow, although Ottawa remained unconvinced of the value of such massive expenditures in the isolated and voter-less frontier.

In 1938, the United States government established an Alaska Highway Commission to investigate the various proposals for a road to Alaska. At the Americans' urging, Pattullo then pressed Ottawa to establish a similar commission in Canada. Although King did so, he appointed as chairman of the Canadian Highway Commission a man named Charles Stewart, who happened to be very seriously ill and thus unable to devote himself fully to the commission's work. The commissions made extensive studies and visited the north, and in 1940 they wrote their reports. The American study supported the construction of a coastal route, running behind the Alaskan panhandle and providing for future access to coastal areas. The Canadian commissioners offered an uninspired and inconclusive summary of the two main routes proposed, favouring the interior route — north from Prince George to Dawson City — over the line preferred by the Americans. Ottawa was obviously counting on the commission to stall deliberation of a serious and, to the people of the northwest, important issue, and much to Pattullo's chagrin, it worked. Pattullo resigned as premier in 1941, and was not around when new circumstances forced a hasty re-examination of the 1930s work of the highway promoters.

At the same time that British Columbia's Duff Pattullo and Warren Magnusson of Washington State were promoting a highway north through British Columbia, politicians on the Canadian and American prairies were also talking of a highway to Alaska. A well-organized group, the United States–Canada–Alaska Prairie Highway Association, drew financial and political support from North Dakota, Saskatchewan, and Alberta, particularly Edmonton, which saw itself as the natural gateway to the northwest. The organization was slower off the mark than Pattullo in British Columbia, but by the early 1940s it had established a political pressure campaign, hoping to convince American and Canadian decision-makers to opt for a prairie route to Alaska. F. S. Wright, a tireless promoter of northern development provided much of the inspiration and data for the campaign.[5]

As talk of a highway went on, work was underway on the improvement of airplane facilities in the far northwest. The most enthusiastic promoters talked of a "Great Circle Route," connecting the Canadian northwest, Alaska, Siberia, and China. For British and Canadian authorities anxious to tap into the Far East, the proposal was especially attractive. As early as 1935,

Dan McLean, an employee of the Department of Transport, flew an aerial reconnaissance throughout the northwest with the famous northern bush pilot Punch Dickens, and just before the outbreak of war in Europe, the federal government authorized preliminary survey work on the planned airway to the Orient. Airfields were laid out at Grande Prairie, Alberta; Fort St. John and Fort Nelson, B.C.; and Watson Lake and Whitehorse in the Yukon. Later work led to the establishment of similar emergency flight strips between the major fields. The route was usable for daylight flying in 1941; radio stations had been opened along the flight path by the end of the year.[6]

As the war progressed, the function of these fields, initially intended for commercial traffic, was transformed. The Northwest Staging Route became particularly important with the entry of Russia into the war in 1941. An extensive "lend-lease" system was established, by which Allied war machinery was shipped by air through the northwest, across Siberia to the front lines of the battle with the forces of Nazi Germany. The Red Star became a routine sight in the skies of the northwest, as a steady stream of planes headed to Fairbanks, where Russian pilots took them over. Even this, however, was only a preliminary to the main show.

On December 7, 1941, Japanese fighter planes and bombers attacked Pearl Harbor. The daring raid had caught the United States unprepared. Where would the next attack come? Residents of the Pacific coast, their already discriminatory attitudes towards Orientals now tinged with a genuine fear of Japanese militarism, prepared for an attack. Although a realistic appraisal of the military significance of the region suggested that the danger was less than it appeared, North America's northern flank was unprotected. Something had to be done quickly, if only to soothe public opinion.

It is difficult to recreate the fear and unease of those troubled days of late 1941 and early 1942. The forces of freedom around the world were in retreat. France had fallen and Britain faced the ferocious attacks of the Battle of Britain. The American fleet in the Pacific had been badly damaged; Hong Kong, Manila, and Singapore had been captured, and the British navy had lost the cornerstone of its Pacific fleet. As time marched on, matters only worsened. Allied forces were in retreat across North Africa as Rommel pressed towards the Nile, and German armies had the Soviet forces on the run on the Eastern Front. For Canadians, confirmation of the severity of the wartime situation came in August 1942 when the fatally flawed attack on Dieppe struck at the heart of Canadian confidence. One could well understand how, in those desperate days, North Americans might wonder if their continent too was about to face the full power and destruction of an enemy invasion.

Alaska and the Canadian northwest seemed particularly vulnerable. The Aleutian Island chain reached to within twelve hundred miles of Japan, and in 1942 the Japanese began to move up the islands, capturing Kiska,

Attu, and attacking Dutch Harbor. While the military challenge was met by a combined Canadian and American force in several bloody battles in what has been labelled "The Forgotten War," the broader question of North American defence had yet to be addressed. Within days of Pearl Harbor, in fact, discussions had started on how best to protect the region from Japanese attack. Even as the military response was being mounted, work was underway on solving the long-term defence requirements of the northwest.

Before the war, Canadian and American planners had dismissed the need for a highway to Alaska, claiming that the advantages of such a costly venture were "negligible," but with the attack on Pearl Harbor, political pressure for the highway increased dramatically. President Roosevelt and others who had supported the project before the war, notably delegate Anthony Dimond of Alaska, welcomed the reopening of the discussion. The politicians asked their advisors in the War Plans Division to examine the strategic value of the highway. Professional soldiers studied the pre-war surveys and weighed the project against the country's many pressing needs. Their advice went against the prevailing political wisdom. Not only was a highway not needed for military purposes, but expenditures on a project of this type would take away from more urgent military requirements. The rationale was simple. The U.S. Navy argued that it could continue to supply Alaska with all strategic goods. Moreover, the major military sites in Alaska were located along the coast, and would not be accessible via the highway in any case. As M. V. Bezeau concluded in his study of the strategic planning process, the road was "a magnificent achievement carried out as a military project in time of war. But it was not needed for defence. The highway was actually planned and built for other reasons."[7] On February 12, 1942, the United States government ignored the professional advice and decided to proceed with the highway.

There was another potential stumbling block. Although the highway ended in Alaska, it had to cross vast reaches of Canadian territory. It followed, therefore, that Canadian permission had to be secured before construction started. Canadian authorities disagreed with the American decision to build the highway, echoing the concerns of the U.S. military about the lack of strategic value. But they would not — and perhaps could not — block it. The Americans were going to pay the entire cost; Canada could scarcely stand in the way. As Hugh Keenleyside, Assistant Under-Secretary of State for External Affairs, noted, "the United States is now so insistent...that the Canadian Government cannot possibly allow itself to be put into the position of barring...land access to Alaska." Further, he pointed out, "this argument should be recognized, in our own minds at least, as being based on political and not strategic grounds. The political argument, given the attitude of Washington, is inescapable; the strategic argument, in my opinion, is a most dubious egg."[8] On March 5, 1942, the

Top: *Brigadier General Bill Hoge was in command of the first phase of Alaska Highway construction. He surveyed much of the route from Les Cook's plane. Hoge was relieved of his duties before the pioneer road was completed.* NATIONAL ARCHIVES OF THE U.S.A.

Centre: *Bulldozers were the work-horses of the Alaska Highway construction, pushing through miles of unmarked wilderness every day as the construction crews worked steadily toward completion.* NATIONAL ARCHIVES OF THE U.S.A.

Below: *While the bulldozers cut a quick and rough slash through the wilderness, construction crews still had a great deal of clean-up to do before the road was ready for any traffic. As the army worked on the pioneer road, civilian contractors supervised by the Public Roads Administration were already building a permanent highway.* NATIONAL ARCHIVES OF THE U.S.A.

Canadian government approved the Americans' request. Construction could begin on the Alaska Highway.

As yet, no one knew which route the highway would take. A public hearing was called before the Committee of Public Roads in Washington in early February to deal with submissions on possibilities. Halvor Halvorson, President of the United States–Canada–Alaska Prairie Highway Association, spoke for proponents of the prairie route. Halvorson faced considerable opposition to his presentation, particularly from the many supporters of the inland highway through British Columbia. To his delight, however, the U.S. government decided to proceed as he had recommended; a prairie route would be built under treaty with Canada, and not as a project undertaken by Congress and therefore subject to political pressure. As he later wrote, somewhat sanctimoniously, "We won the fight on the merits. What political pressure was used, was entirely from the opposition, who carried their story and opposition to not only the Army, and the Secretary of State, but directly to the President of the United States himself."[9]

Seldom has a project of this magnitude been undertaken with such haste and so little planning. The earlier work of the Canadian and American highway commissions was consulted and then rejected, so that the whole project had to begin as if the idea were entirely new. The task of managing this unwieldy project fell to the solid, thick-jawed Colonel William Hoge, a veteran of the U.S. Army Corps of Engineers. Hoge had impressive First World War battle credentials, advanced study in engineering at M.I.T., and considerable experience with frontier road construction. He faced an enormous challenge. He had little to work with, except an order to push through the pioneer road in the first year (1942) and a requirement that his highway link up the existing airfields of the Northwest Staging Route. Beyond that, Hoge had no idea of where the highway would go.

Hoge could call on the assistance of Canadian surveyors already in the area. Knox McCusker, Dominion Land Surveyor, offered to guide the trailblazing crews into the field before spring break-up called a halt to winter operations. Hoge relied heavily on McCusker and his crews, who played a major role in laying down the initial path north from Fort St. John.[10]

Hoge divided the highway into two sections: north of Watson Lake and south of it. Fort St. John was named the southern headquarters; the main administrative centre was located in Whitehorse — the centre with the best combination of river, rail, and air facilities north of Edmonton. Hoge separated the two commands, retaining control of the northern sector and placing Colonel James "Patsy" O'Connor in charge of the Fort St. John headquarters. In addition to the crews working north and south from Whitehorse, north from Fort St. John, and south from Big Delta, Alaska, Hoge, again with McCusker's assistance, rushed a work crew into the Fort Nelson area before the spring thaw of 1942. This manoeuvre allowed construction to begin north of the Peace River through the spring and early summer.

Work on the pioneer road proceeded at a break-neck pace, for almost fifteen hundred miles had to be finished before winter. Carefully managed work-crews pushed into the forest:

> Two men . . . blazed the initial rough trail. After them came the stadia party. Its members ran the preliminary line and cut a pack trail of sorts for the use of advance transport. The surveyors were quickly followed by a single bulldozer cutting a swath through tree growth along the centre line so that the next bulldozers, in squads of six, could concentrate on cleaning up the resulting debris. This clearing operation made way for rough as well as finished grading work all along the line of construction. After the Cats had levelled the roadway for grading, subsequent parties located the final route, building corduroy roads wherever required. The general scene was one of intense activity. Pack trains threaded their way through tangles of tractors, graders and men. Radio equipment enabled workers to keep in close, constant touch with each other's work all along the line. At this stage of the project, men worked extremely long shifts. Motors were seldom turned off. Trucks moved night and day.[11]

Work was off to a great start: the actual route had still not been finalized!

Hoge worked on the road survey with engineers from the Public Roads Administration, an American civilian agency that would be responsible for turning the army's hastily built pioneer road into a usable, year-round highway. While the area north of Whitehorse was well-known — there was a wagon trail of sorts from Whitehorse to Kluane Lake — selecting the route from Fort St. John to Whitehorse was another matter. Indian guides were extremely useful for local work, helping army crews find their way through river valleys and around the mountains that the natives knew so well. They could not, however, help with the siting of the entire road. That task fell largely to Bill Hoge.

Knowing only that he had to connect up the airfields, Hoge set out to select a route. After exhausting all the available information, he turned to Les Cook, one of the region's best bush pilots. Day after day, Cook and Hoge flew over the land between Fort Nelson and Whitehorse. Cook was instrumental in locating a suitable pass between the Mackenzie River and Yukon River watersheds. By early June, reconnaissance parties had travelled the route laid out by Cook and Hoge.[12] Construction crews could now proceed with reasonable confidence that they knew where they were going.

Few Canadians were consulted on the general path of the highway, a cause for concern in some quarters:

> While there is unanimous approval of the decision to build the highway and almost equally unanimous satisfaction that the advice of qualified

Highway engineers and workers had little experience dealing with northern conditions. The onset of spring, sudden rains, and, especially, muskeg, played havoc with road. NORTHERN HERITAGE CONSULTING PHOTOGRAPH

Bridge construction was labour intensive, as the workers put together the makeshift structures. Few of the bridges survived the first year, and were quickly replaced with more permanent crossings. NATIONAL ARCHIVES OF THE U.S.A.

military experts is being relied upon, especially in the controversial matter of the choice of route, nevertheless there have been a few isolated expressions of discontent on the choice made.[13]

Hoge's problems were not over once the route was selected. He did not get along well with Brigadier General Clarence Sturdevant, who had overall responsibility for the highway. Nor did his operation mesh well with the Public Roads Administration activities in the area. Their initial plan had called for the improved highway to follow the route set out by army crews. He faced numerous difficulties managing the large number of workers under his direction. The men often were sent into the field without the proper equipment and supplies. As one regimental historian recounted, work north of Whitehorse started slowly; the soldiers worked "in coolie fashion, bending pick points in frozen ground and mucking around in rivers of mud, going nowhere." The heavy equipment eventually arrived, allowing the men to proceed in a proper fashion. Ice, snow, spring rains, hot summers, and mosquitoes complicated the work and added to the workers' frustrations. From an engineering perspective, permafrost and muskeg presented the greater challenges. Where possible, the highway was routed around the muskeg; otherwise, corduroy roads were built over the surface. Dealing with permafrost was more difficult. In numerous places, surface soil and vegetation was scraped off, exposing an apparently hard surface underneath. Within hours, as the hitherto-insulated soil thawed, the hard pack turned into a quagmire. Only slowly did the engineers discover the need to build up a "blanket," or extra level of insulation, over the permafrost.

In the middle of 1942, Bill Hoge was abruptly fired. His superior officer, Brigadier General Sturdevant, had visited the highway in July 1942 and liked what he had seen, but suggested that Hoge try to co-ordinate his work more closely with the Public Roads Administration. News that the highway was well ahead of schedule, coupled with mounting criticism of the route selected, convinced Lieutenant General Brehon Somervell, commanding general for services and supply, that he too, should visit the area. Somervell, "whose reputation for pomp, show, and grand designs was unrivaled in the United States Army,"[14] was not impressed by the apparent chaos throughout the northwest. With little warning, and little justification beyond a dislike for Hoge, Somervell relieved the highway commander of his duties. Colonel "Patsy" O'Connor was given charge of a revamped administrative structure, called the Northwest Service Command and based in Whitehorse. Hoge's career picked up with little interruption. He played a major role in the Allied landing in Europe, continued up the ranks, and ended his career as Commander-in-Chief of the United States Army in Europe.[15]

Under Hoge and O'Connor, the U.S. Army Corps of Engineers completed their assigned task on schedule. The more than ten thousand men assigned to the project (including several regiments of black engineers),

Top: *The initial highway left a great deal to be desired. Steep hills provided a major impediment, particularly when the road was icy or wet.* NATIONAL ARCHIVES OF THE U.S.A.

Centre: *The pioneer road, pushed through by the late fall of 1942, was little more than a rough trail blazed through the northwest. The bridges were temporary structures, subject to frequent wash-outs.* NATIONAL ARCHIVES OF THE U.S.A.

Below: *The Canol project held great promise for the northwest, offering the foundation of a prosperous industrial future. The undertaking was so poorly conceived, however, that it foundered from the beginning. The Whitehorse refinery was closed shortly after it opened, and the entire plant was shipped south.* NATIONAL ARCHIVES OF THE U.S.A.

pushed the pioneer road through expeditiously. The highway was officially opened to much fanfare on November 20, 1942, at Soldier's Summit near Kluane Lake. It was a striking engineering accomplishment. Some fifteen hundred miles of rough pioneer road had been pushed through the northwest in a single year. Despite all the celebration, and a sense throughout North America that the project was all but finished, a major part of it still lay ahead.

The Public Roads Administration had been involved with the project from the beginning. Their task, using staff engineers and civilian contractors, was to improve the military road to the appropriate civilian standard, to replace temporary bridges, and otherwise to make the Alcan Highway useable on a year-round basis. It was wartime and supplies were hard to come by, but fortunately the P.R.A. had numerous warehouses filled with material left over from Depression-era construction projects. In the haste of the moment, the contents of these warehouses were loaded, almost intact, onto rail cars and shipped north to Dawson Creek, in northern British Columbia. Much of the stuff was unnecessary — only a certain number of typewriters and filing cabinets could be used — and was discarded upon arrival in the northwest. P.R.A. crews took most of 1942 to get started, although their engineering divisions were extremely active, laying the plans for an extensive push in 1943 to complete the highway.[15]

Starting in 1942, however, the P.R.A. lined up the contractors. Most were American — Dowell Construction, Okes Construction, Lytle and Green Construction, and W. Green Co. — with one major Canadian participant, R. Melville Smith Co. These companies managed major sections of the highway and hired sub-contractors (forty-seven in 1942 and eighty-one the following year) to handle specific tasks. Together, these companies supervised the work of 7,500 workers in 1942 and over 14,000 in 1943. Work was done on a cost-plus basis, eliminating the need for time-consuming tendering delays.

The division of labour between the Corps of Engineers and the P.R.A. caused some difficulties. The P.R.A. found their men and equipment being diverted to assist with the high-priority task of completing the Alcan Highway in the first year. According to one estimate, P.R.A. crews built, alone or together with the army, over three-quarters of the pioneer road. In 1943, the P.R.A. turned to the task of improving it. They quickly discovered that huge sections of the original road were unusable and would have to be abandoned. Engineers of the P.R.A. began surveying a route for the new road that often deviated by miles from the army one. In many places, the pioneer road would serve as little more than an access road to the new road, eliminating much of the value of the initial project.

The American government was understandably angered by this costly and seemingly unnecessary duplication. In 1943 they admitted that the

232

Alcan Highway was not needed for military and supply purposes, beyond providing a land link for the airfields. The project was downgraded considerably; the U.S. government even approached Canadian authorities and asked them to take over control of the route. Boastful newspaper and radio accounts still talked of the "high-quality, well-finished road" to Alaska, but Canadian authorities, well-informed by their liaison officer in the area, C. K. LeCapelain, knew better. The United States government had reneged on their promise to complete a proper civilian road, although Canada could hardly object, since the Americans were dedicated to a major war effort and had built the road without Canadian involvement. However, the federal government could, and did, ignore American requests in 1944 that Canada assume responsibility for the highway, since the initial agreement required that the United States would maintain the highway until six months after the war.[16]

The Alcan Highway was but one arm of the American "invasion" of the Canadian northwest. In one of the most ill-conceived construction projects of the war, the American government authorized the development of the Norman Wells oilfield in the Mackenzie River Valley, the building of a pipeline overland to Whitehorse, and the erection of a modern refinery in Whitehorse. The pipeline cut across one of the most isolated portions of the Yukon Territory, providing access to the MacMillan Pass area, crossing the Pelly River at the village of Ross River, and joining the Alaska Highway north of Teslin Lake. Known as the Canol (for Canadian Oil) project, the undertaking promised the highway and associated airfields a ready supply of inexpensive fuel, which would be delivered throughout the north by pipelines running from Whitehorse south to Watson Lake and north to Fairbanks. Another branch connected Whitehorse to the coast at Skagway. The undertaking was beset with problems from the beginning, not the least of which was building a pipeline through hundreds of miles of undeveloped territory. Shoddy construction of the line, a lack of understanding of northern conditions, and a shocking lack of attention to fiscal concerns inflated the project's costs wildly. The project was completed but "was allowed to wither, subject to some fancy diplomatic footwork which upset the Americans, and remained a junkyard monument to military stupidity."[17]

The transformation of the northwest was clearly underway; there was more to come. The backlog of supplies at Skagway and along the White Pass and Yukon Route convinced the Americans that an additional access road was required. As work continued on the main Alcan Highway, workers pushed south from what is now Haines Junction toward the coast. Other crews started from the fishing town of Haines, Alaska, and worked north. The construction of the Haines Road allowed for the movement of supplies from the coast into the interior, without relying on the Skagway-Whitehorse railway. There were other projects as well. Airfields were upgraded, hangars

Many small native settlements and trading centres in the Yukon were swamped by the arrival of thousands of American soldiers and civilian workers. The old villages were quickly taken over as centres for construction activity. PUBLIC ARCHIVES OF CANADA

built, and access roads constructed. Additional emergency strips were constructed. A telephone system was built along the highway, providing greater contact with the outside than Yukoners had ever known.

The impact of all this on the Yukon Territory went far beyond the provision of a new road, airfields, a pipeline, and a telephone line. The Yukon had had fewer than five thousand people in 1941, 30 per cent of whom were natives. The white population lived in a few communities — Whitehorse, Dawson, Mayo — with only a few missionaries, police officers, and fur traders in the outlying areas. Almost overnight, ten thousand American military and an equally large number of civilian workers, some Canadians but mostly American, flooded into the northwest. By the end of 1942, the Whitehorse area alone had a population four times that of the pre-war Yukon. The American invasion affected all aspects of the Yukon life, created the greatest boom since the Klondike gold rush, and set the Territory on a markedly different course.

It was not a course that Yukoners directed or even influenced. They had, of course, petitioned often for the construction of a highway and, regardless of the circumstances, they were pleased that they were about to get their connection to the outside. More than a few expressed severe disappointment with the selected southern route, which entirely missed the heavily mineralized Mayo area and ran far south of Dawson City. Only the residents of Whitehorse could be pleased with this highway, which ignored the social and economic realities of the Territory.

The disruptions hit at all levels of Yukon society. In 1942 the American army leased the White Pass and Yukon Route. Only two months after the American take-over, a Canadian official reported that Yukoners were furious:

The U.S. Army has taken over the White Pass Railway on a lease. Before the lease was given, Ottawa was consulted and approved of the transfer. It was distinctly understood that shipments for the Canadian Government Departments and for the needs of the civilian population of the Yukon, were to be handled with reasonable dispatch. The operation of the railway under the U.S. Army has been very unsatisfactory and the service rendered to the people of the Yukon has been just about as bad as could be. The military handling the operation of the railway simply takes the attitude that the army comes first and Canadian Government, airport supplies and freight for the civilian population can take what is left, which, at the present time is NOTHING.[18]

The Americans ran the railway hard, pushing it twenty-four hours a day during the summer and keeping trains going all winter long. They did not, unfortunately, pay much attention to roadbed and running-stock mainte-nance, leaving the railway in bad shape when their lease ended. The army gave highway-related shipments top priority on the railway, making it difficult for commercial and domestic consumers to plan for their own needs. Repeated protests by Controller George Jeckell, the highest ranking territo-rial official, on behalf of the Yukon government were ignored, and it was only when construction demand slowed after 1943 that civilian needs were given a reasonable priority. This was wartime, after all, and Yukoners knew they had little right to complain about such comparatively trifling inconven-iences. The federal government helped out somewhat by not applying national rationing to the Territory, although shortages of key commodities ensured long line-ups in front of the stores — especially the liquor store — when supplies arrived.

The construction projects also created opportunities. Workers from around the Territory were drawn to the high-paying jobs along the highway or pipeline, making it extremely difficult for local employers to find suitable employees. C. J. Rogers, president of the White Pass and Yukon Railway, complained to George Black:

> Our Labour and Wage situation is all snarled up here on account of the arrival of American contractors who are competing for local labour and paying a wage scale away in excess of that prevailing for any similar kind of work such as on the airfield here. They initially agreed not to disturb the local scale.[19]

Yukoners, not surprisingly, preferred the high-paying American jobs to low-paying Canadian work. Eventually Humphrey Mitchell, Canadian Minis-ter of Labour, stepped in and ruled that only Americans were eligible for work with American companies. Horace Moore, publisher of the *Whitehorse Star*, protested the policy as "manifestly unfair and might reasonably be construed as placing a penalty on one's nationality....As long as Canadian labour is available here there is no real necessity or reason for the U.S. contractors being compelled to import U.S. citizens, none of whom will contribute a single cent toward Canadian taxation and whose earnings, for the most part, will be transmitted to the United States."[20] As the initial agreements took effect, moreover, Yukoners found that they did not have equal access to all the jobs.

Because the Americans were supervising and paying for the construction of the defence projects, the Canadian government agreed to their request that American wage rates and wartime regulations would apply to American nationals working in the northwest. Canadians came under the jurisdiction of the Western Regional Labour Board, which decided whether labour could be spared for specific tasks and set wage rates for all Canadian workers. Canadian contractors and sub-contractors hired Canadian personnel; Americans sought their employees in the United States. Given that most of the contractors were American, this meant that the majority of the work was undertaken by United States citizens. While a general shortage of workers throughout the northwest limited Canadian protests, there were occasions when Yukoners found themselves barred from high-paying jobs in favour of workers brought in from the states.[21]

The regulations were not rigidly enforced, particularly in the isolated camps along the highway and the Canol pipeline, far removed from the watchful eyes of highway administrators. Canadians raised no objections when an employer agreed to pay the prevailing American scale, a better option perhaps than having a bitter employee. Most workers, imported from the outside, approached highway work in a "get rich quick" frame of mind, preventing the strict imposition of the rules. Rigidity on this question, officials realized, "would probably have created some friction particularly when most Canadians were looking for some of this 'easy American money.' "[22]

The wage differentials were substantial enough to create considerable hostility. Bechtel, Price, Callahan, one of the largest contractors on the northern defence projects, paid its American labourers on the Canol project $1 per hour (U.S. funds); a Canadian employee, doing the same job, would receive 50¢ (Canadian, and the Canadian dollar was worth less than the American). The pattern was the same for other job classifications: American truck drivers received $1.40; Canadian 85¢. An electrician from the United States was paid $1.50 an hour; his Canadian counterpart, working in his own country, received $1. Other companies followed the same basic scale. Although the difference was narrowed through the war years, high American salaries remained a major grievance for Canadian workers in the Yukon.

The grievances over wage rates spilled over into intense controversies concerning the application of American laws in Canada's north. Negotiations between Ottawa and Washington resulted in the establishment of concurrent jurisdiction in the northwest. While Canadian laws remained in

Although the wages for northern work were high, conditions were rough, as the Bechtel, Price, Callahan company made clear to potential employees.
PUBLIC ARCHIVES OF CANADA

force, American soldiers and workers came under the authority of United States military and civilian regulations. Initially, these regulations applied only within the confines of American work camps, a situation few Canadians found unsettling. As time passed, and as it became increasingly evident that the Canadian government was reluctant to press its own authority in the region, Americans expanded their authority beyond their own establishments.

Although the American legal arm was generally benign, there were enough unsettling situations to cause concern among Yukoners. In a number of criminal cases, for instance, American military police arrested the offenders and spirited them back to the United States before the Royal Canadian Mounted Police even had a chance to question them. In a controversial case, a doctor escorting two young ladies home from a dance at the airport was accosted and beaten by two American soldiers. By the time the police had been alerted, the men were in a truck heading for the Alaskan border. Numerous protests were registered, including a strongly worded letter by Yukon Member of Parliament George Black, but to no avail. In such instances, the Americans preferred to try their soldiers and civilians under American military law rather than let the Canadian legal process run its course.

The system generated considerable anger, particularly among Canadians who wondered if justice was truly being served. In some cases, such as one in which two soldiers entered the Carcross Residential School girls' dormitory, severe penalties were handed out, much more severe, in fact, than they would have received under Canadian law (in this case, almost certainly because the culprits were black). But the opposite was also true. Two soldiers found guilty of having sex with under-age girls were fined $24 and $20 each by an American military court; a conviction for the same

237

offence in front of a Canadian judge probably would have carried a jail sentence.

The situation could, and did, work in reverse. There were occasions when American military law provided for much faster and more severe punishment than would have been possible through the Canadian courts. In what became known as "Sofa Laws," (as in the phrase "to hide under the sofa"), Canadian authorities would deliver the accused to American officials and leave the dispensation of the case in their hands. However, the judicial systems were only intermittently in conflict, for, as with other aspects of highway work and administration, co-operation was more the norm. If there was a problem on the legal front, it had to do with enforcement, where charges of American high-handedness were more commonplace.

Although the Royal Canadian Mounted Police moved its Yukon head-quarters to Whitehorse in 1943–44, the thirty-man detachment could not patrol the entire southern Yukon. The United States Army Military Police, therefore, had an important enforcement role. They took to the task with enthusiasm, often overstepping legal and national barriers. For example, they arrested the Assistant Fire Chief of the Whitehorse Volunteer Fire Brigade for investigating the fire that followed a plane crash on the streets of his town.

The activities of the American Military Police were evident throughout the Territory. Security investigations were carried out on a number of Yukon citizens, sometimes over the protests of Canadian authorities. The numerous military sites around Whitehorse were off-limits to Canadian personnel, sparking a series of confrontations between the police and local residents. The Military Police controlled access to the Alaska Highway, barring even local traffic, although the residents had been promised relatively free use of the road after initial construction. They similarly enforced highway regula-tions, once more stepping beyond their authority, and were accused on several occasions of handling civilians in a rude and abrasive fashion. While the complaints resounded with the moral indignation of people who felt they had been unfairly treated, they contained the additional frustration of being mistreated by foreign nationals. Whose country, they could ask with some justification, *was* this? Indeed, the problem would have broader connota-tions.

For the soldiers and workers, northern work quickly lost its lustre. The excitement of the journey northward was offset by the isolation and frontier conditions of the land they now worked in. They found themselves working ten- to sixteen-hour shifts, made possible by the long summer days. Not many complained about the workload, in part because they had little reason for being there except to make money and also because there was little else to do. Construction camps were rudimentary affairs; most soldiers spent the winter in dome-style tents. As time passed, the ubiquitous Quonset huts sprang up in the construction and maintenance camps along the highway.

The Alaska Highway was a military road, and a rough one at that. Traffic along the highway was strictly controlled; all drivers had to report at the highway stations along the highway. The check-points proved particularly important for stopping bootlegging along the highway.
NATIONAL ARCHIVES OF THE U.S.A.

Eventually, wooden barracks were erected at the more important centres; Whitehorse was filled with the long, low "temporary" buildings that housed the workers and offices of the Northwest Service Command.

As the workers soon discovered, the northern climate had its vicious side. Most were not familiar with the dangers of a sub-Arctic winter. Several men died when they ignored the oft-repeated warning to stay with their vehicles if they broke down along the road; they froze to death while trying to walk to the nearest highway camp. The cold weather made it hard to operate machinery, limited outside activities, and generally made life miserable for the men. They also complained about the summer, when the long days made it possible for their bosses to extend the workday and for the mosquitoes to feast on them. The food offered little relief from what rapidly became a dreary existence. Difficulties with supply forced the army and construction cooks, never known for creativity, to feed the workers a distressingly monotonous menu of Yukon Shrimp (Vienna sausages), hash, and chili.

Army and civilian managers recognized the dangers of unhappy work crews and sought to provide some recreation for them. The American government asked for and received permission for its men to hunt along the highway, subject to a one-dollar licence fee. The charge was the same as that for resident Yukoners, and substantially less than the standard non-resident fee of $75 for British subjects and $100 for foreign nationals.[23] While locals, particularly the native people, complained about over-hunting and wastage of game, the government accepted such losses as necessary evils. As General Hoge also noted, "if permission was not granted the men would hunt anyway."[24]

Top: *Facilities along the pioneer road were few and far between. Construction crews and truck drivers, particularly those caught by bad weather or poor road conditions, often had to bunk down along the highway.* OFFICE OF HISTORY, U.S. ARMY CORPS OF ENGINEERS

Centre: *Whitehorse was the headquarters of the construction activity, selected for its position at the railhead, excellent airfield and access to the Yukon river system. Hundreds of troops were housed in a tent city located on the escarpment overlooking the community.* PUBLIC ARCHIVES OF CANADA

Below: *The highway and the sub-Arctic winter conditions claimed a large number of victims. Within days of the highway opening, over-turned and abandoned trucks could be found along the route.* OFFICE OF HISTORY, U.S. ARMY CORPS OF ENGINEERS

And hunt the Yankees did. The slaughter was too much for one employee of the E. W. Elliott Company: "There are guns in every camp killing everything from the smallest to the largest....The soldiers kill anything. What is your people [R.C.M.P.] going to do? Stand by and see your game destroyed? It hurts a lot of us to see these trusting animals killed."[21] The area surrounding construction and maintenance camps faced the greatest pressure, for few of the visitors risked the journey into the back-country. Although the long-term damage was comparatively slight, the impact on local game resources was noticeable. The Fur Supervisor, Indian Affairs Branch, observed that "the decimation of the big game resources in the area was the direct result of too intensive big game hunting by whites generally and particularly by U.S. Army personnel."[26]

Allowing Americans to hunt also revealed a fundamental truth about federal policy towards Yukon Indian harvesting. R. H. Gibson, a federal official, noted that:

> there has always been a fundamental difference in wild life management in the Yukon and Northwest Territories. In the Yukon hunting for sport has been encouraged. In the Northwest Territories the wild life is reserved for those who depend on it for a living, chiefly our increasing population of Indians and Eskimos.[27]

While the natives did not appreciate or agree with the distinction, the federal decision permitted the Americans at least one outlet for their energies.

There were, of course, others. Card-playing competed with complaining about the weather and food as a major pastime. The "beer bust" was an important part of an otherwise dreary social life, and workers near the major centres joined the long line-ups at the liquor stores. The United States Army established a radio network along the highway which reached most construction camps, providing the best of modern music and timely newscasts to the widely scattered crews. The army also delivered first-run movies, fresh out of Hollywood and preceded by patriotic newsreels outlining the progress of the war overseas. On occasion, U.S.O. troops visited the area, bringing attractive female performers to the northern camps to entertain the soldiers and construction workers. Word of these and other events was spread along the highway via the *Northwest Newscast*, a newspaper printed especially to bring the international and local news to the camps.

There were many other recreational opportunities. Camp officials and local residents ensured that national celebrations, both Canadian and American, were suitably marked with parties, competitions, music, and other special events. The camps and divisional offices organized their own baseball, basketball, hockey, and bowling leagues where facilities and manpower permitted. Highway rivalries developed as teams travelled to other camps for competitions. In settlements with a sizable civilian population, the locals competed with army and construction teams, adding the spice of competition to their generally friendly relations. Boxing matches always attracted good crowds; skilled fighters travelled up and down the highway staging exhibition matches in front of enthusiastic audiences. At most camps, and particularly in the administrative centre at Whitehorse, out-trips were organized for those wishing to put their days off to productive use. Buses travelled from Whitehorse to Teslin for a day of sight-seeing and fishing, or north to Haines Junction for some time in the mountains. In Whitehorse, dances were held almost nightly. Local dance bands worked constantly as the various military and civilian branches took turns sponsoring an active social round. There were occasional problems, particularly if alcohol flowed too freely.

Given the sexual imbalance in the Territory, the range of social activities kept the small number of unmarried women in the area very much the centre of attention, and there were a number of suitably romantic highway marriages. Of course, prostitutes could be found in all highway communities, and venereal disease reached almost epidemic proportions. The Yukon territorial government gave itself the authority to imprison anyone carrying the infection, a law applied primarily to prostitutes and native women, but seldom to men. The United States authorities struggled with the problem as well, offering medical advice, requiring attendance at films on the evils of casual sex, and operating twenty-four-hour prophylactic stations for the men. The warnings and attempted controls did not always work. There were a number of reported rape cases, and several dozen convictions for indecent assault.

The United States authorities provided alternatives for such behaviour, and tried to control it in other ways as well. Native villages were placed off-limits to all American personnel, although to little effect. Strongly worded directives circulated through the camps, describing the punishments for rape and sexual assaults, and advising highway workers to respect the rights of local residents.

The shortage of white women guaranteed that native women would be drawn into short-term liaisons with construction workers, often in the context of party drinking. Some, evidently victims of what in those days was called a "line," believed that their relationship would be permanent, only to be disillusioned when the man involved left the Territory. The territorial birth rate jumped sharply during the construction years, especially among the native population.[28]

The Territory's racial mix was also enriched during the construction by the black troops used in the building of the pioneer road. Although American military regulations officially discouraged the use of black troops in northern settings, wartime necessity forced the dispatch of several battalions of black engineers to the Yukon. They were, as one official noted, sent to do the "dirty work," in isolated areas, away from the white population. Local residents were warned not to get too friendly with them, a warning that

Despite American regulations restricting the use of black soldiers in northern climates, thousands of black engineering troops were sent to the northwest to work on the Alaska Highway and the Canol Pipeline. PUBLIC ARCHIVES OF CANADA

reinforced existing racial stereotypes. Whitehorse residents, consequently, were relieved to hear that the black troops were being sent further up the highway, rather than being stationed in the town to work on the airport construction.[29]

The Yukon's Indians suffered in a variety of other ways from the arrival of the soldiers and civilian workers. The highway improved access to hunting grounds throughout the southern Yukon for the natives, while providing others with access to the same resources. Thus, as already mentioned, the workers competed for pleasure for the same game and fish resources that the natives needed for survival. The Indians found a few job opportunities, particularly in 1942 and 1943, when their skills as guides and labourers were in demand. It was soon obvious that the wartime projects, like the earlier economic booms, meant lots of work for whites from the outside but few jobs for Yukon native people. As the Indians had done in the past, they took the short-term and occasionally high-paying jobs when available. The Americans, in fact, did not take rapidly to the high salaries demanded by the natives. The president of the White Pass and Yukon Route had little sympathy:

> In Whitehorse, key to the whole northland, the rate is $7.50 minimum for a 10-hour day, with the Indians getting the same rate . . . the [Indians] are among the best workers we ever had. Immediately there was a holler. . . that the idea of paying an Indian $7.50 a day was unheard of, immoral, ridiculous, fantastic and all that stuff. Well, we won't have any Jim Crow laws up here. If labour gets $7.50 and labour is Indian, then an Indian gets $7.50.[30]

But the natives also maintained their seasonal movements. Fur harvests remained steady through the first construction years, then expanded rapidly thereafter. In 1944–45 and again in 1945–46, Yukon trappers brought in close to $670,000 worth of furs, the highest returns in the first half of the twentieth century.

While the economic impact on the native people was comparatively light, the same could not be said of the health impact. Many of the Yukon Indians affected by the Alcan Highway had had little earlier contact with non-natives. Now, suddenly, thousands of strangers entered their lands, carrying a variety of diseases against which they had little natural protection. Dr. J. F. Marchand, stationed at Teslin during the winter of 1942–43, recorded successive attacks of measles, dysentery, jaundice, whooping cough, mumps, and meningitis — all in a single community in one year.[31] Several of these epidemics, notably measles and influenza, swept along the Alaska Highway and cut a deadly swathe through all the native communities in the southern Yukon. Many of the deaths, some never officially recorded but well-remembered in the oral traditions of the affected communities, were of infants and young children, contributing to a horrifying infant mortality rate.

Army and civilian doctors did what they could. Both Canadian and American authorities made their facilities available to the Indians, although there was a short controversy over whether or not American doctors would be permitted to practise medicine on the Territory's civilians. On balance, however, the medical effects were devastating. C. K. LeCapelain described the problem:

> There is no question but what the impact of all the construction in the Southern Yukon and its consequent influx of white people is having a very harmful effect upon the natives, and it is noticeable that the degree of this harm is in direct proportion to the closeness of the association that the natives have with the whites. The new era is here to stay and is and will continue to present many problems....One of these problems is how to soften the blow upon the natives and ameliorate conditions so as to prevent their complete devastation.[32]

The highway also meant that the southern natives came under the scrutiny and influence of the Canadian government. While this brought improved medical service and access to hospitals and government relief, it also resulted in demands that the Indians send their children to school. The increased population in the region also resulted in the transfer of the Royal Canadian Mounted Police headquarters from Dawson to Whitehorse in 1943–44. The combination of greater police attention and increased access to alcohol resulted in a dramatic increase in the number of natives convicted of drinking offences (under the Indian Act, not the Criminal Code).

Although the incidence of serious crime among the Indian population was low, a number of native people found themselves before the courts with some regularity, a process that unfortunately helped confirm white stereotypes.

Protests about over-hunting in the southwest corner of the territory stimulated an unexpected action. At the urging of C. K. LeCapelain, federal liaison officer, the Canadian government moved quickly to block further development in the land west of the Alcan Highway, and in December 1942, within two weeks of the official opening of the pioneer road, the government set the land aside.[33] The following year, the Territorial Council seconded the federal effort by banning all hunting, including that by native people, in the region. Indians in the area, working through Burwash trader and guide Eugene Jacquot, protested the government's action. Some revisions were made — a strip of land near the White River was exempted from the freeze; the bulk of the land, however, remained closed to all hunting. Although expressing some concern for native rights, federal authorities decided that the land and resources took higher priority. The game sanctuary remained, to become, in 1972, Kluane National Park, one of Canada's most impressive wilderness areas and a UNESCO World Heritage Site. For the natives, displaced from a valued and traditional hunting ground, there were official regrets, some help with muskrat hunting, and the two-edged benefits of a slowly expanding welfare state.

The building of the Alaska Highway, particularly after Hoge's decision to follow a southern route, caused consternation in Dawson City, whose residents had always pushed for a road that would connect their town with the south, thus ensuring their continued dominance over the Territory. But now Whitehorse was booming and Dawson, already on the skids as a result of the declining gold industry, faced the most serious threat in its history.

Although home to a summer population of around a thousand, Dawson City had little reason for optimism in the early years of the war. The seasonal pattern of the past remained in evidence, forcing Dawson into a cocoon-like existence every fall. The city's structures were aging, many of them were abandoned; the community was drained of its life. The presence of a truncated civil service could not offset the dominance of the Yukon Consolidated Gold Corporation; for all of its former glory and its pretenses as capital city, Dawson was really a company town tied to a declining industry.[34]

There was real pain for Dawsonites in watching Whitehorse's spectacular growth and the frenetic activity in the south. As J. E. Gibben noted with some bitterness in 1943, "The people in Dawson and Mayo Districts are receiving no pecuniary benefit from war industries or war projects, and increased taxation has brought about a self-imposed liquor rationing." Many simply surrendered to the new realities and headed south. Workers left the dredges for better prospects along the highway; all through the winter of 1942–43, the exodus continued. Businessmen moved specialized equipment, including the Cascade Laundry dry-cleaning plant, to Whitehorse, where greater markets and handsome boom-town profits awaited.

Dawson's already battered armour began to fall away in large chunks. The demands of government work forced key officials to spend long periods of time in the south. Some succumbed to the new pressures of business and relocated in Whitehorse. The R.C.M.P. moved out, as did several key federal departments, including the Wartime Prices and Trade Board. Prominent citizens followed suit; George and Martha Black shifted their residence in 1944, as did the Anglican bishop. Dawson, suffering the ignominy of losing government offices, the basis of its claim to territorial prominence, now suffered the pain of watching many of its leading citizens leave forever.

Not everyone gave up hope. George Jeckell resisted all suggestions that he move to Whitehorse, or even spend more time there. His reluctance to travel restricted his ability to do his job properly, but his staunch defence of Dawson City encouraged others. The town still had its boosters, and now Jeckell provided it with a rallying cry — Dawson needed a highway of its own. Dawsonites believed — they had to — that Whitehorse would collapse at the end of the war, and felt that if a connector road was built they could overcome their isolation and be able to serve the entire Territory. Jeckell's intransigence ensured that Dawson retained the capital, for now at least. The seat of government was all it had left, for power and wealth had clearly shifted to Whitehorse.

Whitehorse bore the full weight of changes — both creative and destructive changes — accompanying the wartime construction projects. Previously an isolated, seasonal community, tied to the rhythms of river travel and controlled by the White Pass and Yukon Route, Whitehorse had attracted little attention before the war. Virtually all goods and people entering the Territory passed through Whitehorse, but they seldom stayed long, or thought much of the slow, rough-hewn town on the edge of the Yukon River. Local businesses, with a few exceptions like the still extensive Taylor and Drury operations, were tied to the rail and steamer system, and there were no expectations of growth. There was copper still in the hills, but Whitehorse residents had long learned not to pin their hopes on the resource.[35]

The town was laid out on the river plain below Miles Canyon and the Whitehorse Rapids, a picturesque setting, flanked on the east by rounded, tree-covered mountains and on the west by high clay hills and a level plateau. The White Pass and Yukon Route railyards and docks dominated the landscape, and provided a focus for the community. Main Street ran perpendicular to the river, and boasted a few retail stores, government offices, and hotels. The private homes of civil servants, leading company officials, and businessmen surrounded the business district. The Indians occupied their reservation, removed from the downtown, sporadically. The workers' commitment to the town was little different; many squatted on

W.P.Y.R. lands in semi-permanent shacks. Whitehorse was, to all but a few businessmen and citizens, a way station, a place to earn a few dollars before escaping.

William Hoge and the highway roused the town from its slumber. The selection of Whitehorse as the administrative centre of the construction projects made sense, for it had an excellent airfield on the escarpment overlooking the community, had rail access to the ocean, and was the base for navigation on the Yukon River. The community was jolted into the twentieth century in June of 1942, when more than three thousand soldiers of the United States Army Corps of Engineers camped west of the town. While many of these men moved on, shifted to construction camps further along the highway, others took their places and added to a growing chaos. As the headquarters for the army and the Public Roads Administration, Whitehorse quickly became a temporary home for thousands of administrators, maintenance workers, soldiers, and construction workers, for project managers and support personnel, the site for the Canol refinery, and a supply depot for much of the northwest. A year after construction started, Whitehorse had some ten thousand people, the vast majority from the United States. It had exploded from a sleepy river depot to a major military and construction complex. That these changes were directed by outsiders was nothing new for a Territory used to external control and the instability of a boom-and-bust economy.

Yukoners once more found themselves swamped by foreign nationals and, like the Klondike in 1897–98, Whitehorse was ill-equipped to deal with the onslaught. With few houses and only three hotels, the town faced a shortage of bed space. For a while, soldiers and construction workers were housed in tent cities, then civilian contractors, working under the Public Roads Administration, built dozens of barracks, office buildings, and other facilities. The urban landscape of Whitehorse was completely transformed. Local residents participated in the boom; Martin Berrigan built several "log skyscrapers" as rental units in response to an almost unlimited demand. Canadian citizens, denied housing by the United States Army's insatiable appetite, moved into the rapidly growing squatter settlements of Whiskey and Moccasin flats.

Americans, aided by a few Canadians, built the highway, altered the communities, and made the decisions. On an individual level, the challenge for Canadians in the Yukon during the Second World War was living with the Yankees. That they did so with surprisingly little strife reflected well on their shared commitment to continental defence and the war effort. However, as one Canadian official complained, "Some of these people do not seem to know that Whitehorse is in Canada and it is high time that proper steps were taken to acquaint them of the fact."[36] The Northwest Service Command headquarters were erected atop the bluff, near the Alaska

Highway. The town began to move up the hill, out of the river valley. A subdivision of "cemesto" family homes in Camp Takhini added to the office and housing complex on the plateau. Unlike the temporary structures built in the lower town, the cemestos were designed for long-term use, although their southern designers had made few adaptations for the special needs of the northern environment. The buildings offered only minimal protection from the cold, and residents of both barracks and family homes faced many nights when uninsulated oil pipelines froze, forcing a dependence on wood stoves.[37]

Little was done to protect local residents from the effects of this American reconstruction of their town. Government officials did nothing to stop the spread of squatters' homes onto crown and private land. George Jeckell, who was responsible for the administration of Whitehorse, was indifferent to the town's problems. Believing that the wartime changes would prove temporary, Jeckell refused to commit the Territory to major expenditures in Whitehorse. In fact, even though Whitehorse was generating sizeable revenues at this time, particularly through the local liquor store, Jeckell felt no obligation to turn that money back into the community. It was instead set aside in a reserve fund for post-war use when, Jeckell expected, the *status ante bellum* would return. Even when civil servants, transferred to Whitehorse from Dawson, faced astronomical rents, Jeckell remained unmoved and rejected their requests for financial assistance.

The combination of inadequate planning, American military initiative, and limited local control over the transformation of the community had serious implications. Whitehorse's rudimentary sewage and water system could not contend with the massive invasion. Water was delivered by private contractors; septic fields and pit toilets handled human waste. The American army feared widespread dysentery and built chlorination plants to provide water for its personnel. In the interests of preventing epidemics in the community, the army made its water available to all residents and to local water dealers. Unbeknownst to Canadian authorities, American plans were underway for the construction of a proper sewage and water system for the community. C. K. LeCapelain wrote to R. A. Gibson, Director, Lands, Parks and Housing: "As far as I know neither you nor the Controller, Yukon Territory, are aware of this proposed work."[38] Their subsequent protests were noted and extensive negotiations on the project began. Finally, the Americans abruptly scrapped the plan agreed to with the Canadians, to proceed instead unilaterally with a cheaper, scaled-down version. The system served the army's needs in the downtown area and the homes of a few well-to-do citizens, private businesses, and government offices who, at their own expense, hooked into the system. Many civilian residents and businesses, however, remained without adequate water and sewage facilities. Canadian health officials were far from pleased; one government agent, A. H. Perry, called the townsite "an undeveloped island of cesspits."[39]

A pattern had been set. American activities transformed and disrupted the community, local citizens clamoured for attention to their needs, and George Jeckell and the territorial government ignored them. In 1944, for example, residents angry over the dense dust from construction blanketing the community through the summer petitioned Jeckell for assistance. Nothing could be done, he claimed, because of a lack of oil and equipment to spread it. The residents' complaints received a more favourable reception in Ottawa. R. A. Gibson, now Director of the Bureau of Northwest Territories and Yukon Affairs learned of the problem, contacted American officials, and secured an offer of oil, free of charge, from the newly opened Canol refinery in town.

The arrogance of some of the American soldiers and construction workers brought about other difficulties. They showed a decided lack of knowledge of the area, and an indifference to the diplomatic niceties, a sentiment well summarized in one soldier's note to his mother: "You know, Mom, the British have got this country now, but don't you worry, we'll soon get it back."[40] The American bravado showed up on a variety of fronts — their disrespect for Canadian authorities, their casual use of Canadian resources, and their lack of attention to the symbols of Canadian sovereignty — at some camps, the Canadian flag was not flown; at others, displayed inappropriately. The lack of attention to Canadian sensitivities rankled, although local residents had difficulty complaining, given the almost complete inattention of their own government to such matters.

The Americans, for their part, were not always pleased with Canadian workers and administrators. Commissioner George Jeckell was viewed as a foot-dragger, and after several unsuccessful attempts at dealing with him, the Americans simply began to ignore his office. Complaints from local residents, funnelled through civil servants such as C. K. LeCapelain, only irritated American officials, who sensed that Canadians were not as keen as they were about the northern projects, even though they stood to reap the lion's share of the benefits. The U.S. ambassador to Canada summarized a general American sentiment when he wrote, "Do not think...that I am giving the Canadians a clean bill of health and damning the Americans. Canadian construction work is dishearteningly slow, they are short in most modern construction equipment, and their labour is casual and at times dishearteningly apathetic."[41]

The Americans' arrival brought dozens of other changes to Whitehorse. Little money was spared in providing the soldiers and civilian workers with a full set of recreational facilities, to help them survive the long winters in this Canadian outpost with their morale intact. Military and civilian authorities built outdoor hockey rinks and cleared a number of baseball fields. Baseball took root with a vengeance during the war, sparked by intense, if friendly, rivalries between the army and the "townies"; the community's love affair with the sport outlived the war.

Top: *Although the government made special arrangements to ensure a steady supply of liquor to workers and soldiers in the northwest, the demand was usually greater. Long line-ups outside the Whitehorse Liquor Store were the norm during the construction years.* YUKON TERRITORIAL ARCHIVES

Below: *Troops and civilians in the far northwest kept abreast of international affairs, aided by a U.S. Army radio station and a regular army newspaper, Northwest Newscast. Americans and Canadians gathered to celebrate V-E day at a Whitehorse baseball field, May 8, 1945.* NATIONAL ARCHIVES OF THE U.S.A.

With thousands of potential patrons in town, many on short-term furlough from highway camps, local businessmen seized the opportunity and opened bars (aided by the federal government's decision not to impose wartime liquor rationing in the Yukon), restaurants, and two new theatres. Whitehorse had had only one restaurant in 1941; two years later, it could claim ten. One café alone claimed to have served up to nine hundred meals a day during the first year. As well, more rooms were added to schools and the hospital, and the Americans built a small medical facility of their own. Local hotels faced an almost unlimited demand for their rooms. While government regulations prohibited price-gouging, there were ways around such rules. Patrons, it seemed, rented the bed, not the room, and had to sleep in shifts, for there was always someone around to take up any empty beds. Barbers and taxi drivers, once marginal and seasonal operators, found a steady supply of customers. So did drycleaners, laundries, and the local bank, which increased its staff from three to twelve in 1942. Not just in Whitehorse but all along the route, Indian women found work as seamstresses, cooks, or taking in laundry; they also worked to fill an almost inexhaustible demand for native-made products, especially mukluks, mittens, and coats.

Everyone in Whitehorse seemed to be enjoying the boom. Even though the army provided its own messing facilities, and brought in most of its supplies, they still purchased large quantities from local retailers. At the beginning of 1942, according to one report, American government spending in the town quadrupled from one month to the next. But local citizens began to wonder about what would happen when the Americans pulled out. After all, the highway was not being completed to civilian standards. If it stayed open, it was clear that the highway would not be the catalyst for regional economic growth that its promoters had foreseen. The Whitehorse refinery had proven a major disappointment and it had been hoped that the hundreds of workers brought north with their families to work at the refinery would have become the backbone for an expanding industrial economy. The decision, taken within months of opening it, to mothball the entire operation, was a blow to those looking for a greater measure of stability. Could it be that Whitehorse was about to experience a classic "boom and bust"?

While they wondered about the possibility of a bust, Yukoners got on with the business of living, and in the Yukon of the war years, that meant dealing with ten thousand distant cousins camped in your backyard. Although relations between Canadians and Americans were generally peaceable and friendly, as might be expected given the long history of national mixture in the Yukon River Valley, many were troubled by the scale and pervasiveness of United States involvement. The Americans made virtually all the decisions and had assumed *de facto* control of much of the Yukon Territory. J. D. Hickerson of the United States Department of State recognized that the scale of American interests created certain problems:

> Our relations with Canada are excellent. The only cloud on the horizon is that the extent of our War Department expenditures and activities in western Canada has been so great in connection with the war effort... that some people feel that we may have a vested interest there and be reluctant to leave when the war is over. That is of course nonsense but not all Canadians realize it.[42]

251

While American control made sense from a logistical and administrative perspective, it represented an alarming loss of sovereignty on Canada's part. C. K. LeCapelain, who served as a liaison between the U.S. authorities and the federal government, travelled extensively throughout the region. Although his reports reveal a first-rate understanding of the circumstances and consequences of the wartime projects, he could do little more than observe. With George Jeckell only occasionally venturing out of Dawson City, the territorial interests were not well protected, leaving the Americans to locate the road, place the airfields, construct buildings and facilities, and otherwise make decisions that would shape the future development of the Yukon Territory.

Ottawa, it seemed, was unconcerned about the situation. True, the nation was pre-occupied with the pressing challenges of fighting an international war and managing a rapidly expanding domestic economy. But the complete indifference to the activities of thousands of American nationals in a large segment of the Canadian northwest was nonetheless astonishing. Historian Donald Creighton, a vigorous critic of the King government's handling of the national war effort, waxed vitriolic in his criticisms of the administration of the Alaska Highway:

> [The Americans] enjoyed the power of numbers and the authority of command; and the Canadian efforts to regulate their activities, which consisted chiefly in paper commands and exhortations despatched at long range from Ottawa, were singularly ineffectual. The Canadian government showed, in fact, an inexcusable lack of responsibility in its failure to protect one of the nation's greatest assets. No member of the King cabinet ever thought it worth his while to visit the Canadian north and really find out what was going on there.[43]

Canada was ultimately jolted into action at the urging of Malcolm MacDonald, British High Commissioner to Canada. At the request of his government and an informal group of Ottawa-based "Northern Nationalists," MacDonald visited the north in 1942 — one of his duties was to stop at Old Crow and extend his thanks, on behalf of the British people, for the Indians' donations to war relief projects. The High Commissioner returned the following year, concerned about continued reports of American liberties in the north and rumours of Yankee designs on the region. Upon his return to Ottawa, MacDonald laid a blunt report on his findings before the Canadian War Cabinet. Canada, he argued, might lose its northern possessions if Americans plans came to fruition:

> But certainly many influential American individuals who have had a hand in these developments in the North-West have no serious thought that the interests which they represent shall withdraw. American money, energy and labour have been spent on an immense scale whilst the

Canadians have had comparatively little to do with some of the most important undertakings. One can imagine some of these people stirring up quite an unpleasant agitation in Congress circles to force the hands of the Administration, if they feel so disposed.[44]

While there was a certain hysteria (tinged with British self-interest), in MacDonald's rhetoric, there was also a good deal of truth. MacDonald drew attention to the limited federal presence in the area — a few officials, with scant resources, scattered throughout an area now host to tens of thousands of Americans who jokingly called themselves the "Army of Occupation." The High Commissioner had a solution. He recommended that the federal government immediately appoint a civil servant to represent Canadian interests in the northern defence projects. In May 1943, fully a year after the major construction projects had started and after most of the decisions affecting them had been made, the King government dispatched General W. W. Foster as Special Commissioner on Defence Projects in the Northwest. Canada had, once more belatedly, recognized the threat to its ownership of the far northwest.[45]

Based in Edmonton with a small staff, there was little that Foster could actually do. His presence, however, had a salutary influence on the Americans, who now passed most decisions through his office for approval. In a way, it did not matter much. By the end of 1943, work on the Alaska Highway had slowed and construction standards had been relaxed considerably. By the following spring, public revelations from the Truman Commission about grotesque over-spending on the Canol pipeline dampened American interest in that project as well, although work continued until the pipeline and refinery were completed. In September 1944, the United States government formally asked Canada to take over maintenance responsibility for the Alaska Highway. When a report indicated that the cost of such work would be $6 million for the first two years alone, Ottawa decided that that exceeded the reasonable costs of regaining sovereignty and refused.

By now, however, it was evident that Canada *would* eventually take over the road; doubts about American intentions in the north had been laid to rest, if only because the oilfields, pipeline, and refinery had proved such monumental disasters. The federal government would wait out the contract and would take over control of the highway as agreed, six months after the war ended. In the interim, the United States government left a small military staff to maintain the highway and airfields. The Public Roads Administration pulled its people out as their work on highway relocation and bridge construction was completed, and moved them back to the United States. Most major projects were stopped by 1944, and the Americans unilaterally and in violation of international agreements closed down the Haines Lateral, the road connecting Haines, Alaska, and the military highway, a reflection of the changing face of the Pacific War and a grudging admission that the highway did not serve an important military purpose.

The Canadian government now faced a troubling dilemma. Reports from LeCapelain, MacDonald, and others made it clear that the Alaska Highway was neither the road sought by northern residents nor that expected by North Americans. Major expenditures were required to bring the road and bridges up to proper standards. It would not do to criticize the Americans for failing to live up to the initial agreement; they had, after all, built the highway without cost to Canadians. On the other hand, the Canadian government knew it would face much criticism if and when the highway was opened to civilian traffic. That could be prevented during the war years, when civilian traffic was severely limited, but as the end of the confrontations in Europe and Asia neared, it was clear that a decision on the highway was necessary.

The reasons for Canadian reluctance were evident; there was little pleasure in taking over a road that Canada had not wanted and that did not address the economic and social needs of the northwest. As one civil servant bitterly noted, Canada now had to "build and maintain the kind of road that the United States promised but did not construct." To make matters worse, Canada was put in the uneasy situation of having to buy back its sovereignty in the north. The federal government eventually paid $123,500,000 to the United States for permanent installations along the Alaska Highway and the staging route. According to Prime Minister King, the payments were essential, for it was "undesirable that any other country should have financial investment in improvements of permanent value such as civil aviation facilities for peacetime use in this country." Wisely, the government refused American requests that Canada purchase the physical assets of the Canol pipeline, already moth-balled before the end of the war.[46]

The Yukon had been truly transformed. Native people had been hit with yet another wave of epidemics; the numerous new graves in Indian cemeteries at Upper Liard, Teslin, Whitehorse, Champagne, and elsewhere offered mute but poignant testimony to the great personal loss that would always be associated with the highway. Whitehorse was no longer a sleepy river town; instead, it was the most modern and populous community in the north, with the facilities and problems of a city twice its size. Dawson had slipped further down the path towards oblivion, outpaced by its southern rival. The Mayo-Keno mines, for two decades the engine of the territorial economy, had closed down, but the current boom was so great that few commented on the temporary loss. Long isolated from the southern world, the Yukon now found itself astride a major highway and airway and with a new telephone system. Yukoners had long seen the lack of contact with the outside as a major impediment to regional growth. Had the Territory's time come once again?

While there was reasonable excitement about the changes, Yukoners,

The Yukon River system proved surprisingly important in carrying supplies for highway construction. River steamers moved supplies up the Yukon River to Whitehorse and along some of the major tributaries to isolated construction camps. NATIONAL ARCHIVES OF THE U.S.A.

Before construction started on the Alaska Highway, Whitehorse was a seasonal company town, its prosperity dependent upon river navigation and rail traffic. The community would be quickly transformed by the arrival of the U.S. Army and the construction crews. NATIONAL ARCHIVES OF THE U.S.A.

In the days of the pioneer road, all traffic along the Alaska Highway was by convoy. Spare parts were at a premium, and any truck left abandoned on the side of the road was soon cannibalized by army or civilian drivers. NATIONAL ARCHIVES OF THE U.S.A.

used to the boom-and-bust lifestyle, faced the future with some trepidation. No one knew what would follow the withdrawal of American troops, and the noises emanating from Ottawa about the highway were not encouraging. The closure of the Haines Lateral and of the Whitehorse refinery, once touted as the cornerstone of the city's economy, raised doubts about the future of the Alaska Highway itself. Many Yukoners were far from pleased with the highway and airfields. They had had no say in the location of the facilities, and the traditional corridors of territorial development — from Whitehorse to Mayo and Dawson — had been almost completely ignored.

But the bust never came, at least not for Whitehorse. Under the influence of the Northwest Service Command headquarters and the growing number of federal and territorial offices in town, Whitehorse had taken on a bureaucratic aura. The civilians had brought a measure of stability that the town had seldom known in the past, even though the population did drop dramatically from the heights of 1942. In the summer of 1944, Whitehorse still had six thousand residents, many of them temporary. Americans began to pull out in droves that year, as the civilian contractors finished their work and headed south. The Public Roads Administration reduced their northern staff and the American army moved to cut costs on their expensive northern defence projects. When word came of the final transfer of the facilities to Canadian authorities, Whitehorse held its collective breath. Would the federal government keep the highway open — and Whitehorse alive? For once, there was little hesitation on Ottawa's part. Thousands of Canadian army personnel headed north to take over the construction, maintenance, and administrative tasks associated with the Alaska Highway. Whitehorse remained the centre of highway operations and hence retained most of the highway personnel. Five years after the Americans left, Whitehorse still had some five thousand residents, fewer than in the heady days of 1942, but a much larger and more stable population than that of the tiny frontier community of the pre-war days.

The legacy of the war would live on in Whitehorse. The community had been pushed up onto the hill, creating an artificial separation between government and civilian residents that would last for another three decades. The highway also by-passed the city on the west side, forcing a reorientation of Whitehorse away from the waterfront. A drastically inadequate sewage and water system, and large squatters' settlements lingered. So did the dozens of American buildings — barracks, offices, warehouses, and recreation facilities — that filled in much of the lower town and served as the foundation of the military and civilian complexes on the bluff. Within forty years, most of the physical legacy of the war projects would be gone, but the shape of Whitehorse continued to reflect the decisions — largely American ones — made during the Second World War.

The entire Yukon was forced to adjust quickly to the end of the war.

Highway communities, some new, some older, became maintenance depots for the Canadian work crews. The airfields did not fare as well. The fields in Fort St. John, Fort Nelson, Watson Lake, and Whitehorse were maintained for post-war civilian use; others were maintained as emergency strips. Some of the airfields, like the one near Aishihik Lake, were mothballed and abandoned. Facilities constructed for the Canol project, including the pipe, transmission stations, and the Whitehorse refinery were dismantled after the war and shipped to Alberta, where they found new life in the Leduc oilfield. Maintenance shops along the route were abandoned, often on only a few days' notice; bridges were not repaired and the Canol road was allowed to deteriorate, so much so that the northern section (from Ross River to Norman Wells) was closed and the southern portion could only be used by heavy trucks equipped with winches to get across the rivers.

The Americans left quickly and with little planning — much the same way as they had arrived. Millions of dollars worth of equipment and buildings were declared surplus and attempts were made to sell them off. In Whitehorse, surplus army barracks were bought as private homes, donated to the Whitehorse Baptist Indian School, and otherwise pressed into service by a community still short of housing. The Canadian government, which took over many of the buildings and maintenance facilities for its own uses, prevented an extensive sell-off of the American supplies, fearing a total collapse of the northern retail market. Tons of usable materials, everything from heavy equipment to office supplies, were simply dumped, burned, or abandoned. The highway camps, especially along the Canol road, were slowly cannibalized, leaving behind empty buildings, the windows smashed, and piles of garbage. One observer, commenting on the Peace River district, described a reaction felt uniformly across the north:

> It is difficult to overestimate the dismay and disgust which has greeted recent revelations of waste and destruction in the Peace River. Scattered throughout that district are hundreds of families to whom just one of those blankets would be a Godsend; families that will not buy stoves, coats, blankets, etc. because they cannot afford them. Yet here, before their very eyes, goes on the senseless destruction of the very articles which they need but cannot pay for.[47]

The mounds of smashed and cannibalized bulldozers, the rusting equipment and decaying buildings which now lined the Alaska Highway left a sour taste in the mouths of northerners, a sorry legacy of the enthusiasm, energy, and expenditures of wartime.

YUKON TERRITORY
1987

0 — 100 — 200 Miles

Beaufort Sea

Pacific Ocean

GREAT BEAR LAKE

RICHARDSON MOUNTAINS

SELWYN MOUNTAINS

MACKENZIE MOUNTAINS

ST ELIAS MOUNTAINS

KLUANE NATIONAL PARK

Firth River

Porcupine River

Peel River

Klondike R.

Stewart River

YUKON RIVER

Pelly River

Teslin

Nahanni River

Liard River

Stikine River

Dease Lake

Kluane Lake

Aishihik Lake

Lake Laberge

Marsh Lake

Bennett Lake

Tagish Lake

Atlin Lake

Frances Lake

Aklavik

Inuvik

Old Crow

Fort McPherson

Fort Good Hope

Fort Norman

Dawson

Elsa

Keno

Mayo

Beaver Creek

Pelly Crossing

Carmacks

Ross River

Tungsten

WHITEHORSE

Haines Junction

Carcross

Skagway

Johnsons Crossing

Teslin

Atlin

Watson Lake

Fort Nelson

DANIEL 87

CHAPTER NINE

The New Yukon, 1946–1987

At the beginning of April 1946, after a stay of four years, the last of the American forces left the Yukon, to be replaced as keepers of the Alaska Highway by the Royal Canadian Engineers. The presence of American military and civilian personnel had breathed life into the Territory, particularly the Whitehorse region. The Yankees had brought with them boundless energy, a "can-do" spirit, and lots of money — things the Yukon badly needed at the end of the 1930s. Now they were gone, leaving the Territory to its native people, still living largely outside the settled communities, and to its small white population. Yukoners said farewell to the Americans with a mixture of sorrow, relief, and apprehension, wondering if the Canadian government was planning to continue its pre-war policy of stinginess towards the north, if the bad times were about to return.

Fortunately for the Yukon, there had been two important changes since 1940. The Cold War, which began as soon as the shooting in Europe stopped, guaranteed that the northwest of Canada would have to play a part in continental defence; thus some military presence would be necessary in the Yukon. Second, the advent of the welfare state, heralded by the Family Allowance plan, meant that the bad old days of careful, parsimonious government were over, and a new era of spending, transfer payments, and social assistance of various kinds was about to begin. Within a generation, the era when Comptroller Jeckell could rejoice over a $10,000-increase in the federal appropriation for the Territory seemed like a bad dream; by the 1960s the talk was not of a few thousands, but of many millions.

The Canadian army was glad to take on the responsibility for the Alaska Highway — not because they thought it of much military significance, but because it provided good training for the Engineers. While the Canadian Army busied itself with snow removal, grading, culvert replacement, and bridge construction (the latter particularly urgent because of the temporary nature of many of the American bridges), the defence of the region was scaled down. In the early days of the Cold War, Canadian and American military planners shared a common concern about the prospect of a Russian invasion along the Alaska Highway. Steps had to be taken, the military urged, to protect the vulnerable route by means of garrisons at several communities. The government rejected this costly option and instead established a Mobile Striking Force, with the capacity to move armed personnel swiftly into isolated areas. But a series of post-1946 manoeuvres, including Exercise North, Exercise Eagle, and Exercise Sweetbriar, demonstrated that the Mobile Striking Force could not handle the defence requirements of the northern terrain. In subsequent years, military advisors debated the options at great length and reluctantly agreed that there was no cost-effective solution. A token army and air force detachment remained at Whitehorse until the 1960s, but the Canadian government's new-found urge to spend money did not extend to the military, and no systematic attempt was made to mirror the substantial military build-up underway in Alaska. Except for the highway, the Yukon was returned to the civilians.[1]

With comparatively reliable access to the outside, Yukoners now hoped for economic development, a booming tourist industry, and the beginning of a new era in the Territory. The federal government was sympathetic. The Americanization of the northwest during the Second World War had frightened federal officials out of their lethargy and, led by the "Northern Nationalists," a loosely formed group of northern promoters and activists, Ottawa now aggressively sought to control the north's future. With the support of the government and with public interest in the region kindled by the highway, Yukon boosters hoped that for the first time their dreams for their Territory might be fulfilled.

The most dramatic changes brought by the war had occurred in Whitehorse. In 1946 it bore only slight resemblance to the small, seasonal company centre of decades past. Whitehorse now had the facilities of a small modern city, with theatres, baseball diamonds, skating rinks, dance halls, a radio station (which continued to operate for a number of years with programs supplied by the United States Army), new roads, dozens of new buildings, water and sewage systems, warehouse and maintenance space, and a rapidly growing commercial district.[2] Residents had worried that the town would collapse when the Americans left — Dawsonites had hoped it would. But the arrival of the Canadian soldiers provided the base for continued prosperity, and there were other favourable omens. After the war, the shift of population to the town continued. The federal government continued to transfer its administrative offices; by 1950, the public administrator, liquor controller, and sanitary engineer were there, as well as the forestry officer, airways engineer, and chief of the telegraph service. The civil servants still in Dawson City discovered that much of their work had shifted southward, forcing prolonged absences from their home offices. Even more offices would have moved had it not been for George Jeckell, who supported Dawson and

The City of Whitehorse in 1986, a modern, cosmopolitan government centre.
GOVERNMENT OF YUKON PHOTO

resisted the shift to Whitehorse, spending as little time as possible there. His replacement in 1948 by J. E. Gibben removed a major impediment to the administrative rationalization of the Yukon Territory.[3]

Dawson City, which had watched its remaining power dwindle during the war, had no intention of going down without a fight. Its boosters rallied in a desperate attempt to preserve their community. Led by George Jeckell, they presented a simple solution. Whitehorse's claim to territorial pre-eminence rested largely on year-round road access. A road to Dawson City, with connections to the mining camps in the Mayo area, would bring it prosperity as well. But this would cost a great deal of money, and the federal government was not eager to make such commitments in a losing cause.

Dawson's supporters did not give up easily, for they recognized the importance of the road project to the future of their community, but their cause lost ground steadily. There were even rumours that the territorial capital was to be moved. In 1950, a road north of Whitehorse was completed, but to Mayo rather than Dawson, which had to face the troubling fact that it was now the Yukon's third largest city. When Dawson did finally receive its connection to the Alaska Highway in 1951, the road went west into Alaska and not south through the Yukon.[4]

The failure to build the road between Dawson and Whitehorse was the writing on the wall for Dawson. In 1950 the axe fell; the federal government announced that the territorial council would be transferred to Whitehorse. Desperate appeals to overturn the decision fell on deaf ears. Robert Winters, Minister of Resources and Development, made it clear that there really was nothing to discuss, that the decision to move the capital was based not on the heritage of the Yukon, nor on a desire for balanced growth, but on administrative convenience:

261

Whitehorse has good communications with the rest of Canada and with the United States, including airplane and air mail service six days a week, regular and frequent train, bus and truck connections, and telegraph and telephone service. On the other hand, Dawson has scheduled airplane service three times a week, air mail service twice a week, river boat service during the summer months only, no rail connections with the "outside," no all-weather road connections with the "outside," and no long distance telephone. Whitehorse, as the railhead, is the point through which all incoming supplies are distributed and all outgoing concentrates are shipped. Every person and every article of commerce entering the Territory must pass through Whitehorse. Under these circumstances, the result has inevitably been that most of the problems with which administrative officials have to deal can now be handled much more efficiently from Whitehorse than from Dawson.[5]

The formal transfer of power did not take place immediately, although by this time many administrative offices had already been moved. Construction of a federal government building began in Whitehorse in 1952; the following year, the Yukon Territorial Council met in Whitehorse, ending the battle for administrative control of the Yukon Territory. Dawsonites would struggle on, but with limited success, for even the gold-mining sector was in serious trouble. Dawson finally received its road to the south in 1955, when a spur from Stewart Crossing to Dawson opened. This put an end to steam-boat travel, and the last boat was pulled out of the Yukon River that same year. Dawson now had its connection to the south, but it no longer had the government offices and status that accompanied the Territorial Council. Already devastated by the continued erosion of the gold economy, the once-proud and dynamic city sank into a sad somnolence, which many thought was only the inevitable precursor of a slow and lingering death.

Whitehorse, however, also had problems. To the consternation of regional promoters, access to the south via the Alaska Highway did not guarantee prosperity, nor did it immediately usher in the years of growth that many had counted on. Part of the problem lay with the road itself. Poorly sited, unfinished, and without commercial facilities, the Alaska Highway was kept closed to civilian traffic until 1947. The Royal Canadian Engineers lacked the manpower, equipment, and money to upgrade the highway. All they could do was to repair its most severely damaged portions, conduct routine maintenance, and bear the brunt of the criticism about the "rough road north."[6]

As early as 1954, the federal government considered passing responsibility for the highway from the Department of National Defence, which was anxious to be rid of it, to the Department of Public Works, the agency responsible for federal construction projects. The public prodded Ottawa to undertake a major reconstruction of this now vital route. Alaskans seconded the cry, calling for another Canadian-American enterprise to complete the work started during the war. These demands received substantial backing with the release in 1961 of a report by the Batelle Memorial Institute, a private research agency working on Alaska's behalf, which estimated that paving the road would cost some $103 million, money that would be quickly recovered through tourism and expanded economic activity.[7] When a Royal Commission on Government Reorganization recommended that the army be relieved of its highway duties, the federal government finally acted, and on April 1, 1964, transferred responsibility for the highway to the Department of Public Works.[8]

Public Works was interested in rebuilding the highway rather than in supervising its routine maintenance, a job which belonged to provincial and territorial authorities. Even before the transfer, the government gave control of the southernmost eighty-four miles of the road to the British Columbia government; in 1972, responsibility for maintaining the Yukon portions of the highway went to the Yukon Department of Highways. The remaining sections in British Columbia, still in federal hands, remained in limbo. Although the B.C. government had a constitutional responsibility for roads within the province, it steadfastly refused to assume control of remaining sections of the highway, which were maintained by private contractors.

For Yukoners hoping for the immediate paving of the Alaska Highway, only disappointment followed. The federal government commissioned its own study of the feasibility of paving the road. The Stanford Research Institute report, issued in 1966, offered a gloomy forecast; paving the highway could not be justified. The report recommended a limited improvement project, in which the worst portions would be upgraded and paved.[9] The federal government proceeded on this basis, building new bridges, improving major sections of the highway, and continuing negotiations with the British Columbia government for final transfer of the provincial sections of the highway.

In 1973, the United States government offered to pay for the reconstruction and paving of the Haines Road and portions of the Alaska Highway northwest of Haines Junction. This stretch of the highway was lowest on Ottawa's priority list, since most of the traffic in this area was American, but the generous offer could not be ignored. This Shakwak Project, ran into difficulty in the early 1980s, when key Congressional supporters lost their seats in the Reagan sweep, slowing, but not stopping, construction work. Once the poor relation of the Yukon highway system, the Haines Road has become, at least in sections, a paved road of top quality.[10]

The same cannot be said of rest of the Alaska Highway. The road, which still carries thousands of tourists every summer, remains a patchwork. There are few signs of the 1946 road (and even fewer places where one can

263

Top: *Once a rough, dusty road, the Alaska Highway has been significantly upgraded over the past two decades. There are few remaining signs of the wartime highway left by the United States Army. This view is of the highway near Jakes Corner, southeast of Whitehorse.* YUKON GOVERNMENT PHOTO

Below: *In 1942, a homesick American soldier placed a sign at Watson Lake, indicating the distance to his home. Other workers followed his lead. Tourists travelling the highway now carry signs with them to add to the collection.* YUKON GOVERNMENT PHOTO

see the original pioneer road of 1942). More than one-third of the Canadian portion of the road is paved; much of the rest has been specially treated to control the notorious Alaska Highway dust that long plagued travellers. The bridges, all new since the war, are of the highest quality. But if it is not the road the Americans left behind, it is also not the highway that northern promoters have longed for since the 1940s. The Alaska Highway, like the Yukon itself, is full of promise only partially fulfilled.

Nonetheless, the highway has become the lifeline of the north, as was aptly demonstrated in 1974. Extremely heavy rains in the Muncho Lake area wiped out more than twenty miles of road surface and undermined several key bridges. The same storm destroyed bridges and broke up portions of the Stewart-Cassiar Road, the only other road access out of the Yukon. Truckers and travellers congregated in Watson Lake, where roadblocks had been established to prevent people from moving farther down the highway. Congestion at the highway community was intense; people slept in shifts in the hotels, and the restaurants quickly ran out of food. Every available piece of construction equipment in the region was rushed into service, and contractors worked around the clock to reopen the road. Dozens of detours were carved out of the roadside and temporary bridges erected before convoys were permitted to move up and down the highway. When the first convoy of several dozen car-loads of people who had been trapped during the storm at Muncho Lake reached Watson Lake, crowds lined the highway to cheer their arrival.

Perhaps the greatest irony of the Alaska Highway is that though the road has been a blessing to Whitehorse, it has actually had only a minor impact on the economy of the Territory. While it has breathed life into the tourist trade (even though a high percentage of the traffic on the road passes through the Yukon to and from Alaska), it has not provided the stimulus to economic growth that its promoters had counted on. The main reason for this is its location. The highway did not follow the route that Yukoners had wanted; it misses the mid-Yukon corridor, the Mayo mines, and the Dawson area. The areas of the southern Yukon opened by the highway had few exploitable mineral resources and thus did not contribute much to the post-war development of the Territory.

Although the Yukon did enjoy considerable post-war growth, the stability and security that its supporters had long sought still escaped it. In the forty years since the end of the war, the Yukon economy has continued through its boom-and-bust cycles. The immediate post-war period was a time of disappointment, with the highway failing to produce the benefits so long expected. By the mid-1950s, increased federal expenditures in the Yukon had fueled a boom that brought a new level of prosperity. After a slump in the early 1960s, there was another boom, based on the opening of new mines and continued government spending. The Yukon seemed to have found a new level, based on a solid core of well-paid federal and territorial employees, long-term mining projects, and continued exploration. Although the years of prosperity continued throughout the 1970s, the boom came to an abrupt end early in the 1980s, when the closure of all of the Yukon's major mines and the collapse of plans for an Alaska Highway natural gas pipeline crippled the territorial economy. Continued federal government expenditures propped up the Yukon economy (to a greater degree than the Territory's doctrinaire free-enterprisers like to admit) but the confidence built up through the post-war period was badly shaken. The downturn ended in the mid-1980s, giving way to stability rather than another boom. The pattern of territorial economic development is still based on the success and failure of Yukon mines, with a safety net of government spending. In the past, this structure harmed the Territory; in the present era of government spending and talk of a new commitment to the north, dependence on federal and territorial expenditures has brought fiscal stability, if not prosperity.

The Territory's economic ebbs and flows had not meant a great deal to the Yukon's Indian population until the post-war years. Throughout the first half of the twentieth century, the mining sector had provided few opportunities for the native people — primarily seasonal, unskilled work as labourers and woodcutters. For a few, there was guiding for big-game hunters; for most, trapping provided what income they required. After the Second World War, the market for furs and wild game all but collapsed, destroying one of the foundations of Yukon Indian society. By 1950, new regulations, the registration of traplines, and reduced fur markets had led to a restructuring of the manner in which Indians and other Yukoners viewed and used the natural resources of the Territory.[11]

The establishment of the Yukon Fish and Game Association in 1945 reflected a change in attitude towards the environment. Under the leadership of Geoff Bidlake and W. D. MacBride, the association began to lobby for changes in the management of territorial game resources. They advocated the registration of individual traplines, a system adopted more than two decades earlier in British Columbia and in general use across the country. At their urging, in 1949, a Director of Game, Them Kjar, was hired to bring trapping practices in line with those in the south. They convinced the government to import new species to be hunted, including bison, elk, and mule deer, and to undertake a widespread wolf kill program. The arrival of American big-game hunters, particularly publicist James Bond and Carson Shade, who introduced fly-in hunting camps, made big-game hunting in the Yukon an international sport. The comparatively unregulated conditions of the past, based on limited demand, harvesting for personal use, and a seeming abundance of game, could no longer be tolerated.[12]

In 1947 the territorial government made substantial amendments to the Yukon Game Ordinance, several of which struck at the heart of native commercial harvesting practices. From the early days of the Yukon fur trade, Indians had sold meat to traders, miners, and townsfolk. In 1947, without warning, the government prohibited the sale of wild game. Comptroller George Jeckell commented that the change was rooted in squeamishness on the part of white Yukoners:

> In past years the white population was small and the amount of game meat sold to the white population by the Indians was insignificant, and this was particularly due to the fact that white people generally do not care to purchase game from Indians because the game they take is not slaughtered carefully and not kept clean and wholesome.[13]

The proposed moves could not have come at a worse time. The long-vital fur trade had entered a prolonged decline shortly after the war, a victim of lost European markets and shifting fashions in North America. Yukon trappers had harvested over $650,000 worth of pelts in 1945–46; two years later, their returns fell to $230,000, despite thirty thousand additional pelts brought to

Old Crow, an isolated Indian community in the northern Yukon, is inaccessible by road. The village depends on trapping, especially in the nearby Old Crow Flats, and its harvest from the Porcupine River caribou herd. YUKON GOVERNMENT PHOTO

the trading posts, and the trade stayed at this level. Many small traders left the industry and Taylor and Drury closed some of their posts. The changes sapped much of the vitality from the Yukon Indian economy.[14]

When Kjar drafted the 1949 legislation for trapline registration, he included a $10 annual fee to cover the costs of administration. Natives around the Territory petitioned the government to scrap the fee, arguing that the diminished returns from their traplines made it impossible for them to pay it. But there was no malice behind the decision to require trapline registration; it was intended to forestall conflict between trappers and to guarantee access to the resource for established hunters. In fact, many Indians, faced with competition for areas they had trapped for years, had urged the government to act.

What began as an exercise to ensure the access of natives and other Yukon veterans to their traplines was quickly turned on its head. Although many Indians registered their traplines, over the years a number surrendered or lost their rights. The registration process provided individual ownership of a resource that, for the Indian people at least, had always been collective property. Now trappers might sell their traplines or lose their rights through non-use of the area, in which case someone else could claim it. Five years after registration started, 430 traplines were in use; by 1960, only 190. The fur trade had not died, for native attachment to harvesting sustained it through some bad years, but declining markets and the registration system had clearly altered what had long been a cornerstone of the territorial economy.[15]

The fur trade retained a particular importance in native settlements like Ross River and Old Crow. In the latter community, the school year was arranged so that children could accompany their families on the annual spring muskrat hunt in the nearby Old Crow flats. Although governments seemed to write off trapping as a vestige of the distant past, it contributed significantly to native incomes. In the 1970s, the emergence of the animal rights movement and international campaigns against trapping once more challenged it. National native organizations rallied to the defence of the industry which, they pointed out, was essential to the survival of their culture. Although the threat of protests and boycotts continues to hang over the industry, steady demand for the Yukon's prime furs keeps the trade alive in the Territory, where the annual value of fur production currently averages about $1 million, with lynx pelts making up half that total.[16]

The fur trade was not the only sector of the Yukon economy to suffer in the post-war years. Declining international markets for gold and falling returns from the Klondike fields continued to plague this once prosperous industry. In 1947 the federal government passed the Emergency Gold Mining Assistance Act, offering production subsidies for companies and individuals willing to sell gold to the Canadian mint.[17] The program was, in fact, designed for major gold producers in central Canada rather than the dredging companies and the many small operators still active in the Yukon. But many of these applied for federal support, and kept their mines in operation despite high costs and small returns.

The collapse of the fur trade and decline of the gold-mining sector, once fiercely independent but now tied to government subsidies, signalled the onset of more troubled times for the Yukon. Once again a single company, this time United Keno Hill, propped up the entire regional economy. The company initially worked on the Galena Hills property, but by 1950 had started development work at the Elsa, Silver King, No Cash, and Calumet properties and exploration on the Ladue, Sadie, Lucky Queen, Porcupine, and King claims. The company experienced many difficulties. Finding and holding a trained work force proved a constant headache, supplies were difficult to procure and ship, and shortages of mining equipment plagued expansion plans. In June 1949 the processing mill was lost in a fire, forcing a temporary halt to development and exploratory work. With all available manpower and equipment devoted to rebuilding, United Keno Hill was back in operation by October of the same year. The subsequent addition of expanded milling capacity, the construction of a concentrating mill at Keno, the upgrading of transportation facilities, and the expansion of the work force from 90 men in 1947 to 360 four years later, 476 in 1955, symbolized the steady growth of this vital cog in the territorial economy.[18]

The generous returns from the company's Galena Hill property justified the effort and the expense. In 1948 the mine produced over $2.4 million worth of silver and lead, along with small quantities of gold. Company profits mounted steadily through the 1950s, as the benefits of the investments in the physical plants began to pay dividends. By the mid-1950s,

United Keno Hill's revenues climbed to nearly $10 million, producing a net profit of over $2 million in 1956.[19]

The effects of the mining activity filtered throughout the territorial economy. High mineral prices in the post-war period fueled greatly expanded exploration throughout the Yukon. Prospectors, assisted by a skilled band of bush pilots, scoured the creeks and mountainsides with sophisticated equipment. In 1952, mineral production topped $11 million, with silver, lead, and zinc providing most of the returns. There were failures as well as successes. There had been great hopes that new, mineable deposits would be found in the Mayo area, but after considerable expenditure, hundreds of claims on Stand-to Mountain, Lynx Dome, and Lime Creek were permitted to lapse. Despite the withdrawal of many prospectors, a number of companies — Ankeno Mines, Bellekeno Mines, Comstock, Keno, Jersey Yukon, Klondike Keno Mines, Mackeno Mines, Mount Keno Mines, Yukeno Mines, and, of course, United Keno Hill Mines — continued their development or extraction work.[20]

Returns from the Whitehorse mining district seemed even more promising. Three prospectors working for the Yukon Mining Company uncovered a promising nickel deposit on the west side of Kluane Lake in June 1952. The discovery touched off a mini-boom. By December of that year, over sixteen hundred claims had been staked. Prospectors fanned out in various directions, finding additional deposits west of the Donjek River and near the Alaska Highway and generating another 1,247 claims. Hudson Bay Exploration and Development Company optioned most of the properties and began development work on the claims around Quill Creek. The Yukon Exploration and Development Company began prospecting in the Wheaton River area; Prospectors Airways had started work in the MacMillan River district, but later joined the rush to Quill Creek; American Smelting and Refining Company sought lead and zinc deposits near Quartz Lake. Independent prospectors, some working under contract to speculative mining companies, pushed the search throughout the White River and Kluane Lake regions.

While most prospecting and exploratory activity focused on lode mining, placer operations remained important. Over eleven hundred placer claims, most in the Dawson City area, remained in good standing in 1952. The self-sufficient Yukon Consolidated Gold Corporation ran extensive hydraulic and dredging activities in the Klondike fields. Their power plant on the north fork of the Klondike River supplied all their own power needs and the surplus went to the town of Dawson. The massive hydraulic operations processed almost 2 million yards of earth in 1952. Cold-water thawing operations, in which water was run over permafrost, thawed out more than 4,250,000 cubic yards of material. Yukon Consolidated operated seven dredges during 1952, keeping each in operation for an average of 187 days. The efforts paid off, although not as handsomely as in the past, for the company produced 56,332 fine ounces of gold and over 12,000 ounces of silver, with a total value of $1,918,000. The mining operation ran from late April to the beginning of December, when the last dredge shut down. As if to symbolize the declining fortunes of Yukon Consolidated, one of its largest dredges was mothballed in 1952, after more than forty years' service. The machine was later cannibalized to keep the firm's other aging dinosaurs in operation. Although the company was gradually shrinking, it remained one of the Territory's largest employers. In May 1952, at the height of the season, the firm had over 450 employees in the field. As had traditionally been the case, many of the seasonal employees left the Territory for the winter, and by December only 28 people remained on the company's payroll.

Yukon Consolidated did not have the Klondike field to itself, although it dwarfed its competitors. Yukon Placer Mining Company, Clear Creek Placers, and Yukon Gold Placers ran small dredges or hydraulic operations. Smaller mines, usually one- or two-man operations, kept alive the flavour of gold rush prospecting, though the technology had changed since 1898. R. E. Troburg, working on Bonanza Creek, used a bulldozer and one employee to extract 281 ounces of gold, worth about $10,000. Over on Quartz Creek, R. Hastle and J. E. Lundin, adopting the drifting techniques of the late nineteenth century, worked eight months for a meagre return of 44 ounces of gold. Operators small and large prospected in new areas, retraced miners' paths through old claims, and used new technology in the search for a new Eldorado. The rush to Quill Creek, the persistence of the Klondike placer miners, the conservative professionalism of the United Keno Hill operators, and the fantasies of speculators and foot-slogging prospectors echoed age-old patterns in the Yukon. But with gold prices locked at $35 an ounce, it was clear that even with the government subsidies of the Emergency Gold Mining Assistance Act, placer mining in the Dawson area was rapidly becoming uneconomical.

In the Mayo area, most of the small operators had pulled out, leaving United Keno Hill Mines to dominate the area. Development continued in each of its principal properties, as new shafts were cut, mining schedules adjusted to capitalize on rich veins of ore, and exploratory work expanded. The effort paid off, for the company's employees produced 7.3 million ounces of silver, 22 million pounds of lead, and over 15 million pounds of zinc. Other lode-mining operations near Mayo slipped into a holding pattern. Most claim holders did only the minimal amount of work required to maintain title to the properties.

The Whitehorse district attracted more activity, as prospectors again chased the retreating spring snows into the Kluane, Frances Lake, Sheldon Lake, Quiet Lake, Carmacks, Dezadeash, and Flat River regions. Small operations, extracting rich nodes of ore, were brought into production, but no large mines started up.

There are few communities in the Territory; Whitehorse alone has more than three-quarters of the Yukon's population. The smaller villages, like Carmacks, have few facilities and a very meagre economic base. YUKON GOVERNMENT PHOTO

Better days lay ahead for the Yukon mining industry. The modest successes of the 1950s would be replaced by real boom-times in the next decade, as major new mines came on stream, stimulating a major expansion of the territorial economy. The prospecting activities continued in a variety of directions. Calgary-based Western Minerals struck oil on the Eagle Plains in 1959, sparking short-lived dreams of an oil-rich future.[21] By the 1970s, much attention was focused on the mineral-rich MacMillan Pass area, where promising discoveries held much hope for the future. Although few of these explorations resulted in producing mines — the opening of the Mount Skookum property was a welcome exception — the search continued, pouring millions of dollars annually into the territorial economy.

The search continued because the Yukon still occasionally produced a winner. One mine, even if it lasted only a few years, could produce enough money to make its prospectors rich and pay handsome dividends to its investors. Throughout the 1960s and 1970s, activity centred on the death and rebirth of the Klondike goldfields, the opening of an asbestos mine at Clinton Creek, renewed development of the Whitehorse copper belt, and, most importantly, the discovery of Canada's largest lead and zinc property in the Ross River area.

In the goldfields, Yukon Consolidated Gold Corporation had almost run its course by the early 1960s. The dredging and hydraulic equipment was rusting and in ill-repair; as one machine was shut down, its usable parts were cannibalized to keep the others working. Returns had fallen steadily, eroding profits, although dividends continued to be paid until 1965. There was still gold in the ground — a 1965 estimate identified over $4 million

271

worth of gold at $35 an ounce — but the high operating costs rendered extracting it unprofitable. In November 1966, the last three Yukon Consolidated dredges shut down for the season, and forever. The company sold off what it could, leased out its claims, and wound down its operations. Ironically, it had acted too soon; in 1973, the American decision to let the price of gold float on international markets led to an amazing price surge. Gold-bearing ground that was barely profitable at $35 an ounce was once more rich at over $800 an ounce. Small operators, most with two or three employees and a bulldozer or two, returned to the creeks in large numbers and pressed the Klondike gold properties into service once more. New extraction techniques, particularly the development of more advanced sluice boxes, allowed miners to go through the old diggings once more. The Klondike, which had made rich men of the original stampeders and had sustained the large corporate operators for many years, once more provided handsome returns to those willing to risk the vagaries of Yukon placer operations.

Early in the century, prospectors had found deposits of asbestos not far from Dawson. The thin, string-like mineral found a market from the 1960s until health concerns in the 1970s and 1980s eliminated many of its uses. In the early 1950s, Conwest Exploration, headed by Fred Connell, had developed the rich Cassiar Asbestos property in northern British Columbia. While that mine was being brought on stream, Connell turned his attentions to reported discoveries on Cassiar Creek, some thirty miles from Dawson. When news later surfaced of another strike on nearby Clinton Creek, Connell was immediately interested. In 1965, Cassiar Asbestos Corporation decided to proceed with mine development; a townsite was quickly built and two years later the mill opened.[22]

The Clinton Creek property proved expensive to operate; the only primary access to the mine was by the Yukon River ferry — there was no bridge, except an ice bridge during the winter. When the river was impassible, supplies and ore had to be transported across the river on a cable skyline. Rich returns from the asbestos property, however, gave the company enough confidence to predict a long mine life. Cassiar Asbestos built a modern, well-equipped company town, complete with a small hospital, school, recreational facilities, and housing, but when expenses proved unexpectedly high, the owners decided to exploit the property, taking out the ore as quickly as possible without worrying about the long-term prospects for the area. Although the Clinton Creek mine had proved highly profitable for Cassiar Asbestos Corporation, the returns to the Yukon were negligible, except insofar as they provided an impetus for further exploration. Ten years after the mine opened, and ten years ahead of schedule, the Clinton Creek mine was closed.

There are few things as final as the closing of a company town. Workers

272

had no reason to stay and quickly moved on to other mining communities. Usable equipment, particularly the milling facility, was dismantled and shipped out. Even the houses were shipped out; auctioned to the highest bidder, most were hauled to Dawson City to replace the town's aging housing stock. By the mid-1980s, Clinton Creek could not even be called a ghost town, for little remained of what had once been a flourishing community, except basement shells where the homes once stood and a water-filled hole where the company mined the asbestos.

The Whitehorse mines followed a similar course, although the impact on the community was much less noticeable. The Whitehorse copper belt had been known for years, but had attracted only sporadic interest. In 1957, Aubrey Simmons, the Yukon's Member of Parliament, created New Imperial Mines to bring the Whitehorse properties into production. As always, low prices continued to confound development prospects, and it was not until 1967 that New Imperial Mines started work on an open-pit mine on the Little Chief claim. The company remained in operation only four years. A short-term surge in the price for copper in the early 1970s led to the reorganization of the New Imperial interests into Whitehorse Copper Mines. The new company abandoned the open pits (one of them is now the Whitehorse garbage dump) and instead tunnelled into the copper veins. The economic imperative could not, however, be avoided. When copper prices fell again, the always marginal Whitehorse properties had to be abandoned and, in 1981, Whitehorse Copper Mines ceased operations.[23]

The demise of Clinton Creek and Whitehorse Copper received comparatively little attention because of the dominance of another new mine, the Cypress-Anvil property producing zinc and lead at Faro. Like all other Yukon mines, this property owed its existence to the persistence of prospectors and investors who had faith in the Territory. The story of the Cypress-Anvil property begins with Al Kulan. He had been in the north since 1947, moving about the Territory in hopes of striking it rich. Kulan had the special qualities of the determined prospector:

> He was a featherweight, as supple as a willow and as strong as a telephone pole. But he was not a scrapper — not belligerent or antagonistic in any way — and avoided arguments and confrontations at any cost. He did everything fast. He made decisions fast; moved toward goals fast; walked fast; ate, and even drank, fast.[24]

Kulan was fixated on the Ross River and, usually in the company of Indian guides, he scoured the river valleys and hillsides for signs of minerals. Although he made several promising discoveries, especially on Vangorda Creek, Kulan's initial work came to nothing, although he nevertheless found himself embroiled in a series of lawsuits with former partners and employ-

Faro, townsite for the Cypress-Anvil mine, was built in 1968, destroyed by fire and rebuilt the following year. The community all but closed down in the early 1980s, but has enjoyed a revival with the recent re-opening of the mine. YUKON GOVERNMENT PHOTO

ees. Undeterred, Kulan continued his efforts and remained optimistic about the Ross River area.

In the early 1960s, Kulan joined with Dr. Aaro Aho to form Dynasty Explorations. Aho was the antithesis of the rough-hewn Kulan; he was well-educated (with a PhD from the University of California), sophisticated, and well-connected with the mining industry. Like Kulan, he had extensive Yukon experience and he was convinced that the Yukon held major mineral deposits, as yet undiscovered. Dynasty Exploration moved crews into the field to work on the promising properties Kulan had identified. Short of funds to carry on the expensive exploration scheme, Dynasty turned to Cypress Mines, a Los Angeles mining company, for enough money to sustain their development program. It was not like the old days. In 1965 Dynasty Explorations had a full crew of 117 in the field, river barges, two helicopters, and an air strip. The work cost over $50,000 per month.

Drilling results exceeded the most optimistic expectations. Dynasty kept the news private for a time, taking advantage of the discovery to stake more claims and secure their hold on the property. When word of the strike leaked out, prospectors from around the Territory rushed in, marking out more than seventeen thousand claims in the area in 1966 alone. Additional development only confirmed the scale of the discovery. The Yukon had its first truly world-class mine. Negotiations with two Japanese companies, Mitsui Mining and Smelting and Toho Zinc Company, resulted in an agreement with Cypress-Anvil, as the new mine was called, to purchase all the concentrates from the mine for a period of eight years. As the confirmed ore reserves expanded, the company signed additional contracts with other smelters, including Cominco's Trail plant, and firms in Germany, France, and England. Production began in December 1969.[25]

There was much work above and beyond the mining to be done. A forest fire destroyed the townsite in the middle of construction, forcing a second start on the apartment complexes, dormitories, and houses. Additional facilities, including a small shopping centre, hotel, and recreation complex, were added shortly thereafter. Transportation problems also had to be solved. The Cypress-Anvil mine was more than 200 miles by road from Whitehorse, which in turn was 110 miles from tidewater. Discussions with the White Pass and Yukon Route resulted in the construction of a combined trucking and rail transport system, organized around the Utah shipping yards just south of Whitehorse, and a new docking facility in Skagway. Although the new facilities cost the W.P.Y.R. over $22 million, the guaranteed work injected new life into the company, which had previously funded exploration and promoted northern mines in the hopes of providing greater traffic for its trucking and rail operations.[26]

The mine and community also placed considerable demands on the Yukon power grid. In the early 1970s, work began on a controversial project to dam the Aishihik River at Otter Falls, a scene which once graced the back of Canada's $5 bill, to provide direct power service to Faro and the mine. The power, it turned out, was not really needed, as the mine drew on regional coal deposits; the project proved extremely costly to the Yukon consumers, who paid off the cost of the Aishihik dam through their monthly electricity bills.

The federal government also provided generous support for the mine project. According to a 1972 estimate, Ottawa provided over $28 million in infrastructure support, including the road from Carmacks to Faro and the power line from Whitehorse to the mine site. The government also provided a three-year tax holiday on corporate profits.

There were a number of problems during the first year of operation. Although the company had made vague promises to provide work for local Indians, only a few native people (who ironically had played an important role in the initial discovery) found temporary work. There was a major leak of sodium cyanide in 1976. Mine officials did not inform the government as required, and the company was fined $49,000.

By the mid 1970s the Cypress-Anvil mine was the backbone of the Yukon economy. It directly employed over a thousand workers and provided other benefits throughout the territorial economy. Faro was something of a min-ers' enclave, isolated from the rest of the Territory. Most miners were recruited in the south, took their holidays in warmer climates, and stayed in the town for only a few years. They were well looked after in Faro, where thanks to a strong union, wage scales were among the most generous in the Yukon. Other benefits included inexpensive housing, living allowances and recreational facilities.

But like the Yukon's earlier booms, this one was built on shaky founda-tions. Despite the public investments in the mine, and the seemingly

The Faro mine has been the backbone of the Yukon economy from its opening in the late 1960s. YUKON GOVERNMENT PHOTO

inexhaustible ore body, the Cypress-Anvil mine closed in 1981, victim of international corporate finance. Cypress-Anvil had been purchased by Hudson's Bay Oil and Gas, which in turn was bought by Dome Petroleum, darling of the federal government's plan to nationalize the oil industry. Cypress-Anvil was, to Dome, a minor component of the larger transaction. When Dome subsequently faced bankruptcy, it lacked the resources to keep Cypress-Anvil afloat during a temporary down-turn in the world prices for lead and zinc. When the company attempted a major retrenchment, largely at the workers' expense, the union went out on strike. To the dismay of many Yukoners the Faro mine shut down. The strike proved fortuitous for the Company, which had negotiated in a desultory manner, for when the mine closed there was no need to pay severance pay to the striking employees.

Several hundred workers hung on, hoping that government and corporate salvage operations would reopen the mine. Periodic government grants provided short-term work, such as stripping over-burden from the ore body to prepare for future mining operations, but the rescue effort seemed to have failed. By 1984, the bustling community, second-largest in the Yukon, had all but closed down. Once home to over 2,000 people, in 1985 it could claim only 320 residents. Territorial and federal politicians made every effort to get the mine back in operation, for it had clearly become the one stabilizing force in the vulnerable territorial economy. The White Pass and Yukon Route was devastated by the closure; the loss of its major customer contributed to the decision in 1981 to close the historic railway between Whitehorse and Skagway. The ripple effect worked its way through the entire economy, forcing hundreds to leave the Territory and ushering in the deepest depression in the Yukon since the First World War.

In 1986, after negotiating with several potential operators, federal and territorial officials finally struck a deal with little-known Curraugh Resources. The package included generous subsidies, including an agreement to maintain the newly opened Carcross-Skagway road (which had been intended for summer travel only) through the winter months. The historic W.P.Y.R. railway, one of the Territory's leading tourist attractions, as well as a useful supply route, remained closed. The mine reopened that year, but under very different labour conditions. Initially a non-union operation, the Curraugh mine offered few of the generous bonuses, housing subsidies, or high wages of the early Cypress-Anvil operation. Employee turn-over was, from the first, extremely high as the men discovered the high cost of living in an unsubsidized company town. The deal did, however, put the Yukon's largest mine back into operation, providing the basis for a strong revival of the territorial economy in the mid-1980s.

What remained of Dawson had been left out of the excitement of the post-war mining booms, and had pinned its hopes instead on tourism. In the years before the Second World War, Dawson had done little to develop a tourist trade; the town's most famous site, Robert Service's cabin, was maintained by a small committee of the local Imperial Order Daughters of the Empire. As the community collapsed further with the expansion of Whitehorse after 1942, even the Service shrine fell on hard times and was taken over by the city government.

Dawson's desperation intensified during the 1950s, as the capital was lost, the sternwheelers were pulled off the Yukon River, and the dredging operations all but shut down. Finally, in desperation, the few remaining local boosters turned to tourism. In the early 1950s, the community established the Klondike Visitors Association. The KVA's hopes of success rested in large measure on the writings of a former Dawsonite, Pierre Berton. Although Berton had long since left the Yukon, his magazine articles and, in 1957, his popular book, *Klondike*, did more than any other single factor to resurrect flagging interest in the gold-rush legends. This, coupled with a growing interest in the north generally, made Dawson's desperate attempt to save itself more than just a fantasy.

The effort, however, required money. The city kept a few key attractions open — the Service cabin, a museum, and a partially restored Palace Grand Theatre — but these were hardly enough to convince thousands of tourists to undertake the long journey to the Yukon. In an era of rapidly expanding dependence on government assistance, it was only a matter of time before the city approached the wellhead of money in Ottawa. The federal government was amenable, and in 1962 announced a hastily conceived Dawson City Gold Rush Festival for two years later. There was little local input into the planning, which was dominated by a federally controlled Dawson City Festival Foundation, National Historic Sites, and the National Parks Branch. As part of the undertaking, the government moved an old W.P.Y.R.

Top: *The last of the Klondike dredges closed down in 1966. The goldfields have been brought back into production, but at a much smaller scale than in the past.* YUKON GOVERNMENT PHOTO

Centre: *Restored and refurbished as part of a general reclamation of Dawson City, the Palace Grand Theatre is host of the Gaslight Follies revue.* YUKON GOVERNMENT PHOTO

Below: *The s.s.* Klondike, *one of the fleet of river steamers that plied the Yukon River, has been restored by Parks Canada and is now a prominent tourist attraction in Whitehorse.* YUKON GOVERNMENT PHOTO steamer, the *Keno*, to Dawson, where it was turned into a museum. The festival drew eighteen thousand tourists — more than twice as many as came to the town in a normal year — but did not stimulate lasting interest. The federal government had invested more than $1.6 million; the visitors spent an estimated $1.9 million. The festival may have failed to revitalize Dawson City completely, but local residents were imbued with hope.[27]

Realizing that the government was willing to fertilize their plans for renewal of the gold-rush heritage with cash, Dawson's citizens now organized a more sustained request for federal assistance. The Klondike Visitor's Association sought new means of attracting tourists, such as offering legalized gambling aboard the *Keno* — an idea which initially sent tremors of apprehension through the federal bureaucracy. By the late 1960s, the National Historic Sites Branch recognized that an amateur effort would not be enough to save the city's tourist resources. In 1967, representatives of the Historic Sites and Monuments Board of Canada visited Dawson and made a strong recommendation that the federal government make a major commitment to the preservation of Dawson City.

The establishment of the Klondike National Historic Site was a crucial turning point for Dawson City. Over the next decade, the federal government, working with the Klondike Visitors Association, poured millions of dollars into Dawson and the surrounding area, restoring old buildings, providing things for tourists to see and do in the town and the goldfields, opening Diamond Tooth Gertie's as a gambling saloon and turning the Palace Grand Theatre into a Klondike repertory theatre. The effort worked, and Dawson gained a new lease on life. Businesses returned to the city, new hotels, restaurants, and stores opened to cater to a rapidly expanding tourist market.

The revitalization of Dawson City in the 1960s and 1970s was only part (albeit the largest part) of the attempt to capitalize on the Territory's tourist potential. In Whitehorse, the federal government moved another steamer, the s.s. *Klondike*, to a new site and restored it. (The other two remaining sternwheelers, *Casca* and *Whitehorse* would later be destroyed in a spectacular blaze on the Whitehorse waterfront.) The Anglican church maintained its Old Log Church in downtown Whitehorse, resisting federal efforts to have the old buildings relocated next to the s.s. *Klondike*. In the late 1970s the territorial government began to add to the stock of tourist attractions — a sternwheeler at Carcross, decaying for years, was saved at the last minute and preserved as an historic site. Private investors jumped on the bandwagon. In Whitehorse, the Frantic Follies drew hundreds of visitors each night to its Gay Nineties revue; boat tours of Miles Canyon allowed travellers to recreate part of the Trail of '98 (in much calmer waters than the stampeders had encountered). The efforts reached across the border. Increased cruise ship travel through the Inside Passage inspired Skagway to capitalize on the rapidly growing tourist trade. In a welcome example of Canadian-American co-operation, the historic Chilkoot Trail was preserved, with guides and facilities placed along the route to assist those desiring to retrace the footsteps of the stampeders.

The promotion of tourism did not stop with the Klondike story. The Yukon's natural wonders, ever more precious in an era of environmental awareness and the rapid loss of wilderness elsewhere in North America, found a ready market, especially in the United States and in Germany. Big-game hunters, fishermen, photographers, white-water travellers, hikers, and naturalists were sought out aggressively by the tourism promoters. The Yukon Pavilion at Expo '86 in Vancouver, B.C., brought together these themes and the days of the Klondike, attracting visitors with the brilliantly colourful entrance-way painted by Ted Harrison, the Yukon's most famous artist.[28]

If there is an irony in all this tourist promotion, it is the concentration on the Klondike and the comparative lack of attention to other aspects of Yukon history. The building of the Alaska Highway receives surprisingly little attention; few of the wartime buildings remain in use, and there are few monuments or displays highlighting this equally intense and internationally known side of the Yukon's history. While tourist promotions are, to a certain extent, market-driven, the Yukon has so far missed an opportunity to overcome the narrow southern image of the Territory's history and to present a more balanced impression of its past.

The federal government's investments in the mining sector and the redevelopment of Dawson City represented only the most obvious signs of a massive national commitment to the Yukon Territory, and to the Canadian north generally. In contrast to the earlier years of the neglect, the federal government now offered generous subsidies to the territorial administration and made substantial investments of its own in the Yukon. The new commitment emerged fairly quickly after the Second World War, in the form of a new federal Department of Northern Development. In the early 1950s, the government had maintained the Alaska Highway and provided money for the construction of other new roads in the Territory. Much of the Yukon, however, remained virtually inaccessible.

The Territory's Member of Parliament, Liberal Aubrey Simmons, argued in favour of more roads, particularly one to the Mackenzie Delta, and eventually he carried the day. Early in 1957, just before the election of John Diefenbaker and the Conservatives, Simmons announced that work on the road would start shortly. The Tory government followed through on the promise. Alvin Hamilton, Minister of Northern Affairs and National Resources, supported the plan, declaring "I visualize making every corner of the Yukon accessible. We can't develop without access. I see a network of trunk roads branching out from Dawson City. The great development

280

possibilities in the northwest corner certainly justify road investments into the Mackenzie River delta area.''[29]

Northern roads, unexpectedly, became a major element in the 1958 federal election. In the opening speech of the campaign, Prime Minister Diefenbaker electrified his audience with his plan for northern development: "We intend to start a vast roads program for the Yukon and Northwest Territories which will open up for exploration vast new oil and mineral acres — thirty million acres! We will launch a seventy-five-million-dollar federal-provincial program to build access roads. THIS IS THE VISION....We are fulfilling the visions and dreams of Canada's first prime minister — Sir John A. Macdonald. But Macdonald saw Canada from East to West. I see a new Canada. A CANADA OF THE NORTH!" After the victory, Diefenbaker and Hamilton announced the allocation of $100 million for the northern roads program.

Work began shortly thereafter on the highway to the Mackenzie Delta. Even as construction was beginning, Hamilton announced that oil had been discovered on Eagle Plains, proof of the value of the access roads. But by 1960, only the first seventy miles of the highway had been finished; winter roads allowed convoys to move supplies further out onto Eagle Plains. When the energetic Hamilton left his Northern Affairs portfolio, responsibility passed to the more pedestrian Walter Dinsdale. Highway construction slowed and then stopped. Yukoners gained a minor victory in having the highway named after W. J. D. Dempster, the popular old-time R.C.M.P. officer then in his mid eighties, but when work on the Eagle Plains oilfield sputtered, federal interest fell even further. The Diefenbaker administration, awash in a sea of political difficulties, lost interest in northern development.

There the highway remained for another decade, some seventy-five miles of road heading northwest from Dawson City. The vision of a link to the Mackenzie had been put on hold; the highway served as an access road for exploration crews and provided hunters with a route to the massive caribou herds that migrated annually across Eagle Plains. Not until the early 1970s did funding return to what had once been a flagship project for the Canadian government. Much of the renewed interest was based on proposed plans for a pipeline down the Mackenzie River Valley. The Canadian Armed Forces built the bridges at Ogilvie and Eagle rivers (another money-saving venture disguised as a northern training exercise). Private contractors worked on the highway under the direction of the Department of Public Works, battling with the environmental and engineering challenges posed by permafrost and Arctic weather conditions. Initially slated to cost from $5 to $8 million and to be finished in five years, the Dempster Highway cost nearly $103 million, and was finally opened nineteen years after work started. Initial work cost $55,000 per mile; the last segments of the road, between Rock

Started in the late 1950s, the Dempster Highway was not completed for more than a decade. The road now links Dawson City and Inuvik, Northwest Territories.
GOVERNMENT OF YUKON PHOTO

River and the border between the Yukon and Northwest Territories, cost ten times that.

The government's commitment was not, however, limited to roads and the promotion of tourism. The communication system built by the U.S. Signal Corps during the Second World War had significantly upgraded the Yukon's connections to the south. In 1960–61, the existing land-line system was enlarged by the addition of a high-capacity microwave radio system.[30] The Yukon's integration into the broader communications and information networks took much longer. The U.S. Army had left behind the radio station in Whitehorse, which was run on a volunteer basis. The Canadian Broadcasting Corporation opened a station in Whitehorse and began broadcasting throughout the Territory. The CBC Northern Service offered a variety of national programming, community news, and message services, providing links between Yukon communities and between the Territory and the rest of the country. The national network was later joined by a private radio station in Whitehorse, CKRW, which offered more contemporary music and was aimed more specifically at the local market.

Television came much later than radio. In Whitehorse, CFWH, one of the many Yukon enterprises owned by the Hougen family, provided an extensive cable system, based on taped programs flown in from the south. Live programs were not available; the landing of Americans on the moon in 1969, for example, was seen in the north on a tape. In the fall of 1972, while much of the rest of the country watched the final game of the Canada-Russia hockey series, Yukoners listened attentively on their radios and then watched the game the next day on tape flown in by the television station.

That was the year that Canada deployed Anik-1, the first satellite devoted exclusively to domestic communications. The Anik system permitted transmission of live broadcasts from the south, initially offered only in the late afternoon and evening. The limited service caused numerous scheduling problems — the complaints of those who were not sports fans led to the unexpected cancellation of Friday-night Montreal Expos baseball for instance, but wiser heads quickly prevailed, and the Expos took back their weekly slot. The CBC later went to a full-service program, with some special northern programming. In 1986, the weekly program *NEDAA* commenced production in Whitehorse, under the auspices of Northern Native Broadcasting. This program, like its counterpart, *Focus North*, offered a northern insight into contemporary northern issues. Commercial television also expanded in the 1980s. The Cancom system, under the leadership of Rolf Hougen, received a licence from the Canadian Radio and Television Commission in 1981 to beam several southern stations into a large number of communities throughout the Yukon and Northwest Territories.

These services, combined with the generally available satellite programming represent something of a cultural revolution for the north. In all communities, English- and French-language programming is available throughout the day; the American-made programs that dominate the television networks have become part of the cultural baggage for all Yukoners, including native people in previously isolated hunting villages like Old Crow. The new technology, while posing a threat to existing cultures, also provides new opportunities. The *NEDAA* program, CHON-FM, a native-run FM radio station based in Whitehorse, the CBC Northern Service, film work by the Northern Native Broadcasting Company, and a variety of native-language programs on the various media have provided a previously unavailable opportunity for native people to respond to the intrusion of southern culture.

The renaissance of native culture through radio and television programming represents one of the most promising signs of the revitalization of Yukon Indian society. For decades the only constant in the Territory, the Yukon native people faced massive social and economic dislocations; their communities and families still bear the many scars of the difficult transition to the realities of the industrial and administrative revolution that has transformed the Yukon over the past forty years.

While the standard economic indicators suggest that the Yukon enjoyed reasonable prosperity after 1946, the Yukon Indians did not share in the new wealth. The new mines were operated by whites, with a white workforce; the roads brought thousands of whites into areas known before almost only to the Indians. The Indians' nomadic and harvesting lifestyle had co-existed with the advance of the mining frontier and white settlement, but the accommodations of the past no longer worked. Government programs lay at the root of the transformation, which coincided with the collapse of the North American fur market. In the early years of the Canadian welfare state, the federal government decided that its poorest citizens, the Indians, should be given special encouragement and assistance as they struggled to adapt to the Canadian mainstream. Business incentive grants, pensions, and welfare programs targeted specifically at Indians expanded rapidly in the 1950s. For the natives in the Yukon, all but ignored in the previous decades, the new level of intervention brought marked changes in their lifestyles.

The Indians became increasingly reliant on government support payments. The establishment of the Family Allowance in 1945, for example, gave authorities the ability to force regular attendance at public schools; failure to send the children resulted in the quick elimination of the monthly payments, which, though small, were important to people with little cash income. The government's underlying paternalism toward northern natives was further reflected in the policy, enforced until the mid 1950s, that the Family Allowance be provided in kind rather than in cash, allowing the authorities to determine how the money was spent. Welfare payments, all but ignored by the Indians before the war, became an increasingly important part of their economy. Before 1944, the government had paid out less than $12,000 in welfare payments each year; welfare spending on the Yukon's Indians alone reached $90,000 by 1954–55 and over $200,000 by the mid 1960s.[31]

While such subsidies as old-age pensions, welfare, and emergency relief provided a short-term solution, the government's hope was that the Indians could be integrated into the broader economy — on, of course, the dominant society's terms. Loans for native entrepreneurs, community housing projects, and training programs were provided in the expectation that the Indians would gain the skills and acquire the values of the modern industrial age. There was little room left in this new economy for traditional harvesting practices and seasonal movements and as the fur trade declined in importance, natives had no choice but to accept government support. Having done so, they were required to follow the instructions of federal administrators.

Government agents were particularly anxious that Indian children attend school regularly. Families wanting to maintain their government support payments now had no choice but to move to communities where schools were available. While some families resisted the transition, either remaining in the bush or leaving the father behind while the rest of the family moved closer to the school, most reluctantly left the camps for villages. Many students were sent to residential schools — either the Catholic school at Lower Post, B.C., the Anglican School at Carcross (reopened in expanded quarters), or, after 1949, the Baptist Indian Mission School housed in war-surplus buildings in Whitehorse. By 1954, the Department of Indian Affairs could claim that "only a score of school-age children in the entire Yukon Territory were not enrolled in school."[32]

Schooling, as always, proved a mixed blessing. While the children

The modern Indian residential school at Carcross, built in the 1950s, was the cornerstone of the federal government's plan for the assimilation of the Yukon Indians. Most children resented their treatment at the institution, and the government gradually realized that education was best offered closer to the children's homes. The school served for a short time as an "alternative school" and has now been abandoned. ANGLICAN CHURCH ARCHIVES

gained new skills, they also discovered a system that was culturally insensitive, offering virtually no support or recognition of native culture. The residential school children, often forcibly removed from their parents and kept away for months or years at a time, faced particular difficulties. Cut adrift from their own culture but not readily accepted within the mainstream Yukon society, these children often left school before graduation only to face grave difficulties in adapting back into their home communities. Both the government and the teachers were aware of the problem, and sought more workable techniques. In 1960 Yukon Hall opened in Whitehorse, replacing the Baptist School. It provided a dormitory for Indian children who would then attend the regular public schools. Similarly, Catholic students were boarded in Catholic dormitories and attended the local Catholic schools. By the late 1960s, all the residential schools had been phased out — Lower Post was closed down; Carcross operated for a few years as an "alternative" school. As the territorial school system expanded, bringing classrooms closer to the Indian communities, some of the problem was eliminated.

But the legacy of Yukon Indian education could not be quickly overcome, and most natives remained unconvinced of the benefits of the Canadian educational system. Their suspicion rested, in large measure, on the enormous gap between their lifestyle and the curriculum in the schools, which was based on the B.C. system. Within the central school program, Indian culture and traditions were considered irrelevant, at best an historical curiosity. Textbooks, problems, and materials related to a world that few

Yukon Indians had experienced. In the past ten years, however, some significant changes have been made. The Yukon Department of Education is beginning to produce its own curriculum materials and is using the output of the northern communications companies to add further Yukon content.

The most promising initiative has been housed for a number of years in a small facility in Whitehorse Elementary School. The Yukon Native Languages Project, under the administration of linguist John Ritter, seeks to preserve Yukon Indian languages, several of which face extinction, and to encourage the use of native languages in the classrooms. In a number of communities, native speakers assist teachers in the use of traditional languages and share legends and cultural traditions with the children. As the territorial school system moves to accept native culture as an important component of the curriculum — for all students, not just those of Indian background — it is likely that the long-standing hostility of Yukon Indians to formal education will ease.[33]

It was for economic as well as educational reasons that government agents encouraged the Indians to move out of the bush to permanent communities. As one official noted about the Champagne Indians in 1958, "Some of the younger Indians are being encouraged to locate on the Haines Junction Reserve to improve employment opportunities and to be closer to services." Similar advice was offered to the Ross River band which was "a welfare problem and the younger Indians are to be encouraged to move to Upper Liard Bridge permanently and transfer to that Band." Such administrative restructuring of native society was commonplace after the war.[34]

Indians accustomed to a harvesting, nomadic lifestyle found the transition to the sedentary life of a government-controlled reserve difficult and stressful. There were, it turned out, few opportunities for Indians in the communities, forcing an even greater dependence on government assistance. The difficulties that followed have been well-documented — alcoholism and related problems with the law, poor educational attainment, and poverty. The housing provided on the reserves was exceptionally bad, adding to the already serious health problems facing the Indians. Overriding all of these concerns, however, was the cultural dislocation, reinforced by government agents and a white population that seemed not to value Indian culture.

This was evident in federal government economic development programs for Indians. While native harvesting remained (and remains) important, government efforts sought to integrate the natives into the industrial economy. Through such programs as the Indian Economic Development Fund, Special Agricultural and Rural Development grants, and a myriad of other initiatives, the government offered loans, advice, supervision, and training for native entrepreneurs, industrial workers, employers willing to hire Indians, and villages prepared to undertake community development projects. The individualism required for such capitalist ventures, however, ran counter to the co-operative ethos imbedded in Indian culture. While there were a few success stories, including the construction company started by the Champagne-Aishihik Band, most of the government-funded businesses did not succeed. Affirmative action programs and government-funded native organizations provided many new jobs, but carried the danger of creating an internal elite within Yukon native society, a small number of well-paid professionals set against the larger, comparatively impoverished Indian population. In the past few years, the reason for the repeated failures has finally struck home, leading to greater attention to native harvesting and alternative methods of Indian economic development.[35]

The economic and social turmoil of the post-war period struck at the very heart of Indian culture. Pulled into highway communities, forced into a culturally insensitive education system, and encouraged to adapt to an economic system that offered few prospects, Yukon Indians sank into despair, a dislocated and colonized people. Whites reacted often with disapproval, occasionally with concern, to the visible signs of that despair — the startlingly impoverished villages, drunken people on the streets of Whitehorse, Indians outside grocery stores discounting their welfare chits for cash, and a surfeit of Indian names on the court docket — but were slow to appreciate the deep cultural loss that had attended the collapse of the harvesting economy and the far-reaching effects of the modernization of the Yukon.

Traditional native leaders, raised in the bush, lacked the skills necessary for the bureaucratic age. The new communities, most of them inhabited by people from several bands, came under the official control of elected band councils. In fact, government agents made most of the decisions, leaving the councils to carry the word to the community. Native people became increasingly suspicious of these officials who apprehended their children and sent them off to distant boarding schools, forced elderly people into hospitals, and made most of the important decisions. The agents, for their part, struggled with the obligations of their jobs, and often suffered in silence with their native clients, though a few made their protests public. But they persevered in their tasks, convinced that the government's plan was in the Indians' long-term interests.

It would fall to the Indians themselves to force greater awareness of their condition. In the mid 1960s, a number of prominent Indian leaders began to discuss the need for a Territory-wide Indian organization. Led by the quiet eloquence of Elijah Smith, they formed the Yukon Native Brotherhood, determined, as Smith said, to end the "welfare thinking of Indian Affairs and our people." The sense of shared grievance, often heightened by a common experience in residential school, drew the Indians behind the Yukon Native Brotherhood and turned that organization into an influential territorial force. The Indians did not stand alone: the Christian churches had, in the main, overcome their traditional paternalism, and now declared their intention to support the Indians' search for social justice, and many white individuals offered their assistance to the movement.[36]

The Yukon Indians had an ace in the hole. They had never been taken under treaty, contrary to the Canadian government's often-stated commitment to the terms of the Royal Proclamation of 1763, which required a treaty before Indian lands were developed. The growing confidence and radicalism of the Yukon Native Brotherhood culminated in the 1973 publication of *Together Today for Our Children Tomorrow*, the first salvo in the Yukon land claims process.[37] The thoughtful, provocative, and wide-ranging document called for the transfer of substantial tracts of land to the Indians, cash payments to compensate for previous losses, resource revenues, sweeping education reforms, and other benefits. Perhaps recognizing the government's legal vulnerability on the question of Yukon land claims, the Trudeau government agreed to negotiate the Brotherhood's land claim, the first comprehensive land claim accepted for negotiation in Canada.[38]

White Yukoners responded with considerable bitterness and some fear to this proposal, and wondered aloud if the federal government would adequately protect their rights. The declaration of native intentions injected an element of uncertainty into the territorial economic climate and placed some major projects in doubt. In the pro-development atmosphere of the 1970s, such interference with the ''natural'' process of regional economic expansion seemed perverse to some people. The territorial government, controlled by the Conservative Party, favoured the pro-business position, particularly when the Indians combined a demand for greater self-government with their land claim. The territorial government went one step further, demanding that its outstanding claim for control of natural resources be settled before the natives' claim was finally addressed.[39]

Settling the claim has proved difficult. A tentative agreement was reached between the Council of Yukon Indians (which combined the Yukon Native Brotherhood and the Yukon Association of Non-Status Indians in 1973), only to be rejected by the communities when a ratification vote was taken. Representatives returned to the bargaining table, the native work funded out of advance payments from the eventual settlement, and seemed to have reached a favourable conclusion in 1984. The federal Liberal government, facing an election, reached an agreement in principle with the Council in early summer, leaving the rest of the year for final negotiations and ratification. The Conservative sweep of September 1984 quickly altered the equation. Although ten of the twelve Yukon Indian bands accepted the deal, the federal government pulled out of subsequent discussions. Negotiations continue, although the parameters for discussion seem to be shifting constantly. The Yukon Indians, only too aware of the problems in Alaska,

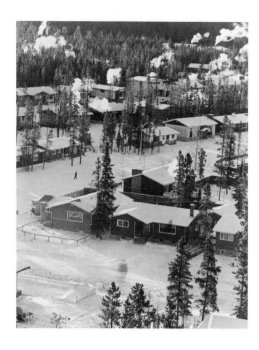

Riverdale, a residential subdivision across the river from the Whitehorse townsite, is a sign of the continuing modernization and expansion of the territorial capital.
YUKON GOVERNMENT PHOTO

where the natives accepted a deal they later regretted, battle on, determined to achieve a fair and lasting settlement of their aboriginal entitlement. In 1973 the Yukon Native Brotherhood pointedly noted: "We will not accept promises — because we have very little faith any more in Whiteman promises."[40] The bitterness and uncertainty linger.

The politicization of the Yukon Indians has had its effects. The government can no longer ignore their many pressing needs. New housing projects are being undertaken on reserves around the Territory; even Old Crow, the Yukon's most northerly village, has its own modern "suburb." The change is particularly noticeable in Whitehorse. The local Indian reserve, relocated several times, sat for many years next to the industrial area, one of the most unattractive locations in the community. When a planned housing development atop the bluff surrounding Whitehorse fell through, the Indians petitioned for the right to move their reserve there. After lengthy negotiations, the proposal was accepted. New houses are being built and the reserve is shifting to its new site, chosen this time by the Indians and in one of the best locations in the community. The change can also be seen in the growing integration of native and white segments of the Yukon community. Once firmly divided, particularly in the residential sphere, the communities are now growing together. Riverdale, across the river from Whitehorse and long a white preserve, now has a growing native population, a sign of one of the most important social shifts in the Yukon.

The painful and complex process of modernization in the north is further illustrated by the dispute over the Whitehorse squatters. Squatters had set up temporary but highly visible shacks in Whiskey and Moccasin flats during the Second World War, responding to the acute shortage of housing in the area. Government officials, particularly federal ones, recoiled at the informality and illegality of these settlements, which they considered a blight on the new Whitehorse. The squatters were, to them, an affront to Whitehorse's status as a territorial capital. Contrary to official perceptions, however, the squatters were not all ne'er-do-wells; in fact, most were gainfully employed, but the tightly controlled Whitehorse land market kept them from building their own homes. The development of Riverdale and of Porter Creek in the 1960s gave an exit to some, but many remained. Whitehorse City Council, although reluctant to take action, under pressure from the federal government offered these remaining residents a deal. Their homes would be moved outside the city limits — some ten miles south of town after the city had expanded its boundaries — where they would be freed from taxes. The flats were cleared out in the early 1970s; Whiskey Flats, which sat in front of the handsome new Territorial Building, was developed into an attractive park by the local Rotary Club.[41]

Though Yukon society is changing on a variety of other fronts, the dominance of Whitehorse continues. In 1987, nearly 19,000 of the Yukon's 27,000 people lived in the community. The political, administrative, economic, and cultural centre, Whitehorse controls much of the life of the Yukon, and it increasingly shows signs of its growing maturity. Most of the wartime buildings are gone, replaced by impressive (and expensive) public facilities, a trend begun in the 1950s when the hospital and the high school were built across the river from downtown. Since that time, a new territorial government building, the Kwanlin Mall, the city's commercial centre, Rolf Hougen's ever-growing retail complex along Main Street, new recreation facilities around the city, a new justice building, a territorial jail in Camp Takhini, and suburban developments in Porter Creek and Wolf Creek have modernized Whitehorse considerably. So, too, has the construction of a new campus of Yukon College. Initially housed in the Yukon Vocational School, the college offers a wide range of vocational and academic courses, including a recently expanded university transfer program. Whitehorse has facilities and conveniences that few towns its size anywhere in Canada could match, a mark of its position as territorial capital and generous government spending over the past two decades.

The Yukon's other communities have not developed as rapidly. Dawson City remains a seasonal centre, crowded in the summer with tourists and students who have come north to work; shrinking to its core in the winter months. Several of the key businesses, including some of the hotels and the placer operations, close down for the winter, adding to the sense of isolation.

Most of the smaller communities are built on a similarly seasonal foundation, dependent on tourist traffic along the Alaska Highway or summer mineral exploration. Their permanence rests, in large measure, on the stable native population and the few regular (mostly government) jobs based in the community.

The mining communities have had a different history. During the days of Cypress-Anvil, Faro had a measure of stability, but when the mine closed, most workers left the Territory in search of new opportunities. The reopened mine, with its less generous terms of employment, has had trouble keeping workers, adding to the transient nature of the community. Faro and Clinton Creek may, in fact, be the last of the Yukon's company towns. Plans for new mines in the MacMillan Pass region call for workers based in existing communities (probably Whitehorse) to be flown in and out on rotation.

The sizable emigration of about three thousand people during the 1981–85 depression was only the most visible sign of a deeply entrenched social pattern. Most of those who come north to work in the mines, government offices, and private businesses stay only a few years before moving south again. This pattern began to change only in the latter half of the 1970s, a welcome trend that continued over the next decade. The gradually increasing social stability has an important commercial dimension. In years past, much of the Yukon's wealth was exported to the south, often by business people who lived outside for the winter. While that pattern has not been broken entirely, there are noticeable signs of change. Individuals like Rolf Hougen, whose investments blanket the Yukon, have stayed in the north, re-investing their profits in the region. Hougen's family started a retail business on Whitehorse's Main Street, an outlet he used over the years as the cornerstone of holdings that now include a radio and television station, a car dealership, real estate, and other ventures. Another example of a businessman who has stayed on in the north is Con Lattin, who arrived in the Yukon after the war and lived for a time in Whiskey Flats. Lattin and his family first invested in a pop- and milk-bottling plant. The milk-processing business collapsed when milk trucked in from the south cornered the market; the pop-bottling enterprise ended with a fire that destroyed the plant. But the company remained in business, eventually expanding into every corner of the Territory and diversifying in other service ventures. These people, much like Taylor and Drury in an earlier era, hold promise for the future of a society struggling for stability. The roots of a self-sustaining community rest in this type of commitment, one that has long been missing in the Yukon Territory.

On the political level, the elected Territorial Council has continued to provide an increasing measure of representative government. Two additional members were added to the council in 1951. Two years later, the council received the authority to borrow money, subject to a federal veto. In

Erik Nielsen, first elected in 1957, served as the Yukon's Member of Parliament for thirty years. During his tenure, he earned a reputation as a staunch defender of territorial rights and a strong parliamentarian. He held several government portfolios, including Minister of Public Works, Deputy Prime Minister, and Minister of Defence. He resigned his seat in 1987.
CONSERVATIVE PARTY OF CANADA

the main, however, the Territory remained under the control of a commissioner, appointed by Ottawa and answering to no territorial authorities. As federal investment in the Yukon escalated, the commissioner's status likewise improved. No longer an administrator, the commissioner became a political force, having a great deal to do with the Territory's direction.

The Yukon went through three commissioners from the mid 1950s to the end of the 1960s. Frederick Collins was an outsider, well-connected in Ottawa and an able administrator. The government appointed Gordon Cameron to succeed him. Cameron, as a Yukoner, was expected to quiet growing territorial demands for greater local autonomy. He grew frustrated when he found himself trapped between the wishes of Territorial Council and the demands of his federal superiors. As he reportedly commented on many occasions "You can't drive a team of horses with reins 4,000 miles long. By the time you give the signal, you've missed the turn."[42]

Led by Erik Nielsen, who would serve as the Yukon's Member of Parliament for more than a quarter of a century, territorial politicians demanded greater local control and freedom from the old colonial structures. As one territorial councillor commented in 1958, "As the voice of the Yukon's population, we have a mandate, I believe, to push with all the aggressiveness at our command to improve the local scene and make the Yukon an attractive place for people to live and prosper. The mandate includes laying of the foundations for the day of responsible government — a day which may not be so far distant."[43] Erik Nielsen was more blunt: "There is a rising tide of resentment in both Territories against the continuing

292

situation whereby people living in the Territories have no direct control over the development of their respective territories....We believe that we in the Territories exist in a state of vassalage...ignored in all high-level deliberations."[44] The protests culminated in 1966 with the demand that the Yukon be granted provincial status.

The lack of control, and the fact that the federal government continued to make major decisions without involving territorial politicians, forced elected officials and their public allies into extreme, often radical positions. The selection in 1966 of a new commissioner, well-respected local businessman James Smith, was intended to smooth the waters, but major decisions, including the contract with Cypress-Anvil, were made without consulting territorial councillors, and like Cameron, Smith found himself taking the heat for federal actions. Nonetheless, he handled the job with tact and aplomb; no one doubted his commitment to the Yukon and his desire to see the Territory move towards political maturity.

During Smith's tenure, the balance of power began to tip toward the Territorial Council. Always a forum for colourful debate, the Territorial Council also proved itself capable of serious work. In 1969, the federal government established an executive council, consisting of the commissioner, appointed officials, and several members of the assembly, who were empowered to handle the routine business of the government. Another eight years would pass before elected members secured a majority of the seats on the executive council, thus gaining some measure of responsible government for the Yukon.[45]

The concerted campaign for local autonomy obscured, at least in part, the very different views of the future of the Yukon. The business community, whose political interests were well-represented by Erik Nielsen, sought territorial control of resources and a pro-development approach to government. Native people (who gained representation on the Territorial Council by the drafting of electoral boundaries which created several largely Indian constituencies) and some white sympathizers had a different view, which favoured native rights, environmental concerns, and a more cautious development program. Dislodging the territorial Conservatives would prove a difficult challenge, although the opposing forces came close on a few occasions. In the federal election of 1972, for example, the Liberal candidate nearly defeated Nielsen.

It was the Conservatives who decided that party distinctions should be brought to Territorial Council. In the 1978 territorial election, Chris Pearson's Conservative caucus won eleven of the sixteen seats. As Government Leader, Pearson selected the executive council from within his caucus, marking a watershed in territorial politics. Tory power gathered steam. In the federal election of 1979, the Conservatives squeaked into office; Erik Nielsen was named Minister of Public Works, a crucial post given the importance of highway construction and government investment in the Yukon. The federal government acted quickly to reduce the powers of the commissioner further, granting greater autonomy to local officials. Not all were pleased with the change. Commissioner Ione Chrisstensen resigned over the reduction in the commissioner's role. As the council became more powerful, the commissioner became less so; by the mid 1980s the position was largely ceremonial.

Promising signs showed up on other fronts as well. The election of Joe Clark and the Conservatives seemed particularly fortuitous. As early as 1976, Clark had announced his determination to grant the Yukon Territory full provincial status. To Clark's surprise, he discovered that Yukoners were not as pleased with the proposal as he had expected. Serious critics of the proposition wondered about the cost to Yukoners, and queried whether the emphasis on political reform might be better expended on economic and social improvements. As one commentator noted, "To talk about province hood under such circumstances seems to be unrealistic and even dangerous because someone might just say yes."[46]

The election of the Conservative government in 1984 — and Erik Nielsen's elevation to the position of Deputy Prime Minister — seemed to hold considerable promise for the Territory. But Nielsen, near retirement and distracted by the many problems of the early Mulroney years, put little public effort into the Yukon political campaigns. Provincial status would remain on hold, replaced by rather more pressing concerns, including a prolonged debate over the high charges and massive debt of the Northern Canada Power Commission.

The most immediate of these concerns, which held the Yukon's attention for much of the late 1970s, revolved around proposed pipeline developments. In the early 1970s, the Arctic Gas consortium came forward with plans for a pipeline to deliver Alaskan natural gas down a Mackenzie River corridor. Facing opposition from native and environmental organizations, the federal government agreed to place the matter before a Royal Commission chaired by Thomas Berger, a former NDP politician whose support for Indian rights and concern about the environment were well-known. Berger launched a high-profile inquiry that visited the affected communities in the Northwest Territories and the Yukon and brought the concerns of northern natives before the Canadian people in a way that no other forum has done before or since.[47]

The Berger Commission recommended that the Mackenzie Valley pipe line project be delayed and called the government's attention to the pressing need to settle native land claims and protect the environment. It also suggested alternative routes, including a proposal brought forward by the Foothills Pipe Lines Company of Bob Blair. Blair, the upstart in the pipeline wars, had proven surprisingly persuasive and it appeared that his project would carry the day. The federal government established another investigative commission, this time under the leadership of Kenneth Lysyk, from the University of British Columbia's Faculty of Law, with Yukon representatives Willard Phelps and Edith Bohmer, to examine the proposal. The Alaska Highway Pipeline Inquiry report, issued in 1977, called for careful attention to the needs of the Yukon Indian people and to the social, economic, and environmental changes that would accompany the massive project.[48] The government was, however, determined to proceed, and the Yukon braced for another construction boom, one that promised to match the building of the Alaska Highway in intensity. Yukon businesses expanded operations in anticipation; the city of Whitehorse opened new lots and a new subdivision (now the Indian reserve) in expectation of a building boom. Just as excitement peaked, Blair's dream began to unravel. Declining oil and gas prices, combined with reduced demand in the United States, scuttled the project. Although the plans remain in place, and hope remains that the project will be revived, the much-awaited construction explosion proved illusory.

The collapse of the pipeline project, combined with the depression of the early 1980s, raised serious questions about the viability of the Yukon's economy. Government expenditures made up a strikingly high percentage of the territorial economy, particularly with the Faro mine shut down. The demise of the mining sector and the pipeline also called into question the territorial Conservative Party's dependence on development as the basis for the regional economy. Chris Pearson resigned the government leader's chair in 1985, assuming a patronage appointment as Canada's representative in Dallas, Texas. He was replaced by Willard Phelps, a man with deep Yukon roots but wedded to the standard Tory model of regional development. Less than three months after his selection, Phelps faced his first major test. To the surprise of many, the May 1985 election saw the election of a New Democratic Party minority government, led by Tony Penikett. The NDP gained eight seats — half of those available — in the exceptionally close campaign, while Phelps's Tories fell to only six. The Liberals, with the remaining two seats, held the balance of power. Sam Johnston of Teslin was appointed Speaker, the first native in Canada to hold such a post. The Liberals supported the government initially, until their leader Roger Coles was charged and found guilty of possession of cocaine, and a February 1987 by-election in the Tatchun constituency returned an NDP member, solidifying the government's hold on office.

The new government faced no shortage of challenges, the most serious of which was attending to the collapsing territorial economy. Penikett and the government moved quickly to reassure the business community that their socialist leanings would not bring startling changes in government policy. The successful reopening of the Faro mine provided substantial evidence that the government was not opposed to development. The government also paid particular attention to the concerns of native people and the outlying communities. Perhaps surprisingly, however, the sizable native representation in the governing party and the assembly did not quickly translate into a major political power block. Perhaps the NDP's greatest success lay in the revitalization of the territorial bureaucracy. The former Conservative government, staunch defenders of the individualistic, growth-oriented frontier ethic, had given the civil servants little latitude to propose new programs. Under the NDP, initiative and innovation from civil servants was clearly welcomed, breathing new life into this large and important sector of Yukon society.

Evidence of the new spirit of innovation was the establishment of the "Yukon 2000" process in the spring of 1986. The government invited all Yukoners to participate in a lengthy territorial economic planning process, including extensive research and numerous opportunities for community consultation. Yukon 2000 centred on a series of public forums — in Faro and Whitehorse in 1986 and Dawson in 1987 — in which representatives from all sectors of Yukon society and economy debated the region's future. Although the process produced few new ideas, it did reveal a strong consensus on the need for economic diversification and measures to ensure economic equality and social stability within the Territory.

In 1986, Erik Nielsen announced his resignation from the House of Commons to the solitude of his Quiet Lake retreat. For the first time in a quarter-century, the federal Yukon seat was truly open. The NDP put its considerable resources and expertise into the campaign of Audrey McLaughlin and won a narrow victory over popular Whitehorse mayor Don Brannigan, the Liberal candidate. The Conservatives finished third. The success of the NDP campaign rested, at least in part, on the strong opposition of McLaughlin and the Yukon government to an announced constitutional deal involving the federal government and the provinces.

In the spring of 1987, Prime Minister Brian Mulroney and the ten provincial premiers emerged from a marathon meeting at a resort at Meech Lake in Quebec to announce the signing of a constitutional accord. Most political leaders rushed to support the deal, which brought Quebec into the constitution and expanded provincial influence over Senate and judicial appointments and future constitutional change. To their dismay, Yukoners discovered that no one had stood up for northern concerns. The Yukon government would have no say in the new appointment processes nor would they be able to negotiate solely with the federal government on future provincial status, as had all other late entries into Confederation. Under the terms of the proposed accord, such changes would be subject to approval by the federal government and the ten provincial premiers, a level of unanimity seldom achieved in Canada.

It was a constitutional slap in the face of the worst kind. The governments of the Yukon and the Northwest Territories protested the provisions in the strongest terms. Tony Penikett spoke out loudly against the deal, as did Audrey McLaughlin, who broke ranks with her national party over the issue. The Yukon government went even further, challenging the constitutional deal in the courts. The campaign against the Meech Lake accord has, ironically, drawn Yukoners together, providing the kind of common cause for protest that so often forms the basis of a regional identity. As such, it may contribute to the development of political and social stability in a region not noted for either. At the same time, Meech Lake reveals the Yukon's continuing vulnerability to federal politics and southern Canadian priorities. Once more the Yukon had been sacrificed to a greater Canadian ambition. It now seems that the Yukon Territory could well be doomed to the status of a permanent colony, denied even the ambition of constitutional evolution that sits at the base of the Canadian political tradition.

Epilogue

To most North Americans, the Yukon remains locked in the legacy of the Klondike gold rush. That single, intense episode, two years in duration and ninety years in the past, remains deeply imbedded in the southern consciousness. The Yukon has, not altogether unwittingly, allowed itself to be a captive of the gold rush. Klondike lore dominates Yukon tourist promotion to the detriment of other aspects of the Territory's vibrant and diverse past. The psychology of the gold rush also remains in evidence — in modern-day speculators playing the tables at Diamond Tooth Gertie's, and in the prospectors' continued search for the Yukon's next "Bonanza." The belief that prosperity lies buried in the next hill, along the next creek, or in some other commercial *deus ex machina*, has long diverted Yukoners' attention from the less dramatic but vital task of planning for a more lasting future.

Much of the contemporary Yukon reflects the patterns of the past. The economic instability graphically demonstrated in the depression of 1981–85, brought home the Territory's continued dependence on international markets and investors whose interests lie outside the Territory. Similarly, the Meech Lake accord and the Yukon's inconsequential role in the now-routine First Ministers' conferences provide constant, if painful, reminders of the general lack of southern interest in northern concerns.

The old Yukon can be seen everywhere, in paternalistic federal policies, in the continued transiency of much of the white population, in the lack of diversification of the economy away from minerals, in the social and economic isolation of the Yukon Indians outside the mainstream of white society, and in the dominance of a single city. For the pessimist there is ample evidence that little has changed.

For those who look more closely, there are promising signs that the colonial patterns are being resisted and that the Yukon is developing toward a more stable future. A more sustained political response, rooted in a commitment to long-term growth rather than short-term development, both reflects and sustains the base of Yukon population. The politicization of the

298

Yukon Indians, which has stimulated a dramatic renaissance of native culture and society, promises that the Indians will never again be shunted aside and ignored. While the failure to resolve the land-claim issue hangs like Damocles' sword over the Territory, the Indians' determination to attain a settlement that honours their aboriginal land rights and provides the means for dealing with the problems of the present and future must be seen as the foundation of any revitalized Yukon society. No more will it be possible for whites, as they did so often in the past, to proceed with development as though the Indians did not exist.

There is hope, too, in what appears to be a sincere federal commitment to the north. While public attention is distracted by the flashy projects — submarines capable of operating under Arctic ice, Arctic ice-breakers — there is a subtle revolution underway at the administrative level. For years, the federal government simply shipped money north, pulling the strings from Ottawa and looking primarily to the national implications of its northern investments. The slow, but inexorable, devolution of authority, which transfers the decision-making power to the Yukon government augurs well for the Territory's future. While provincial status seems unlikely (and seemed so even before Meech Lake), there is a full range of constitutional and administrative possibilities that lies just short of that over-rated goal.[1] The settlement of native land claims and the passage of significant powers, particularly over resources and development, to the territorial government would offer Yukoners of all races the ability to control their destiny for the first time since the Klondike gold rush.

Perhaps the greatest sign of the Yukon's maturity is the gradual submergence of grandiose dreams of imminent prosperity. Visions of that type have, in the past, only clouded national and territorial perceptions of the realistic prospects for the Yukon Territory. More moderate expectations, based on gradual economic diversification, local autonomy, legitimate authority for the Indians, greater federal dedication to the north, re-investment of locally produced wealth, and more Yukoners committed to putting down their roots in the Territory — these are the means by which the Yukon can escape its past. History tells us how the Yukon developed and explains how the problems and promises of the present are firmly imbedded in the experiences of the past. The past need not, however, become a blueprint for the future. There is an old saying that those who forget the past are condemned to relive it. This is nowhere more true than in the Yukon.

Footnotes

Chapter One

1. On the subject of Canadian thinkers and the north, see W. L. Morton, "The North in Canadian History," in A. B. McKillop, ed., *Contexts of Canada's Past* (Ottawa: Carleton University Press, 1980); L.-E. Hamelin, *Canadian Nordicity: It's Your North Too*, trans. W. Barr (Montreal: Harvest House, 1978); K. S. Coates and W. R. Morrison, "Northern Visions: Recent Writing in Northern Canadian History," *Manitoba History*, (Fall 1985). On the nationalistic rhetoric of Canadian nordicity, see Carl Berger, "The True North Strong and Free," in Peter Russell, *Nationalism in Canada* (Toronto: McGraw-Hill, 1966). On the history of the Canadian north, see K. S. Coates, *Canada's Colonies: A History of the Yukon and Northwest Territories* (Toronto: James Lorimer and Company, 1985).
2. See Thomas Berger, *Northern Frontier/Northern Homeland: the Report of the Mackenzie Valley Pipeline Inquiry, Vol. 1* (Ottawa: Department of Supply and Services, 1977) and Robert Page, *Northern Development: The Canadian Dilemma* (Toronto: McClelland and Stewart, 1986).
3. R. Coutts, *Yukon Places and Names* (Sidney, B.C.: Gray's Publishing, 1980) deals with the question of place names, although the historical materials are not always reliable.
4. The following section draws heavily on Brian M. Fagan, *The Great Journey: the Peopling of Ancient America* (New York: Thames and Hudson, 1987), and Catherine McClellan, *Part of the Land, Part of the Water: a History of the Yukon Indians* (Toronto: Douglas and McIntyre, 1987), pp. 44–62.
5. McClellan, *Part of the Land*, pp. 4–5.
6. There is a vast anthropological and ethnographic literature on the aboriginal inhabitants of the Yukon River basin. Among the best sources are McClellan, *Part of the Land*; June Helm, ed., *Handbook of North American Indians, Vol. 6: Subarctic Indians* (Washington: Smithsonian Institution, 1981); C. Osgood, *Contributions to the Ethnography of the Kutchin* (New Haven: Yale University Press, 1970); C. Osgood, *The Han Indians* (New Haven: Yale University Press, 1954); John Honigmann, *The Kaska Indians* (New Haven: Yale University Press, 1954); C. McClellan, *My Old People Say: An Ethnographic Survey of Southern Yukon Territory* (Ottawa: National Museum of Canada, 1975); James Van Stone, *Athapaskan Adaptations: Hunters and Fishermen of the Subarctic Forests* (Chicago: Aldine, 1975). The following description draws on these sources, among others.
8. For a solid, if somewhat dated, survey of the history of the Inuit in Canada, see Diamond Jenness, *Eskimo Administration II: Canada* (Montreal: Arctic Institute of North America, 1964).
9. General Synod Archives, M56-2, Series C-23, Canham Papers, T. H. Canham, "Untitled Comments on the Indians of the Far North."

Chapter Two

1. A. A. Wright, *Prelude to Bonanza: The Discovery and Exploration of the Yukon* (Whitehorse: Arctic Star Printing, 1980), pp. 1–58; Alexander Mackenzie, *Voyages from Montreal, on the River St. Lawrence, through the Continent of North America to the Frozen and Pacific Oceans in the Years 1789 and 1793* (London: Noble, 1801), p. 54.

2. Theodore Karamanski, *Fur Trade and Exploration: Opening the Far Northwest, 1821–1852* (Vancouver: University of British Columbia Press, 1983), pp. 3–38.

3. Peter C. Newman, *Caesars of the Wilderness* (Toronto: Penguin, 1987).

4. Stephen Johnson, "Baron Wrangel and the Russian-American Company," unpublished PHD thesis, University of Manitoba, 1978.

5. Johnson, "Baron Wrangel"; K. S. Coates, "Furs Along the Yukon: Hudson's Bay Company–Native Trade in the Yukon River Basin, 1830–1893," unpublished MA thesis, University of Manitoba, 1979, pp. 25–56.

6. Coates, "Furs Along the Yukon"; Karamanski, *Fur Trade and Exploration*, ch. 5.

7. Hudson's Bay Company Archives (HBCA) D.4/24, fol. 5, Simpson to McPherson, 28 February 1838.

8. For a sympathetic portrayal of Robert Campbell, see Wright, *Prelude to Bonanza* and Clifford Wilson, *Campbell of the Yukon* (Toronto: Macmillan, 1970). For a more critical analysis of his career, see Coates, "Furs Along the Yukon."

9. HBCA, D.5/15, fol. 47. Governor and Committee to Governor and Council, 1 June 1838.

10. Thomas Simpson, *Narrative of the Discoveries on the North Coast of America* (London: Richard Bentley, 1843); HBCA, D.5/14, fol. 326, P. W. Dease and T. Simpson to Governor Simpson, 5 September 1837. *See also* K. S. Coates, "The Commerce of Discovery: The Hudson's Bay Company and the Simpson and Dease Expeditions," unpublished paper presented at a conference.

11. Coates, "Furs Along the Yukon, pp. 46–48;" Karamanski, *Fur Trade and Exploration*, pp. 161–69.

12. HBCA, D.5/14, fol. 212–15, Bell to Simpson, 1 August 1845.

13. Karamanski, *Fur Trade and Exploration*, pp. 214–44.

14. HBCA, D.5/5 fol. 326b, Campbell to Simpson, 30 September 1840.

15. Karamanski, *Fur Trade and Exploration*, pp. 210–14.

16. Coates, "Furs Along the Yukon," pp. 67–90.

17. Karamanski, *Fur Trade and Exploration*, pp. 244–55.

18. HBCA, D.4/71, fol. 241, Simpson to Campbell, 20 June 1850.

19. HBCA, B.200/b/22, fol. 15, Murray to McPherson, 20 November 1847; HBCA, B.240/a/1, fol. 45, Youcon Journal, 27 November 1847. *See also* Alexander Hunter Murray, *Journal of the Yukon 1847–1848*, L.J. Burpee, ed., Publications of the Canadian Archives, no. 4 (Ottawa: Government Printing Bureau, 1916).

20. For the Hudson's Bay Company's side of this story, see Coates, "Protecting the Monopoly: The Hudson's Bay Company and Scientific Knowledge of the Yukon Valley," Yukon Museums and Historical Association, *Proceedings, 1982*, pp. 3–12. For the Russian perspective, see Katherine Arndt, "Russian-American Company Trade on the Middle Yukon River, 1839–1867," unpublished paper presented at a conference.

21. Coates, "Furs Along the Yukon," pp. 67–84. For a more favourable portrait, based largely on Campbell's memoirs, see Karamanski, ch. 8 and 9.

22. HBCA, D.5/20, fol. 510, McPherson to Simpson, 23 November 1847; HBCA, D.5/21, fol. 341, McPherson to Simpson, 1 March 1848.

23. This encounter can be followed in greater detail in Wright, *Prelude to Bonanza*, pp. 70–77. The Tlingit trade with the interior is documented in William Ostenstat,

"The Impact of the Fur Trade on the Tlingit During the Late Eighteenth and Nineteenth Centuries," unpublished MA thesis, University of Manitoba, 1976.

24. Robert Campbell, *Two Journals of Robert Campbell, 1808 to 1853* (Seattle: John W. Todd, Jr., 1951). The accounts by Wright and Karamanski draw rather uncritically on these memoirs.

25. HBCA, D.4/37, fol. 183, Simpson to Campbell, 12 June 1848.

26. HBCA, D.5/34, fol. 71, Anderson to Simpson, 10 July 1852.

27. Public Archives of Canada, MG 19, A-25, Pelly Banks Journal.

28. Lorne Hammond, "Any Ordinary Degree of System: The Columbia Department and the Harvesting of Wildlife, 1825-1849," unpublished MA thesis, University of Victoria, 1988.

29. The following analysis of the Hudson's Bay Company's trade can be followed in Coates, "Furs Along the Yukon," and, in shortened form, in K. S. Coates, "Furs Along the Yukon: Hudson's Bay Company–Native Trade in the Yukon River Basin, 1840-1893," *BC Studies* No. 55 (Autumn 1982), pp. 50-78. See also Shepherd Krech III, "The Eastern Kutchin and the Fur Trade, 1800-1860," *Ethnohistory*, 23/3 (Summer 1976), 213-35.

30. Arndt, "Russian-American Company Trade."

31. Ibid.

32. Hudson Stuck, *Voyages on the Yukon and Its Tributaries* (New York: Scribner's Sons, 1917), pp. 136-37.

33. Shepherd Krech III, "On the Aboriginal Population of the Kutchin," *Arctic Anthropology*, vol. 15 (1978), 89-104; S. Krech III, "Throwing Bad Medicine: Sorcery, Disease and the Fur Trade Among the Kutchin and Other Northern Athapaskans," in S. Krech III, ed. *Indians, Animals and the Fur Trade* (Athens: University of Georgia, 1982).

34. HBCA, B.200/b/36, fol. 58, McDougall to Hardisty, 5 July 1866; ibid., fol. 42, Flett to Hardisty, January 1866.

35. W. W. Kirkby, "A Journey to the Youcon, Russian America," Smithsonian Institution, *Annual Report, 1864*, pp. 416-20.

36. Frank Peake, "Fur Traders and Missionaries: Some Reflections on Attitudes of the H.B.C. Towards Missionary Work Among the Indians," *Western Canadian Journal of Anthropology*, vol. 3, no. 1 (1977), 77-93.

37. Frank Peake, "Robert McDonald (1829-1913): The Great Unknown Missionary of the Northwest," *Journal of the Canadian Church Historical Society*, vol. 17, no 3 (1975), 54-72.

38. On the Anglican Church generally, see T. C. B. Boon, *The Anglican Church from the Bay to the Rockies* (Toronto: Ryerson Press, 1962); for a hagiographic portrait of Bompas, see H. A. Cody, *An Apostle of the North* (New York: E. P. Dutton, 1908); on the difficulties of recruiting for the north, see K. S. Coates, "Send Only Those Who Rise a Peg: The Recruitment and Use of Anglican Missionaries in the Yukon, 1858-1932," *Journal of the Canadian Church Historical Society* (Summer 1986), pp. 3-18.

39. On Kennicott, see James G. James, *The First Scientific Exploration of Alaska, and the Purchase of Alaska* (Evanston: Northwestern University, 1942).

40. This analysis of Kennicott's Yukon career can be followed in K. S. Coates, "The Kennicott Network: Robert Kennicott and the Far Northwest," Yukon Museums and Historical Association, *Proceedings, 1982*, pp. 25-33.

41. Wright, *Prelude to Bonanza*, ch. 4; Melody Webb, *The Last Frontier: A History of the Yukon Basin of Canada and Alaska* (Albuquerque: University of New Mexico Press, 1985), ch. 3. *See also* two very good memoirs, William Dall, *Alaska and it*

Resources (Boston: Lee and Chepard, 1870); Frederick Whymper, *Travel and Adventure in the Territory of Alaska* (Ann Arbor: University Microfilms, 1966).

42. Coates, "Protecting the Monopoly."
43. Coates, "Furs Along the Yukon," pp. 123-52.
44. For Raymond's report on this exercise, see United States Government, *Compilation of Narratives of Explorations in Alaska* (Washington: Government Printing Office, 1900).
45. Coates, "Furs Along the Yukon."

Chapter Three

1. K. S. Coates, "Furs Along the Yukon: Hudson's Bay Company–Native Trade in the Yukon, 1830-1893," *B.C. Studies*, no. 55, (Autumn 1982).
2. G. Sealey, "The History of the Hudson's Bay Company, 1870-1910," unpublished MA thesis, University of Western Ontario, 1967.
3. Hudson's Bay Company Archives (HBCA) B/200/b/40, fol. 65-67, McDougall to Hardisty, 4 November 1872.
4. HBCA, B/200/b/40, fol. 68. Hardisty to Smith.
5. HBCA, B/200/b/37, fol. 255, Hardisty to Council, 2 August 1870.
6. K. S. Coates, "Furs Along the Yukon: Hudson Bay Company–Native Trade in the Yukon River Basin, 1830-1893," unpublished MA thesis, University of Manitoba, 1979.
7. R. G. McConnell, "Report of an exploration in the Yukon and Mackenzie Basins, N. W. T.," *Canadian Geological Survey Annual Report, 1888-1889* (Ottawa: King's Printer, 1890). On the history of the Geological Survey, see Morris Zaslow, *Reading the Rocks: The Story of the Geological Survey of Canada, 1842-1872* (Toronto: Macmillan, 1975).
8. J. H. Turner, "The Boundary North of Fort Yukon," Part II of "The Alaska Boundary Survey," *National Geographic*, vol. 4 (February 1893).
9. HBCA, B.200/b/43, fol. 755, Camsell to Chipman, 30 March 1892.
10. The following section draws from Melody Webb, *The Last Frontier: A History of the Yukon Basin of Canada and Alaska* (Albuquerque: University of New Mexico Press, 1985), ch. 3.
11. W. R. Hunt, *North of '53: the Wild Days of the Alaska-Yukon Mining Frontier, 1870-1914* (New York: Macmillan, 1974).
12. On the history of the Yukon before the gold rush, see Allen A. Wright, *Prelude to Bonanza: The Discovery and Exploration of the Yukon* (Whitehorse: Arctic Star Printing, 1980).
13. William Ogilvie, *Early Days on the Yukon & the Story of Its Gold Finds* (Ottawa: Thorburn and Abbott, 1913), pp. 85-87.
14. L. N. McQuesten, *Recollections of Leroy N. McQuesten*, Yukon Archives, Coutts Collection, Pamphlets 1952-53, p. 3.
15. Ibid., p. 7.
16. Ibid., pp. 4-7.
17. Alan Cooke and Clive Holland, *The Exploration of Northern Canada, 500 to 1920: a Chronology* (Toronto: Arctic History Press, 1978), p. 228. For a description of Tlingit attempts to control the passes, see William Ostenstat, "The Impact of the Fur Trade on the Tlingit During the Late Eighteenth and Nineteenth Centuries," unpublished MA thesis, University of Manitoba, 1976.

18. H. B. Goodrich, "History and Conditions of the Yukon Gold District to 1897," in J. E. Spurr, ed., *Geology of the Yukon Gold District, Alaska — Eighteenth Annual Report of the United States Geological Survey to the Secretary of the Interior, 1896–97. Part 3* (Washington: Government Printing Office, 1898), pp. 103–33.

18. Webb, *The Last Frontier*, p. 71.

19. W. H. Pierce, *Thirteen Years of Travel and Exploration in Alaska, 1877–1889* (Anchorage: Alaska Northwest Publishing, 1977), quoted in Webb, *The Last Frontier*, p. 78.

20. Webb, *The Last Frontier*, p. 78.

21. Coates, "Furs Along the Yukon."

22. "Report of Inspector Constantine, 20 January 1896," *Annual Report of the North-West Mounted Police, 1896* (Ottawa: King's Printer, 1897).

23. Public Archives of Canada (PAC), Department of Indian Affairs papers, RG 10, vol. 3962, file 147,654-1, part 2, W. C. Bompas to Indian Commissioner, 5 September 1896.

24. PAC, Ogilvie papers, MG 20, B-22, W. C. Bompas to Lieutenant Governor, 3 December 1891.

25. K. S. Coates, "Best Left as Indians: Indian–White Relations in the Yukon Territory, 1840–1950," unpublished PhD thesis, University of British Columbia, 1984.

26. HBCA, B.200/b/43, fol. 698, Camsell to Wrigley, 25 March 1891; B.200/b/43, fol. 719, Camsell to Chipman, 11 September 1891.

27. R. Stuart and J. Gould, "Permafrost Gold: a Treatise on Early Klondike Mining: History, Methods, and Technology," microfiche report, (Ottawa: Parks Canada, 1983).

28. Webb, *The Last Frontier*, p. 82.

29. Ibid., p. 85.

30. The term *creole* was used in Alaska to describe people of mixed Russian-native parentage.

31. Goodrich, "History and Conditions of the Yukon Gold District to 1897," p. 332.

32. Pierre Berton, *Klondike: The Last Great Gold Rush* (Toronto: McClelland and Stewart, 1972), p. 17.

33. Ibid., p. 17.

34. This discussion of mining society is indebted to the work of Thomas Stone, particularly "Atomistic Order and Frontier Violence: Miners and Whalemen in the Nineteenth Century Yukon," *Ethnology*, vol. 22, (October 1983); "Flux and Authority in a Subarctic Society: the Yukon Miners in the Nineteenth Century," *Ethnohistory*, 30(4), 1983; "The Mounties as Vigilantes: Perceptions of Community and the Transformation of Law in the Yukon, 1885–1897," *Law and Society Review*, vol. 14, no. 1, (Fall 1979).

35. Stone, "Atomistic Order," p. 328–29.

36. This account is taken from Stone, "Flux and Authority," pp. 204–206.

37. Goodrich, p. 127, quoted in Stone, "The Mounties as Vigilantes," p. 87.

38. By E. Colson, in *Tradition and Contract: The Problem of Order* (Chicago: Aldine Publishing, 1974), p. 54.

39. Hugh Brody, *The Living Arctic*, (Vancouver: Douglas and McIntyre, 1987).

40. William Ogilvie tells the story in *Early Days on the Yukon*, ch. 3, but calls Leslie "the Discoverer," perhaps to avoid a libel suit.

41. Stone, "Atomistic Order," p. 332.

42. Roger D. McGrath, *Gunfighters, Highwaymen and Vigilantes: Violence on the Frontier* (Berkeley, 1984) discusses violence on the American mining frontier.

43. Stone, "The Mounties as Vigilantes," p. 93.
44. Frederick Schwatka, *A Summer in Alaska*, pp. 83–84, quoted in Allen A. Wright, *Prelude to Bonanza*, p. 144.
45. G. M. Dawson, *Report on an Exploration in the Yukon District, N. W. T. and Adjacent Northern Portion of British Columbia, 1887* (Ottawa: King's Printer, 1888), gives his account of the trip. Ogilvie's version is in *Early Days on the Yukon*. On the Canadian Geological Survey, see Zaslow, *Reading the Rocks*.
46. Dawson, *Report*, p. 33, quoted in Wright, *Prelude to Bonanza*, p. 180.
47. See Roy Minter, *The White Pass: Gateway to the Klondike* (Toronto: McClelland and Stewart, 1987).
48. Quoted in Wright, *Prelude to Bonanza*, p. 191.
49. Ogilvie, *Early Days*, p. 139.
50. McConnell, "Extracts Relating to the Yukon District...." in Dawson, *Report*, quoted in Wright, *Prelude to Bonanza*, p. 203.
51. McConnell, "Extracts," quoted in Wright, *Prelude to Bonanza*, pp. 232–33.
52. Ogilvie, *Early Days*, p. 143.
53. He died the next year, 1892, age forty-three, of an overdose of laudanum taken to treat stomach ulcers. Webb, *The Last Frontier*, p. 118.
54. K. S. Coates, *The Northern Yukon: A History*, Manuscript Report No. 309, (Winnipeg: Parks Canada, 1979) p. 42.
55. K. S. Coates, "Send Only Those Who Rise a Peg: The Recruitment and Use of Anglican Missionaries in the Yukon, 1858–1932," *Journal of the Canadian Church Historical Society* (Summer 1986).
56. Quoted in Coates, "Send Only Those."
57. M. Wesbrook, "A Venture into Ethnohistory: the Journals of V. C. Sim," *Polar Notes*, no. 9, (1969).
58. Quoted in Coates, "Send Only Those."
59. A. S. Archer, *A Heroine of the North: Memoirs of Charlotte Selina Bompas* (London: Macmillan, 1929), p. 132. See also H. A. Cody, *An Apostle of the North: Memoirs of the Right Reverend William Carpenter Bompas* (Toronto: Musson, 1908).
60. George E. Gartrell, "The Work of the Churches in the Yukon During the Era of the Klondike Gold Rush," unpublished MA thesis, University of Western Ontario, 1970, quoted in Wright, *Prelude to Bonanza*, p. 255. The letter is to be found originally in Public Archives of Canada, Charles Constantine Papers, vol. 3.
61. Public Archives of Canada (PAC), RG10, vol. 3906, file 105,378, Bompas to Minister of the Interior, 5 June 1894.
62. K. S. Coates, "Asking for All Sorts of Favours: the Anglican Church, the Federal Government and the Indians of the Yukon Territory, 1891 to 1909," unpublished paper presented at a conference.
63. A copy of this is in Constantine Papers, vol. 3.
64. He later rose to the rank of superintendent, and died while on sick leave in 1912. See R. Stewart, *Sam Steele: Lion of the Frontier* (Toronto: Doubleday, 1979).
65. *Report of the North-West Mounted Police, 1894* (Ottawa: King's Printer, 1895), C, p. 81.
66. *Report of the North-West Mounted Police, 1895*, (Ottawa: King's Printer, 1896) p. 7.
67. *Report of the North-West Mounted Police, 1894*, C, p. 77.
68. *Report of the North-West Mounted Police, 1894*, p. 78.
69. PAC, R.C.M.P. Papers, Commissioner's Office, RG 18, B-2, vol. 2182.
70. J. N. E. Brown, "The Evolution of Law and Government in the Yukon Territory," in S. M. Wickett, ed., *Municipal Government in Canada* (Toronto:

University of Toronto Press, 1907), p. 198. The districts of Franklin, Ungava, and Mackenzie were created at the same time.

71. M. H. E. Hayne and H. W. Taylor, *The Pioneers of the Klondyke* (London: Sampson Low, Marston, 1897).

72. The incident is recounted in Constantine's report to Frederick White, Comptroller of the N.W.M.P., 13 July 1896, in PAC, R.C.M.P. Papers, RG 18 A-1, Comptroller's Correspondence, vol. 123.

73. William R. Hunt, *Distant Justice: Policing the Alaska Frontier* (Norman: University of Oklahoma Press, 1987), shows the evolution of law and order west of the 141st meridian.

Chapter Four

1. H. A. Innis, *Settlement and the Mining Frontier* (Toronto: Macmillan, 1936); W. R. Hunt, *North of '53: the Wild Days of the Alaska–Yukon Mining Frontier, 1870–1914* (New York: Macmillan, 1974).

2. Andrew H. Malcolm, *The Canadians* (Toronto: Fitzhenry and Whiteside, 1985), pp. 342–45, tells the story.

3. He became known to the world as Tagish Charlie, or Charley.

4. A. A. Wright, *Prelude to Bonanza* (Whitehorse: Arctic Star Printing, 1980), pp. 247–90.

5. Pierre Berton, *Klondike: The Last Great Gold Rush* (Toronto: McClelland and Stewart, 1972), p. 44.

6. A. A. Wright, *Prelude to Bonanza*, p. 295.

7. This discussion is drawn from Melody Webb, *The Last Frontier: A History of the Yukon River Basin of Canada and Alaska* (Albuquerque: University of New Mexico Press, 1985); Pierre Berton, *Klondike*; Morris Zaslow, *The Opening of the Canadian North, 1870–1914* (Toronto: McClelland and Stewart, 1971); Hal Guest, "A History of Dawson City, Yukon Territory," Microfiche Report Series No. 7, Parks Canada, 1983.

8. Berton, *Klondike*, pp. 73–74.

9. Norbert MacDonald, "Seattle, Vancouver, and the Klondike," *Canadian Historical Review*, vol. XLIX, no. 3 (September 1968).

10. J. G. MacGregor, *The Klondike Rush through Edmonton, 1897–1898* (Toronto: McClelland and Stewart, 1970); K. S. Coates, *The Northern Yukon: A History*, Manuscript Report #309 (Winnipeg: Parks Canada, 1979).

11. S. B. Steele, *Forty Years in Canada* (London: Jenkins, 1915), p. 296.

12. Richard J. Friesen, *The Chilkoot Pass: A History of the Great Gold Rush of 1898*, Manuscript Report No. 276, (Ottawa: Parks Canada, 1978).

13. Steele, *Forty Years*, p. 296.

14. Martha Black, *My Ninety Years*, (Anchorage: Alaska Northwest Publishing Co., 1976), p. 30.

15. Ibid., p. 30.

16. Lewis Green, *The Boundary Hunters* (Vancouver: University of British Columbia Press, 1982).

17. Quoted in Berton, *Klondike*, pp. 143–44.

18. Gordon Bennett, *Yukon Transportation: A History*, (Ottawa: Parks Canada, 1978), pp. 24–58.

19. Steele, *Forty Years*.

20. W. R. Morrison, *Showing the Flag: The Mounted Police and Canadian Sovereignty in the North, 1894-1925* (Vancouver: University of British Columbia Press, 1985) recounts the history of the police force during the gold rush.
21. Quoted in Morrison, *Showing the Flag*, p. 37.
22. *Report of the North-West Mounted Police, 1897* (Ottawa: King's Printer, 1898), p. 309.
23. Quoted in Morrison, *Showing the Flag*, p. 40.
24. See A. L. Disher, "The Long March of the Yukon Field Force," *The Beaver* (Autumn 1962).
25. Morris Zaslow, "The Yukon: Northern Development in a Canadian American Context," in Mason Wade, ed., *Regionalism in the Canadian Community, 1867-1967* (Toronto, 1969).
26. Quoted in A. L. Disher, "The Long March."
27. His reminiscences are in "Klondike Memories," *The Beaver* (March, June, September 1951); see also H. S. Bostock, "Prospecting on Russell Creek," *North*, vol. 17 (November-December 1970).
28. Hal Guest, "A History of Dawson City;" *See also* Hal Guest, "A Socioeconomic History of the Klondike Gold Fields, 1896-1966," Microfiche Report Series 181 (Ottawa: Parks Canada, 1985).
29. The Yukon had been made a District of the North-West Territories in 1895.
30. David Hall, *Clifford Sifton*, 2 vols (Vancouver: University of British Columbia, 1982 and 1985). *See also* Lewis H. Thomas, *The Struggle for Responsible Government in the Northwest Territories* 2nd Edition (Toronto: University of Toronto Press, 1970).
31. Berton, *Klondike*, p. 308.
32. The following section is drawn from Michael R. Booth, "Gold Rush Theatres of the Klondike," *The Beaver* (Spring 1962).
33. C. E. S. Franks, "How the Sabbath Came to the Yukon," *Canadian Public Administration*, vol. 10 (March 1967).
34. Guest, "A History of Dawson City."
35. Laurence E. Karp, "The Writing of Dan McGrew," *North*, vol. 21 (September-October 1974).
36. W. R. Morrison, "Policing the Boom Town: The Mounted Police as a Social Force on the Gold Rush Frontier," unpublished paper presented at a conference.
37. Steele, *Forty Years*, p. 327.
38. Thomas Stone, "The Mounties as Vigilantes: Perceptions of Community and the Transformation of Law in the Yukon, 1885-1897," *Law and Society Review*, vol. 14, no. 1 (Fall 1979).
39. David Hall, *Clifford Sifton*, Vol. 1, ch. 7.
40. The activities of the Yukon Indians during the gold rush are examined in K. S. Coates, "Best Left as Indians: Native–White Relations in the Yukon Territory, 1840-1950," unpublished PHD thesis, University of British Columbia, 1984.
41. K. S. Coates, "Best Left as Indians: The Federal Government and the Indians of the Yukon Territory, 1894-1950," *Canadian Journal of Native Studies*, vol. 4, no. 2 (Fall 1984), pp. 179-204.
42. For a general description of the impact of the gold rush on the sub-arctic Indians, see Alice Kehoe, *North American Indians: A Comprehensive Account* (Englewood Cliffs: Prentice Hall, 1981). See also June Helm, ed., *Handbook of North American Indians*, Vol. 6: *The Sub-Arctic* (Washington: Smithsonian Institution, 1981).
43. George Gartrell, "The Work of the Churches in the Yukon During the Era of the Klondike Gold Rush," unpublished MA thesis, University of Western Ontario, 1970.

44. Public Archives of Canada (PAC), Indian Affairs Records, RG 10, vol. 4001, file 207,418, Congdon to Pedley, 28 May 1903. On this general theme, see K. S. Coates, "Asking for All Sorts of Favours: The Anglican Church, the Federal Government and the Indians of the Yukon Territory, 1891 to 1909," unpublished paper.
45. The best study of this is Roy Minter, *White Pass: Gateway to the Klondike* (Toronto: McClelland and Stewart, 1987). See also, Bennett, *Yukon Transportation*.
46. Paul Korischil, "Whitehorse: The Company Town, 1899–1945," unpublished paper presented at a conference.
47. David Hall, *Clifford Sifton*, Vol. 1, p. 189. See also Lewis Green, *The Gold Hustlers* (Vancouver: J. J. Douglas, 1972).

Chapter Five

1. P. J. Usher, "The Canadian Western Arctic: A Century of Change," *Anthropologica* no. 5, 13(1–2), pp. 169–83.
2. Quoted in Daniel Francis, *The Discovery of the North* (Edmonton: Hurtig, 1986), p. 72.
3. Ibid., p. 96.
4. Fred Bruemmer, "Herschel, the Big Town," *The Beaver* (Winter 1980), p. 26.
5. Francis, *Discovery of the North*, p. 117.
6. Alexander Simpson, *The Life and Travels of Thomas Simpson, the Arctic Discoverer* (London: Richard Bentley, 1845).
7. On the northern whaling industry, see Daniel Francis, *Arctic Chase* (St. John's: Breakwater Books, 1984).
8. John R. Bockstoce, *Steam Whaling in the Western Arctic* (New Bedford, Mass.: Old Dartmouth Historical Society, 1977), p. 36. Bockstoce is the best source on the history of whaling in this area.
9. Bruemmer, "Herschel, the Big Town," p. 28.
10. Quoted in Bockstoce, *Steam Whaling*, p. 39. Bodfish was later master of the *Beluga*.
11. Ibid., p. 40.
12. Ibid.
13. Ibid., p. 40.
14. There were only thirteen ships there that year, and since there were not a hundred men on each ship (the average crew was closer to thirty), this total is either inaccurate, or includes all the Inuit employees of the whalers as well as those Inuit who simply lived on the island.
15. Bruemmer, "Herschel, the Big Town," p. 28.
16. Public Archives of Canada (PAC), R.C.M.P. Papers, RG 18, Comptroller's Correspondence, vol. 309, Inspector D. M. Howard's report, August 1906.
17. On the economics of the whaling industry, see Bockstoce, *Steam Whaling*, and Francis, *Arctic Chase*, ch. 2.
18. Thomas Stone, "Atomistic Order and Frontier Violence: Miners and Whalemen in the Nineteenth Century Yukon," *Ethnology*, XXII/4 (October 1983). Also, Bockstoce, *Steam Whaling*, p. 43.
19. Stone, "Atomistic Order."
20. Stone, "Atomistic Order," quoting from H. H. Bodfish, *Chasing the Bowhead* (Cambridge, Mass.: Harvard University Press, 1936), pp. 159–60.

21. Stone, "Atomistic Order."
22. Bockstoce, *Steam Whaling*, p. 46.
23. A. Stevenson, "Whaler's Wait" quoted in Thomas Stone, "Whalers and Missionaries at Herschel Island," *Ethnohistory*, 28/2 (Spring 1981).
24. Diamond Jenness, *Eskimo Administration: II. Canada* (Montreal: Arctic Institute of North America, 1964), p. 14.
25. Bodfish, *Chasing the Bowhead*, quoted in Peter Usher, "Canadian Western Arctic: A Century of Change," *Anthropologica*, vol. 13, no. 1/2 (1971), p. 174.
26. F. A. Peake, *The Bishop Who Ate His Boots: A Biography of Isaac O. Stringer* (Don Mills: Anglican Church of Canada, 1966).
27. Quoted in Thomas Stone, "Whalers and Missionaries."
28. Ibid.
29. Bruemmer, "Herschel, the Big Island," p. 33.
30. PAC, Constantine Papers, MG 30, E55, vol. 3, file 4, Fitzgerald to Commanding Officer, G Division, 6 September 1903.
31. Maurice Metayer, trans., *I, Nuligak* (New York: Pocket Books, 1971), p. 29.
32. Quoted in W. R. Morrison, *Showing the Flag*, p. 74.
33. Quoted in Stone, "Whalers and Missionaries."
34. Quoted in Bruemmer, "The Big Island," p. 26.
35. Quoted in Morrison, *Showing the Flag*, p. 75.
36. Quoted in Bockstoce, *Steam Whaling*, p. 43.
37. *R.N.W.M.P. Report, 1908* (Ottawa: King's Printer, 1909), K, p. 140.
38. PAC, RG 18, R.C.M.P. Papers, Comptroller's Correspondence, vol. 293, J. A. Smart, memo, n.d. (probably Summer 1903).
39. See Morrison, *Showing the Flag*, ch. 6.
40. C. E. Whittaker, "Memoranda" (July 1907), Archives of the Ecclesiastical Province of Rupertsland, Public Archives of Manitoba, MG 7, A-1, box N, #4003. See also Dick North, *The Lost Patrol* (Anchorage: Alaska Northwest Publishing, 1978).
41. The episode is discussed in Morrison, *Showing the Flag*, ch. 10.
42. Peter J. Usher, *Fur Trade Posts of the Northwest Territories 1870–1970* (Ottawa: Department of Indian Affairs and Northern Development, 1971); K. S. Coates, *The Northern Yukon: a History*, Manuscript Report, Series no. 403, (Winnipeg: Parks Canada, 1979).
43. Quoted in Bruemmer, "Herschel, the Big Town," p. 34.
44. R. Amundsen, *The North West Passage* (London: Constable, 1908).
45. R. J. Diubaldo, "Wrangling Over Wrangel Island," *Canadian Historical Review*, Vol. XLVIII, no. 3 (September 1967).
46. The best biography of the explorer is R. J. Diubaldo, *Stefansson and the Canadian Arctic* (Montreal: McGill-Queen's University Press, 1978). See also W. R. Hunt, *Stef: A Biography of Vilhjalmur Stefansson, Canadian Arctic Explorer* (Vancouver: University of British Columbia Press, 1986).
47. PAC, R.C.M.P. Papers, Comptroller's Correspondence, vol. 353.
48. PAC, Department of Mines, RG 45, vol. 67, file 4078, Acting Chief, Biological Division, Victoria Memorial Museum to Camsell, January 4, 1912.
49. PAC, Chipman Papers, MG 30, "Diary of Canadian Arctic Expedition," entry for April 4, 1914.
50. PAC, R.C.M.P. Papers, Comptroller's Correspondence, vol. 353.
51. His autobiography is Henry Larsen, *The Big Ship* (Toronto: McClelland and Stewart, 1967).

52. For a discussion of the case, see Morrison, *Showing the Flag*, ch. 10. For a similar case, see R. G. Moyles, *British Law and Arctic Men* (Saskatoon: Western Producer Prairie Books, 1979).

53. Hudson's Bay Company Archives, B.434/a/1. Shingle Point Journal, 1937–38; B.419/a/104, Herschel Island Journals.

54. PAC, Northern Administration Branch, RG 85, vol. 792, file 6271, extract from the report of M. Meikle, July 30 1937.

55. Margaret Alstrom, *Draft History of Yukon Education*, unpublished manuscript, ch. 8, "Native Education: Residential Schools, 1906–1940."

56. PAC, Chipman Papers, MG 30, B66, Diary No. 2, entry for 27 April 1914.

57. PAC, Osborne Papers, MG 30, D66, Stringer to Osborne, 14 March 1927.

58. A. Tanner, "The Structure of Fur Trade Relations," unpublished PHD thesis, University of British Columbia, 1966, p. 21.

59. PAC, Northern Administration Branch, RG 85. vol. 792, file 6271, Finnie to Gibson, 2 January 1929.

60. On this subject, see the excellent study by Robert Page, *Northern Development: The Canadian Dilemma* (Toronto: McClelland and Stewart, 1987).

61. On the controversy over the future of the region, see Thomas R. Berger, *Northern Frontier, Northern Homeland: The Report of the Mackenzie Valley Pipeline Inquiry* (Ottawa: Queen's Printer, 1977); also W. R. Morrison, *A Survey of the History and Claims of the Native Peoples of Northern Canada* (Ottawa: Treaties and Historical Research Centre, Department of Indian and Northern Affairs, 1984).

Chapter Six

1. Robert McCandless, *Yukon Wildlife: A Social History* (Edmonton: University of Alberta Press, 1985), pp. 108–109.

2. Hal Guest, "A History of Dawson City, Yukon Territory, 1896–1920," Microfiche Report Series No. 7, Parks Canada, 1983.

3. Guest, "A History of Dawson City," p. 67.

4. Melody Webb, *The Last Frontier: A History of the Yukon Basin of Canada and Alaska* (Albuquerque: University of New Mexico Press, 1985), pp. 201–202.

5. Guest, "A History of Dawson City," p. 103.

6. Guest, "A History of Dawson City." See also Morris Zaslow, *The Opening of the Canadian North, 1870–1914* (Toronto: McClelland and Stewart, 1971), pp. 124–46 for an analysis of the decline of Dawson City. For a comparison with British Columbia, see S. D. Clark, "The Gold Rush Society of British Columbia and the Yukon," in *The Developing Canadian Community* (Toronto: University of Toronto Press, 1970).

7. Zaslow, *The Opening of the Canadian North*, p. 137.

8. Guest, "A History of Dawson City," p. 246.

9. Ibid., pp. 245–58.

10. Ibid., p. 291.

11. Laura Berton, *I Married the Klondike* (Toronto: Little, Brown, 1954), pp. 44–45.

12. Ibid., p. 52.

13. Ibid., pp. 46–48.

14. Frank Peake, *The Bishop Who Ate His Boots* (Don Mills, Anglican Church of Canada, 1967), p. 142. On the relationship between the Indians and the white population, see K. S. Coates, "Best Left as Indians: Native-White Relations in the Yukon Territory, 1840–1950," unpublished PHD thesis, University of British Columbia, 1984.

15. Berton, *I Married the Klondike*, p. 63.
16. David Morrison, *The Politics of the Yukon Territory, 1898–1909* (Toronto: University of Toronto Press, 1968).
17. Berton, *I Married the Klondike*, pp. 59–61.
18. Ibid., pp. 68–72.
19. Kenneth J. Rea, *The Political Economy of the Canadian North* (Toronto: University of Toronto Press, 1968), p. 99.
20. For a thorough analysis of Sifton's activities relating to the Yukon, see David Hall, *Clifford Sifton*, 2 vols. (Vancouver: University of British Columbia Press, 1982 and 1985).
21. The advance of the dredging mining sector is ably traced in Lewis Green, *The Gold Hustlers* (Vancouver: J. J. Douglas, 1972).
22. Hall, *Clifford Sifton*, vol. 2, p. 133.
23. Green, *The Gold Hustlers*, p. 62.
24. Hall, *Clifford Sifton*, vol. 2, p. 139.
25. Green, *The Gold Hustlers*, p. 71. The word is actually *simoom*; a hot desert wind.
26. Quoted in Green, *The Gold Hustlers*, pp. 91–92.
27. This survey of Boyle's career is drawn from Green, *The Gold Hustlers* and the two biographies of the man, William Rodney, *Joe Boyle: King of the Klondike* (Toronto: McGraw-Hill Ryerson, 1974) and Leonard Taylor, *The Sourdough and the Queen* (Toronto: Methuen, 1983).
28. Rea, *The Political Economy of the Canadian North*, p. 105.
29. R. Coutts, *Yukon Places and Names* (Sidney: Gray's Publishing, 1980), p. 162.
30. Hope Morritt, *Land of the Fireweed: A Young Woman's Story of the Alaska Highway Construction Days* (Anchorage: Alaska Northwest Publishing Company, 1985), pp. 153–54.
31. K. S. Coates, *The Northern Yukon: A History*, Manuscript Report no. 403 (Winnipeg: Parks Canada, 1979), p. 129.
32. Diane Johnston, "Carrying the Yukon: Silver-Lead Mining in the Mayo District, 1919–1942," unpublished paper, presented at a conference.
33. Zaslow, *The Opening of the Canadian North*, p. 121; Paul Korischil, "Whitehorse: The Company Town, 1899–1945," unpublished paper, presented at a conference.
34. Thomas Riggs, "Running the Alaska Boundary," *The Beaver* (September 1945), p. 42.
35. Quoted in R. McCandless, *Yukon Wildlife: A Social History* (Edmonton: University of Alberta Press, 1985), p. 105.
36. McCandless, *Yukon Wildlife*, pp. 112–14.
37. This analysis of the development of Yukon transportation is drawn from Gordon Bennett, *Yukon Transportation: A History*, Canadian Historic Sites: Occasional Papers in Archeology and History, no. 19 (Ottawa: National Historic Parks, 1978). See also Roy Minter, *The White Pass: Gateway to the Klondike* (Toronto: McClelland and Stewart, 1987).
38. This theme is explored in a work in progress by K. S. Coates and W. R. Morrison, *Taking the North Down with Her: The Sinking of the s.s. Princess Sophia*.
39. Korischil, "Whitehorse: The Company Town."
40. Bennett, *Yukon Transportation*, p. 77.
41. Ibid., p. 77.
42. Lewis Thomas, *The Struggle for Responsible Government in the Northwest Territories, 1870–97* 2nd Edition (Toronto: University of Toronto Press, 1970), p. 208; David Morrison, *The Politics of the Yukon Territory*, p. 23.

43. W. R. Morrison, *Showing the Flag: The Mounted Police and Canadian Sovereignty in the North, 1894-1925* (Vancouver: University of British Columbia Press, 1985). See also Coates, *The Northern Yukon: A History.*
44. K. S. Coates, "Send Only Those Who Rise a Peg: The Recruitment and Use of Anglican Missionaries in the Yukon, 1858-1932," *Journal of the Canadian Church Historical Society* (Summer 1986), p. 10.
45. Peake, *The Bishop Who Ate His Boots.*
46. Zaslow, *The Opening of the Canadian North*, pp. 128-29; George Gartrell, "The Work of the Churches in the Yukon During the Era of the Klondike Gold Rush," unpublished MA thesis, University of Western Ontario, 1970.
47. Cecil Swanson, *The Days of My Sojourning* (Calgary: Glenbow-Alberta Institute, 1979), p. 36.
48. Coates, "Send Only Those," p. 12. On the missionary-Indian relations, see K. S. Coates, "Best Left as Indians: Native-White Relations in the Yukon," unpublished PHD thesis, 1984, ch. 9.
49. Quoted in K. S. Coates, "A Very Imperfect Means of Education: Indian Day Schools in the Yukon Territory, 1890-1955," in Jean Barman, Y. Hebert and D. McCaskill, eds. *Indian Education in Canada*, Vol. 1: *The Legacy* (Vancouver: University of British Columbia Press, 1986), pp. 132-49.
50. General Synod Archives, Anglican Church of Canada, M75-103, Series 2-14, MSCC, Frank Oliver to A.C.C., 28 January 1908.
51. K. S. Coates, "Betwixt and Between: The Anglican Church and the Children of the Carcross (Chouttla) Residential School, 1911-1955," *BC Studies*, no. 62 (Winter 1984-85), pp. 27-47.
52. Charles Maier, "Responsible Government and Federal Administrators in Yukon, 1898-1913," unpublished paper presented at a conference.
53. Hal Guest, "The Incorporation and Disincorporation of Dawson City," unpublished paper presented at a conference. See also Guest, "A History of Dawson City."
54. This section draws on the work of Burt Harris, currently completing a Master of Arts thesis at the University of Calgary on the evolution of the Yukon legal system in the post-Gold Rush era.
55. The political battles described in the following paragraphs are best followed in David Morrison, *The Politics of the Yukon Territory* and David Hall, *Clifford Sifton*, 2 vols. The latter is particularly good on relations between the national Liberal government and local Liberal politicians. See also Laura Berton, *I Married the Klondike* and Martha Black, *My Seventy Years* (Toronto: Thomas Nelson, 1938).
56. Berton, *I Married the Klondike*, p. 108.
57. Morrison, *The Politics of the Yukon Territory*, p. 94.
58. Berton, *I Married the Klondike*, p. 128.
59. Black, *My Seventy Years*, p. 255.
60. This issue is examined in Coates and Morrison, *Taking the North Down with Her.* The specific references are located in Yukon Territorial Archives (YTA) IODE Records, Acc. 82/463, fol. 717 and YTA, Yukon Record Group One, vol. 44, file 29461.
61. The total number of volunteers from the Yukon during the war was 2,327—a third of its population. This remarkable figure was more than three times the next highest rate (Manitoba, at 9.8%). It was partly due to the dominance of single males in the Territory's population, but is dramatic proof of the Yukon's enthusiasm for the war.
62. Black, *My Seventy Years*, p. 238.
63. Green, *The Gold Hustlers*, Chapter 9. See also the biographies of Boyle by Rodney and Taylor cited above.

64. *Dawson News*, 12 October 1914.
65. M. Black, *My Ninety Years* (Anchorage: Alaska Northwest Publishing, 1976), p. 106.
66. *Dawson News*, 23 June 1916.
67. *Whitehorse Star* and *Dawson News*, May to September 1916 carry the details and rhetoric of the debate.
68. Berton, *I Married the Klondike*, p. 96.
69. This disaster is discussed in full in the forthcoming work by Coates and Morrison, *Taking the North Down with Her: The Sinking of the* S.S. *Princess Sophia*.
70. L. Thomas, *The Struggle for Responsible Government in the Northwest Territories*, 2nd Edition, (Toronto: University of Toronto Press, 1978), ch. 10, "Reflections on Territorial Government."

Chapter Seven

1. Kenneth Rea, *The Political Economy of the Canadian North* (Toronto: University of Toronto Press, 1968). See, in particular, the statistical material assembled in the tables at the end of the book.
2. The following discussion of the Keno-area mines relies heavily on Diane Johnston, "Carrying the Yukon: Silver-Lead Mining in the Mayo District, 1919-1942," unpublished paper, presented at a conference.
3. Gordon Bennett, *Yukon Transportation: A History* (Ottawa: National Historic Parks, 1978), pp. 96-104.
4. Rea, *The Political Economy of the Canadian North*, pp. 394-95.
5. The evolution of gold-mining activity in the Yukon can be followed in Lewis Green, *The Gold Hustlers* (Vancouver: J. J. Douglas, 1972).
6. Green, *The Gold Hustlers*, p. 238 and *passim*.
7. Ibid., p. 263.
8. The fur trade is analysed in Robert McCandless, *Yukon Wildlife: A Social History* (Edmonton: University of Alberta Press, 1985), pp. 103-36 and K. S. Coates, "Best Left as Indians: Native-White Relations in the Yukon Territory, 1840-1950," unpublished PHD thesis, University of British Columbia, 1984, pp. 92-125.
9. Quoted in McCandless, *Yukon Wildlife*, p. 121.
10. For an anthropological analysis of the twentieth-century trading system, see Adrian Tanner, "The Structure of Fur Trade Relations," unpublished MA thesis, University of British Columbia, 1965.
11. The nature of social relations in the fur trade districts is examined in Coates, "Best Left as Indians."
12. On big-game hunting, see McCandless, *Yukon Wildlife*, pp. 42-63. There are a number of memoirs written by big-game hunters, including Nevill A. D. Armstrong, *After Big Game in the Upper Yukon* (London: John Long, 1937), H. A. Auer, *Camp Fires in the Yukon* (Cincinnati: Stewart and Kidd, 1916), Thomas Martindale, *Hunting in the Upper Yukon* (Philadelphia: George W. Jacobs, 1913).
13. Quoted in McCandless, *Yukon Wildlife*, p. 60.
14. On railroads in the Territory, see Bennett, *Yukon Transportation*, pp. 24-50.
15. Laura Berton, *I Married the Klondike* (Toronto: Little, Brown, 1954), p. 154.
16. Bennett, *Yukon Transportation*, p. 110.
17. A second firm, with the same name, lost all three of its planes in less than six months, and had to close down.

18. Carol Livermore, "Percy DeWolfe: Iron Man of the Yukon," *The Beaver* (Autumn 1977), pp. 16-20.

19. Berton, *I Married the Klondike*, p. 145. For another perspective on life in the Dawson area in the 1920s, see Pierre Berton, *Starting Out, 1920-1947* (Toronto: McClelland and Stewart, 1987).

20. Berton, *I Married the Klondike*, p. 151.

21. Paul Korischil, "Whitehorse: The Company Town, 1899-1945," unpublished paper.

22. Berton, *I Married the Klondike*, pp. 135-36.

23. There is some excellent material available on the Yukon Indians in this period. See Catherine McClellan, *Part of the Land, Part of the River: A History of the Yukon Indians* (Vancouver: Douglas and McIntyre, 1987). For ethnographic materials on the Yukon Indians, see C. Osgood, *The Han Indians* (New Haven: Yale University Press, 1971), C. Osgood, *Contributions to the Ethnography of the Kutchin* (New Haven: Yale University, 1936), Catherine McClellan, *My Old People Say: An Ethnographic Survey of Southern Yukon Territory* (Ottawa: National Museum of Canada, 1975). For an historical analysis of this period, see Coates, "Best Left as Indians."

24. Yukon Territorial Archives (YTA), Anglican Church Records, Fort Yukon file, Grafton Burke to John Hawksley, 21 May 1926.

25. Berton, *I Married the Klondike*, p. 169.

26. The government's involvement with this is described in K. S. Coates, "Best Left as Indians: The Federal Government and the Indians of the Yukon, 1894-1950," *Canadian Journal of Native Studies*, vol. 4, no. 2 (Fall 1984), pp. 179-204.

27. K. S. Coates, "Send Only Those Who Rise a Peg: The Recruitment and Use of Anglican Missionaries in the Yukon, 1858-1932," *Journal of the Canadian Church Historical Society* (Summer 1986), pp. 3-18.

28. Cecil Swanson, *The Days of My Sojourning* (Calgary: Glenbow-Alberta Institute, 1977), p. 36.

29. Frank Peake, *The Bishop Who Ate His Boots* (Don Mills: Anglican Church of Canada, 1967); T. C. B. Boon, *The Anglican Church from the Bay to the Rockies* (Toronto: Ryerson Press, 1962).

30. K. S. Coates, "Betwixt and Between: The Anglican Church and the Children of the Carcross (Chouttla) Residential School, 1911-1955," *BC Studies*, No. 62 (Winter 1984-85), pp. 27-47.

31. YTA, Anglican Church Records, McCullum file, Wood to Stringer, 14 April 1926.

32. YTA, Anglican Church Records, Carmacks-Little Salmon file, Report of Missionary Work carried on from May 23 to August 31, 1934, in and about Carmacks.

33. Peake, *The Bishop Who Ate His Boots*, pp. 108-109.

34. Public Archives of Canada (PAC), Department of Indian Affairs Records, RG 10, file 941-1, pt. 1, Bishop Geddes to Dr. H. W. McGill, 27 January 1943.

35. YTA Anglican Church Records, St. Agnes Hostel file, Extract from *Mayo-Keno Bulletin*, 8 September 1925.

36. This section draws on Coates, "Best Left as Indians."

37. YTA, Yukon Record Group 1, Series 3, vol. 8, file 12-15, Camsell to Gibson, 14 September 1935.

38. Rea, *The Political Economy of the Canadian North*, pp. 314-18.

39. Martha Black, *My Seventy Years* (Toronto: Thomas Nelson, 1938). On the later part of her life, see Martha Black, *My Ninety Years* (Anchorage: Alaska Northwest Publishing Co., 1976).

40. Jim Lotz, *Northern Realities: The Future of Northern Development in Canada* (Toronto: New Press, 1972), p. 80. On the pattern of government development, see also Richard Stuart, "Undeveloping the Yukon, 1840-1940," unpublished paper, presented at a conference.
41. Richard Stuart, "Duff Pattullo and the Yukon Schools Question of 1937," *Canadian Historical Review*, LXIV, no. 1 (1983), pp. 25-44.
42. Lotz, *Northern Realities*, p. 79.

Chapter Eight

1. Lewis Green, *The Gold Hustlers* (Vancouver: J. J. Douglas, 1972), p. 286.
2. Richard Stuart, "The Impact of the Alaska Highway on Dawson City," in K. S. Coates, ed., *The Alaska Highway: Papers of the 40th Anniversary Symposium* (Vancouver: University of British Columbia Press, 1985), p. 195.
3. Diane Johnston, "Carrying the Yukon: Silver-Lead Mining in the Mayo District, 1919-1942," unpublished paper, presented at a conference.
4. David Remley, "The Latent Fear: Canadian-American Relations and Early Proposals for a Highway to Alaska" and Robin Fisher, "T. D. Pattullo and the British Columbia to Alaska Highway" in Coates, *The Alaska Highway*, offer different perspectives on this issue. See also David Remley, *The Crooked Road: The Story of the Alaska Highway* (Toronto: McGraw-Hill, 1976). This section draws primarily on Robin Fisher's work.
5. This debate can be followed in Edmonton Municipal Archives (EMA), RG 11, Class 90, files 28-32.
6. Don Thomson, "Surveying the Line: The Canadian Participation" in Coates, *The Alaska Highway*.
7. M. V. Bezeau, "The Realities of Strategic Planning: The Decision to Build the Alaska Highway" in Coates, *The Alaska Highway*, p. 33.
8. Ibid., p. 32.
9. EMA, RG 11, Class 90, file 32, Report of Halvor Halvorson, President, United States-Canada-Alaska Prairie Highway Association, 23 October 1942.
10. John Greenwood, "General Bill Hoge and the Alaska Highway" and D. W. Thompson, "Surveying the Line" in Coates, *The Alaska Highway*.
11. D. W. Thomson, "Surveying the Line" in Coates, *The Alaska Highway*, pp. 78-79.
12. Cook died shortly afterwards, crashing his plane on a Whitehorse street.
13. National Archives of the United States (NAUS), RG 59, file 842-154, Lewis Clark to U.S. Secretary of State, 14 March 1942.
14. Greenwood, "General Bill Hoge" in Coates, *The Alaska Highway*, p. 49.
15. Heath Twichell, "Cut, Fill and Straighten: The Role of the Public Roads Administration in the Building of the Alaska Highway," in Coates, *The Alaska Highway*.
16. Richard Diubaldo, "The Alaska Highway in Canada-United States Relations" in Coates, *The Alaska Highway*.
17. Diubaldo, "The Alaska Highway in Canada-United States Relations" in Coates, *The Alaska Highway*. See also Diubaldo, "The Canol Project in Canadian-American Relations," Canadian Historical Association, *Historical Papers, 1977*, pp. 178-95.
18. Public Archives of Canada (PAC), Northern Administration Branch, RG 85, vol. 1160, file 331-2/200-1, Memorandum, December 1942.

19. U.S. Army Corps of Engineers, Historical Division, Acc. 72-A-3173, Box 15, file 50-19, Rogers to Black, 20 May 1942.
20. PAC Department of Labour, RG 27, vol. 676, file 6-5-75-3, Moore to Mitchell, 4 July 1944.
21. The authors of this book are currently working on a monograph on the northwest during the Second World War, tentatively entitled *The Army of Occupation: Americans in the Canadian Northwest, 1942–1946.*
22. PAC, RG 27, vol. 676, file 6-5-75-1, Memo, Cabinet War Committee, 5 March 1943.
23. PAC, Northern Administration Branch, RG 85, vol. 944, file 12743, Part 1, R. A. Gibson Memorandum, 27 May 1943.
24. NAUS, RG 59, file 842.154, Moffat to Hickerson, 29 July 1942.
25. PAC, Northern Administration Branch, RG 85, vol. 944, file 12743, part C, Phillips to R.C.M.P., 17 August 1944.
26. Robert G. McCandless, in *Yukon Wildlife: A Social History* (Edmonton: University of Alberta Press, 1985), ch. 4, argues that the harmful effects on the wildlife have been exaggerated.
27. Yukon Territorial Archives (YTA), Yukon Record Group 1, Series 3, vol. 10, file 12-20B, Gibson to Hoffmaster, 23 January 1943.
28. See the statistics in K. S. Coates, "The Indians of the Southern Yukon and the Construction of the Alaska Highway, 1942–1950: A Case Study in Native Response to Northern Construction," in Coates, *The Alaska Highway*, pp. 151–71.
29. On the subject of black troops, see Ulysses Lee, *The United States Army in World War II: The Employment of Negro Troops* (Washington, D.C.: Dept. of the Army, 1966); A. Russell Buchanan, *Black Americans in World War II* (New York: Oxford, 1977).
30. "Money Makes Indian Squaws Fashion Leaders," *Edmonton Journal*, 12 July 1941. See also Coates, "The Indians of the Southern Yukon and the Construction of the Alaska Highway, 1942–1950," in Coates, *The Alaska Highway*.
31. J. F. Marchand, "Tribal Epidemics in Yukon," *Journal of the American Medical Association*, 123 (1943), pp. 1019–20.
32. PAC, Yukon Government Records, RG 91, vol. 9, file 1490, pt. J, LeCapelain to R. A. Gibson, 17 July 1943.
33. McCandless, *Yukon Wildlife: A Social History*, p. 79.
34. This section on Dawson City, including the quotations, is drawn from Richard Stuart, "The Impact of the Alaska Highway on Dawson City," in Coates, *The Alaska Highway*.
35. The impact of the construction phase on Whitehorse is described in K. S. Coates and Judith Powell, "Whitehorse and the Building of the Alaska Highway," *Alaska History* (forthcoming).
36. PAC, Northern Administration Branch, RG 85, vol. 1160, file 331-2/200-1, Memorandum, December 1942.
37. Hope Merritt, *Land of the Fireweed: A Young Woman's Story of the Alaska Highway Construction Days* (Anchorage: Alaska Northwest Publishing Company, 1985) details the post-war problems with these buildings.
38. PAC, Northern Administration Branch, RG 85, vol. 1160, file 331-2/200-1, LeCapelain to Gibson, 13 March 1943.
39. See Dwight Oland, "The Army Medical Department and the Construction of the Alaska Highway," in Coates, *The Alaska Highway*.
40. "Alaskan Highway: An Engineering Epic," *National Geographic*, (February 1943).

41. PAC, RG 338, Box 1, NWSC 092, Foreign Affairs and Relations, Pierrepont Moffat, American Minister to Canada to J. D. Hickerson, 23 October 1943.
42. NAUS, RG 59, file 711.42/255, J. D. Hickerson, Department of State, Memorandum, 20 May 1943.
43. Donald Creighton, *The Forked Road: Canada, 1939-1957* (Toronto: McClelland and Stewart, 1976), pp. 73-74. Creighton was wrong, not the only mistake in a flawed book, for Ian Mackenzie, B.C. member of the cabinet, attended the opening ceremonies. Robin Fisher, "T. D. Pattullo and the British Columbia to Alaska Highway," in Coates, *The Alaska Highway*, p. 9.
44. Curtis Nordman, "The Army of Occupation: Malcolm MacDonald and U.S. Military Involvement in the Canadian Northwest," and "Appendix: Note on Development in North-Western Canada, by Malcolm MacDonald," in Coates, *The Alaska Highway*, pp. 83-101.
45. Shelagh Grant, of Trent University, is currently completing a detailed examination of federal government activities in this period.
46. Diubaldo, "The Alaska Highway in Canada-United States Relations," in Coates, *The Alaska Highway*.
47. PAC, Special Commissioner on Northern Defence Projects, RG 36/7, vol. 36, file 11-16, T. M. Dauphine to W. L. Mackenzie King, Prime Minister, 12 July 1944.

Chapter Nine

1. Stephen Harris, "Really a Defile Throughout its Length: The Defence of the Alaska Highway in Peacetime," in K. S. Coates, ed. *The Alaska Highway* (Vancouver: University of British Columbia Press, 1985).
2. For a good description of Whitehorse after the war, see Hope Morritt, *Land of the Fireweed: A Young Woman's Story of the Alaska Highway Construction Days* (Anchorage: Alaska Northwest Publishing Company, 1985).
3. Richard Stuart, "The Impact of the Alaska Highway on Dawson City," in Coates, *The Alaska Highway*. On Whitehorse, see K. S. Coates and Judith Powell, "Whitehorse and the Building of the Alaska Highway, 1942-1946," *Alaska History* (forthcoming).
4. Stuart, "The Impact of the Alaska Highway."
5. *Dawson News*, 22 March 1951 quoted in Stuart.
6. David Remley, *The Crooked Road: The Story of the Alaska Highway* (Toronto: McGraw-Hill, 1976).
7. Batelle Memorial Institute, *An Integrated Transport System to Encourage Economic Development of Northwest North America* (Columbus, Ohio: Batelle, 1960). The report was released to the public early in 1961.
8. K. S. Coates, "The Civilian Highway: Public Works Canada and the Alaska Highway, 1964-83," in Coates, *The Alaska Highway*.
9. Stanford Research Institute, *Improvement Program for the Alaska Highway: An Analysis of Economic Benefits* (Ottawa: Queen's Printer, 1966).
10. K. S. Coates, "The Civilian Highway."
11. This issue is examined in Julie Cruikshank, "The Gravel Magnet: Some Social Impacts of the Alaska Highway on Yukon Indians," in Coates, *The Alaska Highway*.
12. Robert McCandless, *Yukon Wildlife: A Social History* (Edmonton: University of Alberta Press, 1985).

13. Yukon Territorial Archives (YTA), Series 3, vol. 10, file 12-20C, Jeckell to Gibson, 13 January 1944.
14. Kenneth Rea, *The Political Economy of the Canadian North* (Toronto: University of Toronto Press, 1968).
15. Adrian Tanner, *Trappers, Hunters and Fishermen* (Ottawa: Department of Northern Affairs and Natural Resources, 1966).
16. One of the best statements of the continued importance of harvesting is Ross River Indian Band, *So That the Future Will Be Ours* (Ross River: Ross River Indian Band, 1984). See also Frank Duerden, *Teslin: The Indian Village and Community Economy* (Toronto: Ryerson Polytechnical Institute, 1986).
17. Pierre Lasserre, "L'aide aux mines d'or ou les silences du fantôme de Bretton Woods," *Canadian Public Policy* IX:4 (1983): pp. 446–57.
18. Rae, *The Political Economy of the Canadian North* offers a good survey of mining activity in the 1950s.
19. R. L. Debicki, *Yukon Mineral Industry, 1941 to 1959* (Ottawa: Department of Indian and Northern Affairs, 1982).
20. The following is drawn from R. L. Debicki, *Yukon Mineral Industry*; Jane Griffen, *Cashing In* (Whitehorse: Word Pro, 1980); Kenneth J. Rea, *The Political Economy of Northern Development* (Science Council of Canada Background Study No. 36. Ottawa: Science Council of Canada, 1976).
21. Walter Campbell, "The Search for Oil in the Yukon Territory," *Canadian Geographical Journal*, vol. 62 (October 1961).
22. Griffen, *Cashing In*, recounts this process.
23. Again, see Kenneth Rea, *The Political Economy of Northern Development*.
24. Griffen, *Cashing In*.
25. Janet MacPherson, "The Cypress-Anvil Mine," in E. Peterson and Janet Wright, *Northern Transitions, Vol. 1* (Ottawa: Canadian Arctic Resources Committee, 1978).
26. The post-war development of the White Pass and Yukon Route is discussed in Gordon Bennett, *Yukon Transportation: A History*. Canadian Historic Sites: Occasional Papers in Archeology and History, no. 19 (Ottawa: National Historic Parks, 1978), pp. 145–46.
27. A good account of this exercise is provided in Jim Lotz, *Northern Realities: The Future of Northern Development in Canada* (Toronto: New Press, 1972).
28. Nick Tueli, "Studied Naïvete: The Art of Ted Harrison," *Northern Review*, vol. 1, no. 1 (1988).
29. William G. MacLeod, "The Dempster Highway," in E. Peterson and Janet Wright, *Northern Transitions, Vol. 1* (Ottawa: Canadian Arctic Resources Committee, 1978).
30. R. A. C. Caldwell, "Communications to — and for — the North," *North*, vol. 11 (Sept./Oct. 1964), pp. 1–8.
31. K. S. Coates, "Best Left as Indians: The Federal Government and the Indians of the Yukon Territory, 1894–1950," in Robin Fisher and K. S. Coates, eds. *Out of the Background: Readings in Native History* (Toronto: Copp Clark-Pitman, 1988).
32. K. S. Coates, "A Very Imperfect Means of Education: Indian Day Schools in the Yukon Territory, 1890–1955," in Jean Barman, Y. Hebert and D. McCaskill, eds. *Indian Education in Canada*, Vol. 1: *The Legacy* (Vancouver: University of British Columbia Press, 1986).
33. Ronald Wright, "Beyond Words," *Saturday Night*, vol. 103, No. 4 (April 1988), pp. 38–46.
34. K. S. Coates, "Upsetting the Rhythms: The Federal Government and Native Communities in the Yukon Territory, 1945 to 1973," in Gurston Dacks and

K. S. Coates, eds. *Northern Communities: The Prospects for Empowerment* (Edmonton: Boreal Institute, 1988).

35. *Participation of Indians in the Economy.* Discussion Paper prepared for the Yukon 2000 Whitehorse Fall Conference, 1986.
36. Charles Hendry, *Beyond Traplines* (Toronto: Ryerson Press, 1969). See also Hugh and Karmel McCullum, *This Land Is Not for Sale* (Toronto: Anglican Book Centre, 1975).
37. Yukon Native Brotherhood (YNB) *Together Today for Our Children Tomorrow* (Whitehorse: Yukon Native Brotherhood, 1973).
38. W. R. Morrison, *A Survey of the History and Claims of the Native Peoples of Northern Canada* (Ottawa: Treaties and Historical Research Centre, 1983).
39. The best review of northern politics is Gurston Dacks, *A Choice of Futures* (Toronto: Methuen, 1981).
40. YNB, *Together Today*, p. 73.
41. Jim Lotz, *The People Outside: Studies of Squatters, Shack Town and Shanty Residents and Other Dwellings on the Fringe of Canada* (Ottawa: Saint Paul University, 1971) pp. 114–28.
42. Lotz, *Northern Realities*, p. 87.
43. Morris Zaslow, "Recent Constitutional Developments in the North," *Canadian Public Administration* 10 (June 1967), pp. 167–80.
44. Lotz, *Northern Realities*, p. 93.
45. Dacks, *A Choice of Futures*.
46. Anthony Alexander, "On Provincehood," *Whitehorse Star*, 7 February 1976.
47. Robert Page, *Northern Development: The Canadian Dilemma* (Toronto: McClelland and Stewart, 1986).
48. Kenneth Lysyk, E. Bohmer and W. Phelps, *Alaska Highway Pipeline Inquiry* (Ottawa: Supply and Services, 1977).

Epilogue

1. Gordon Robertson, *Northern Provinces: A Mistaken Goal?* (Ottawa: Institute of Public Policy Research, 1986).

Select Bibliography

Amundsen, Roald. *The North West Passage.* London: Constable, 1908.

Archer, A. S. *A Heroine of the North: Memoirs of Charlotte Selina Bompas.* London: Macmillan, 1929.

Bennett, Gordon. *Yukon Transportation: A History.* Canadian Historic Sites: Occasional Papers in Archeology and History, no. 19. Ottawa: National Historic Parks, 1978.

Berger, Carl. "The True North Strong and Free." In Peter Russell, *Nationalism in Canada.* Toronto: McGraw-Hill, 1966.

Berger, Thomas. *Northern Frontier/Northern Homeland: the Report of the Mackenzie Valley Pipeline Inquiry, Vol. 1.* Ottawa: Department of Supply and Services, 1977.

Berton, Laura. *I Married the Klondike.* Toronto: Little, Brown, 1954.

Berton, Pierre. *Klondike: The Last Great Gold Rush.* Toronto: McClelland and Stewart, 1972.

Black, Martha. *My Ninety Years.* Anchorage: Alaska Northwest Publishing, 1976.

Black, Martha. *My Seventy Years.* London: Thomas Nelson, 1938.

Bockstoce, John R. *Steam Whaling in the Western Arctic.* New Bedford, Mass.: Old Dartmouth Historical Society, 1977.

Boon, T. C. B. *The Anglican Church from the Bay to the Rockies.* Toronto: Ryerson Press, 1962.

Booth, Michael R. "Gold Rush Theatres of the Klondike." *The Beaver* (Spring 1962).

Bostock, H. S. "Prospecting on Russell Creek." *North*, Vol. 17 (November–December 1970).

Brody, Hugh. *The Living Arctic.* Vancouver: Douglas and McIntyre, 1987.

Brown, J. N. E. "The Evolution of Law and Government in the Yukon Territory." In *Municipal Government in Canada* edited by S. M. Wickett. Toronto: University of Toronto Press, 1907.

Bruemmer, Fred. "Herschel, the Big Town." *The Beaver* (Winter 1980).

Campbell, Robert. *Two Journals of Robert Campbell, 1808 to 1853.* Seattle: John W. Todd, Jr., 1951.

Clark, S. D. "The Gold Rush Society of British Columbia and the Yukon." In *The Developing Canadian Community.* Toronto: University of Toronto Press, 1970.

Coates, K.S., ed. *The Alaska Highway: Papers of the 40th Anniversary Symposium.* Vancouver: University of British Columbia Press, 1985.

____. "Best Left as Indians: The Federal Government and the Indians of the Yukon Territory, 1894-1950." In *Out of the Background: Readings in Native History* edited by Robin Fisher and K. S. Coates. Toronto: Copp Clark Pitman, 1988.

____. "Best Left as Indians: Indian-White Relations in the Yukon Territory, 1840-1950." Unpublished PHD thesis, University of British Columbia, 1984.

____. *Canada's Colonies: A History of the Yukon and Northwest Territories.* Toronto: James Lorimer, 1985.

____. "Furs Along the Yukon: Hudson's Bay Company–Native Trade in the Yukon River Basin, 1830-1893." Unpublished MA thesis, University of Manitoba, 1979.

____. "Furs Along the Yukon: Hudson's Bay Company–Native Trade in the Yukon River Basin, 1840-1893." *BC Studies* No. 55 (Autumn 1982).

____. "The Kennicott Network: Robert Kennicott and the Far Northwest." In Yukon Museums and Historical Association *Proceedings, 1982.*

____. *The Northern Yukon: a History.* Manuscript Report No. 403. Winnipeg: Parks Canada.

____. "Protecting the Monopoly: The Hudson's Bay Company and Scientific Knowledge of the Yukon Valley." Yukon Museums and Historical Association *Proceedings, 1982.*

____. "Send Only Those Who Rise a Peg: The Recruitment and Use of Anglican Missionaries in the Yukon, 1858-1932." *Journal of the Canadian Church Historical Society* (Summer 1986).

____. "A Very Imperfect Means of Education: Indian Day Schools in the Yukon Territory, 1890-1955." In *Indian Education in Canada, Vol. 1: The Legacy* edited by Jean Barman, Y. Hebert, and D. McCaskill. Vancouver: University of British Columbia Press, 1986.

____ and W. R. Morrison. "Northern Visions: Recent Writing in Northern Canadian History." *Manitoba History,* (Fall 1985).

Cody, H. A. *An Apostle of the North: Memoirs of the Right Reverend William Carpenter Bompas, DD.* New York: E.P. Dutton, 1908.

Cooke, Alan and Clive Holland. *The Exploration of Northern Canada, 500 to 1920: A Chronology.* Toronto: Arctic History Press, 1978.

Coutts, R. *Yukon Places and Names.* Sidney, B.C.: Gray's Publishing, 1980.

Creighton, Donald. *The Forked Road: Canada, 1939-1957.* Toronto: McClelland and Stewart, 1976.

Dacks, Gurston. *A Choice of Futures*. Toronto: Methuen, 1981.

___ and K. S. Coates, eds. *Northern Communities: The Prospects for Empowerment*. Edmonton: Boreal Institute, 1988.

Dall, William. *Alaska and its Resources*. Boston: Lee and Chepard, 1870.

Dawson, G. M. *Report on an Exploration in the Yukon District, N. W. T. and Adjacent Northern Portion of British Columbia, 1887*. Ottawa: King's Printer, 1888.

Debicki, R. L. *Yukon Mineral Industry, 1941 to 1959*. Ottawa: Department of Indian and Northern Affairs, 1982.

Disher, A. L. "The Long March of the Yukon Field Force." *The Beaver*, (Autumn 1962).

Diubaldo, R. J. *Stefansson and the Canadian Arctic*. Montreal: McGill-Queen's University Press, 1978.

___. "The Canol Project in Canadian-American Relations." Canadian Historical Association, *Historical Papers, 1977*.

___. "Wrangling Over Wrangel Island." *Canadian Historical Review*, vol. XLVIII, no. 3 (September 1967).

Duerden, Frank. *The Development and Structure of the Settlement System in the Yukon*. Whitehorse: Government of Yukon, 1981.

___. *Teslin: The Indian Village and Community Economy*. Toronto: Ryerson Polytechnical Institute, 1986.

Fagan, Brian M. *The Great Journey: The Peopling of North America*. New York: Thames and Hudson, 1987.

Francis, Daniel. *Arctic Chase*. St. John's: Breakwater Books, 1984.

___. *The Discovery of the North*. Edmonton: Hurtig, 1986.

Franks, C. E. S. "How the Sabbath Came to the Yukon." *Canadian Public Administration*, Vol. 10 (March 1967).

Gartrell, G. E. "The Work of the Churches in the Yukon During the Era of the Klondike Gold Rush." Unpublished MA thesis, University of Western Ontario, 1970.

Goodrich, H. B. "History and Conditions of the Yukon Gold District to 1897." In *Geology of the Yukon Gold District, Alaska — Eighteenth Annual Report of the United States Geological Survey to the Secretary of the Interior, 1896-97. Part 3* edited by J.E. Spurr. Washington, D. C.: Government Printing Office, 1898.

Green, Lewis. *The Gold Hustlers*. Vancouver: J. J. Douglas, 1972.

Griffen, Jane. *Cashing In*. Whitehorse: Word Pro, 1980.

Hall, David. *Clifford Sifton*. 2 vols., Vancouver: University of British Columbia Press, 1982 and 1985.

Hamelin, L.-E. *Canadian Nordicity: It's Your North Too*. Translated by W. Barr. Montreal: Harvest House, 1978.

Hammond, Lorne. "Any Ordinary Degree of System: The Columbia Department and the Harvesting of Wildlife, 1825-1849." Unpublished MA thesis, University of Victoria, 1988.

Hayne, M. H. E. and H. W. Taylor, *The Pioneers of the Klondyke*. London: Sampson Low, Marston, 1897.

Helm, June, ed. *Handbook of North American Indians, vol. 6: Subarctic Indians*. Washington: Smithsonian Institution, 1981.

Honigman, John. *The Kaska Indians*. New Haven: Yale University Press, 1954.

Hunt, W. R. *North of '53: the Wild Days of the Alaska-Yukon Mining Frontier, 1870–1914*. New York: Macmillan, 1974.

____. *Stef: A Biography of Vilhjalmur Stefansson, Canadian Arctic Explorer*. Vancouver: University of British Columbia Press, 1986.

____. *Distant Justice: Policing the Alaska Frontier*. Norman: University of Oklahoma Press, 1987.

James, James G. *The First Scientific Exploration of Alaska, and the Purchase of Alaska*. Evanston: Northwestern University Press, 1942.

Jenness, Diamond. *Eskimo Administration II: Canada*. Montreal: Arctic Institute of North America, 1964.

Johnson, Stephen. "Baron Wrangel and the Russian-American Company." Unpublished PHD thesis, University of Manitoba, 1978.

Karamanski, Theodore. *Fur Trade and Exploration: Opening the Far Northwest, 1821–1852*. Vancouver: University of British Columbia Press, 1983.

Karp, Lawrence E. "The Writing of Dan McGrew." *North*, Vol. 21, (September–October 1974).

Kirkby, W. W. "A Journey to the Youcon, Russian America." *Annual Report, 1864*. Washington, D.C.: Smithsonian Institution, 1865.

Krech, Shepherd III. "On the Aboriginal Population of the Kutchin," *Arctic Anthropology*, Vol. 15 (1978).

____. "The Eastern Kutchin and the Fur Trade, 1800–1860," *Ethnohistory*, 23/3 (Summer 1976).

____. "Throwing Bad Medicine: Sorcery, Disease and the Fur Trade Among the Kutchin and Other Northern Athapaskans." In *Indians, Animals and the Fur Trade* edited by Shepherd Krech III. Athens: University of Georgia, 1982.

Larsen, Henry. *The Big Ship*. Toronto: McClelland and Stewart, 1967.

Lasserre, Pierre, "L'aide aux mines d'or ou les silences du fantôme de Bretton Woods," *Canadian Public Policy* IX:4 (1983), 446–57.

Lee, Ulysses. *The United States Army in World War II: The Employment of Negro Troops*. Washington, D.C., 1966.

Lotz, Jim. *Northern Realities: The Future of Northern Development in Canada*. Toronto: New Press, 1972.

Lysyk, Kenneth, E. Bohmer, and W. Phelps, *Alaska Highway Pipeline Inquiry*. Ottawa: Supply and Services, 1977.

MacDonald, Norbert. "Seattle, Vancouver, and the Klondike," *Canadian Historical Review*, Vol. XLIX, no. 3, (September 1968).

MacGregor, J. G. *The Klondike Rush Through Edmonton 1897-1898*. Toronto: McClelland and Stewart, 1970.

Mackenzie, Alexander. *Voyages from Montreal, on the River St. Lawrence, through the Continent of North America to the Frozen and Pacific Ocean in the Years 1789 and 1793*. London: Noble, 1801.

Malcolm, Andrew H. *The Canadians*. Toronto: Fitzhenry and Whiteside, 1985.

Marchand, J. F. "Tribal Epidemics in Yukon." *Journal of the American Medical Association*, 123 (1943).

McCandless, Robert. *Yukon Wildlife: A Social History*. Edmonton: University of Alberta Press, 1985.

McClellan, Catherine. *My Old People Say: An Ethnographic Survey of Southern Yukon Territory*. Ottawa: National Museums of Canada, 1975.

_____. *Part of the Land, Part of the Water: a History of the Yukon Indians*. Vancouver: Douglas and McIntyre, 1987.

Hugh McCullum, *This Land Is Not for Sale*. Toronto: Anglican Book Centre, 1975.

McConnell, R. G. "Report of an exploration in the Yukon and Mackenzie Basins, N.W.T." *Canadian Geological Survey Annual Report, 1888-1889*. Ottawa: King's Printer, 1890.

McQuesten, L. N. *Recollections of Leroy N. McQuesten*. Whitehorse: Yukon Archives, Coutts Collection, Pamphlets 1952-53.

Metayer, Maurice, trans. *I, Nuligak*. New York: Pocket Books, 1971.

Minter, Roy. *The White Pass: Gateway to the Klondike*. Toronto: McClelland and Stewart, 1987.

Morrison, David. *The Politics of the Yukon Territory, 1898-1906*. Toronto: University of Toronto Press, 1968.

Morrison, William R. *A Survey of the History and Claims of the Native Peoples of Northern Canada*. Ottawa: Treaties and Historical Research Centre, Department of Indian and Northern Affairs, 1984.

_____. *Showing the Flag: the Mounted Police and Canadian Sovereignty in the North, 1894-1925*. Vancouver: University of British Columbia Press, 1985.

Morritt, Hope. *Land of the Fireweed: A Young Woman's Story of the Alaska Highway Construction Days*. Anchorage: Alaska Northwest Publishing Company, 1985.

Morton, W. L. "The North in Canadian History." In *Contexts of Canada's Past* edited by A. B. McKillop. Ottawa: Carleton University Press, 1980.

Moyles, R. G. *British Law and Arctic Men*. Saskatoon: Western Producer Prairie Books, 1979.

Murray, Alexander Hunter. *Journal of the Yukon 1847-1848*, edited by L. J. Burpee. Publications of the Canadian Archives, no. 4. Ottawa: Government Printing Bureau, 1916.

Newman, Peter C. *Caesars of the Wilderness*. Toronto: Penguin, 1987.

North, Dick. *The Lost Patrol*. Anchorage, Alaska: Northwest Publishing, 1978.

Ogilvie, William. *Early Days on the Yukon & the Story of its Gold Finds*. Ottawa: Thorburn and Abbott, 1913.

Osgood, C. *The Han Indians*. New Haven: Yale University Press, 1954.

Ostenstat, William. "The Impact of the Fur Trade on the Tlingit During the Late Eighteenth and Nineteenth Centuries." Unpublished MA thesis, University of Manitoba, 1976.

Page, Robert. *Northern Development: The Canadian Dilemma*. Toronto: McClelland and Stewart, 1986.

Peake, F. A. *The Bishop Who Ate His Boots: A Biography of Isaac O. Stringer*. Don Mills: Anglican Church of Canada, 1966.

____. "Fur Traders and Missionaries: Some Reflections on Attitudes of the H.B.C. Towards Missionary Work Among the Indians." *Western Canadian Journal of Anthropology*, Vol. 3, no. 1 (1977).

____. "Robert McDonald (1829–1913): The Great Unknown Missionary of the Northwest." *Journal of the Canadian Church Historical Society*, Vol. 17, no. 3 (1975).

Peterson, E. and Janet Wright, *Northern Transitions, Vol. 1*. Ottawa: Canadian Arctic Resources Committee, 1978.

Pierce, W. H. *Thirteen Years of Travel and Exploration in Alaska, 1877–1889*. Anchorage: Alaska Northwest Publishing, 1977.

Rea, Kenneth J. *The Political Economy of Northern Development*. Science Council of Canada Background Study No. 36. Ottawa: Science Council of Canada, 1976.

____. *The Political Economy of the Canadian North*. Toronto: University of Toronto Press, 1968.

Remley, David. *The Crooked Road: The Story of the Alaska Highway*. Toronto: McGraw-Hill, 1976.

Riggs, Thomas. "Running the Alaska Boundary." *The Beaver*, (September 1945).

Robertson, Gordon. *Northern Provinces: A Mistaken Goal?* Ottawa: Institute of Public Policy Research, 1986.

Rodney, William. *Joe Boyle: King of the Klondike.* Toronto: McGraw-Hill Ryerson, 1974.

Ross River Indian Band. *So That the Future Will Be Ours*. Ross River: Ross River Indian Band, 1984.

Sealey, G. "The History of the Hudson's Bay Company, 1870–1910." Unpublished MA thesis, University of Western Ontario, 1967.

Simpson, Alexander. *The Life and Travels of Thomas Simpson, the Arctic Discoverer*. London: Richard Bentley, 1845.

Simpson, Thomas. *Narrative of the Discoveries on North Coast of America*. London: Richard Bentley, 1843.

Steele, S. B. *Forty Years in Canada*. London: Jenkins, 1915.

Stewart, R. *Sam Steele: Lion of the Frontier*. Toronto: Doubleday, 1979.

Stone, Thomas. "The Mounties as Vigilantes: Perceptions of Community and the Transformation of Law in the Yukon, 1885-1897." *Law and Society Review*, Vol. 14, no. 1, (Fall 1979).

___. "Atomistic Order and Frontier Violence: Miners and Whalemen in the Nineteenth Century Yukon." *Ethnology*, Vol. 22, (October 1983).

___. "Flux and Authority in a Subarctic Society: the Yukon Miners in the Nineteenth Century." *Ethnohistory*, 30(4), 1983.

Stuart, Richard. "Duff Pattullo and the Yukon Schools Question of 1937." *Canadian Historical Review*, LXIV, no. 1 (1983).

Stuck, Hudson. *Voyages on the Yukon and its Tributaries*. New York: Scribner's Sons, 1917.

Swanson, Cecil. *The Days of My Sojourning*. Calgary: Glenbow-Alberta Institute, 1979.

Tanner, Adrian. *Trappers, Hunters and Fishermen*. Ottawa: Department of Northern Affairs and Natural Resources, 1966.

Taylor, Leonard. *The Sourdough and the Queen*. Toronto: Methuen, 1983.

Thomas, Lewis. *The Struggle for Responsible Government in the Northwest Territories, 1870-97*. 2nd Edition. Toronto: University of Toronto Press, 1970.

Tueli, Nick. "Studied Naïvete: The Art of Ted Harrison," *Northern Review*, Vol. 1, no. 1 (1988).

Turner, J. H. "The Boundary North of Fort Yukon." Part II of "The Alaska Boundary Survey." *National Geographic*, Vol. 4 (February 1893).

United States. *Compilation of Narratives of Explorations in Alaska*. Washington: Government Printing Office, 1900.

Usher, Peter J. *Fur Trade Posts of the Northwest Territories 1870-1970*. Ottawa: Department of Indian Affairs and Northern Development, 1971.

___. "Canadian Western Arctic: a Century of Change." *Anthropologica*, Vol. 13, no. 1/2 (1971).

Van Stone, James. *Athapaskan Adaptations: Hunters and Fishermen of the Subarctic Forests*. Chicago: Aldine, 1975.

Webb, Melody. *The Last Frontier: A History of the Yukon Basin of Canada and Alaska*. Albuquerque: University of New Mexico Press, 1985.

Wesbrook, M. "A Venture into Ethnohistory: the Journals of V. C. Sim." *Polar Notes*, no. 9, (1969).

Whymper, Frederick. *Travel and Adventure in the Territory of Alaska*. Ann Arbor: University Microfilms, 1966.

Wilson, Clifford. *Campbell of the Yukon*. Toronto: Macmillan of Canada, 1970.

Wright, A. A. *Prelude to Bonanza: The Discovery and Exploration of the Yukon*. Whitehorse: Arctic Star Printing, 1980.

Yukon Native Brotherhood, *Together Today for Our Children Tomorrow*. Whitehorse: Yukon Native Brotherhood, 1973.

Zaslow, Morris. *Reading the Rocks: The Story of the Geological Survey of Canada,
1842-1872*. Toronto: Macmillan of Canada, 1975.

——. *The Opening of the Canadian North, 1870-1914*. Toronto: McClelland and
Stewart, 1971.

——. "Recent Constitutional Developments in the North." *Canadian Public
Administration* 10 (June 1967), 167-80.

Index

Brown, Staff Sgt. Charles, 73
Buckley, Charles, 35
Bunoz, Rev., 171
Burgess, A.M., 68
Burke, Grafton, 205
Burrall and Baird Company, 190
Burwash, 170, 196
Buxton Mission, 70

Cadzow, Dan, 165, 196, 205
Cameron, Gordon, 292
Campbell, Robert, 20–26, 34, 36, 46
Camp Takhini, 248
Camsell, Charles, 212
Canadian Airways, 201
Canadian Armed Forces (*see*
    Department of National Defence)
Canadian Arctic Expedition, 138–39
Canadian Broadcasting Corporation,
    282
Canadian Highway Commission, 223
Canadian Klondyke Mining
    Company, 157, 159, 161, 190
Canadian Mounted Rifles, Yukon
    Detachment, 181
Canadian Pacific Steamship
    Company, 197
Canadian Patriotic Fund, 182
Canham, T.H., 13, 70
Canol Project, 233, 247, 249, 251,
    253, 254, 256
Carcross, 4, 112, 171, 197
Carcross Residential School, 173,
    208–10, 211, 237, 284–85
Carcross-Skagway Road, 277
Carmack, George W., 66, 79–82
Carmacks, 210
Cassiar Asbestos Corporation, 272
Chambers, Shorty, 193, 205
Champagne, 171
Champagne Indians, 286, 287
Cheechako Hill, 101
Chernesky, Sergi Gologoff, 57
Chilkoot Pass, 50, 63, 73, 85, 86, 88,
    91
Chilkoot Trail, 280
Chipman, K.G., 142
Chrisstensen, Ione, 294
Church Missionary Society, 31, 32,
    69, 128, 171
Circle City, 57, 58, 62

Citizens' Committee, 175–76
Clark, Rt. Hon. Joe, 294
Clarke, Joe, 176, 177
Clarkson, G.T., 192
Clear Creek Placers, 270
Clinton Creek, 270, 272, 291
Cody, Rev. H.A., 170
Coles, Roger, 295
Collins, Frederick, 292
Collins, Percy McDonough, 35
Committee for Original Peoples'
    Entitlement (COPE), 143
Congdon, F.T., 148, 165, 176, 178
Connel, Fred, 272
Conrad, 163, 170
Consolidated Mining and Smelting
    Company, 163, 274
Constantine, Insp. Charles, 73–75, 83,
    101, 132
Conwest Exploration, 272
Cook, Les, 228
Council of Yukon Indians, 143, 288
Craig, Judge J.A., 174–75
Creighton, Donald, 252
Cruikshank, Andy, 201
Curragh Resources, 277
Cypress-Anvil Mine, 273–76, 291, 293
Cypress Mine, 274

Dall, William, 34, 36, 37, 46
Dalton, Jack, 68
Dalton Post, 169
Daly, T.M., 72
Davidson, Jacob, 162
Dawson Charlie, 66, 79–82, 189
Dawson City: 4, 100–109, 145, 146,
    147, 154, 184, 203, 205, 223, 234,
    245, 260–61, 269, 273, 277, 279,
    280, 290; crime in, 108–109;
    gambling in, 106, 147, 148; Gold
    Rush Festival, 277; Festival
    Foundation, 277; municipal
    government, 174; prostitution in,
    106, 147, 148; public school, 210;
    saloons, 148; social life, 149–50,
    203; theatre in, 103–104
Dawson Creek, 232
Dawson Daily News, 203
Dawson, George M., 65, 84
Dease River, 19
Dease, Peter Warren, 20, 119

329

Haines Junction, 233, 263
Haines Mission, 68
Haines Road, 233, 253, 254, 263
Hall, Billy, 197
Halvorson, Halvor, 227
Hamilton, Alvin, 280
Hardisty, William, 42–43
Harper, Arthur, 48, 49, 52
Harrington, Richard, 7
Harrison, Ted, 280
Hawksley, John, 207, 211
Healey, John J., 59, 60, 72
Healy, John, 72
Henderson, A., 177
Henderson, Robert, 79–82, 148, 149
Herschel Island: 4, 45, 46, 55,
   117–144; social life, 128; Territorial
   Park, 144
Hickerson, J.D., 251
Historic Sites and Monuments Board
   of Canada, 277, 279
Hoge, Col. William, 227, 228, 230,
   247
Holt, George, 49, 50
Hougen, Rolf, 282, 283, 290, 291
Hudson Bay Exploration and
   Development Company, 269
Hudson's Bay Company, 2, 15–39
   passim, 20, 41, 42, 45, 52, 54, 87,
   123, 128, 137, 195
Hudson's Bay Oil and Gas, 276
Hughes, Col. Sam, 181
Hunker Creek, 82
hunting, 11, 27, 238–39
Hutchinson, John, 20
Hutchinson Khol and Company, 37,
   39

Iditarod, Alaska, 167
Imperial Order Daughters of the
   Empire, 182, 277
Indian Act, 244
Indian Economic Development Fund,
   286
Indians, see Native Peoples
Inuit, see Native Peoples
Irving, William, 7

Jacquot, Eugene, 161, 165, 196, 205,
   245
Jacquot, Louis, 162

Jeckell, George, 215, 235, 246, 248,
   249, 252, 259, 261, 266
Jenness, Diamond, 128
Johns, Johnny, 193, 196, 197, 210
Johnson, C.F., 210
Johnson, George, 197
Johnston, Sam, 295
Jones, Strachan, 29, 35
Judge, Father William, 112
Juneau, Alaska, 85

Kane, Jimmy, 196
Karluk, 127, 138
Kaska, 9, 12, 13
Keenleyside, Hugh, 225
Kendi, Julius, 152, 172, 208
Kennicott, Robert, 34, 35, 36, 46
Keno, 185, 188, 190, 216, 221
Ketchum, Frank, 36, 37
King William Island, 137
King, Rt. Hon. William Lyon
   McKenzie, 216, 222–23, 254
Kirkby, W.W., 208
Kiska, Alaska, 224
Kittigazuit, 129
Kjar, Them, 266, 267
Klondike, 200, 279
Klondike City, 106, 148
Klondike Mines Railway, 154, 168
Klondike Visitors Association, 277–78
Kluane: 2; National Park, 245
Krause, Aurel and Arthur, 63
Krech, Shepherd III, 30
Kulan, Al, 273–74
Kunizzi, K., 208

Ladue, Joseph, 50, 52, 55, 56, 85, 161
Lakes: Bennett, 4, 86, 95–6; Dease,
   19, 20; Dezedeash, 4; Finlayson,
   22; Frances, 19, 21, 22, 24, 65;
   Kluane, 4, 161, 269; Kushawa, 4;
   Laberge, 4, 199; Lindeman, 63,
   86, 95–6; Marsh, 4, 64, 199;
   Mintokh, 28; Muncho, 264;
   Simpson, 19; Tagish, 4; Teslin, 87;
   Watson, 224, 256, 264–65; Wolf,
   212
Lamore, Gussie, 102
Lapierre House, 22, 23, 35, 41, 45, 67
Larsen, Henry, 140
Lattin, Con, 291

331

gathering, 12; and the gold rush, 110; Han Indians, 9, 11, 13, 48, 112; Indian Agreement, lack of, 206, 286; Inuit: 8, 12, 13, 61, 117, 118, 120, 125, 142; Alikomiak, 140; and Christianity, 130–31; and education, 141–42, 172, 173; and missionaries, 141–42; Nuligak, 131, 137, 140: Nuklako, 48; Tlingit, 9, 13, 24, 25, 50; and trade goods, 27, 28; Tutchone, 9, 13; social organization of, 12

New Imperial Mines, 273
New Northwest Corporation, 190
Nielsen, Erik, 292–93, 294, 296
Njootli, Amos, 172, 208, 210
Nome, Alaska, 1, 114, 145, 167
Norman Wells, 233
Northern Airways, 201
Northern Canada Power Corporation, 294
northern nationalists, 252, 260
Northern Native Broadcasting, 283
North American Trading and Transportation Company, 59, 85
Northern Light, Power and Coal Company, 160
North West Company, 15, 16
Northwest Corporation, 190
Northwest Hydraulic Mining Company, 155
North West Mounted Police, (see R.C.M.P.)
Northwest Service Command, 230, 256
Northwest Staging Route, 224, 254
Northwest Territories, 1, 103, 143, 294
Nulato, 23, 28, 37

Oblates of Mary Immaculate, 31
O'Connor, Col. James (Patsy), 227, 230
Ogden, Peter Skene, 19
Ogilvie, William, 55, 65–67, 72, 83, 103, 146, 175
oil, exploration, 144
Okes Construction Company, 232
Old Crow; 7, 211, 212, 267, 289; basin, 7; Flats, 268; region, 8
Oliver, Frank, 172, 177
Otter Falls, 275

Overland Telegraph Company, 35–36
Overland Trail, 168–69, 198, 201

Pacific Steamship Company, 197
Pacific Steam Whaling Company, 121, 122
Palace Grand Theatre, 104, 277, 279
Partridge, Mr. and Mrs. Otto, 198
patronage, 151
Patton, Tom, 191, 192
Pattullo, T. Duff, 215–16, 222
Pauline Cove, 121, 122, 143
Peace River, 228, 256
Pearl Harbor, 224
Pearson, Chris, 293, 295
Pedro, Felix, 146
Peel's River Post, (see Fort McPherson)
Pelisse, J., 208
Penikett, Tony, 295, 297
Perry, A.H., 248
Peters, Joseph, 161
Phelps, Willard, 295
Pierce, Walter H., 51–52
Pillage Point, 118
Pioneer Company, 46
Point Barrow, 119, 121
politics: 151, 176–79; federal election (1911), 151; (1918), 178
Porcupine River, 8, 21, 38, 41
Porter Creek, 290
Powell, Georgia, 99
Presbyterian church, 171
Prince George, 223
Princess Sophia, 183, 184
Pringle, Rev. John, 14, 171
Prospector Airways, 269
Public Roads Administration, 228, 230, 232, 247, 253, 256
Purdy, E.P., 170

Quaker Oats Company, 78
Quill Creek, 269

Rabbit Creek, 80
Rampart House, 39, 41, 43–45, 70, 123–24, 126, 171, 196
Rea, Kenneth, 161
Red River, 20, 27, 34
Reed, Harper, 212
Reeve, Bishop William, 129
Reid, Frank, 88

333